VISUAL QUICKPRO GUIDE

# PREMIERE PRO 1.5

## FOR WINDOWS

Antony Bolante

 Peachpit Press

Visual QuickPro Guide
**Premiere Pro 1.5 for Windows**
Antony Bolante

**Peachpit Press**
1249 Eighth Street
Berkeley, CA 94710
510/524-2178
800/283-9444
510/524-2221 (fax)

Find us on the World Wide Web at: www.peachpit.com
To report errors, please send a note to errata@peachpit.com

Peachpit Press is a division of Pearson Education.

Editor: Rebecca Gulick
Project Editor: Judy Ziajka
Contributing Writer: Steven Gotz
Production Coordinator: Andrei Pasternak
Compositor: Christi Payne
Indexer: Karin Arrigoni
Cover Design: The Visual Group
Cover Production: George Mattingly / GMD

ISBN 0-321-26791-5

9 8 7 6 5 4 3 2 1

Printed and bound in the United States of America

# Dedication

For all my pals; I miss you when we're not in the same town.

## Thank You

Steven Gotz, who was essential to revising this book swiftly and accurately. Thanks for the great work and excellent screen shots. You're a real quick pro.

Everyone involved in creating the earlier editions of this book. I hope the latest does you proud.

Rebecca Gulick and Judy Ziajka.

Andrei Pasternak, Christi Payne, Karin Arrigoni and all the good people at Peachpit Press.

The clever folks at Adobe Systems, Inc., especially everyone in Instructional Communications.

Family and friends who've let me share their beautiful photos and faces, but especially Yuuki Hayashi and Lucia Elena Geddes.

My family, of course.

# TABLE OF CONTENTS

**Introduction**   **Premiere Pro: Making the Move**       **xiii**
The Visual QuickPro Series . . . . . . . . . . . . . . . . . xiv
Using This Book . . . . . . . . . . . . . . . . . . . . . . . . . xiv
How Premiere Pro Works . . . . . . . . . . . . . . . . . . . xv
Editing Strategy: Offline and Online Editing . . . xvi
DV and Premiere Pro . . . . . . . . . . . . . . . . . . . . . . xviii
Your Desktop Editing Suite . . . . . . . . . . . . . . . . . xix
Workflow . . . . . . . . . . . . . . . . . . . . . . . . . . . . . . . xxi
New Features . . . . . . . . . . . . . . . . . . . . . . . . . . . xxii
The Digital Video Collection . . . . . . . . . . . . . . . xxiii
System Requirements . . . . . . . . . . . . . . . . . . . . . xxiv
Suggested System . . . . . . . . . . . . . . . . . . . . . . . . xxv
Professional System Additions . . . . . . . . . . . . . xxvi
System Configurations . . . . . . . . . . . . . . . . . . . . xxvii

**Chapter 1**   **Premiere Pro Basics**       **1**
A Look at the Interface . . . . . . . . . . . . . . . . . . . . . 2
A Glance at Secondary Windows . . . . . . . . . . . . . . 3
Arranging the Workspace . . . . . . . . . . . . . . . . . . . 5
Using Context Menus . . . . . . . . . . . . . . . . . . . . . . . 7
Using Tabbed Windows . . . . . . . . . . . . . . . . . . . . . 8
Using Keyboard Shortcuts . . . . . . . . . . . . . . . . . . . 9
Customizing Keyboard Shortcuts . . . . . . . . . . . . 10
Correcting Mistakes . . . . . . . . . . . . . . . . . . . . . . . 12
Using the History Palette . . . . . . . . . . . . . . . . . . . 13
Using the Events Window . . . . . . . . . . . . . . . . . . . 15

**Chapter 2**   **Starting a Project**       **17**
Starting a Project . . . . . . . . . . . . . . . . . . . . . . . . . 18
Specifying Project Settings . . . . . . . . . . . . . . . . . 20
Choosing Built-in Presets . . . . . . . . . . . . . . . . . . 21
Selecting Custom Project Settings . . . . . . . . . . . 22
Saving Custom Settings as a Preset . . . . . . . . . . . 23
Saving Projects . . . . . . . . . . . . . . . . . . . . . . . . . . . 24
Saving Projects Automatically . . . . . . . . . . . . . . . 26
Opening Projects . . . . . . . . . . . . . . . . . . . . . . . . . 27
Locating Missing and Offline Files . . . . . . . . . . . 29

**Chapter 3  Capturing & Importing Footage     33**

Understanding Capture ...................... 34

Capturing DV vs. Digitizing Analog .......... 36

Optimizing Your System for Capture ......... 38

Understanding Capture Options ............. 39

Using the Capture Window .................. 40

Choosing Capture Settings ................. 42

Choosing a Capture Location ............... 44

Using Device Control ...................... 45

Using Playback Controls in the Capture Window  48

Capturing Audio and Video ................. 49

Importing Footage .......................... 62

Importing Projects ......................... 64

Importing Stills ............................ 66

Importing Illustrator Files ................... 67

Importing Layered Photoshop Files .......... 68

Importing Still-Image Sequences ............. 72

Creating a Photoshop File ................... 73

Generating Synthetic Media ................. 74

**Chapter 4  Managing Clips     79**

Working with the Project Window ............ 80

Working with Project Window Views ......... 81

Working with Icon View .................... 84

Working with List View .................... 86

Using Labels .............................. 90

Selecting and Deleting Items in the Project
Window .............................. 92

Using the Preview Area of the Project Window . 93

Organizing Clips in Bins .................... 96

Duplicating and Copying Source Clips ........ 100

Renaming Clips ........................... 103

Finding Clips ............................. 104

Interpreting Footage ....................... 105

Viewing Clip Properties .................... 107

Unlinking and Relinking Media ............. 108

Using the Project Manager ................. 111

**Chapter 5  Viewing Clips in the Monitor Window  115**

Using the Monitor Window ................. 116

Modifying the Monitor Window ............. 118

Viewing Clips ............................. 119

Opening Audio Clips ....................... 122

Using Playback Controls ................... 124

Cuing Clips Numerically ................... 126

Using the Monitor Window's Time Ruler
    Controls . . . . . . . . . . . . . . . . . . . . . . . . . . . . . 128
Viewing Video Safe Zones . . . . . . . . . . . . . . . . . . 131
Choosing a Quality Setting . . . . . . . . . . . . . . . . . 132
Changing the Magnification . . . . . . . . . . . . . . . . 133
Choosing a Display Mode . . . . . . . . . . . . . . . . . . 134
Setting Waveform and Vectorscope Display
    Options . . . . . . . . . . . . . . . . . . . . . . . . . . . . . 136
Using a Reference Monitor . . . . . . . . . . . . . . . . . 141
Ganging the Source and Program Views . . . . . . 143

**Chapter 6    Creating a Sequence    145**
Comparing Editing Methods . . . . . . . . . . . . . . . 146
Setting In and Out Points . . . . . . . . . . . . . . . . . . 148
Setting Split Edit Points . . . . . . . . . . . . . . . . . . . 151
Setting Precise Audio In and Out Points . . . . . . 152
Setting Clip Markers . . . . . . . . . . . . . . . . . . . . . . 153
Cuing to and Clearing Clip Markers . . . . . . . . . 156
Specifying Source and Target Tracks . . . . . . . . 158
Comparing Overlay and Insert Edits . . . . . . . . 160
Adding Clips by Dragging . . . . . . . . . . . . . . . . . 161
Editing with Monitor Window Controls . . . . . . 166
Three-Point Editing . . . . . . . . . . . . . . . . . . . . . . . 167
Four-Point Editing . . . . . . . . . . . . . . . . . . . . . . . . 168
Performing an Edit Using Monitor Window
    Controls . . . . . . . . . . . . . . . . . . . . . . . . . . . . . 169
Lift and Extract . . . . . . . . . . . . . . . . . . . . . . . . . . 173
Storyboard Editing . . . . . . . . . . . . . . . . . . . . . . . 176
About Multiple and Nested Sequences . . . . . . . 179
Using Multiple Sequences . . . . . . . . . . . . . . . . . 180
Nesting Sequences . . . . . . . . . . . . . . . . . . . . . . . . 184

**Chapter 7    Editing in the Timeline    189**
Customizing the Time Ruler . . . . . . . . . . . . . . . . 190
Customizing Track Views . . . . . . . . . . . . . . . . . . 192
Resizing Tracks . . . . . . . . . . . . . . . . . . . . . . . . . . 195
Adding, Deleting, and Renaming Tracks . . . . . . 197
Monitoring Tracks . . . . . . . . . . . . . . . . . . . . . . . . 201
Locking and Unlocking Tracks . . . . . . . . . . . . . 202
Getting Around the Timeline . . . . . . . . . . . . . . . 203
Playing the Sequence in the Timeline . . . . . . . . 207
Cuing to Edits . . . . . . . . . . . . . . . . . . . . . . . . . . . . 209
Using Sequence Markers . . . . . . . . . . . . . . . . . . 210
Viewing Clip Information . . . . . . . . . . . . . . . . . . 212
Using Linked Clips . . . . . . . . . . . . . . . . . . . . . . . 213

TABLE OF CONTENTS

Selecting Clips in the Timeline . . . . . . . . . . . . . . 214
Grouping Clips . . . . . . . . . . . . . . . . . . . . . . . . . . . 216
Deleting Clips and Gaps from the Timeline . . . 218
Enabling and Disabling Clips . . . . . . . . . . . . . . 220
Splitting Clips . . . . . . . . . . . . . . . . . . . . . . . . . . . 221
Cutting, Copying, and Pasting Clips . . . . . . . . . 224
Playing Clips at a Different Speed or in
    Reverse . . . . . . . . . . . . . . . . . . . . . . . . . . . . . . . 228
Creating a Freeze Frame . . . . . . . . . . . . . . . . . . 232

## Chapter 8   Refining the Sequence   235

Using the Snapping Feature . . . . . . . . . . . . . . . . 236
Editing by Dragging . . . . . . . . . . . . . . . . . . . . . . 238
Choosing a Trimming Method . . . . . . . . . . . . . . 243
Trimming Clips in the Timeline . . . . . . . . . . . . . 244
Making Ripple and Rolling Edits . . . . . . . . . . . . 246
Making Slip and Slide Edits . . . . . . . . . . . . . . . 249
Using the Trim Window . . . . . . . . . . . . . . . . . . . 252
Previewing and Applying Edits in the Trim
    Window . . . . . . . . . . . . . . . . . . . . . . . . . . . . . 257
Working with Links . . . . . . . . . . . . . . . . . . . . . . 258
Creating Split Edits . . . . . . . . . . . . . . . . . . . . . . 259
Breaking and Creating Links . . . . . . . . . . . . . . 262
Keeping Sync . . . . . . . . . . . . . . . . . . . . . . . . . . . 264
Finding Source Clips . . . . . . . . . . . . . . . . . . . . . 265
Finding the Match Frame . . . . . . . . . . . . . . . . . 266

## Chapter 9   Adding Transitions   267

Using the Effects Palette . . . . . . . . . . . . . . . . . . 268
Understanding Transitions . . . . . . . . . . . . . . . . 272
Understanding Transition Duration and
    Alignment . . . . . . . . . . . . . . . . . . . . . . . . . . . 274
Setting the Default Transition Duration . . . . . . 275
Specifying a Default Transition . . . . . . . . . . . . . 276
Applying a Transition . . . . . . . . . . . . . . . . . . . . . 277
Using the Effect Controls Palette with
    Transitions . . . . . . . . . . . . . . . . . . . . . . . . . . . 279
Adjusting a Transition's Duration and
    Alignment . . . . . . . . . . . . . . . . . . . . . . . . . . . 283
Customizing Transition Settings . . . . . . . . . . . . 286
Using Special Transitions . . . . . . . . . . . . . . . . . 292

## Chapter 10   Previewing a Sequence   293

Using Real-Time Rendering . . . . . . . . . . . . . . . . 294
Viewing a Sequence via a DV Device . . . . . . . . 295
Rendering the Work Area . . . . . . . . . . . . . . . . . 298

Storing Preview Files . . . . . . . . . . . . . . . . . . . . . . . 302
Deleting Preview Files . . . . . . . . . . . . . . . . . . . . 305

**Chapter 11    Mixing Audio    307**
Planning an Audio Mix . . . . . . . . . . . . . . . . . . . 308
Specifying Audio Hardware Options . . . . . . . . . 310
Understanding Audio Tracks and Channel Types 312
Converting Mono and Stereo Clips . . . . . . . . . . . 313
Adjusting a Clip's Gain . . . . . . . . . . . . . . . . . . . . 315
Creating Cross-Fades with Audio Transitions . 317
Viewing Audio Data in the Timeline . . . . . . . . 319
Using the Audio Mixer . . . . . . . . . . . . . . . . . . . . 321
Customizing the Audio Mixer . . . . . . . . . . . . . . 323
Monitoring Tracks in the Audio Mixer . . . . . . . 327
Recording with the Audio Mixer . . . . . . . . . . . . 328
Fading, Panning, and Balancing . . . . . . . . . . . . . 330
Mixing 5.1 Audio . . . . . . . . . . . . . . . . . . . . . . . . . 331
Selecting an Automation Mode . . . . . . . . . . . . . 333
Routing Track Output . . . . . . . . . . . . . . . . . . . . . 335
Working with Sends . . . . . . . . . . . . . . . . . . . . . . . 336
Adding Track Effects . . . . . . . . . . . . . . . . . . . . . . 339
Specifying Audio Keyframe Optimization . . . . . 344
Mixing with the Audio Mixer . . . . . . . . . . . . . . . 345

**Chapter 12    Creating Titles    349**
The Title Designer Window . . . . . . . . . . . . . . . . . 350
Creating a Title . . . . . . . . . . . . . . . . . . . . . . . . . . . 351
Using Title Templates . . . . . . . . . . . . . . . . . . . . . 353
Viewing the Video Safe Zones . . . . . . . . . . . . . . 354
Viewing the Video in the Background . . . . . . . . 355
Adjusting Values . . . . . . . . . . . . . . . . . . . . . . . . . . 356
Creating Text Objects . . . . . . . . . . . . . . . . . . . . . 357
Setting Word Wrap . . . . . . . . . . . . . . . . . . . . . . . 360
Setting Tabs . . . . . . . . . . . . . . . . . . . . . . . . . . . . . . 361
Creating Path Text . . . . . . . . . . . . . . . . . . . . . . . . 363
Selecting Text . . . . . . . . . . . . . . . . . . . . . . . . . . . . 365
Setting Text Properties . . . . . . . . . . . . . . . . . . . . 366
Using the Font Browser . . . . . . . . . . . . . . . . . . . . 368
Using Styles . . . . . . . . . . . . . . . . . . . . . . . . . . . . . . 370
Creating Rolls and Crawls . . . . . . . . . . . . . . . . . . 373
Creating Shape Objects . . . . . . . . . . . . . . . . . . . . 376
Understanding Control Points and Segments . 377
Using the Pen Tools . . . . . . . . . . . . . . . . . . . . . . . 379
Reshaping a Bézier Curve . . . . . . . . . . . . . . . . . . 381
Specifying Line and Path Properties . . . . . . . . . 384
Converting Shapes to Filled Bézier Shapes . . . . 386

Setting Fill Options . . . . . . . . . . . . . . . . . . . . . . . . . 387
Setting Gradient Options . . . . . . . . . . . . . . . . . . . . 388
Setting Sheen Options . . . . . . . . . . . . . . . . . . . . . . 390
Applying a Texture . . . . . . . . . . . . . . . . . . . . . . . . 391
Setting Stroke Options . . . . . . . . . . . . . . . . . . . . . 393
Adding Drop Shadows . . . . . . . . . . . . . . . . . . . . . 397
Inserting Logos . . . . . . . . . . . . . . . . . . . . . . . . . . 398
Transforming Objects . . . . . . . . . . . . . . . . . . . . . . 400
Positioning Objects Automatically . . . . . . . . . . . 402
Arranging Objects . . . . . . . . . . . . . . . . . . . . . . . . 403
Aligning Objects . . . . . . . . . . . . . . . . . . . . . . . . . 404
Distributing Objects . . . . . . . . . . . . . . . . . . . . . . 405

**Chapter 13**  **Working with Effects**  **407**

Comparing Effect Types . . . . . . . . . . . . . . . . . . . . 408
Setting and Animating Effect Properties . . . . . . 410
Viewing Effect Property Values . . . . . . . . . . . . . 411
Choosing a Keyframing Method . . . . . . . . . . . . 413
Viewing Property Values in the Timeline
    Window . . . . . . . . . . . . . . . . . . . . . . . . . . . . . 414
Changing Property Values in the Timeline . . . . 416
Animating Opacity and Volume . . . . . . . . . . . . 421
Adding Standard Effects . . . . . . . . . . . . . . . . . . . 424
Viewing Effect Properties in the Effect
    Controls Window . . . . . . . . . . . . . . . . . . . . . 426
Disabling and Resetting Effects . . . . . . . . . . . . . 429
Customizing the Effect Controls Window . . . . 431
Using Multiple Effects . . . . . . . . . . . . . . . . . . . . 433
Viewing Motion Effects . . . . . . . . . . . . . . . . . . . 435
Setting Spatial Properties in the Program View 437
Basic Keyframing in the Effect Controls
    Window . . . . . . . . . . . . . . . . . . . . . . . . . . . . . 441
Using Keyframes in the Effect Controls
    Window . . . . . . . . . . . . . . . . . . . . . . . . . . . . . 445
Understanding Interpolation . . . . . . . . . . . . . . . 450
Interpolation Types . . . . . . . . . . . . . . . . . . . . . . 454
Specifying a Spatial Interpolation Method . . . . 456
Specifying a Temporal Interpolation Method . . 457

**Chapter 14**  **Effects in Action**  **461**

Working with Effect Presets . . . . . . . . . . . . . . . . 462
Superimposing Images . . . . . . . . . . . . . . . . . . . . 467
Using Keying Filters . . . . . . . . . . . . . . . . . . . . . . 471
Using Alpha-Based Keys . . . . . . . . . . . . . . . . . . . 472
Using Luminance-Based Keys . . . . . . . . . . . . . . 474
Using Chrominance-Based Keys . . . . . . . . . . . . 477

Using Matte-Based Keys ................... 481
Using Garbage Mattes ..................... 487
Using Adjust Filters ........................ 489
Using the Color Corrector Filter ............ 496
Other Filters ............................. 504

**Chapter 15    Creating Output                              507**
Choosing Export Options and Settings ....... 508
Considering Output Goals .................. 509
Exporting File Types ....................... 511
Exporting to Tape ......................... 512
Exporting Directly to DVD ................. 514
Exporting a Movie File ..................... 518
Specifying the General Export Settings ....... 520
Keyframe and Rendering Settings and Audio
        Settings ............................. 522
Exporting Still-Image Sequences ............. 523
Exporting Single Still Images ............... 525
Specifying GIF Options ................... 528
Exporting Audio-Only Files ................ 530
Using the Adobe Media Encoder ............ 532
Specifying Pre- and Post-Encoding Tasks ..... 536
Modifying, Saving, and Deleting Presets ...... 538
Exporting an AAF File .................... 540
Exporting an Edit Decision List (EDL) ....... 541

**Chapter 16    Video and Audio Settings                    543**
Choosing Settings ........................ 544
Timebase ................................ 545
Frame Rate .............................. 546
Timecode ................................ 547
Drop-Frame and Non–Drop-Frame Timecode . 548
Video Display Format ...................... 549
Audio Display Format ...................... 550
Interlaced and Progressive Scan Video ........ 551
Interlacing Problems ...................... 553
Overscan and Safe Zones ................... 555
Safe Colors ............................... 556
Frame Size ............................... 557
Image Aspect Ratios ....................... 558
Pixel Aspect Ratio ........................ 560
Image Bit Depth .......................... 561
Compression ............................. 562
Codecs .................................. 563
Data Rates ............................... 564
Keyframes ............................... 565

Audio Sample Rate .......................... 566
Audio Bit Depth ........................... 567
Audio Channels ........................... 568
Audio Interleave .......................... 570
Audio Compression ........................ 571

**Index** **573**

# PREMIERE PRO: MAKING THE MOVE

It was a big move. Even though we cherished the old Premiere, it was a little rundown. The new program has everything the old one had and much more. Premiere Pro isn't just newer; it has a more modern design, and a sturdier construction. And instead of just fixing up the old software, these improvements were built-in from the ground up. Premiere Pro has a new look, a streamlined editing model, and a more unified interface—not to mention a host of new features. Naturally, the transition was a bit of a shock, and it took a little getting used to the new environment. But it was worth the effort. And though we look back on the old Premiere fondly, we hardly miss it at all.

For a time, it wasn't clear whether we should think of Premiere Pro as version 7 in a long line of software, or as a break with the past called version 1.0. Now we know: Adobe has labeled the latest version Premiere Pro 1.5.

Sure, after the excitement of moving to Premiere Pro, version 1.5's improvements seem relatively humble. Even so, they're significant. After proudly showing off the new program, Adobe has been busy rearranging things, making improvements, and adding features that didn't make it in the first time around. Improvements are evident throughout the program: better integration with other software, enhanced and new effects, better audio keyframing, a refurbished title designer, and better import and export functions. This version also includes enhanced waveform and vectorscope displays and some eagerly awaited media management features, like a project trimmer. If Premiere Pro represented a bold fresh start, then version 1.5 feathers the nest.

Whether you've moved to Premiere Pro to create video for multimedia, video broadcast, DVD, or the Web, this book shows you around the new digs. It guides you through this expansive and complex program in a thorough, concise, visually appealing way. It also conducts you to the new additions and points out the recent renovations. If you're new to editing with Premiere Pro, this QuickPro Guide will ease your transition; if you're coming back, it should help you settle in.

# The Visual QuickPro Series

Chances are good that you're already familiar with Peachpit Press's QuickStart series of books. They're known for their concise style, step-by-step instructions, and ample illustrations.

The *Pro* in *QuickPro*, as in *Premiere Pro*, implies that the software under discussion appeals to more advanced users. For this reason, this QuickPro guide is designed for intermediate to advanced users and assumes that you have significant experience not only with computers, but also with the use of some form of digital media.

That said, the QuickPro series remains true to the essential QuickStart traditions. The approach still emphasizes step-by-step instructions and concise explanations. If the book looks a little thick for a "concise" guide, consider that it contains over 1,000 screen shots that clearly illustrate every task. Like other books in this series, *Premiere Pro 1.5: Visual QuickPro Guide* strives to be quick without failing to guide.

# Using This Book

Although the text restricts itself to the task at hand, it doesn't hesitate to give you critical background information, usually in the form of *sidebars* that help you understand the concepts behind the task. If you're already familiar with the concept, feel free to skip ahead; if not, look to the sidebars for some grounding. Also keep an eye out for tips, which point out shortcuts, pitfalls, and tricks of the trade.

Chapters are organized to present topics as you encounter them in a typical editing project, but the task-oriented format and thumb tabs let you jump to the topic that you need. To avoid bogging you down with potentially lengthy and redundant information, technical topics pervasive to digital video and audio settings are compiled in the final chapter, "Video and Audio Settings." Turn to it whenever you need a more thorough explanation of a setting, or use it as a technical handbook.

By explaining how to use Premiere Pro, this book inevitably touches on a multitude of related topics: formats, editing aesthetics, special effects, audio sweetening, Web delivery, and so on. Discussing the fundamentals and background of each of these areas is far outside the scope of this book (and even books that don't have the word *quick* in their title). Nevertheless, this guide tries to provide enough information to keep you moving and point you in new directions.

# How Premiere Pro Works

Premiere Pro is *digital nonlinear editing software*. A breakdown of this description can give you clues about how the program works:

**Digital:** Premiere Pro manipulates digital media: digital video and audio, scanned images, and digitally created artwork and animation stored in various formats. Regardless of the particular format, these materials are stored as files on your computer's hard disk. Strictly speaking, Premiere Pro doesn't convert analog video and audio to digital form, although it does contain controls that do so in conjunction with built-in or add-on hardware, such as a capture card or IEEE 1394 connection.

**Nonlinear:** Editing in Premiere Pro is described as *nonlinear* because your sources aren't constrained to a linear medium, such as videotape. In other words, you can access any source clip instantly, without shuttling tape, and you can change the order of clips in a sequence without rerecording.

**Software:** As a software-only package, Premiere Pro can be installed on any personal computer system that meets or exceeds the program's minimum requirements and doesn't require specialized hardware. But although Premiere Pro isn't an inextricable part of a black box, you can purchase it bundled with a system or with other hardware options.

## Terminology: Digital and Analog

When you record audio and video, sound and light are converted to electrical signals. *Analog* media record these signals as continuously changing values. *Digital* media, on the other hand, record audio and video as a series of specific, discrete values. A playback device converts these values back to audio and video. The accuracy of each conversion greatly influences the picture and sound quality.

Because digital recordings use discrete values, it's easy to reproduce them exactly, time after time. In addition, you can take advantage of the computer's ability to manipulate these values—which means you can more easily alter the sound, color, and brightness and add effects.

**EDITING STRATEGY: OFFLINE AND ONLINE EDITING**

# Editing Strategy: Offline and Online Editing

It can be argued that all projects begin at the same point: the end. Setting your output goal determines the choices you make to achieve it. Therefore, the editing strategy you develop always proceeds from the same question: What is my output goal (**Figure i.1**)?

Whether your animation is destined for film, broadcast video, CD-ROM, or the Web, familiarize yourself with the specifications of your output goal, such as frame size, frame rate, and file format. Often, you must reconcile your output goal with the capabilities and limitations of your system. These factors help determine your postproduction path—particularly whether you perform offline editing or online editing.

*Online editing* results in the final video sequence. You can edit online in Premiere Pro if your system is capable of acquiring, processing, and delivering a sequence at final-output quality. The higher the image quality, however, the greater the system requirements. To achieve your output goal, you may need a fast processor, a high-end capture card, and large, fast hard drives. If your system doesn't meet the output requirements, use another system for the online edit, and use Premiere Pro for your offline edit.

*Offline editing* prepares projects for an online edit. In an offline edit, you often edit with low-quality versions of the video. Rather than produce a final sequence at output quality, you produce an accurate draft version.

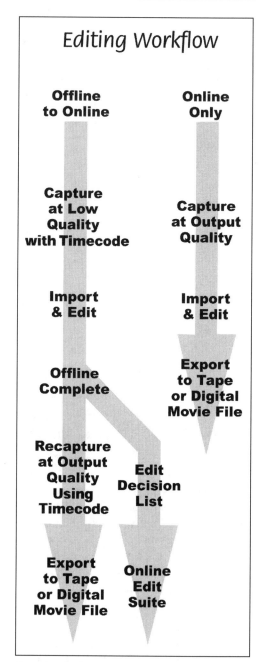

Figure i.1 This flow chart outlines the typical offline and online editing strategies.

The completed offline edit can produce a kind of transcript of all your edits, known as an *edit-decision list* (EDL). You can use the EDL and source tapes to re-create a sequence quickly and easily in a traditional tape-based online-editing suite. You can also use your offline edit and EDL to re-create a sequence on film. Premiere Pro can export a project in the widely accepted Advanced Authoring Format (AAF), which can contain EDL and other data as well as the CMX3600 EDL format.

Alternatively, you can edit offline and online on the same system. Because lower-quality clips are smaller, more of them fit on your hard drive, and your computer can process them faster. For the online edit, you can recapture only the clips that you actually used in the sequence at the final-output quality. Premiere Pro automatically uses the high-quality clips in your final sequence, and no re-editing is required.

For an offline edit to succeed, you must have some way to accurately match your low-quality offline clips with their high-quality counterparts. Without a frame-accurate reference, there's no way to easily reproduce the sequence you created in the offline edit. That frame-accurate reference is known as *timecode*.

Timecode numbers identify each frame of video on a source tape. Premiere Pro and other video technologies use timecode to track edits in the offline edit and accurately re-create them in the online edit. Without timecode, an EDL would be meaningless, and recapturing clips would be impossible.

EDITING STRATEGY: OFFLINE AND ONLINE EDITING

# DV and Premiere Pro

For DV users, all this talk about offline and online editing may seem old-fashioned. DV is a high-quality, inexpensive video standard that not only has made video production more accessible, but simplifies postproduction, as well.

With DV, timecode is no longer a costly option found only in professional gear but is instead an integral part of the video signal. And *generational loss*—the progressive degradation of image and sound quality inherent in duplicating analog signals—isn't a concern with digital.

Because DV cameras record video in a digital format, there's no need to add a capture card to your computer to *digitize*, or convert an analog signal to a digital signal (for more about digitizing, see Chapter 3, "Capturing and Importing Footage"). With the help of an inexpensive IEEE 1394 (also called. FireWire or iLink) interface, Premiere Pro can transfer your footage to the hard drive for editing.

Just as important, IEEE 1394 simplifies postproduction. Whereas digitizing requires separate cables for video and audio, DV transfers both using a single IEEE 1394 cable. The cable also delivers DV's timecode information. Even device control (the ability to control a camera or deck from a computer) is accomplished over this same cable.

Compared to files digitized using older technology, DV footage consumes less storage space and requires only a modestly fast hard drive.

Whereas each type of analog capture card follows unique specifications, DV's characteristics are relatively consistent from one device to another. For this reason, Premiere Pro can include preset project and capture settings for DV, so you don't have to select video and audio settings manually.

# Your Desktop Editing Suite

All nonlinear editing systems use a graphical interface that to some degree refers to their predecessors: film- and tape-based editing tools. Yet as these traditional tools yield to newer technologies, the metaphors lose much of their meaning. These days, many editors have never seen a film splicer or a traditional video-editing suite. Nevertheless, it may help you to understand what Premiere Pro does if you realize what it's designed to replace.

Before programs like Premiere Pro, offline editing was synonymous with inexpensive, but very limited, editing equipment. In a typical offline suite, you'd create a simple *cuts-only* edit (no dissolves or other transitions) using low-quality copies of the camera originals called *window dubs*. In a window dub, timecode numbers were recorded over the picture (not actual timecode, but a "picture" of the timecode). When editing was complete, you could painstakingly transcribe the timecode numbers at the beginning and end of each shot to create the edit-decision list.

Only after you were armed with an EDL would you proceed to an online suite, with its expensive decks and special equipment. At this stage, you'd finally be able to add transitions, effects, and titles and mix audio.

Programs like Premiere Pro blur the line between online and offline editing by offering the online features at the offline stage (and price):

**A/B roll editing:** In a traditional tape-editing suite, any transition other than a cut required two sources: an *A roll* and a *B roll*. As the two tapes played, a video switcher could mix the signal from tape A with that from tape B for recording on the master tape. This way, you could create dissolves, wipes, and other effects. If two scenes were on the same source tape, one had to be copied onto the B roll before dissolves and other transitions could be applied (unless you had a deck with a preread feature, but that's another story). All this was possible only in an expensive online editing suite. Premiere Pro allows you to create an even wider range of transitions during the offline stage.

**Audio mixing and sweetening:** Just as a traditional offline suite permitted only simple cuts-only video editing, audio editing was usually limited to volume control. Better audio editing was left to the online edit or even to a separate audio post session. Premiere Pro allows you to apply complex audio editing and effects from the start, including audio processing to adjust the level, placement, and character of the sound. You can set audio In points based on audio samples, which are more precise than video frames. In addition, you can fade, boost, mix, and pan almost unlimited tracks of audio. Premiere Pro's audio mixer even resembles a traditional mixing board. Moreover, you can sweeten the audio, subtly correcting the sound and adding special effects.

**Digital video effects (DVE):** DVE is the generic term for a device used to process the video signal digitally, in real time, to accomplish all kinds of visual effects. DVEs can rotate, resize, and move an image; change the colors; and add other visual effects. Premiere Pro's effect settings can achieve the same results, as well as many effects you won't find in a DVE. They take more time to process on the desktop, but these kinds of visual effects used to be unavailable outside an online suite.

**Character generator (CG):** A CG is used to create text for video, usually to superimpose over other images. Premiere Pro's Adobe Title Designer brings the tools and ease of desktop publishing to character generation for video.

**Edit-decision list (EDL) import/export:** This feature produces a transcript of the edits in the final sequence so that it can be reproduced on another system—typically, a traditional higher-end system. Alternatively, it can read an EDL from another system. Premiere Pro supports the widely accepted AAF file format for exchanging data with other systems.

**Batch capture:** Batch capture uses timecode references to capture the proper clips automatically from a log or offline edit.

# Workflow

Regardless of whether you choose an offline or online editing path, you should look at your editing workflow as proceeding from simple to complex. You don't need to adhere rigidly to the following outline, but gradually fleshing out the final sequence is usually more efficient than plunging into effects, going back again to rough-cutting, and then discovering that the effects need to be redone. The Premiere Pro workspace options provide for an incremental process, optimizing the interface for editing, audio editing, and effects editing:

**Logging:** The most tedious (and, therefore, the most neglected) part of the editing process involves watching your source tapes and noting the *selects*—the shots you want to use in the project. Premiere Pro's Capture window and device control can make the logging process nearly painless. If your tape has timecode, you can log shots directly to your project; this log can serve as a *batch list*, a list of timecode start and end numbers that can be used to automate the capture process.

**Capture:** If you're using an IEEE 1394 connection, capture simply involves transferring video from your camera or deck to the hard drive. Analog sources require a capture device that can digitize the video. If you have timecode and device control, Premiere Pro can capture shots from a batch list automatically.

**Import:** At this point, you add to a Premiere Pro project the footage you want to use. You can import a variety of digital media: video, audio, stills, image sequences, and so on. Your project uses references to the source footage, not the footage itself.

**Basic edit/rough-cutting:** Arrange and adjust the sequence of clips into an edited sequence, using a variety of flexible and powerful editing tools. Because you're using file references, your decisions are nondestructive—that is, you can make as many changes as you want without permanently altering the source files.

**Preview:** Watch your sequences at any time, with or without transitions or special effects. Premiere Pro can render many effects in *real time*. That is, Premiere Pro can play transitions and other effects right away and at full playback speed using only your system's resources (and without special add-on hardware).

**Fine-tuning/fine-cutting:** Refine the edits in a sequence using any combination of editing controls, direct manipulation in the timeline, and the specialized Trim window.

**Effects and character generation:** Add titles, superimpose clips, add motion or video and audio effects, and animate effects.

**Audio sweetening:** Cut audio with sample-rate precision, mix tracks using a full-featured audio mixer, and enhance audio clips and tracks using a variety of built-in effects or any VST effect.

**Output:** Export the finished sequence directly to tape or DVD, or save a file in any number of formats for playback on other computers, CD-ROM, or over the Web.

# New Features

The **Adobe Title Designer**—the most striking feature introduced in the last version of Premiere—is the only feature that survived the transformation relatively unchanged. So you might think of the following as a list of new features in the new version, or as a list of features included in Premiere Pro that weren't in its forebear, the recently retired Premiere:

**Multiple and nested sequences:** Premiere Pro not only delivers long-awaited support for multiple sequences, but also allows you to *nest*, or embed, one sequence within another. This functionality allows you to group elements and create complex hierarchies and effects you couldn't achieve otherwise.

**Refined editing model:** Premiere Pro discards the A/B roll editing model entirely, opting for the more streamlined single-track editing model. Related innovations include transitions for audio and video transitions for any video track (not just video track 1).

**Unified approach to effects:** You can control all effects (including transitions) in a revised Effect Controls window, which includes a timeline view. Using the timeline view, you can see and adjust transitions in an A/B format and animate any of a clip's effects, including motion, opacity, volume, or any filter. Alternatively, you can animate an effect by *rubberbanding*—manipulating a property graph in the timeline.

**Enhanced audio support:** Using the enhanced audio mixer, you can mix using effects, sends, and submixes. Premiere Pro also supports 5.1 surround, 32-bit floating-point audio, and greatly enhanced waveform displays and subframe editing.

**Enhanced UI:** Each window shows advantages over previous versions of Premiere. The Project window includes a list view with thumbnails of clips, expanded headings, labels, and an icon view that doubles as a storyboard editor. The Monitor window includes viewing area navigational tools, more viewing options, and images that scale with the window. The Timeline window also includes better navigational tools and, with the tools in a separate window, a more streamlined look.

**Enhanced media management:** Premiere Pro helps you keep better track of your media files. You can unlink a clip from its media (and relink it) and delete media from within the project. New to Premiere Pro 1.5 is the Project Manager, which helps you collect and organize your media files as well as trim the project to just the media you used.

**Windows only:** Admittedly, Macintosh users may not find this a feature, but it is undeniably a difference from previous versions of Premiere. With Apple aggressively developing digital video tools for its own platform, it's not hard to imagine why Adobe found it prudent to focus its energies on developing programs for Windows.

# The Digital Video Collection

Although Premiere Pro is dedicated to editing video, you can use it to bring together a range of digital media. But even though Premiere Pro's features sometimes overlap with other types of software, the ideal workflow includes tools specialized for each job. Chances are good that Photoshop is already part of your still-image editing toolkit, and you use Illustrator for advanced typesetting and graphics. For moving media, Adobe hopes you will use Premiere Pro together with After Effects (for motion graphics and effects), Audition (for advanced audio editing and music creation), and Encore DVD (for DVD authoring). You'll enjoy a discounted price if you purchase these programs together as what Adobe calls its *Digital Video Collection*.

In addition to selling these programs as a set, the folks at Adobe are trying their best to make the programs *work* as a set. As these software packages have matured, they have also become more integrated. Over time, it's become easier to move files from one program to another without performing intermediate steps or sacrificing elements of your work. Even the interfaces have grown more consistent with one another. (The landscape is similar; however, the customs aren't always the same. You may find that some shared features don't use exactly the same procedures or keyboard shortcuts.)

Your familiarity with other Adobe programs may give you a head start in learning Premiere Pro. You'll find that Premiere Pro has a lot in common with its sibling, After Effects. If you're thinking about buying Premiere Pro or other Adobe programs, you may find their consistency or bundled pricing appealing. In any case, Adobe's eye toward product integration may be an important consideration for you.

# System Requirements

To use Premiere Pro, your system must meet these requirements:

◆ Intel Pentium III, 800 MHz or better (Intel Pentium 4, 3 GHz recommended)

◆ Microsoft Windows XP Home (XP Professional recommended)

◆ 256 MB of RAM (1 GB of RAM or more recommended)

◆ Large-capacity 7200 RPM UDMA 66 IDE or SCSI hard disk or disk array

◆ 256-color video display adapter and compatible monitor

◆ CD-ROM drive (DVD recordable required for Export to DVD)

◆ DirectX-compatible sound card (multi-channel ASIO compliant for surround-sound support recommended)

◆ IEEE 1394 (also called FireWire or iLink) connection or Adobe Premiere Pro third-party capture card

# Suggested System

These features aren't required, but they can make working with Premiere Pro a lot more satisfying:

**Faster processor:** The faster your system can make calculations, the faster it can process frames of video and create effects.

**Additional RAM:** Like all programs, Premiere Pro relies partly on RAM for performance and stability. In addition, the number of frames you can preview in real time without having to render depends entirely on the amount of RAM you can allocate to Premiere Pro.

**Larger hard drives:** Video files are notoriously large. Five minutes of DV footage, for example, consumes more than a gigabyte of storage space. Ample storage space allows you to work with more footage and with high-quality footage.

**Faster hard drives:** Your system's ability to play back footage smoothly relies partly on how quickly information can be read from the drives. Generally speaking, higher-quality footage requires faster drives. Drive arrays (RAIDs) use multiple drives to increase the overall transfer speed. To use DV footage, for example, your drives should sustain a data rate of around 5 MB per second.

**24-bit displays:** It almost goes without saying that it's best to work in True Colors.

**Larger or multiple displays:** Premiere Pro's interface can take up a lot of screen space. A large monitor can be more comfortable to work with. Many users like to spread out over two monitors, although others consider that arrangement to be overkill.

# Professional System Additions

Other additions can elevate your editing system to a more professional level:

**Video capture/playback device:** Your computer needs an IEEE 1394 connection and a similarly equipped camera or deck to transfer and output video in the DV format. If you want to digitize material from an analog source (VHS, Hi8, or BetacamSP), you may opt for an add-on capture card. You'll also need a deck to play and record tapes in your format of choice.

**Video monitor:** Video monitors and computer monitors display images differently. So if your work is destined for video or broadcast, a good monitor—preferably one with professional inputs and excellent color reproduction—allows you to judge it more accurately. A video capture device typically supports both your computer and video monitor.

**Audio card:** A standard built-in audio card is adequate for many applications, but you'll need a more advanced, ASIO-compliant audio card if you want to use Premiere Pro for multitrack recording or output to 5.1 surround. For more about ASIO and 5.1 surround, see Chapter 11, "Mixing Audio."

**Surround speakers:** Although an advanced audio card helps process multitrack, high-data-rate audio in 5.1, you won't hear the full effect without a set of speakers to match. Like everything else, surround speakers vary greatly in price and quality.

**DVD recorder:** DVD recorders are quickly becoming as commonplace in a desktop editing suite as video tape decks. (Thankfully, they're becoming more affordable as well.) You can use Premiere Pro to output your edited sequence to DVD. To produce more full-featured DVDs (with menus and the like), you'll also need a dedicated authoring program like Adobe Encore DVD.

**Third-party plug-ins:** A multitude of third-party developers offer software plug-ins that expand Premiere Pro's capabilities. These products include improved or additional effects and transitions, audio effects, matchback tools to create EDLs for film, and tools that allow you to better evaluate and adjust the video signal.

**Hardware acceleration:** If rendering speed and turnaround time are of paramount importance, you may want to invest in a Premiere Pro system bundled with hardware to accelerate effects rendering.

## NTSC, PAL, and SECAM

You'll sometimes hear monitors and other video equipment referred to as NTSC, as in *NTSC monitor*. NTSC stands for National Television Standards Committee, a group that develops the television standards used in North America and Japan; its name describes everything that meets those standards.

PAL (which stand for Phase Alternation Line) is the standard used in most of Europe and other countries, whereas SECAM (Sequential Couleur Avec Mémoire) is used primarily in France, the Middle East, and Eastern Europe.

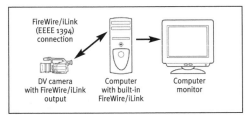

**Figure i.2** This configuration includes a computer equipped for IEEE 1394 (also called FireWire or iLink) and a DV camera.

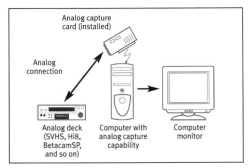

**Figure i.3** This configuration includes a computer equipped with an Adobe-certified capture card and an analog video deck.

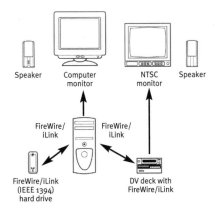

**Figure i.4** This configuration uses several recommended options, such as a television monitor, speakers, external hard drive, and deck.

# System Configurations

As the preceding sections suggest, your Premiere Pro setup can be simple or elaborate. As long as your computer meets the minimum requirements, you can install Premiere Pro and start editing. On the other hand, your system might include a television monitor and a camera or deck. Here's how a few common configurations might look:

**DV camera configuration (Figure i.2):** In this setup, a DV camera is used to transfer source video to your computer's hard drive over an IEEE 1394 connection. The completed edited project can be played back and recorded to a tape in the camera.

**Analog capture configuration (Figure i.3):** In this setup, the computer is equipped with a qualifying video capture card to digitize video from an analog source (such as VHS, Hi8, or BetacamSP). The capture card converts the signal from analog to digital so that it can be stored on the hard drive.

**Enhanced DV configuration (Figure i.4):** In this setup, several recommended options have been added to the system. An external IEEE 1394 drive provides additional storage space for media, a dedicated playback and recording deck reduces wear on the camera's tape transport, a video monitor displays the sequences as they will appear on a television screen, and external speakers provide the audio.

## ✔ Tip

■ Looking for a complete system? Several vendors offer preconfigured editing systems. You may find their pricing and service agreements attractive. In addition, Premiere Pro is often bundled with capture cards and real-time acceleration cards and even offered as an option when you purchase a computer.

# PREMIERE PRO BASICS

Before embarking on a journey, it is useful to survey the landscape and learn a few local customs. In this chapter, you'll get oriented to the Premiere Pro interface and catch a glimpse of what's to come. In addition, you'll learn about the basic workings of the interface: how to use context menus, keyboard shortcuts, and commands, and how to undo mistakes. Once you're familiar with this little travel guide, you can get your passport stamped in Chapter 2, "Starting a Project."

# A Look at the Interface

Most of your editing takes place in three primary windows, which leaves a little room for some helpful tools and palettes (**Figure 1.1**).

The *Project window* lists and organizes the source clips you want to use. It displays important information about each clip that you can use to sort the clips. When you log clips using the Capture window (described in the next section), they are listed in the Project window for batch capture. You can also have Premiere Pro add clips to a sequence automatically, according to how you sort or select clips in the Project window.

The *Monitor window* displays the source clips in the left pane, or *source view*, and displays the clips in your sequence in the right pane, or *program view*. It also contains playback and editing controls.

The *Timeline window* graphically represents your program as video and audio clips arranged in vertically stacked tracks. Time is measured along a horizontal ruler.

The *Tools window* includes an assortment of editing tools that help you arrange and adjust the clips in a sequence. It can be oriented vertically or horizontally.

The *Info palette* provides information pertinent to the task at hand—such as the vital statistics of the selected clip or the current position of the mouse pointer.

The *History palette*, as in other Adobe programs, allows you to view and undo recent actions.

**Figure 1.1** Most editing takes place in three windows, which leaves screen space for a few helpful palettes.

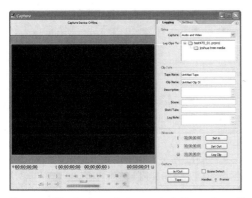

**Figure 1.2** The Capture window controls the capture of video and audio.

**Figure 1.3** The Trim window lets you fine-tune the cut point between clips in a sequence.

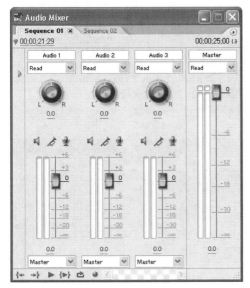

**Figure 1.4** The audio mixer emulates a traditional mixing board.

# A Glance at Secondary Windows

As your project progresses, you'll call upon various other windows and features to fine-tune edits, mix audio, and add effects, as well as capture video and export edit-decision lists.

The *Capture window* controls the capture of video and audio (**Figure 1.2**). (See Chapter 3, "Capturing and Importing Footage.")

The *Trim window* provides special controls for fine-tuning the cut point between clips in the sequence (**Figure 1.3**). (See Chapter 8, "Refining the Sequence.")

The *audio mixer,* which emulates a traditional mixing board, allows you to fade and pan audio tracks in real time and sweeten the audio with effects such as noise reduction and equalization (**Figure 1.4**). (See Chapter 11, "Mixing Audio.")

The *Adobe Title Designer window* allows you to create text and graphics for use in your program (**Figure 1.5**). (See Chapter 12, "Creating Titles.")

**Figure 1.5** The Adobe Title Designer window lets you create text and graphics.

A GLANCE AT SECONDARY WINDOWS

The *Effects palette* lists and organizes video and audio transitions (see Chapter 9, "Adding Transitions") as well as video and audio filters (see Chapter 13, "Working with Effects") (**Figure 1.6**). You can make the Effects palette appear as a tab in the Project window or source view of the Monitor window.

The *Effect Controls palette* consolidates everything you need to adjust transitions and effects in a single palette. It automatically displays the appropriate controls for adjusting a selected transition (**Figure 1.7**) or for setting and keyframing a clip's effects—whether they're fixed effects (motion, opacity, and volume) or filters (**Figure 1.8**). You can make the Effect Controls palette appear as a tab in the Project window or source view.

### ✔ Tip

- You can adjust the brightness of the interface by choosing Edit > Preferences > General and dragging the User Interface Brightness slider.

**Figure 1.6** The Effects palette lists and organizes transitions and filters.

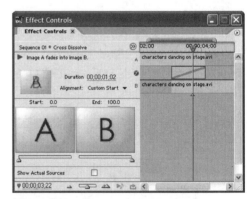

**Figure 1.7** The Effect Controls palette provides controls for adjusting a selected transition . . .

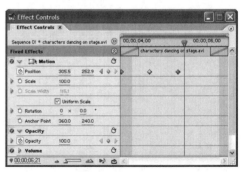

**Figure 1.8** . . . or helps you set and animate effects like motion, opacity, volume, and filters.

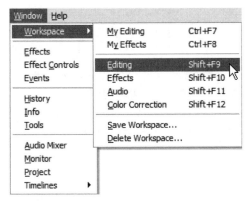

**Figure 1.9** Choose Window > Workspace to select one of the preset workspaces.

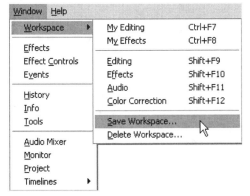

**Figure 1.10** Choose Window > Workspace > Save Workspace.

# Arranging the Workspace

Premiere Pro lets you rearrange the various windows and palettes on the screen to suit different editing tasks. Conveniently, Premiere Pro can memorize each configuration, or *workspace*. This allows you to switch to the most appropriate arrangement with a simple menu command.

Premiere Pro ships with four preset workspaces designed for specific tasks: Editing, Effects, Audio, and Color Correction. You can use them as they are or rearrange them to match your needs. When you save a custom workspace, it appears in the Workspace menu with the name you specify.

## To choose a preset workspace:

◆ Choose Window > Workspace and select one of the preset workspaces (**Figure 1.9**).

## To save a custom workspace:

1. Arrange the windows and palettes in the configuration you want to save as a workspace.

2. Choose Window > Workspace > Save Workspace (**Figure 1.10**).

*continues on next page*

ARRANGING THE WORKSPACE

**3.** In the Save Workspace dialog box, type a name for the workspace and click Save (**Figure 1.11**).

Your new workspace will now appear in the Window > Workspace menu above the supplied presets (**Figure 1.12**).

### ✔ Tips

- You can more quickly switch among your various custom workspaces if you assign keyboard shortcuts as described in "Customizing Keyboard Shortcuts" later in this chapter.

- Starting with Premiere Pro 1.5, custom workspaces remember the stacking order of the windows—a great feature when screen real estate is at a premium. Workspaces saved in the previous version of Premiere Pro will have to be saved again, in a more recent version of the program, if you want Premiere Pro to remember the stacking order.

**Figure 1.11** Type a name for the new workspace and click Save.

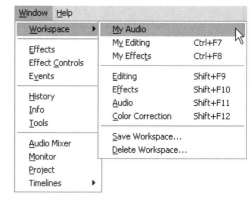

**Figure 1.12** The new workspace is now available in the Window > Workspace menu.

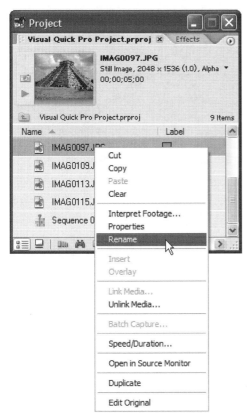

**Figure 1.13** Right-click to view a context menu, which is a menu that relates to the area where you're clicking.

# Using Context Menus

In addition to accessing commands from the menu bar at the top of the screen, you can use context menus. Windows users are already aware that right-clicking, or *context-clicking*, reveals a context menu near the mouse pointer.

As the name suggests, *context menus* contain commands relevant in a particular context or area of the screen. In other words, context-clicking a clip in the Timeline window reveals a menu similar to the one you would see if you selected the clip and chose the Clip menu on the menu bar. The context menu for the Project window contains commands that relate to it, such as the Import command. Like keyboard shortcuts, context menus can be real time savers.

## To access a context menu:

1. Position the pointer on the appropriate window or item and right-click.

   A menu relating to the window or item appears (**Figure 1.13**).

2. Choose a command from the menu as you would from any other menu; then release the mouse button.

   Premiere Pro executes the command.

# Using Tabbed Windows

Premiere Pro helps you optimize your workspace and workflow by letting you view certain palettes separately or as tabs in a single window. However, palettes are compatible only with certain windows. The Project window can contain tabs for the Effects and Effect Controls palettes; in addition to a tab for source clips, the source view can contain the Effect Controls palette and the audio mixer. The program view of the Monitor window and the Timeline window can both contain a tab for each sequence in the project.

### To use tabs:

◆ *Do any of the following:*

▲ To view a palette as a tab, drag the palette to a compatible window.

▲ To view a tabbed palette and bring it to the front of a window, click the tab.

▲ To view a tab as a separate palette, drag the tab out of its current window.

▲ To close a tab, click the tab's close icon ⌧.

### ✔ Tip

■ When there are too many tabs to fit in the available space in the window, a thin scroll bar appears above the tabs. Drag the bar to view hidden tabs.

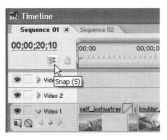

**Figure 1.14** The keyboard shortcut for a menu command appears across from the command.

**Figure 1.15** Hovering the mouse pointer over a button or icon reveals a tool tip, which identifies the item and its keyboard shortcut, if it has one.

**Figure 1.16** Choose Help > Keyboard to learn about the keyboard shortcuts.

# Using Keyboard Shortcuts

One way to increase your speed and efficiency is to take advantage of keyboard shortcuts. A standard set of keyboard shortcuts, the Adobe Premiere Pro Factory Default shortcuts, is built in. Premiere Pro doesn't ship with a quick reference card for keyboard shortcuts, but the interface helps you learn them in other ways. The keyboard shortcut for a menu command appears across from the command in the right column (**Figure 1.14**). You may also have noticed that hovering the mouse pointer over a button or icon reveals a *tool tip*, a small box identifying both the item's name and its keyboard equivalent, if it has one (**Figure 1.15**). Other standard keyboard shortcuts are documented in the online Help system. This book mentions the most common and useful shortcuts in the pertinent sections.

## To view the keyboard shortcuts in Help:

1. Choose Help > Keyboard (**Figure 1.16**). Premiere Pro launches your browser and opens the Help feature (**Figure 1.17**).

2. In the online Help system, click the appropriate related subtopics.

## ✔ Tip

■ Tool tips are turned on by default, but you can turn them off on the General panel of the Preferences dialog box.

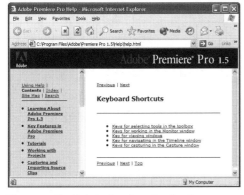

**Figure 1.17** The Help feature launches in a browser window.

# Customizing Keyboard Shortcuts

In addition to offering a standard set of shortcuts, Premiere Pro lets you create your own shortcut for practically every button, tool, and command. Moreover, you can save sets of shortcuts and easily switch among the sets. Sets are great when more than one editor uses the same Premiere Pro system. (Of course, adjusting the chair height is still up to you.) And if you're accustomed to working on a version of Premiere prior to Premiere Pro, or even on a different editing system, you can create sets to match the shortcuts to the ones you're used to.

### To assign custom keyboard shortcuts:

1. Choose Edit > Keyboard Customization (**Figure 1.18**).

   The Keyboard Customization dialog box appears (**Figure 1.19**).

2. In the drop-down menu under the set name, choose the category of shortcut you want to view and edit:

   **Application:** Displays menu commands and other general shortcuts.

   **Windows:** Displays shortcuts related to specific windows and their drop-down menus.

   **Tools:** Displays shortcuts assigned to tools.

3. From the Command list, select the command or tool to which you want to assign a shortcut. If necessary, first click the triangle next to a subcategory to expand it to reveal the commands it contains.

**Figure 1.18** Choose Edit > Keyboard Customization.

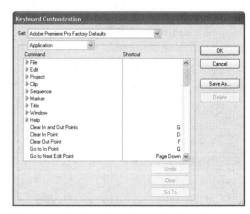

**Figure 1.19** Create custom shortcuts using the Keyboard Customization dialog box.

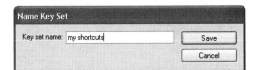

**Figure 1.20** Click Save As to open the Name Key Set dialog box and save your custom set.

**4.** *Do one of the following:*

▲ To assign a new shortcut to the selected item, type the shortcut.

▲ To remove the current shortcut from the selected item, click Clear.

**5.** If you want, *do one of the following when prompted:*

▲ To revert to the previous shortcut assignment, click Undo.

▲ To restore an undone shortcut, click Redo.

▲ To find the command that already uses the shortcut you assigned to the selected item (if any), click Go To.

**6.** Repeat steps 2 through 5 as needed.

## To save a custom set of keyboard shortcuts:

**1.** In the Keyboard Customization dialog box, click Save As.

The Name Key Set dialog box appears (**Figure 1.20**).

**2.** In the Name Key Set dialog box, type the name for the key set and click Save.

## ✔ Tip

■ In addition to the Adobe Premiere Pro Factory Default set, you can choose shortcuts for AVID Xpress DV and Apple Final Cut Pro.

# Correcting Mistakes

Many people judge a program not only by how much it can do, but by how much it can undo. The number of recent actions you can negate in Premiere Pro is limited only by the amount of available memory. So if you change your mind yet again, you can redo the last undone action.

Premiere Pro also includes a History palette, another Adobe standard. The History palette lists your recent actions, so you can choose exactly how many steps back you want to take. This feature is covered in the next section.

And when undoing can't solve the problem, you can revert to the last saved version of the project or open an archived version.

### To undo an action:

◆ Choose Edit > Undo (**Figure 1.21**) or press Ctrl+Z.

If the last action can't be undone, the menu displays the dimmed entry Can't Undo.

### To redo an action:

◆ Choose Edit > Redo (**Figure 1.22**) or press Shift+Ctrl+Z.

If the last action can't be redone, the menu displays the dimmed entry Can't Redo.

### ✔ Tip

■ To cancel an action that Premiere Pro is processing (evidenced by a progress bar), press Esc.

**Figure 1.21** Choose Edit > Undo to negate the preceding action.

**Figure 1.22** Choose Edit > Redo to restore an undone action.

CORRECTING MISTAKES

**Figure 1.23** The History palette lists the actions you've taken; the most recent appears at the bottom.

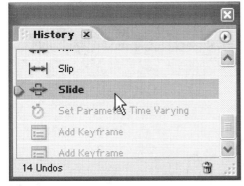

**Figure 1.24** Click an action in the list to return the project to the state it was in when that action was performed.

**Figure 1.25** When you resume editing, the dimmed actions disappear, and your latest actions are added to the list.

# Using the History Palette

If you're familiar with Adobe's other programs, you know that the History palette is like a super-undo—or a time machine. The History palette lists your recent actions, and each new action is added to the bottom of the list. By looking at the list, you can see exactly what you did, and exactly where you went wrong. Clicking an action negates all the subsequent actions listed below it. When you resume editing, the undone actions are removed from the list, and history is rewritten.

## To use the History palette:

1. If necessary, click the History tab to make the History palette visible.

   The palette lists the most recent actions, with the latest action at the bottom of the list (**Figure 1.23**).

2. Click the last action you want to retain (**Figure 1.24**).

   Actions below the selected action become dimmed in the list. The project reverts to the state it was in at the time the selected action was taken. To see the results of various selections, you can select the items even if they are currently dimmed.

3. If you are satisfied with your choice, resume other editing tasks.

   The dimmed actions disappear (**Figure 1.25**), and subsequent actions are added to the list.

## To undo and remove actions from the History list:

1. On the History palette, select an action in the list.

   The project is returned to the state it was in at the time the selected action was taken.

2. *Do one of the following:*
   - ▲ Click the Delete Redoable Actions button 🗑 (**Figure 1.26**).
   - ▲ From the History palette menu, choose Delete.

3. When prompted, click Yes.

   The action and subsequent actions are removed from the list, and the project returns to the state it was in prior to the deleted actions (**Figure 1.27**).

## To clear the History list without undoing actions:

- ◆ In the History palette menu, choose Clear History (**Figure 1.28**).

   All items are removed from the list, but the project remains unchanged.

## ✔ Tips

- ■ The History palette doesn't list every move you make, just actions that affect the project itself.

- ■ Choosing File > Revert eliminates all of the actions listed on the History palette since the project was last saved.

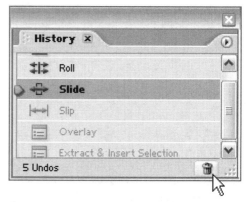

**Figure 1.26** On the History palette, select an action and click the Delete icon.

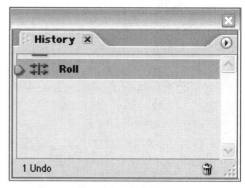

**Figure 1.27** The action and subsequent actions are removed from the list, and the project returns to the state it was in prior to the deleted actions.

**Figure 1.28** In the History palette menu, choose Clear History to clear the list without affecting the project.

**Figure 1.29** Choose Window > Events to open the Events window.

**Figure 1.30** The Events window lists information, warnings, and error messages.

# Using the Events Window

To give third-party plug-in developers a tool for communicating information, warnings, and error messages, Premiere Pro 1.5 includes the Events window. The Events window provides detailed information for users to use to troubleshoot problems with plug-ins. You can clear the Events window to remove the alert icon from the status bar.

## To use the Events window:

1. Choose Window > Events (**Figure 1.29**) or double-click the alert icon on the status bar.

   The Events window opens (**Figure 1.30**).

2. Select the information, warning, or error message you want to know more about and click Details.

## To clear an event:

1. Select the information, warning, or error message you want to clear.

2. Click Clear All (Figure 1.30).

# STARTING A PROJECT

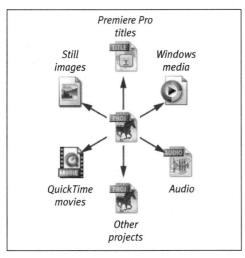

**Figure 2.1** A project file is a detailed set of instructions that refers to—but doesn't contain—source files. Your hard drive must contain both the project (a small file) and the source files to which it refers (larger files).

When you edit with Adobe Premiere Pro, you're actually creating a detailed set of instructions called a *project* (**Figure 2.1**). A project contains a list of all the clips that you intend to use in your edited video program. It also contains a list of all of your editing decisions, including the arrangement of the clips, transitions, audio levels, and effects.

You can think of a project as analogous to a musical score. Just as sheet music refers to instruments and indicates when they should play, the project refers to media files and indicates when they should play. A project doesn't contain the files themselves—only references to those files, called *clips*. As a result, you never alter the source files directly. Hence, editing in Premiere Pro is sometimes referred to as *nondestructive editing*.

Because a project is simply a detailed set of instructions, a project file is small, sometimes less than 1 MB. The source files, on the other hand, tend to consume a lot of hard-drive space. For example, five minutes of DV footage with audio consumes more than 1 GB of storage. Returning to our analogy, you can slip sheet music into your pocket, but the actual orchestra is considerably more bulky.

In this chapter, you'll learn to start a new project, choose audio and video settings, and import a variety of source files as clips.

# Starting a Project

After you launch Premiere Pro, a welcome screen prompts you to start a new project or open an existing one (**Figure 2.2**). Once you're working on a project, you can use a command on the menu bar to switch to another project or start a new one. You can have only one project open at a time, however.

The following steps outline how to start a project without detailing specific settings. For more about choosing project settings or specifying custom presets, continue reading this chapter.

### To start a new project:

1. *Do one of the following:*
   - ▲ Launch Premiere Pro. On the welcome screen, click New Project (**Figure 2.3**).
   - ▲ With Premiere Pro running, choose File > New > Project (**Figure 2.4**).

   The New Project dialog box opens (**Figure 2.5**).

2. In the New Project dialog box, *do one of the following:*
   - ▲ To select the preset appropriate to your project, click the Load Preset tab.
   - ▲ To specify settings (such as format, frame size, frame rate, and audio settings) suited to your project, click the Custom Settings tab.

   A description of the preset's audio and video settings appears on the right side of the dialog box.

**Figure 2.2** Premiere Pro's welcome screen makes starting a new or existing project easy.

**Figure 2.3** To start a new project, click New Project on the welcome screen...

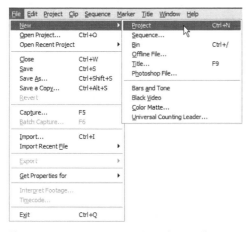

**Figure 2.4** ...or, in an open project, choose File > New > Project.

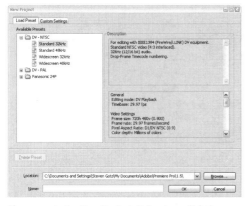

**Figure 2.5** In the New Project dialog box, click the Load Preset tab to use presets, or click the Custom Settings tab to specify the settings manually.

**3.** Specify where you want to save the project file *by doing one of the following*:

▲ Enter the file path in the Location field.

▲ Click Browse to navigate to the location where you want to save the project file.

**4.** For Name, specify the name of the project. Premiere Pro automatically appends the .prproj extension to the file's name.

**5.** Click OK.

An untitled Project window opens, as well as several associated windows, such as the Monitor window and Timeline window.

## ✔ Tips

■ You can close any window except the Project window. Closing the Project window ends the current project and reopens the welcome screen.

■ When you launch Premiere Pro for the first time, it creates a Preferences file in the Application Data folder. If the Adobe Premiere Pro Preferences file becomes corrupted, causing the program to malfunction, delete the Preferences file to force the program to create a new, uncorrupted file.

# Specifying Project Settings

Project settings determine how Premiere Pro processes the audio and video as you edit. In most cases, you can choose one of the built-in presets that are optimized for several common scenarios, such as editing video in the DV format. However, you can also create custom settings to fit your particular needs.

Once you choose project settings, you can't change them for that project. Additionally, the project settings you choose apply to all the sequences in the project. Generally, your choice of settings is based on your source material, your capture device, your computer's ability to process video and audio, and your output goal.

The following sections explain how to select a built-in preset and then provide an overview to help you choose settings yourself.

### ✔ Tip

■ If you discover that you've selected the wrong project settings after you've made significant progress on a sequence, don't panic. You can open a new project with the proper settings and import the sequence into it. Most of your editing decisions should remain intact. However, if the timebases of the two projects differ, clips in the sequence may be misaligned in the new project. In this case, double-check the In and Out points and adjust them where necessary.

## DV Is Easy

You could argue that the greatest advantage of the DV format is not its high quality or affordability, but its ease of use. DV is digitized in the camera, it can be transferred to a hard drive over a single cable, it contains timecode, and it uses a consistent standard. For these reasons, DV users usually don't customize their project settings—they simply choose the appropriate DV preset and move on.

Unlike DV, which uses a widely accepted standard, capture cards generally use their own unique *codecs* (a codec is method of storing and playing video; see Chapter 16, "Video and Audio Settings"). If you're using an analog video-capture card, chances are it comes with its own software, including a preset (which you can add to the list of available presets in the New Project dialog box). You can rely on the documentation that comes with your capture device, and you'll seldom need to stray from the settings designed for it.

If your current project isn't built around DV or a particular capture card, then your choices become more complex. Instead of choosing a ready-made preset, you have to select your own project settings.

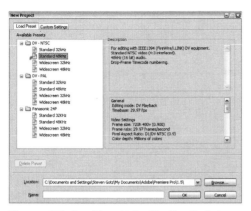

**Figure 2.6** The Load Preset tab of the New Project dialog box presents a choice of built-in or custom-made project presets.

## ✔ Tips

- The DV presets' Default Sequence settings specify a stereo master track, which is suitable for most projects. Because you can't change a sequence's master track, you should use the custom settings to specify a different channel type (mono or 5.1) before you start a project (see the next section). Otherwise, you can create another sequence with the appropriate master audio track in the same project.

- If you're not sure whether your DV footage was shot with 32-kHz or 48-kHz audio, check your camera's documentation or start a project and look at the clips' properties in the Project window (see Chapter 4, "Managing Clips"). If you chose the wrong setting, start another project with the proper setting before you begin editing.

# Choosing Built-in Presets

As you've learned, starting a new project opens the New Project dialog box, which includes a Load Preset tab and a Custom Settings tab.

When you select the Load Preset tab, the left side of the New Project dialog box lists project presets you can use. When you select a preset from the list, a description of the settings appears on the right side of the dialog box (**Figure 2.6**). The built-in presets include project settings optimized for common types of source footage, particularly DV:

**DV – NTSC:** Contains presets for DV footage shot in NTSC, the video standard used in North America, Japan, and other countries.

**DV – PAL:** Contains presets for DV footage shot in PAL, the standard in most of Europe.

**Panasonic 24P:** Contains presets for footage shot using the 24P or 24P Advanced (24PA) format.

These folders each contain the following four options:

**Standard 32kHz:** Used for DV footage shot in television's standard 4:3 aspect ratio, using 32-kHz audio, one of two audio sample rates supported by most DV cameras.

**Standard 48kHz:** Used for DV footage shot in television's standard 4:3 aspect ratio, using 48-kHz audio.

**Widescreen 32kHz:** Used for DV footage shot in a 16:9 aspect ratio, which is supported by some DV cameras and equipment, using 32-kHz audio.

**Widescreen 48kHz:** Used for DV footage shot in a 16:9 aspect ratio, which is supported by some DV cameras and equipment, using 48-kHz audio.

# Selecting Custom Project Settings

You can specify project settings manually on the Custom Settings tab of the New Project dialog box.

When the Custom Settings tab is selected, the left side of the dialog box lists four categories of settings: General, Capture, Video Rendering, and Default Sequence.

If you're new to digital video, the number of options can be daunting at first. Don't worry; making a choice is not as hard as it looks. And even if you make a wrong choice or change your mind later, the mistake usually is not fatal. This section explains only how to access the settings; for more complete explanations of each setting, consult Chapter 16, "Video and Audio Settings."

## ✔ Tip

■ For editing, you're primarily concerned with the General settings category. You'll learn more about the Capture, Video Rendering, and Default Sequence categories in later chapters.

### To select custom settings:

1. Start a new project.

   The New Project dialog box appears.

2. In the New Project dialog box, select the Custom Settings tab.

3. To view settings to adjust them, click a category (**Figure 2.7**):

   **General:** Determines how Premiere Pro processes and displays video and audio. The General category also includes settings that specify safe zones and whether clips are scaled when added to a sequence.

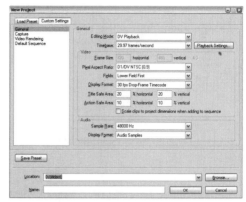

**Figure 2.7** On the Custom Settings tab of the New Project dialog box, click a settings category from the list on the left.

**Capture:** Sets the capture device.

**Video Rendering:** Specifies the way video is compressed and whether stills are optimized for video display.

**Default Sequence:** Sets the initial characteristics of new sequences in the project, such as the number of tracks and the type of audio tracks.

4. Select the settings that suit your project.

5. Specify Location and Name values and click OK.

## ✔ Tip

■ Once you specify the channel type (mono, stereo, or 5.1) of a sequence's master track, you can't change it. However, you can create another sequence with a different type of master audio track in the same project.

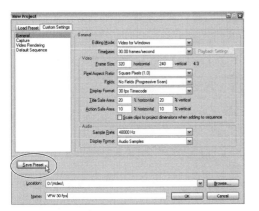

**Figure 2.8** Once you've specified your settings, click Save Preset.

**Figure 2.9** In the Save Project Settings dialog box, type a name and description for your preset.

# Saving Custom Settings as a Preset

Even if you're comfortable selecting project settings, making those choices still can be a chore. Fortunately, you can save settings so that they appear in the Available Presets list on the Load Preset tab of the New Project dialog box. You can also delete presets from the list.

## To save settings:

1. Specify the project settings as explained in the previous section, "Selecting Custom Project Settings."

2. On the Custom Settings tab of the New Project dialog box, click Save Preset (**Figure 2.8**).

   The Save Project Settings dialog box appears (**Figure 2.9**).

3. Type a name for your settings and a description that summarizes your choices.

4. To save settings pertaining to a capture device as part of the preset, select Include Device Control Settings.

5. Click OK to close the dialog box.

6. Click OK to close the New Project dialog box and start your project.

   From now on, your saved preset appears in the Available Presets section of the Load Preset tab of the New Project dialog box. When you select this preset, the description you entered appears in the Description area.

# Saving Projects

Because your project file embodies all your editing decisions, protecting it from possible mishaps is crucial. As with any important file, you should save your project often and keep backups. Premiere Pro can help you protect your project by automatically saving it in the Adobe Premiere Pro Auto-Save folder. In the event of a system crash or file corruption, you can retrieve one of the archived copies.

## To save a project:

**1.** To save a project, *do one of the following:*

▲ Choose File > Save to save the project under the current name and location or to save the project for the first time.

▲ Choose File > Save As (**Figure 2.10**) to save the project under a new name or location and continue working on the new copy of the project.

▲ Choose File > Save a Copy to save a copy of the current project and continue working on the current project.

**2.** If you are prompted by a dialog box, specify a name and destination for the project (**Figure 2.11**).

**3.** Click Save to close the dialog box and save the file.

**Figure 2.10** To save a file under a new name or in a different location, choose File > Save As.

**Figure 2.11** If prompted, specify a name and destination for the project.

**Figure 2.12** Choose File > Revert to revert to the last-saved version.

**Figure 2.13** When prompted, confirm your choice.

## To revert to the last-saved version of a project:

1. Choose File > Revert (**Figure 2.12**).

   Premiere Pro prompts you to confirm your choice (**Figure 2.13**).

2. Click Yes to confirm that you want to revert to the last-saved version.

   The project returns to the state it was in when you last saved it.

**SAVING PROJECTS**

# Saving Projects Automatically

Premiere Pro can back up your project automatically as frequently as you choose. Backup files are saved in a folder called Adobe Premiere Pro Auto-Save, which is located in the same directory as the original project. Backup files use the original project name followed by a dash and a number (*filename*-1.prproj, *filename*-2.prproj, and so on).

## To set automatic save:

1. Choose Edit > Preferences > Auto Save (**Figure 2.14**).

   The Auto Save panel of the Preferences dialog box opens.

2. Click the Automatically Save Projects check box and type the time interval at which you want Premiere Pro to save the current project (**Figure 2.15**).

3. For Maximum Project Versions, enter the number of versions of each project that you want Premiere Pro to automatically save.

   When the maximum number of saved versions is reached, each additional saved version overwrites the oldest saved file.

4. Click OK to close the Preferences dialog box.

**Figure 2.14** Choose Edit > Preferences > Auto Save to set the automatic save option.

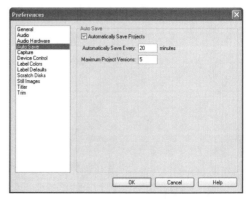

**Figure 2.15** Select Automatically Save Projects and enter a time interval and the maximum number of project versions.

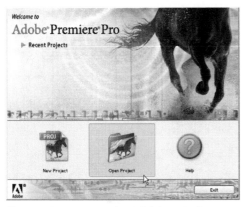

**Figure 2.16** To open a project, click Open Project on the welcome screen...

# Opening Projects

Premiere Pro's welcome screen makes it easy to open a project right after you launch the program. But, naturally, you can switch to another project at any time by using a menu command.

## To open a project:

1. *Do one of the following:*
   - ▲ On the welcome screen, click the Open Project icon (**Figure 2.16**).
   - ▲ In an open project, choose File > Open Project (**Figure 2.17**).

   The Open Project dialog box appears.

2. Select the project file that you want to open (**Figure 2.18**).

   Auto-saved projects are located in the Adobe Premiere Pro Auto-Save folder, which resides in the Premiere Pro folder.

3. Click Open.

**Figure 2.17** ...or, in an open project, choose File > Open Project.

**Figure 2.18** Navigate to the project you want to open and select it.

## To open a recent project:

◆ *Do one of the following:*

▲ On the welcome screen, click the project's name in the Recent Projects list (**Figure 2.19**).

▲ In an open project, Choose File > Open Recent Project and choose the recently open project from the submenu (**Figure 2.20**).

The project opens.

## ✔ Tip

■ Closing a project returns you to the welcome screen, where you can quickly choose whether to start a new or existing project. Clicking Exit on the welcome screen quits Premiere Pro.

**Figure 2.19** To open a recent project, click the name of the project on the welcome screen...

**Figure 2.20** ...or, in an open project, choose File > Open Recent Project and choose the project you want.

# Locating Missing and Offline Files

As you learned at the beginning of this chapter, a project is simply a set of instructions that refers to files on a drive. When you open a project, Premiere Pro looks for the files to which the project refers. If the source files have been moved, deleted, or renamed since the project was last saved, Premiere Pro will have trouble finding them. Premiere Pro attempts to locate the missing clips and prompts you to confirm its choice. (Premiere Pro also attempts to find missing preview files; see Chapter 10, "Previewing a Sequence.")

Sometimes, a project refers to a file that is not currently available, or *offline*. Fortunately, you can tell Premiere Pro to insert a blank placeholder, or *offline clip*, to stand in until you can get the file back on your drive (or *online*) again. Naturally, when you use an offline clip, you can't view the file it is holding a place for, but using the offline clip permits the project to remember the name of the file and recall how you used it in your program.

Once you've accounted for missing files, resave the project. From then on, the updated project will open without incident, because you've told it where to find the files you want and not to look for the ones you don't want. If you say a clip is offline, it doesn't mean the clip is missing; the project simply lists it as offline until you decide to capture it or to relink it with its source media file. For more about creating and capturing offline files, see Chapter 3, "Capturing and Importing Footage." For more about unlinking and relinking clips and media, see Chapter 4, "Managing Clips."

## ✔ Tips

■ In this context, the term *offline* means unavailable, or not on a drive. Don't confuse offline clips with the term *offline editing*, which is the practice of creating a low-quality rough cut in preparation for *online editing*, which produces the final version.

■ When the Project window is set to list view, the Status column indicates a clip's status as Online, Offline, or Offline: File Missing. The clip's icon also indicates whether the clip is online or offline.

LOCATING MISSING AND OFFLINE FILES

## To open a project with missing files that are available:

1. Open a project using any of the methods described in the previous sections.

   If files are missing, the Where Is the File dialog box opens. The name of the missing file appears in quotation marks as part of the name of the dialog box (**Figure 2.21**).

2. To find a file, *do one of the following:*
   - ▲ Allow Premiere Pro to automatically locate a file with the same name as the missing file.
   - ▲ Manually locate the missing file or its replacement.
   - ▲ Click Find to launch the Windows search feature to help locate the file.

3. When you locate the correct file, select it and click the Select button (**Figure 2.22**).

   The missing file is replaced with the selected file.

4. If necessary, repeat steps 2 and 3 when you are prompted to locate other missing clips. If missing clips are not available on your hard drive, follow the instructions in the next task, "To open a project with missing files that are unavailable."

## ✔ Tips

- ■ As a rule, use a consistent organizational method for your files and avoid moving or renaming them until your project has been delivered and is ready to archive.

- ■ Unless you're in the bad habit of moving, renaming, or deleting files, there are only a few reasons Premiere Pro will prompt you for missing files—for example, if you have moved the project and media to another system or restored the files from a backup. In these cases, the media probably isn't on the same drive as when you saved the project.

**Figure 2.21** If files are missing, the Where Is the File *filename*? dialog box appears.

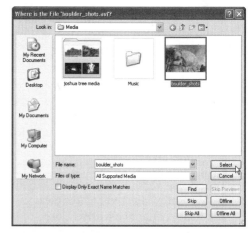

**Figure 2.22** When you locate the correct file, select it and click Select.

**Figure 2.23** If the file is unavailable, skip the file, designate it as offline, or cancel the search.

## To open a project with missing files that are unavailable:

1. Open a project using any of the methods described in the previous sections.

   If files are missing, the Where Is the File dialog box opens. The name of the missing file appears in quotation marks as part of the name of the dialog box.

2. *Click one of the following buttons* (**Figure 2.23**):

   ▲ **Cancel** to close the dialog box without accounting for missing files. Premiere Pro will treat the files as missing the next time you open the project.

   ▲ **Skip** to remove the missing clip from the project. All instances of the clip disappear from the project, including the edited sequence.

   ▲ **Skip All** to have Premiere Pro remove all missing clips from the project without prompting you for confirmation.

   ▲ **Skip Previews** to remove all missing preview files from the project. Preview files are rendered audio and video effects, including transitions (see Chapter 10, "Previewing a Sequence").

   ▲ **Offline** to list the missing file in the project as an offline clip.

   ▲ **Offline All** to have Premiere Pro list all missing files in the project as offline without prompting you for confirmation.

3. Repeat step 2 each time you are prompted to locate a missing file.

   Once you account for all missing files, the project opens.

4. Save the project to update the status of the missing clips.

# CAPTURING & IMPORTING FOOTAGE

**3**

Once you've selected the proper settings for your project, it's time to begin adding footage to it. Usually, this means getting the video from a tape to your hard drive—a process known as video *capture*.

In Premiere Pro, all the controls you need for capture are integrated into a single Capture window. You can control a camera or deck from within the Capture window, which has built-in presets for controlling most DV devices. The Capture window also incorporates tabbed panels for viewing the current capture settings and for logging clips in a batch list.

But you don't have to shoot your own video footage to create a program in Premiere Pro. As explained in Chapter 2, "Starting a Project," you can import a wide range of digitally stored content: movie files in various formats; audio files; still images, including bitmapped and EPS files; numbered image sequences; even other Premiere Pro project files. Maybe you've already started using the files in Premiere Pro's sample folder. In addition, Premiere Pro generates commonly used footage items: black video, color fields, bars and tone, and even a countdown. And starting with version 1.5, you can even create new Photoshop files from inside Premiere Pro. You can also generate titles, but we'll save that topic for Chapter 12, "Creating Titles."

# Understanding Capture

It's not enough to have your video in a digital form; it must also be in a format that's practical to use for editing. In a digital file, every frame of standard (as opposed to high-definition) video consumes nearly 1 MB. Capturing and playing approximately 30 frames per second (the standard frame rate) is impossible for most processors and drives; the *data rate*, or flow of information, is simply too high, and the storage capacity needed to hold such enormous files is too great.

Some professionals use equipment that can process digital video in a relatively pristine, or *uncompressed*, form. However, most users either don't require or can't afford this level of quality; they use equipment that *compresses* the video for use on the computer. Compression is one way to reduce the file size (and thereby the data rate) of the video, making it easier to store, process, and play back. Other audio and video settings, such as frame size and frame rate, also affect the data rate. Along with your final output goal, the equipment you use helps determine the video and audio settings you choose for capturing video.

This chapter illustrates the capture process using a DV video source. Your particular capture device may require slightly different choices and dialog boxes, but the overall process won't vary. Consult the documentation that came with your hardware to learn about the options specific to your system. Chapter 16, "Video and Audio Settings," also offers guidance on selecting and understanding capture settings.

# IEEE 1394

IEEE 1394 provides simple, inexpensive, fast data exchange between electronic devices—most famously, between a video camera and computer. If your computer doesn't already have an IEEE 1394 controller card, you can usually install one yourself. IEEE (pronounced, "eye-triple-E") stands for the Institute of Electrical and Electronics Engineers, Inc., a nonprofit association of professionals who develop standards to foster compatibility between devices. They dubbed their 1,394[th] effort—what else?—IEEE 1394. However, the folks at Apple dubbed it FireWire—a much snappier and more descriptive name. Sony uses name iLink for its IEEE 1394–capable devices. In the spirit of fairness, this book opts for the more generic (albeit more awkward) moniker, IEEE 1394.

In addition, there are two forms of IEEE 1394. The original version is now known as IEEE 1394a, or FireWire 400, because its theoretical transfer rate is 400 Mbps. A newer iteration is called IEEE 1394b, or FireWire 800, because its theoretical transfer rate is 800 Mbps. Of course, there's a big difference between theoretical rates and actual transfer speeds, but even so, IEEE 1394b devices can move data much faster than their IEEE 1394a counterparts. In addition, IEEE 1394b cables—which use a different connector than IEEE 1394a cables—can be much longer.

But these advantages don't come into play when it comes to capturing standard DV footage. After all, IEEE 1394a easily handles DV's data rate. And a faster transfer rate won't make a videotape play any faster. However, the faster throughput could come in handy if you're using formats with higher data rates, or when it comes time to move large files, like video files.

For the sake of simplicity, this book refers to both formats as IEEE 1394, unless there's a reason to distinguish them.

UNDERSTANDING CAPTURE

# Capturing DV vs. Digitizing Analog

If you're using the widely accepted DV format, the capture process couldn't be much easier. DV cameras compress the video in the camera and record the resulting DV signal onto any of several DV tape formats, most commonly, miniDV. If your computer is equipped with the right port—known variously as FireWire, iLink, or IEEE 1394—you can easily transfer footage from a DV camera or deck to your hard disk in much the same way you copy files from one disk to another. A single cable delivers the video, audio, and timecode information (**Figure 3.1**). Assuming that your system is fast enough to play DV (with its relatively lenient 3.6-MBps data rate), you're in business. The DV standard is just that: standard. It narrows down what would otherwise be an intimidating selection of video and audio settings into a single set of options.

Despite the pervasiveness of DV, video and audio are still commonly recorded, stored, and delivered using an analog signal. Common lower-end formats include VHS and Hi8 videotape and conventional audio-cassette tapes.

To use analog media, most computers require a video capture card—add-on hardware that you can install in one of your computer's expansion slots. The capture card *digitizes* analog video and audio, converting it to digital form for storage on your computer. Generally, separate cables deliver the video, audio, and timecode (if timecode is present) (**Figure 3.2**). With some cards, the video is digitized using Motion-JPEG (MJPEG) compression. Other capture devices can convert analog sources to the DV format. Through these processes, you can enjoy some of DV's editing advantages even if you didn't shoot or store the video in DV.

**Figure 3.1** DV footage—including video, audio, and timecode—can be transferred over a single IEEE 1394 connection.

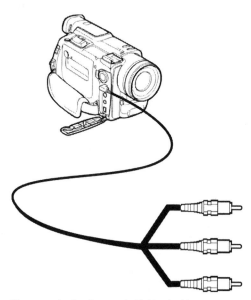

**Figure 3.2** Analog footage is digitized with a capture card. Separate cables deliver the video and audio. A professional deck and a separate device-control cable are often required to deliver timecode.

Of course, DV isn't the only digital format, and IEEE 1394 isn't the only digital interface used to transfer video. A film or broadcast professional may opt for a capture device that uses an uncompressed format, which in turn requires bigger, faster drives and high-speed interfaces. In short, the capabilities, requirements, and prices of capture devices vary widely. Whenever you choose a technology, do your homework and consider the implications from preproduction to distribution.

### ✔ Tips

- Not all capture cards certified to work with earlier versions of Premiere have been certified to work with Premiere Pro. Be sure to check Adobe's Web site for an updated list of certified capture devices.

- When you're putting together a DV editing system, be sure to get enough drive space for your needs: about 1 GB for every 5 minutes of video.

## DV or Not DV

Although *DV* stands for *digital video*, it actually refers to a specific type of signal that can be stored in certain formats.

You may encounter several flavors of DV. Though all of these formats record the same type of DV signal, each records it in a slightly different way:

**MiniDV:** This is the consumer version, often called simply DV. It's used by the DV cameras offered by consumer electronics vendors.

**DVCam:** Sony's professional variation of DV records a DV signal at a different track pitch (the space between tracks), which uses more tape and provides a more reliable signal. Sony's cameras and decks can also read miniDV.

**DVCPro:** Panasonic's professional variety of DV records the signal at an even greater track pitch and uses a more durable metal particle tape. Panasonic's equipment also supports DVCPro50, which doubles the standard data rate to achieve better color reproduction and more detail.

As far as capturing video in Premiere Pro is concerned, it doesn't matter which format you use, but you should understand the difference when you're choosing other equipment, such as cameras, decks, and tapes. Though the essential DV signals are the same, the quality and cost of the equipment differ greatly, and the equipment is not interchangeable.

**CAPTURING DV VS. DIGITIZING ANALOG**

# Optimizing Your System for Capture

As you have already discovered, digital video thrives on a fast processor, speedy drives, and additional hardware. In addition to using powerful hardware, you can take certain steps to maximize your computer's performance:

◆ Quit all other applications.

◆ Turn off file-sharing software, at least temporarily.

◆ Disable other unnecessary operating-system features.

◆ Choose a fast, large disk or disk array as the disk used for capture (see "Choosing a Capture Location" later in this chapter).

◆ Defragment hard disks with a reliable disk utility to optimize their performance.

◆ Select video and audio settings that do not exceed the capabilities of your system.

## ✔ Tips

■ The maximum size for a single file isn't determined by Premiere Pro, but by your operating system, your capture device, and the file system used by your hard disk. Hard disks formatted using FAT32 limit files to 4 GB each. Disks formatted using NTFS don't limit file size. Your capture device, however, may restrict file size; check its documentation.

■ You can capture in the background. On a reasonably high-end system, you can change focus to other applications without interrupting the automated (or batch) capture process. However, Premiere Pro may drop, or fail to capture, frames, especially if you perform system-intensive tasks while capturing. You will need to experiment to determine whether your PC is capable of capturing in the background without dropping frames.

# Understanding Capture Options

At minimum, video capture requires a video source (a camera or deck) and a capture device (an IEEE 1394 connection or analog capture card). Additional options like device control and timecode not only make features such as automated capture—or batch capture—available, they also make it possible to employ an offline/online editing strategy. In fact, most professionals wouldn't consider these to be "options" at all, but crucial tools for a professional workflow.

Device control, timecode, and batch capture are summarized in this section. Later sections put these concepts into practice.

## Device control

As the name indicates, *device control* gives Premiere Pro a means of controlling an external device—usually a videotape deck or camera, although it could also be a digital disk recorder or DAT player, for example. When you enable device control, Premiere Pro's Capture window includes buttons that

### Control without Timecode

To control a camera or deck, device control doesn't require that your tapes contain timecode or that your device read timecode. Some device controllers can even use your deck's counter numbers (which count frames using the tape's control track) to capture a specified shot, although the process won't be frame-accurate. Unlike timecode, counter numbers are arbitrary and can be reset at any time. Counter numbers won't be encoded into the captured clip and can't be used for batch lists or batch capturing.

allow you to control the camera or deck from within Premiere Pro. Device control can also activate a camera or deck to record your finished program (see Chapter 15, "Creating Output"). Premiere Pro can control most DV devices through the IEEE 1394 interface; other cameras and decks may require add-on hardware and software.

## Timecode

Videotapes can be encoded with a signal called *timecode* that identifies each frame of video with a unique number, expressed in hours, minutes, seconds, and frames. Using timecode as a frame-accurate reference, you can create a *batch list*—a list of shots defined by start and end times. Premiere Pro can use timecode combined with device control to capture clips in the batch list automatically. Similarly, timecode makes it possible to recapture clips at different qualities, as when you replace offline-quality clips with clips captured at output quality. Timecode is always included in the DV signal, but for other video formats and devices, timecode is considered a professional option.

## Batch capture

With device control and timecoded source tapes, Premiere Pro can capture clips automatically—a process known as *batch capture*. Device control enables Premiere Pro to cue and play the tape in the camera or deck; timecode makes it possible for Premiere Pro to locate the exact shot logged in the batch list.

### ✔ Tip

■ Unlike previous versions, Premiere Pro doesn't log clips in a separate batch list window or file. Instead, clips are logged in the Project window as "offline." Nevertheless, the term *batch list* is still an industry term that refers to any list of shots awaiting batch capture.

# Using the Capture Window

The Capture window includes two tabbed palettes: Logging and Settings. Selecting the Logging tab reveals controls you can use to set In and Out points, either to define the clips you want to capture right away or to log clips in the Project window so they can be batch captured later. Select the Settings tab to view and change capture settings or to set up scratch disks and device control.

## To open the Capture window:

◆ Choose File > Capture (**Figure 3.3**).

The Capture window appears (**Figure 3.4**).

**Figure 3.3** Choose File > Capture to open the Capture window.

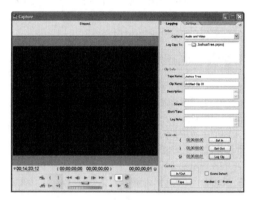

**Figure 3.4** The Capture window.

Figure 3.5 The Logging tab's controls let you log and capture footage.

Figure 3.6 The controls on the Settings tab let you specify settings and scratch disks and set up device control.

Figure 3.7 Choose Collapse Window to hide the tabs.

Figure 3.8 Choose Expand Window to display the tabs.

## To hide or show tabs in the Capture window:

◆ In the Capture window, *do one of the following:*

▲ To display controls for logging and capturing footage, select the Logging tab (**Figure 3.5**).

▲ To display controls for specifying the settings and scratch disks (the disks used to store captured audio and video) and for setting up device control, select the Settings tab (**Figure 3.6**).

▲ To hide the tabs, choose Collapse Window from the Capture window's drop-down menu (**Figure 3.7**).

▲ To display the tabs, choose Expand Window from the Capture window's drop-down menu (**Figure 3.8**).

USING THE CAPTURE WINDOW

# Choosing Capture Settings

As discussed in Chapter 2, "Starting a Project," the Project Settings dialog box includes a Capture category. You can access the Capture panel of the Project settings dialog box from the Capture window. Usually, though, doing so isn't necessary, especially when you're capturing DV over an IEEE 1394 interface; once again, the DV presets take care of everything so you can get to work.

Even so, you should know where to find the settings, if only to tweak a few options. You might check the capture settings if you have more than one capture device installed, or if you want to specify whether to play video and audio in the Capture window only or through your capture device to a television and external speakers as well.

### To specify capture settings in the Capture window:

1. In the Capture window, select the Settings tab.

   The Settings panel appears.

2. In the Capture Settings area of the Capture window's Settings panel, click the Edit button (**Figure 3.9**).

   The Capture panel of the Project Settings dialog box appears.

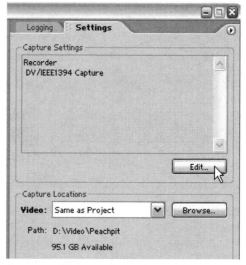

**Figure 3.9** Click the Edit button in the Capture Settings area of the Settings panel.

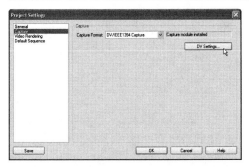

**Figure 3.10** Click the DV Settings button to specify playback settings.

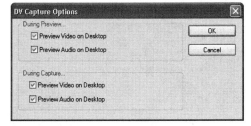

**Figure 3.11** Specify options in the DV Capture Options dialog box.

3. In the Capture Format drop-down menu, select an option.

   For systems using DV over an IEEE 1394 controller, the only option is DV/IEEE 1394 Capture.

4. To specify playback settings when using the Capture window, click DV Settings (**Figure 3.10**).

   The DV Capture Options dialog box appears (**Figure 3.11**).

5. In the DV Capture Options dialog box, specify whether you want to view the video and audio on the desktop while previewing or capturing footage.

   Selecting an item plays the video or audio in the Capture window; leaving it unchecked plays the video or audio on an external video monitor and speakers via the capture device only.

6. Click OK to close the DV Capture Options dialog box and click OK again to close the Project Settings dialog box.

# Choosing a Capture Location

Before you capture, choose the disks that Premiere Pro uses to save video and audio media files. If possible, specify a fast disk with ample storage space to help ensure that all frames are captured successfully.

### To set the capture location:

1. In the Capture window, select the Settings tab.

   The Capture window's Settings panel appears, showing a summary of the capture settings and preferences.

2. In the Capture Locations panel of the Capture window, specify where you want to save captured clips *by doing one of the following*:

   ▲ Choose a folder from the Video drop-down menu (**Figure 3.12**).

   ▲ Click the Video Browse button to navigate to another folder or to create a new one (**Figure 3.13**).

   The path you chose as the location for saving media appears below the Video and Audio drop-down menus.

### ✔ Tips

■ To optimize your system for video editing, use your boot disk (C drive) for your system and software. Dedicate a different disk to media.

■ A capture location is essentially a type of *scratch disk*, a disk you designate for particular tasks. Later in the book, you'll learn how to specify scratch disks for video and audio preview files and for conformed audio files.

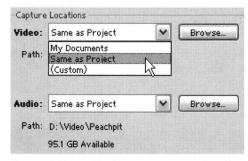

**Figure 3.12** To specify where to save captured media, choose a folder in the Video drop-down menu...

**Figure 3.13** ...or click Browse to navigate to another folder or create a new one.

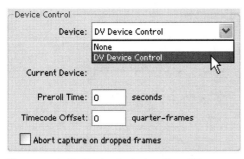

**Figure 3.14** In the Device Control section of the Settings tab, choose one of the options from the Device drop-down menu.

# Using Device Control

DV devices can be controlled over the same IEEE 1394 cable that delivers video and audio, and the plug-ins for controlling most DV cameras and decks come built into Premiere Pro.

If you're not using a DV setup, device control usually includes two components: a hardware cable to connect your computer to your deck and a software plug-in to put in the Premiere Pro Plug-Ins folder. Consult the documentation that came with your device-control equipment to make sure the equipment is set up properly.

## To enable device control:

1. Make sure your device-control hardware is connected.

2. In the Capture window, select the Settings tab.

   The Settings panel appears.

3. In the Device Control section of the Settings panel, choose an option from the Device drop-down menu (**Figure 3.14**):

   **None:** Capture without controlling a camera or deck.

   **DV Device Control:** Use Premiere Pro's built-in ability to control most DV cameras and decks.

   If software for other capture devices is installed in the Premiere Pro Plug-Ins folder, you can select that option from the list.

4. To specify a particular camera or deck, click the Options button.

   See the following task, "To set DV device-control options," for a detailed explanation.

## ✔ Tip

■ If your system doesn't support device control—either because your camera or deck lacks the capability or because you lack device-control hardware or software—you can still capture. The Capture window's playback controls will appear dimmed, but the Stop and Record buttons will still work.

## To set DV device-control options:

1. In the Device Control section of the Capture window, choose DV Device Control from the Device drop-down menu.

2. Under the Device drop-down menu, click the Options button (**Figure 3.15**).

   The DV Device Control Options dialog box appears (**Figure 3.16**).

3. In the DV Device Control Options dialog box, select the options appropriate to your system from the drop-down menus:

   **Video Standard:** The video standard used by your equipment. NTSC is the standard used in North America and Japan. PAL is the standard used in most of Europe.

   **Device Brand:** The brand of the camera or deck you're using. If your brand doesn't appear on the menu, choose Generic (**Figure 3.17**).

   **Device Type:** The model of the camera or deck you're using. If your particular model doesn't appear on the menu, choose a closely related model, or choose Standard.

   **Timecode Format:** The counting method used by your tape and playback device. Most miniDV equipment records drop-frame timecode. Other DV devices may offer a choice between drop-frame and non–drop-frame timecode. (See "Drop-Frame and Non–Drop-Frame Timecode" in Chapter 16.)

4. Click the Check Status button to see if device control is ready:

   **Online:** Indicates that the device is connected and ready to use.

   **Offline:** Indicates that the device is not connected or is not ready to use.

5. To open a browser and connect to Adobe's hardware guide for Premiere Pro, click Go Online for Device Info.

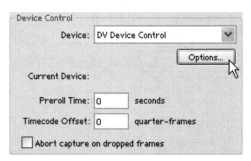

**Figure 3.15** Click Options to open the DV Device Control Options dialog box.

**Figure 3.16** The DV Device Control Options dialog box.

**Figure 3.17** Choose the appropriate options from the drop-down menus, such as the brand of the device you're using.

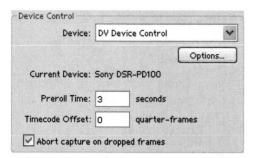

**Figure 3.18** If necessary, specify the preroll time, timecode offset, and whether to abort capture on dropped frames.

6. Click OK to close the DV Device Control Options dialog box.

   The type of device you specified appears in the Device Control area of the Capture window's Settings panel.

## To set other device-control options:

1. In the Capture window, select the Settings tab.

   The Settings panel appears.

2. In the Device Control area of the Settings tab, specify the following options (**Figure 3.18**):

   **Preroll Time:** Enter the number of seconds the deck or camera rewinds before a specified point. Preroll allows the deck to reach normal playback speed before digitizing begins.

   **Timecode Offset:** Enter the number of frames to compensate for discrepancies between the timecode on the tape and that of the captured clips. Use this feature according to the documentation included with your capture device and device controller.

   **Abort Capture on Dropped Frames:** Select this option to stop capture whenever your system drops, or fails to capture, any frames of a clip.

## ✔ Tips

- By default, Premiere Pro generates a report if any frames are dropped during capture. To change this setting, choose Edit > Preferences and select the Capture category in the Preferences dialog box.

- Use the Timecode Offset feature only if the timecode encoded in the captured clips does not match the timecode on the source tape. Check for possible discrepancies the first time you use your capture card, and use the Timecode Offset feature to calibrate your equipment.

# Using Playback Controls in the Capture Window

Once device control is set up, you can control a camera or deck right from the Capture window. Although most of the Capture window's controls should be familiar to you, a few new features are worth reviewing (**Figure 3.19**).

Most notably, you can cue the tape to the frame at which the camera stopped and restarted recording. As you will see, the *scene-detect* feature not only makes it possible to quickly find different shots on the tape, but also allows you to capture an entire tape automatically—each shot becomes a separate clip.

You can also enter timecode numbers to set the current frame, In point, Out point, or duration.

## To cue a tape to a specified timecode:

1. Make sure your device-control hardware is connected.

2. In the Capture window, click the current time display, enter a valid timecode, and press Enter (**Figure 3.20**).

   The tape cues to the frame you specified.

## ✔ Tips

- When the tape is stopped, the playhead is no longer engaged, so that it rewinds and fast-forwards faster but doesn't scan the tape. Instead, the Capture window displays the last frame you viewed until you engage the playhead again by using another playback control.

- Many cameras or decks enter a standby mode after several minutes of inactivity and disengage the playhead so as not to unnecessarily wear the tape.

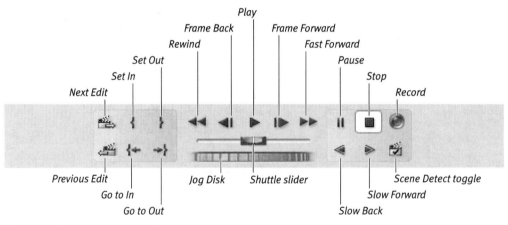

**Figure 3.19** The Capture window's device controls.

*Current time display*

**Figure 3.20** Click the current time display, enter a valid timecode, and press Enter.

**Figure 3.21** Choose File > Capture to open the Capture window.

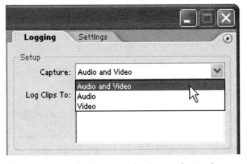

**Figure 3.22** On the Logging tab, choose the tracks you want to capture from the Capture drop-down menu.

# Capturing Audio and Video

Even though it takes the next several tasks to cover the capture process, don't be alarmed: Premiere Pro's Capture window makes capturing a straightforward process. The following sections simply explain the variations. You can capture clips on the fly by playing and recording the footage. Or you can define the start and end times of the clip (its In point and Out point, respectively) before you commit it to the hard drive. Finally, you can use Premiere Pro's scene-detect feature to capture clips automatically, so that each camera shot becomes a separate clip. Overall, the methods are similar and, for the most part, intuitive.

Whatever process you choose, you should first specify the tape name. Then each clip you capture or log will be associated with its source tape, which is essential for keeping track of your material and maintaining a grip on your sanity. You should also specify the tracks you want to capture from the tape: video, audio, or both.

## To specify the tracks and tape name:

1. Choose File > Capture (**Figure 3.21**).

   If device control is set up properly, the Capture window appears with buttons to control the camera or deck. Otherwise, you can use the camera's or deck's controls (sometimes called *local controls*).

2. In the Capture window, select the Logging tab.

   The Logging panel appears.

3. In the Setup area of the Logging tab, choose the tracks you want from the Capture drop-down menu (**Figure 3.22**).

*continues on next page*

**4.** In the Clip Data area of the Logging tab, in the Tape Name field, specify a name for the tape (**Figure 3.23**).

**5.** Capture or log footage using any the methods explained in the following sections.

### ✔ Tips

■ You can also specify the tracks you want to capture in the Capture window's drop-down menu.

■ You can record a voice-over track directly to a track in the timeline using the Audio Mixer window. For details, see Chapter 11, "Mixing Audio."

■ It's impossible to record over a tape using the Capture window, but it *is* possible from your deck or camera controls. Play it safe and set the tape to "record inhibit" by sliding its tab into the save position (for formats like miniDV) or by removing the tab (for formats like VHS).

### To capture a clip without specifying an In point or Out point:

**1.** Open the Capture window and, on the Logging tab, specify the tape name and tracks, as explained in the previous task.

**2.** Using the playback controls in the Capture window or on the deck, play the tape. When it reaches the part you want to capture, click the Capture window's Record button ● (**Figure 3.24**).

**3.** When you have captured the footage you want to save as a clip, press Esc or click the Pause or Stop button.

A Save Captured File dialog box appears (**Figure 3.25**).

**4.** In the Save Captured File dialog box, in the File Name field, type a name for the captured media file.

By default, Premiere Pro provides the proper file name extension, such as .avi.

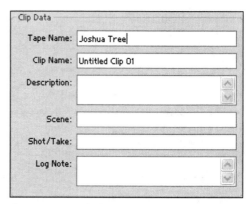

**Figure 3.23** Specify the tape's name in the Tape Name field.

**Figure 3.24** When the tape reaches the part you want to capture, click the Record button.

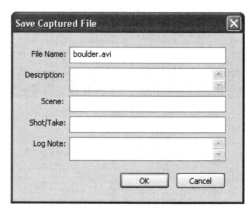

**Figure 3.25** When you press Esc or click Pause or Stop, the Save Captured File dialog box opens.

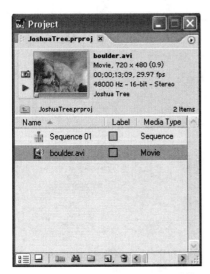

**Figure 3.26** After you save the captured file, it is listed as a clip in the Project window.

5. If you want, enter additional information about the clip in the appropriate fields.

   These fields correspond to clip information categories in the Project window.

6. Click OK to close the dialog box and return to the Capture window.

   The Project window lists the captured file as a clip (**Figure 3.26**).

### ✔ Tips

- The status area at the top of the Capture window displays information about the capture progress.

- If no image appears in the Capture window, the problem is usually something embarrassingly simple. Make sure the camera or deck is on, check your cable connections, and be sure the tape contains (or is cued to) video.

### To capture a clip with a specified In point and Out point:

1. Choose File > Capture to open the Capture window.

2. If necessary, set up device control, as explained in the section "Using Device Control" earlier in this chapter or in the documentation that shipped with the device controller.

   If device control is set up properly, the Capture window appears with buttons to control the deck.

3. In the Capture window, select the Logging tab and specify the tape name and tracks, as explained in the task "To specify the tracks and tape name" earlier in this chapter.

*continues on next page*

**4.** Use the playback controls in the Capture window to cue the tape to the starting point and *do one of the following:*

▲ In the Logging panel, click the Set In button (**Figure 3.27**).

▲ In the Capture window's playback controls, click the Set In button ⟨.

The current time appears as the In point for the captured clip.

**Figure 3.27** When the tape is at the starting point, click the Set In button.

**5.** Use the controls in the Capture window to cue the tape to the end point and *do one of the following:*

▲ In the Logging panel, click the Set Out button (**Figure 3.28**).

▲ In the Capture window's playback controls, click the Set Out button ⟩.

The current time appears as the Out point for the capture.

**Figure 3.28** When the tape is at the ending point, click the Set Out button.

**6.** In the Capture area of the Logging panel, click the In/Out button (**Figure 3.29**).

Premiere Pro automatically captures the video you defined. When it cues the tape, Premiere Pro uses the preroll you specified on the Settings tab (see "To set other device-control options" earlier in this chapter). When digitizing is complete, the Save Captured File dialog box appears.

**7.** In the Save Captured File dialog box, enter a name for the clip and click OK (**Figure 3.30**).

The captured clip appears in the selected bin of the Project window.

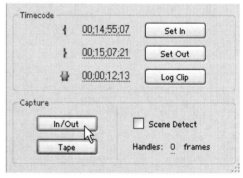

**Figure 3.29** Click the In/Out button to capture the footage you specified.

**Figure 3.30** Enter a name for the clip in the Save Captured File dialog box and then click OK.

## ✔ Tips

- If your deck isn't reaching normal speed before the In point, the device-control software may issue an error message. Try increasing the preroll time on the Settings tab of the Capture window. See "To set other device-control options" earlier in this chapter.

- Some decks have a switch that toggles the controls between local and remote modes. In local mode, you can control the tape only using buttons on the deck itself. To use any type of device control, set the switch to remote.

- In addition to using buttons to set the current frame as an In point or Out point, you can use the In Point, Out Point, and Duration timecode displays. Drag the number or click it and enter a timecode. Changing the duration alters the Out point.

# Capturing using the scene-detect feature

As you have seen, Premiere Pro can detect scene breaks, which are points on the tape where the camera stopped recording and then restarted—you know, where the director called "Roll camera" and "Cut!" You can use the scene-detect feature to capture an entire tape automatically, so that each shot on the tape is captured as a separate media file. The clips use the name you specify plus a sequential number: *filename01, filename02*, and so on.

## To capture using scene detect:

1. Set up device control, as explained in "Using Device Control" earlier in this chapter or the documentation that shipped with the device controller.

2. Choose File > Capture.

3. Using the Capture window's playback controls, cue the tape to the point at which you want to start capturing.
   To capture the entire tape, rewind it to the beginning.

4. In the Capture window, select the Logging tab.
   The Logging panel appears.

5. In the Setup area of the Logging panel, choose the tracks you want from the Capture drop-down menu.

6. In the Clip Data area of the Logging panel, specify the name of the tape by entering a name in the Tape Name field.

*continues on next page*

**7.** In the Capture area of the Logging tab, select Scene Detect (**Figure 3.31**).

**8.** To specify the number of frames, or *handles*, you want to capture beyond the beginning and end of each clip, enter a value for Handles (**Figure 3.32**).

**9.** Click Tape (**Figure 3.33**).

Premiere Pro captures each shot on the tape as a separate file, and each file is listed in the Project window as a clip (**Figure 3.34**).

### ✔ Tips

■ It's a good practice to shoot about 30 seconds of black (or color bars, if your camera can generate them) at the very beginning of the tape. This way, you can capture the first shot with a handle at the beginning and not miss any footage. Also, the very beginning of a tape is more prone to physical damage.

■ If you don't like the naming scheme, you can always change the name of the source clip (or an individual instance of the clip in the Timeline window). See Chapter 4, "Managing Clips," for details.

## Logging clips for batch capture

You can log clips to a batch list in two ways. When you use device control, you can create a batch list as you view the timecoded tape in Premiere Pro's Capture window. If the tape is unavailable (or if a timecode-capable deck is unavailable), you can log a batch list manually. To log manually, you need a written list of accurate timecode starting and ending numbers. Logging manually can help you remain productive (saving you time and money) if you don't always have access to a system that has a deck and device control.

**Figure 3.31** Select Scene Detect in the Capture area of the Logging tab.

**Figure 3.32** For Handles, enter the number of frames you want before the In point and after the Out point.

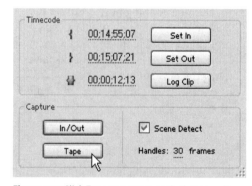

**Figure 3.33** Click Tape to capture each shot as a clip using the scene-detect feature.

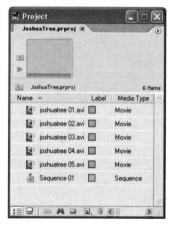

**Figure 3.34** Each clip is listed in the Project window.

**Figure 3.35** When the tape is at the starting point, click the Set In button.

**Figure 3.36** When the tape is at the ending point, click the Set Out button.

**Figure 3.37** Click the Log Clip button.

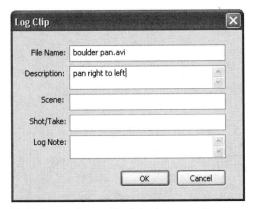

**Figure 3.38** In the Log Clip dialog box, enter the name of the clip and any other information you want to appear in the Project window.

## To log clips for batch capture:

1. Set up device control, as explained in the section "Using Device Control" earlier in this chapter.

2. Choose File > Capture.

3. In the Capture window, click the Logging tab.
   The Logging panel appears.

4. For Tape Name, enter the name of the tape you're using.
   Each tape you use should have a unique name.

5. Use the playback controls in the Capture window to cue the tape to the frame where you want to start the capture and then click the Set In button (**Figure 3.35**).
   The current timecode appears in the In field.

6. Use the deck controls in the Capture window to cue the tape to the frame where you want to stop the capture and then click the Set Out button (**Figure 3.36**).
   The current timecode appears in the Out field.

7. Click Log Clip (**Figure 3.37**).
   A Log Clip dialog box appears.

8. In the Log Clip dialog box, enter a name for the clip (**Figure 3.38**).

9. If you want, enter additional information to be logged with the clip.

*continues on next page*

**10.** Click OK.

The specified clip appears in the Project window. A media offline icon indicates that the clip is not yet linked to a file (**Figure 3.39**).

**11.** Repeat steps 5 through 10 for every clip you want to capture from this tape.

If you change tapes, be sure to enter a new tape name.

## ✔ Tip

- You don't need to have your source tape to log a clip using the Capture window. Just use the In Point, Out Point, and Duration timecode displays to define the clip. Naturally, you'll need a reliable list of timecode numbers to work from.

### To create an offline file without a tape:

**1.** In the Project window, click the New Item button 🖫. and choose Offline File (**Figure 3.40**).

The Offline File dialog box appears (**Figure 3.41**).

**Figure 3.39** The specified clip is listed as offline in the Project window.

**Figure 3.40** Click New Item and choose Offline File.

**Figure 3.41** The Offline File dialog box.

**Figure 3.42** In the Offline File dialog box, choose an option from the Contains drop-down menu.

**Figure 3.43** Specify the Media Start, Media End, and Media Duration timecode numbers.

**Figure 3.44** Double-click the offline file in the Project window.

**2.** In the Offline File dialog box, choose an option from the Contains drop-down menu (**Figure 3.42**): Audio and Video, Audio, or Video.

**3.** For Tape Name, enter the name of the tape that contains the footage you want to capture.

**4.** For File Name, type the name of the clip.

**5.** If you want, specify any of the information in the remaining fields in the General section.

**6.** In the Timecode area of the dialog box, specify the Media Start, Media End, and Media Duration timecode numbers *by doing one of the following* (**Figure 3.43**):

  ▲ Click the timecode number to high-light it and enter a valid timecode number.

  ▲ Drag the timecode number.

  Changing the In point or Out point auto-matically affects the duration. Changing the duration makes a corresponding change in the Out point.

**7.** Click OK to close the dialog box.

  The clip is listed in the Project window as offline.

## To edit an offline file's information:

**1.** In the Project window, double-click the offline file (**Figure 3.44**).

  The Edit Offline File dialog box appears.

*continues on next page*

CAPTURING AUDIO AND VIDEO

**2.** In the Edit Offline File dialog box, edit the information as needed and click OK (**Figure 3.45**).

### ✔ Tip

- The same information (tape name, file name, description, and so on) can be edited in the Project window when it's set to list view.

## Batch capturing

Before you batch capture, check the scratch disk, available disk space, capture settings, device-control settings, and deck, if necessary. (These topics are covered earlier in this chapter.) If everything is set properly, you need to attend to the batch capture only when you are required to change source tapes. If your PC is capable of capturing in the background without dropping frames, then you can work in other applications without interrupting the batch capture.

The clips you log appear in the Project window with the offline icon 🖲. The Media Type and Clip Status columns of the Project window also identify these clips as offline. Clips that have been (intentionally or unintentionally) unlinked from their source media files also appear as offline.

### To batch capture:

**1.** In the Project window, select the offline clips you want to capture (**Figure 3.46**).

**2.** Choose File > Batch Capture (**Figure 3.47**). The Batch Capture window appears.

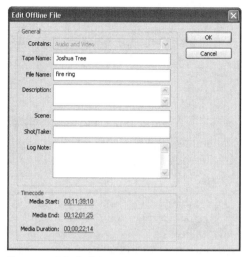

**Figure 3.45** Edit the information as needed and click OK.

**Figure 3.46** Select the offline clips you want to capture.

**Figure 3.47** Choose File > Batch Capture to open the Batch Capture window.

**Figure 3.48** In the Batch Capture window, you can usually leave Override Clip Settings unchecked and click OK.

**Figure 3.49**
When prompted, make sure the proper tape is in the deck and click OK.

**Figure 3.50** The previously offline clips now appear with the movie icon in the Project window.

3. In the Batch Capture window, *do one of the following* (**Figure 3.48**):

   ▲ To change the capture settings, select Override Clip Settings and click the Edit button.

   ▲ Leave Override Clip Settings unchecked and click OK.

   Selecting Override Clip Settings allows you to open a dialog box similar to the one for the capture settings. In most cases, you won't need to edit the capture settings of a clip to make them different from the project capture settings.

4. When you're prompted for a tape, make sure the proper tape is in the deck and click OK (**Figure 3.49**).

   The Capture window appears, and Premiere Pro captures the selected clips automatically.

5. When Premiere Pro notifies you that the batch capture is finished, click OK. If necessary, close the Capture window.

   Previously offline clips appear with the proper movie icon in the Project window (**Figure 3.50**). In addition, Premiere Pro saves a batch capture log alongside the captured files and lists the log file in the Project window.

### ✔ Tip

■ A *gap* (unrecorded area) in the tape, or a *break* (a discontinuity) in the tape's timecode, of longer than three seconds can cause the batch-capture process to be aborted. To avoid these problems while you shoot, understand how your camera works. Otherwise, you may have to copy, or *dub*, your camera original to another tape. Alternatively, you can capture the items where the timecode is continuous and cue the tape manually to prevent Premiere Pro from encountering the gap or timecode break.

# Importing and exporting batch lists

Unlike its predecessors, Premiere Pro doesn't use a Batch List window. Nevertheless, it can import a batch list from Premiere 6.x or a tab-delimited text file and translate the list into a bin of clips in the Project window.

Conversely, you can export a batch-list file for use in an older version of Premiere or in another program. When you export, you have a choice of file formats, depending on your needs: you can export a Premiere 6.x (.pbl) batch list, a Premiere Pro or comma-delimited batch list (.csv), or a text file formatted as a tab-delimited batch list (.tab or .txt).

### To import a batch list:

1. Choose Project > Import Batch List (**Figure 3.51**).

   The Import Batch List dialog box appears (**Figure 3.52**).

2. In the Import Batch List dialog box, navigate to the batch list, select it, and click Open.

   In the Project window, a bin with the same name as the batch-list file appears. The bin contains all the clips in the batch list (**Figure 3.53**).

3. Select and capture the clips from the batch list, as described in "Batch capturing" earlier in this chapter.

**Figure 3.51** Choose Project > Import Batch List.

**Figure 3.52** The Import Batch List dialog box.

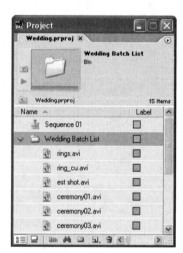

**Figure 3.53** A bin with the same name as the batch-list file contains all the clips in the batch list.

Capturing Audio and Video

**Figure 3.54** Select the Project window, or select individual clips.

**Figure 3.55** Choose Project > Export Batch List.

**Figure 3.56** In the Export Batch List dialog box, specify the file format for the batch list.

## To export a batch list:

1. *Do one of the following:*
   - ▲ To create a batch list of all the clips in the project, select the Project window (but no individual clips).
   - ▲ To create a batch list of a bin of clips, select the bin (**Figure 3.54**).
   - ▲ To create a batch list of particular clips, select the clips.

2. Choose Project > Export Batch List (**Figure 3.55**).

   The Export Batch List dialog box appears.

3. In the Export Batch List dialog box, specify the file format for the batch list (**Figure 3.56**).

4. In the Export Batch List dialog box, specify a name and location for the batch list and click Save.

# Importing Footage

When you want to use a file in your project, you import the file as a clip. You can import one clip at a time, several clips at a time, or an entire folder of clips. You can even import another project into the current project.

Clips can be as big as 4,000 pixels tall by 4,000 pixels wide, and Premiere Pro can support a variety of video and audio formats. Over time, Adobe and other manufacturers undoubtedly will offer plug-in software modules to provide additional file-format support.

### To import files as a clips in the project:

1. In the Project window, specify where you want to import the clip *by doing one of the following:*

   ▲ Navigate to the bin into which you want to import or to the topmost level of the Project window.

   ▲ In list view, select the bin into which you want to import.

2. Choose File > Import (**Figure 3.57**). The Import dialog box appears.

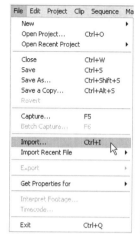

**Figure 3.57** Choose File > Import.

**Figure 3.58** Select one or more files and choose Open, or to import a folder of files, select it and click Import Folder (shown here).

**Figure 3.59** The clips appear in the Project window. A folder of clips appears as a bin in the Project Window. (shown here).

**3.** *Do one of the following:*

▲ To import a single file, double-click the file.

▲ To import multiple files, select the files and click Open.

▲ To import a folder of files, select the folder and click Import Folder (**Figure 3.58**).

The dialog box closes, and the clips appear in the Project window. If you imported an entire folder, then the folder appears as a bin of clips in the Project window (**Figure 3.59**).

## ✔ Tip

■ There are many ways to import files, and chances are that you'll be doing a lot of importing. Now's a good time to learn (or create) shortcuts for the Import command. Use a contextual menu or keyboard shortcut. Instead of choosing File > Import, you can simply double-click an empty part of the clip area of the Project window.

# Importing Projects

In addition to importing media files, you can import an entire project, including all its clips and sequences. An imported project appears as a bin in the current project, which in turn contains all its bins, clips, and sequences.

Why would you import a project rather than just reopen it? Maybe you want to join sequences that were created in different projects or use a "boilerplate" project in several other projects. In Chapter 2, "Starting a Project," you learned that many of a project's attributes—such as its timebase and audio sample rate—can't be changed later. However, you can easily work around this restriction by importing the entire project into another project that uses different settings. Finally, you can open projects created in Premiere 6.x. However, not all of your edit decisions will translate seamlessly into Premiere Pro; see the user guide or online Help for details.

**Figure 3.60** Choose File> Import.

### To import another project into the current project:

1. In the Project window, specify where you want to import the clip *by doing one of the following:*

    ▲ Navigate to the bin into which you want to import or to the topmost level of the Project window.

    ▲ In list view, select the bin into which you want to import.

2. Choose File > Import (**Figure 3.60**).

    The Import Project dialog box appears.

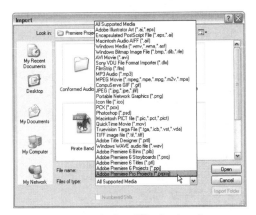

**Figure 3.61** Narrow the list of files by choosing an option in the Files of Type drop-down menu.

**Figure 3.62** In the Import Project dialog box, select a project and click Open.

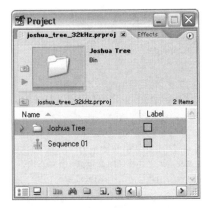

**Figure 3.63** The imported project appears as a bin containing sequences and source clips.

**3.** To make finding the project to import easier, in the Files of Type drop-down menu in the Import Project dialog box, choose the type of project you want to open (**Figure 3.61**): either Adobe Premiere 6 Projects (*.ppj) or Adobe Premiere Pro Projects (*.prproj).

**4.** In the Import Project dialog box, select a project and click Open (**Figure 3.62**).

The imported project appears in the Project window as a bin with the same name as the project file. The bin contains any clips and sequences used in the project (**Figure 3.63**).

**5.** Open the imported bin and double-click the sequences you want to view.

For more about sequences, see Chapter 6, "Creating a Sequence."

# Importing Stills

Although individual images are only single frames, you can set them to play in the program for any duration.

### To set the default duration for still images before you import them:

1. Choose Edit > Preferences > Still Images (**Figure 3.64**).

   The Still Images panel of the Preferences dialog box opens.

2. For Default Duration, type the initial duration of still images, in frames (**Figure 3.65**).

   Hereafter, all still images imported into the project use the default duration. Still images that are already in the project or program remain unaffected. You can change the duration of a still-image clip at any time.

### ✔ Tips

- Photoshop version 7 and earlier displays images using square pixels, or a pixel aspect ratio of 1. DV and D-1 video use a 0.9 pixel aspect ratio. Therefore, you can create artwork for D-1 (720 × 486) projects at 720 × 540, and you can create artwork for DV (720 × 480) projects at 720 × 534. Premiere Pro automatically adjusts for the differences in pixel aspect ratios and displays the image without cropping or distortion. If you create stills with the dimensions 720 × 480, Premiere Pro will interpret them as using rectangular (0.9) pixels. This will result in distorted images. For more about pixel aspect ratios, see Chapter 16, "Video and Audio Settings."

- If you can't remember the proper image sizes for Photoshop files, don't worry; when you create a new file in Photoshop, they're listed in the Preset Sizes drop-down menu.

**Figure 3.64** Choose Edit > Preferences> Still Images.

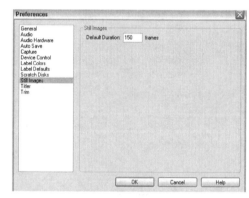

**Figure 3.65** For Default Duration, type the initial duration of still images, in frames.

- Starting with Premiere Pro 1.5, Photoshop can be launched directly from within Premiere Pro. A new file is created using the appropriate dimensions and pixel aspect ratio. Photoshop launches, and the still is automatically imported into the Premiere Pro 1.5 project. (See "Creating a Photoshop File" later in this chapter.)

**Figure 3.66** An image viewed in Illustrator as artwork only...

**Figure 3.67** ...appears rasterized and anti-aliased in Premiere Pro.

# Importing Illustrator Files

Premiere Pro can *rasterize* Illustrator files—a process that converts the path-based (vector) art to Premiere Pro's pixel-based (bitmapped) format. The program *anti-aliases* the art, so that edges appear smooth; it also interprets blank areas as an alpha channel premultiplied with white (**Figures 3.66** and **3.67**).

Set crop marks in the Illustrator file to define the dimensions of the art that will be rasterized by Premiere Pro.

## ✔ Tips

- The term *aliasing* refers to the hard, jagged edges many objects show in digital, pixel-based images. *Anti-aliasing* subtly adds transparency to edges, making them appear smoother.

- For more information on alpha channels and transparency, see Chapter 14, "Effects in Action."

# Importing Layered Photoshop Files

Premiere Pro can import files created in Photoshop 3.0 or later. It can even import a single layer from a multiple-layer Photoshop file. Premiere Pro also recognizes alpha channels in Photoshop files, so you can use alpha channels to define transparent areas (see Chapter 14, "Effects in Action").

## To import a layered Photoshop file:

1. In the Project window, specify where you want to import the clip *by doing one of the following*:

   ▲ Navigate to the bin into which you want to import or to the topmost level of the Project window.

   ▲ In list view, select the bin into which you want to import.

2. Choose File > Import (**Figure 3.68**) or double-click an empty area of the main clip area of the Project window.

   The Import dialog box appears.

3. Locate a layered Photoshop file to import and click Open (**Figure 3.69**).

   The Import Layered File dialog box opens.

4. In the Import As drop-down menu, choose Footage (**Figure 3.70**).

**Figure 3.68** Choose File > Import.

**Figure 3.69** Locate a layered Photoshop file to import and click Open.

**Figure 3.70** In the Import As drop-down menu, choose Footage.

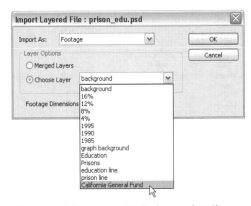

**Figure 3.71** To import a particular layer, select Choose Layer and choose a layer from the drop-down menu.

**Figure 3.72** Single layers can be imported at the document size or the layer size.

5. For Layer Options, *choose one of the following:*

   ▲ To import the image after merging all layers into a single layer, select Merged Layers.

   ▲ To import the single layer as a clip, select Choose Layer and choose a layer (**Figure 3.71**).

6. If you chose a layer in step 5, choose an option for Footage Dimensions (**Figure 3.72**):

   **Document Size:** Imports the layer at the document's pixel dimensions. The layer appears in its proper position; any empty areas are imported as an alpha channel (**Figure 3.73**).

   **Layer Size:** Imports the layer at its individual pixel dimensions (**Figure 3.74**).

7. Click OK.

   Depending on your choice, the single layer or merged layer appears in the selected bin.

**Figure 3.73** Choosing the Document Size option imports the layer using the pixel dimensions of the entire Photoshop document. This makes it easy to reassemble the layers as they appeared in the Photoshop document.

**Figure 3.74** Choosing the Layer Size option uses the layer's individual pixel dimensions.

## To import a file as a layered sequence:

1. Choose File > Import (**Figure 3.75**) or double-click an empty area of the main clip area of the Project window.

   The Import dialog box appears.

2. Locate a layered Photoshop file to import and then click Open (**Figure 3.76**).

   The Import Layered File dialog box opens.

3. In the Import As drop-down menu, choose Sequence (**Figure 3.77**).

**Figure 3.75** Choose File > Import.

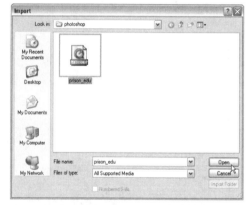

**Figure 3.76** Locate a layered Photoshop file to import and click Open.

**Figure 3.77** In the Import As drop-down menu, choose Sequence.

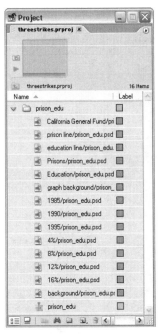

Figure 3.78 The imported file appears as a bin containing each layer and a sequence.

4. Click OK.

A bin appears in the Project window containing each layer as a clip and a sequence that uses the same name as the layered file (**Figure 3.78**).

5. Double-click the sequence to open it in the Timeline window.

In the sequence, each layer appears in a different track (**Figure 3.79**).

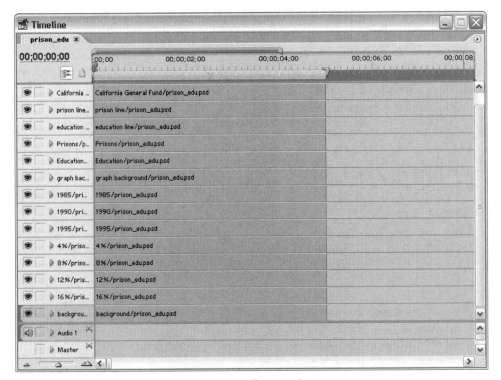

Figure 3.79 In the sequence, each layer appears in a different track.

# Importing Still-Image Sequences

In addition to exporting a single movie file, many programs export movies as a sequence of still images. Don't worry—Premiere Pro has no trouble importing a numbered sequence as a single clip.

### To import numbered still images as a single clip:

1. Confirm that each image in the numbered sequence has the correct extension and that the file names contain an equal number of digits at the end (seq000.bmp, seq001.bmp, and seq002.bmp, for example).

2. In the Project window, specify where you want to import the clip *by doing one of the following:*

   ▲ Navigate to the bin into which you want to import or to the topmost level of the Project window.

   ▲ In list view, select the bin into which you want to import.

3. Choose File > Import (**Figure 3.80**). The Import dialog box appears.

4. Select the first file in the numbered sequence.

5. Select the Numbered Stills check box (**Figure 3.81**).

6. Click Open.

   The image sequence appears in the selected bin as a single clip (**Figure 3.82**).

### ✔ Tip

■ By default, Premiere Pro assumes that the imported image sequence uses the same frame rate as your project. To tell Premiere Pro that the footage uses a different frame rate, use the Interpret Footage command, explained in Chapter 4, "Managing Clips."

**Figure 3.80** Choose File > Import.

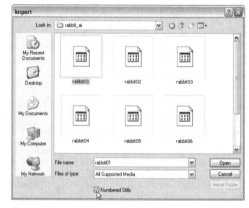

**Figure 3.81** In the Import dialog box, select Numbered Stills.

**Figure 3.82** The image sequence appears in the selected bin as a single clip.

**Figure 3.83** Choose File > New > Photoshop File.

**Figure 3.84** Specify a name and destination for the new Photoshop file and click Save.

# Creating a Photoshop File

If you have Photoshop installed on your PC, you can create a Photoshop file from within Premiere Pro. Photoshop launches automatically with the new file open and ready for use. Since both Premiere Pro and Photoshop will be open on your desktop at the same time, this task requires sufficient memory to operate properly.

Any additions or changes made to the Photoshop file will automatically show up in Premiere Pro once the Photoshop file is saved.

## To create a Photoshop file:

1. Choose File > New > Photoshop File (**Figure 3.83**).

   The Save Photoshop File As dialog box appears (**Figure 3.84**).

   In the Save Photoshop File As dialog box, specify a name and destination for the new Photoshop file and click Save.

   Photoshop opens with the new file ready for use.

# Generating Synthetic Media

In addition to accepting a wide variety of source files, Premiere Pro can generate useful clips of its own. The Project window's New Item button includes options for creating bars and tone, black video, a color matte, and even a standard countdown.

Of the files generated by the New Item command, only titles create an actual file on your hard drive. Everything else—sequences, offline files, color mattes, black video, color bars, and counting leaders—exists only as part of your project, not as independent files.

## To create bars and tone or black video:

1. In the Project window, specify where you want to import the clip *by doing one of the following:*

   ▲ Navigate to the bin into which you want to import or to the topmost level of the Project window.

   ▲ In list view, select the bin into which you want to import.

2. Click the New Item button and choose one of the following (**Figure 3.85**):

   **Bars and Tone:** Creates an NTSC color bars pattern and a 1-kHz audio tone.

   **Black Video:** Creates black video that registers 7.5 IRE on a waveform monitor.

   The footage item you chose appears in the Project window and uses the duration you specified for still images (**Figure 3.86**).

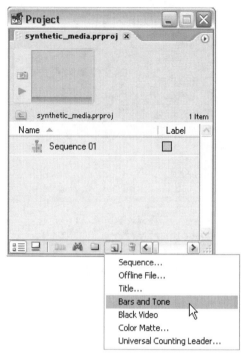

**Figure 3.85** Click the New Item button and choose Bars and Tone or Black Video.

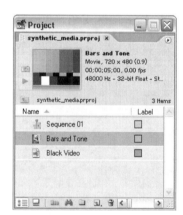

**Figure 3.86** The item you select appears in the Project window and uses the default duration for still images.

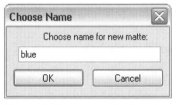

**Figure 3.87** Click the New Item button and choose Color Matte.

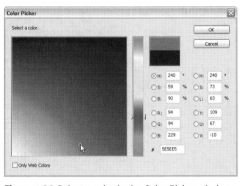

**Figure 3.88** Select a color in the Color Picker window and click OK.

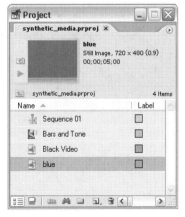

**Figure 3.89** Type a name for the color matte and click OK.

## To create a color matte:

1. In the Project window, specify where you want to import the clip *by doing one of the following:*

   ▲ Navigate to the bin into which you want to import or to the topmost level of the Project window.

   ▲ In list view, select the bin into which you want to import.

2. Click the New Item button and choose Color Matte from the drop-down menu (**Figure 3.87**).

   A Color Picker dialog box appears.

3. In the Color Picker dialog box, choose a color and click OK (**Figure 3.88**).

   A Choose Name dialog box appears.

4. In the Choose Name dialog box, type a name for the color matte and click OK (**Figure 3.89**).

   The color matte appears in the Project window and uses the duration you specified for still images (**Figure 3.90**).

**Figure 3.90** The color matte appears in the Project window and uses the default duration for still images.

GENERATING SYNTHETIC MEDIA

## To create a countdown:

1. In the Project window, specify where you want to import the clip *by doing one of the following:*

   ▲ Navigate to the bin into which you want to import or to the topmost level of the Project window

   ▲ In list view, select the bin into which you want to import

2. Click the New Item button and choose Universal Counting Leader from the drop-down menu (**Figure 3.91**).

   The Universal Counting Leader Setup dialog box appears.

3. Specify the following options (**Figure 3.92**):

   ▲ To open the color picker for each element of the countdown, click the color swatch next to each element.

   ▲ To display a small circle in the last frame of the leader, select the Cue Blip on Out check box.

   ▲ To play a beep at the two-second mark of the countdown, select the Cue Blip on 2 check box.

   ▲ To play a beep at each second of the countdown, select the Cue Blip at All Second Starts check box.

4. Click OK to close the dialog box.

   A Universal Counting Leader clip appears in the selected bin of the Project window (**Figure 3.93**).

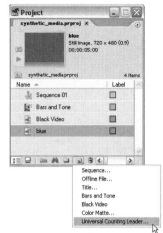

**Figure 3.91** Click the New Item button and choose Universal Counting Leader.

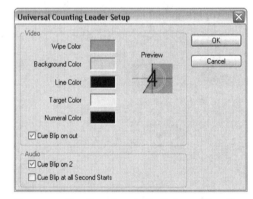

**Figure 3.92** Specify options in the Universal Counting Leader dialog box.

**Figure 3.93** The countdown appears in the Project window.

## ✔ Tips

- To make a slate (containing information such as client, producer, and total running time), you can create a title card, as explained in Chapter 12, "Creating Titles."

- Although an empty space in a sequence appears as black, it doesn't allow you to perform certain edits, and it doesn't appear in edit decision lists. To gain these advantages, add a black video clip.

- Double-clicking black video, color bars, or a counting leader opens the footage in the source view. However, double-clicking a color matte reopens the color picker.

### Creating a Leader

In addition to accepting a wide variety of source files, Premiere Pro provides several useful clips of its own. You can use some of them to create a *leader*, a series of shots that typically appear at the beginning of a master tape. The *master tape* is used to make duplicates (or *dubs*) and usually contains the following:

- **30 seconds of black:** A black screen without sound keeps the program away from the *head*, or beginning, of the master tape, which is more prone to damage.

- **60 seconds of bars and tone:** The color bars and reference tone are used by video technicians to faithfully reproduce your program's video and audio levels.

- **10 seconds of black:** Here, black simply acts as a buffer between the bars and the slate.

- **10 seconds of a slate:** A title screen contains pertinent information about the program and the tape itself, such as the name of the program, the producer, whether the audio is mixed, and so on.

- **8 seconds of countdown:** The visible countdown originally helped a film projectionist know when the program was about to start. It can serve a similar purpose for videotape operators. The standard countdown starts at 8 and ends at 2 (where there is usually a beep, or *2 pop*, to test the sound).

- **2 seconds of black:** Black video immediately precedes the program.

GENERATING SYNTHETIC MEDIA

# MANAGING CLIPS

All the *assets* you intend to use in your project—video clips, audio clips, still pictures, and synthetic media such as leaders and mattes—are listed in the Project window. The longer and more complex the project, the longer the list, and when the list becomes too long, it can become unwieldy. Fortunately, the Project window includes features that help you keep your clips organized and easy to find.

In this chapter, you'll learn how to use the Project window to view, sort, and organize all the assets you learned how to capture and import in the previous chapter. You will also learn how to use the Project Manager to assemble project assets in one location and how to trim the storage requirements of a project by collecting only the footage critical to your project.

# Working with the Project Window

The Project window is the receptacle for all the clips you intend to use. So you can work efficiently, it's vital that the clips be organized, easy to find, and easy to evaluate. Premiere Pro's Project window helps you achieve these goals (**Figure 4.1**).

To help you change the view options or access common commands quickly, several buttons are conveniently located at the bottom of the Project window. As in all the primary windows, you can also access commands associated with the window from an integrated menu named after the window—in this case, the Project window menu. (Some like to call these types of menus fly-out or wingtip menus.)

The preview area displays vital information about selected bins, sequences, and clips, as well as a sample image. You can play movie files in the preview area. In addition, you can choose any frame of a movie clip to represent the clip in the Project window views.

As its name suggests, the Project window is fundamental; you can close other windows, but closing the Project window closes the project and returns you to the welcome screen.

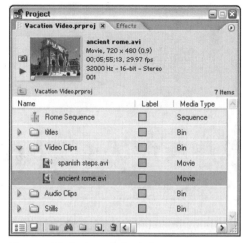

**Figure 4.1** The Project window helps you organize, find, and evaluate your clips.

**Figure 4.2** In icon view, Project window items are arranged in a grid.

**Figure 4.3** In list view, items are listed as rows and columns of information.

List view    Icon view

**Figure 4.4** Click the appropriate button at the bottom of the Project window to switch views.

# Working with Project Window Views

You can view the clips in the Project window in two ways: as icons or as a list. In icon view, items in the Project window are arranged in a grid (**Figure 4.2**). This view tends to take up more space, but it lets you lay out the items like photos on a table. You can use icon view to create a kind of storyboard, which you can assemble into a sequence automatically (using the Automate to Sequence feature, explained in Chapter 6, "Creating a Sequence"). In list view, on the other hand, items are listed with rows and columns of information, which can help you sort and organize your clips (**Figure 4.3**). List view can show more items at once, and its columns are key to managing a large number of clips.

Both view types allow you to choose whether to represent each clip as an icon representing the type of footage or as a thumbnail image of the footage. You can even set the size of the items.

The sections that follow explain how to work with each view, so you can customize the Project window for the task at hand.

### To change the Project window view:

◆ At the bottom of the Project window, click the button that corresponds to the view you want to use (**Figure 4.4**).

**WORKING WITH PROJECT WINDOW VIEWS**

## To toggle thumbnails in the Project window:

◆ In the Project window menu, choose Thumbnails > Off (**Figure 4.5**).

When Off is selected, items appear as icons (**Figure 4.6**); when Off is not selected, items appear as thumbnail images (**Figure 4.7**).

**Figure 4.5** In the Project window menu, choose Thumbnails > Off.

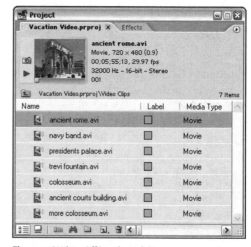

**Figure 4.6** When Off is selected, items appear as icons.

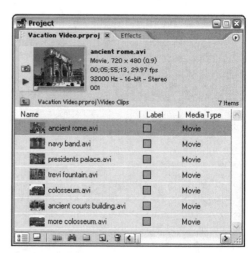

**Figure 4.7** When Off is not selected, items appear as thumbnail images.

**Figure 4.8** In the Project window menu, choose Thumbnails and select a size.

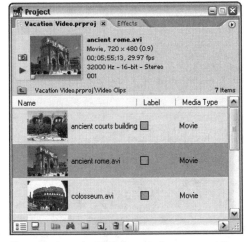

**Figure 4.9** Items in the Project window appear at the relative size you specify.

## To change the size of items in the Project window:

◆ In the Project window menu, choose Thumbnails and select a size (**Figure 4.8**).

Items in the Project window appear at the relative size you specify (**Figure 4.9**).

# Working with Icon View

In icon view 🖳, items in the Project window appear as larger icons arranged in a grid (something like the tiles view in Windows XP). Some editors prefer this view or like to switch to it when working with a client.

Icon view also lends itself to a workflow you might call *storyboard editing.* You can arrange the clips in order, much like the sketches in a storyboard, and then assemble them into a sequence automatically using Premiere Pro's Automate to Sequence command. (See Chapter 6 for more about the Automate to Sequence feature.)

### To arrange items in icon view:

1. With the Project window set to icon view, select one or more items.

2. Drag the selected items to another cell in the grid.

   A bold line between grid cells indicates where the moved items will be inserted (**Figure 4.10**). When you release the mouse, subsequent items are shifted to the right to make room for the moved items (**Figure 4.11**).

**Figure 4.10** When you select items to move to a new position in the grid, a bold line between grid cells indicates where the moved items will be inserted.

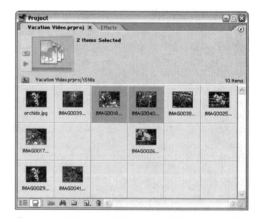

**Figure 4.11** Subsequent items are shifted to the right to make room for the moved items.

**Figure 4.12** Choose Clean Up in the Project window menu.

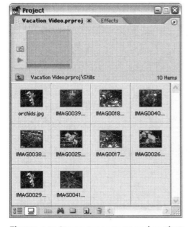

**Figure 4.13** Items are rearranged so that there are no empty cells between items.

## To clean up icon view:

◆ With the Project window set to icon view, choose Clean Up in the Project window menu (**Figure 4.12**).

Items in the Project window are arranged in the visible cells of the grid from left to right and from top to bottom, so that there are no empty cells between items (**Figure 4.13**).

# Working with List View

List view ⬛ lets you organize items according to a number of categories that appear as columns in the Project window. You can select which columns you want to include and add your own custom columns. You can also resize and rearrange the columns to suit your organizational method. However, you can rename or permanently remove only custom columns, and the Name column is always the first column.

### To hide or show columns in list view:

1. In the Project window menu, choose Edit Columns (**Figure 4.14**).

   The Edit Columns dialog box appears.

2. In the Edit Columns dialog box, select the headings for the type of information you want to view when the Project window is set to list view (**Figure 4.15**).

3. Click OK to close the Edit Columns dialog box.

   Only the columns you specified appear in the Project window.

### To add custom columns:

1. In the Project window menu, choose Edit Columns.

   The Edit Columns dialog box appears.

2. In the Edit Columns dialog box, click Add (**Figure 4.16**).

   An Add Column dialog box appears.

**Figure 4.14** In the Project window menu, choose Edit Columns.

**Figure 4.15** In the Edit Columns dialog box, select the headings for the type of information you want to view.

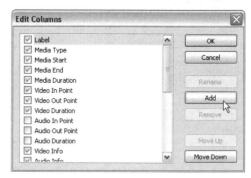

**Figure 4.16** In the Edit Columns dialog box, click Add.

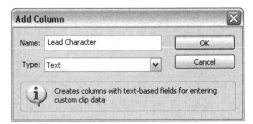

Figure 4.17 In the Add Column dialog box, type the name of the custom column.

Figure 4.18 Choose an option in the Type drop-down menu.

Figure 4.19 Select a column name and choose to rename, remove, or move the column.

3. In the Add Column dialog box, type the name of the custom column (**Figure 4.17**).

4. Choose an option from the Type drop-down menu (**Figure 4.18**):

   **Text:** Creates a column of text fields in which you can enter information.

   **Boolean:** Creates a column of check boxes, which you can use to indicate a yes or no state.

5. Click OK to close the Add Column dialog box.

   The new column appears in the Edit Columns dialog box.

6. When you have finished editing columns, click OK to close the Edit Columns dialog box.

## To edit columns:

1. In the Project window menu, choose Edit Columns.

   The Edit Columns dialog box appears.

2. In the Edit Columns dialog box, select a column name and *click any of the following buttons* (**Figure 4.19**):

   ▲ **Rename:** Renames a custom column.

   ▲ **Remove:** Removes a custom column.

   ▲ **Move Up:** Moves a column one item higher in the list, which moves it to the left in the Project window.

   ▲ **Move Down:** Moves a column one item lower in the list, which moves it to the right in the Project window.

3. Click OK to close the dialog box.

   The Project window reflects your choices.

## ✔ Tip

■ You can't rename or remove any of the default columns, but you can hide them.

## To rearrange headings in list view:

◆ With the Project window set to list view, drag a heading in the Project window to the left or right to place it where you want (**Figures 4.20** and **4.21**).

## To adjust a column's width in list view:

◆ With the Project window set to list view, drag the right edge of a heading in the Project window to resize it (**Figures 4.22** and **4.23**).

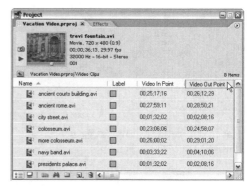

**Figure 4.20** Dragging a heading to the left or to the right...

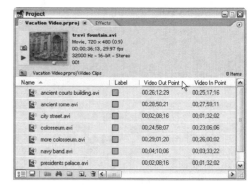

**Figure 4.21** ...changes its relative position in the Project window.

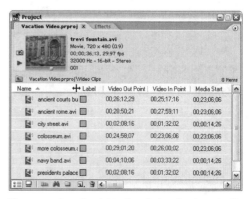

**Figure 4.22** Drag the right edge of a heading to resize it.

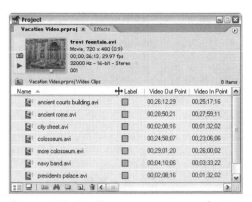

**Figure 4.23** The heading appears narrower or (in this case) wider.

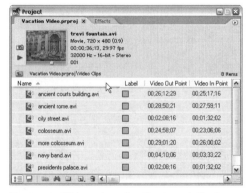

**Figure 4.24** Click a column heading to sort clips by that heading.

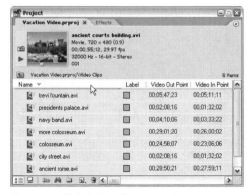

**Figure 4.25** Click the heading a second time to reverse the sort order.

## To sort items in list view:

◆ With the Project window set to list view, *do one of the following:*

▲ To sort clips by a particular column heading, click the heading (**Figure 4.24**).

▲ To reverse the sort order, click a column heading twice (**Figure 4.25**).

A small triangle next to the column name indicates whether items are sorted in ascending or descending order.

**WORKING WITH LIST VIEW**

# Using Labels

By default, the Name column is followed by a Label column. Instead of providing a text field or a check box, the Label column identifies each item by a small color swatch. You can choose from eight colors to represent the six types of items in the Project window: Bin, Sequence, Video, Audio, Movie, and Still. The label helps you identify an item not only in the Project window, but in the Timeline window as well.

Offline files, counting leaders, and bars and tone use the same label color as sequences. Color mattes, black video, and titles use the same label color as stills.

## To set label colors:

1. Choose Edit > Preferences > Label Colors (**Figure 4.26**).

   The Label Colors panel of the Preferences dialog box appears.

2. Click a color swatch to change the selection of colors (**Figure 4.27**).

   A Color Picker dialog box appears.

**Figure 4.26** Choose Edit > Preferences > Label Colors.

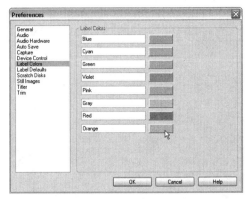

**Figure 4.27** Click a color swatch to change the selection of colors.

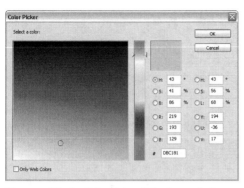

**Figure 4.28** In the Color Picker dialog box, select a color and click OK.

**Figure 4.29** Choose Edit > Preferences > Label Defaults.

3. In the Color Picker dialog box, select a color and click OK (**Figure 4.28**).

4. Repeat steps 2 and 3 to change other colors and then click OK to close the dialog box.

   The color you specified is assigned to corresponding items in the Project window and Timeline window.

## To set default label colors:

1. Choose Edit > Preferences > Label Defaults (**Figure 4.29**).

   The Label Defaults panel of the Preferences dialog box appears.

2. Assign a color to each type of item by choosing an option in the item's drop-down menu (**Figure 4.30**).

   The available colors are determined by the colors you specify in the Label Colors panel of the Preferences dialog box.

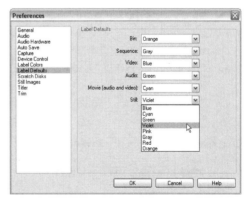

**Figure 4.30** Assign a color to each type of item by choosing an option in the item's drop-down menu.

**USING LABELS**

# Selecting and Deleting Items in the Project Window

You can select items in the Project window in much the same way as you select files in the operating system. However, when you delete an item from the Project window, bear in mind that you're deleting only a reference to a file on the hard disk, not the file itself. So if you delete a clip, the project will no longer require that clip, but its source media remains on the hard disk. When you attempt to delete a clip that's in a sequence, or a sequence that has clips in it, Premiere Pro prompts you to confirm the action.

### To select items in the Project window:

1. If necessary, open the bin that contains the clips you want to view.

2. To select a clip or clips, *do one of the following:*

   ▲ Click an item.

   ▲ Shift-click a range of items.

   ▲ Ctrl-click several noncontiguous items.

   ▲ Drag a marquee around two or more items (**Figure 4.31**).

   ▲ Choose Edit > Select All to select all items.

   ▲ Choose Edit > Deselect All to deselect all items.

### To delete items from the Project window:

1. In the Project window, select one or more items.

2. In the Project window, click the Delete button 🗑, or press Delete on your keyboard.

   Deleting a clip removes it from the project, but the source file remains on the hard disk (**Figure 4.32**). If the clip is used in a sequence, Premiere Pro prompts you to confirm your choice.

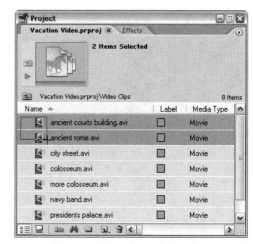

**Figure 4.31** Select items by clicking, or select a range of items by dragging a marquee (shown here).

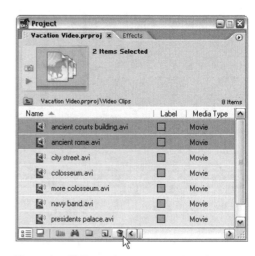

**Figure 4.32** Clicking Delete removes selected items from the project but doesn't remove related media files from the disk.

### ✔ Tip

■ You can use the Project Manager to help with basic housekeeping: remove unused clips, and collect all of the clips you are using in a new location. See "Using the Project Manager" later in this chapter.

**Figure 4.33** The preview area of the Project window displays a thumbnail-sized version of the clip and other clip data.

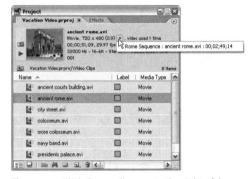

**Figure 4.34** Click the small arrow to the right of the clip's video or audio usage information.

# Using the Preview Area of the Project Window

The preview area of the Project window displays a sample image of the selected bin or clip. The preview area also displays the number of clips in a bin or the vital statistics of a clip—its name, file type, image dimensions, and so on.

If the selected clip is a movie file, you can play the clip—with sound—directly in the Project window. In addition, you can set any frame of the clip as the *poster frame*, the image used to represent the clip when you're viewing thumbnails of the clips in the Project window. This allows you to choose the most appropriate image to represent the clip.

## To display a preview of an item in the Project window:

◆ In the Project window, click a clip to select it.

A sample frame and information appear in the preview area of the Project window. Clip information can include the clip's name, file type, image size, duration, frame rate, data rate, and audio settings; the number of times the clip has been used in sequences; and so on (**Figure 4.33**).

## To show detailed usage information for a clip:

1. In the Project window, click a clip to select it.

2. Click the small arrow to the right of the clip's video or audio usage information (**Figure 4.34**).

A menu lists information about each instance of a clip in a sequence, including the name of the sequence, the name of the clip, and the clip's In point.

## To play a movie clip in the preview area:

1. In the Project window, click a movie clip to select it.

   A sample image and information appear in the preview area of the Project window.

2. To play the preview image, *do one of the following:*

   ▲ To the left of the preview image, click the Play button (**Figure 4.35**).

   ▲ Press the spacebar.

3. To stop playback, click the Play button or press the spacebar again.

4. To cue the preview image, drag the slider below the image (**Figure 4.36**).

**Figure 4.35** Play the preview image by clicking its Play button...

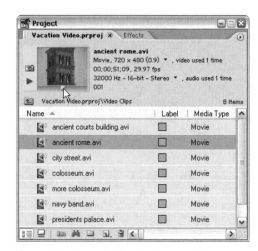

**Figure 4.36** ...or scrub it by dragging its slider.

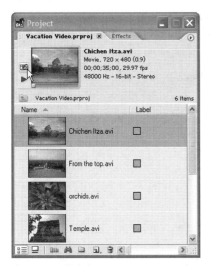

**Figure 4.37** Click the camera icon to set the clip's poster frame.

**Figure 4.38** The frame you specify represents the clip when you view thumbnails.

## To set the poster frame for a movie clip:

1. In the Project window, click a movie clip to select it.

   A sample image and information appear in the preview area of the Project window.

2. Below the preview image, drag the slider to cue the preview to the frame you want to set as the poster frame.

3. To the left of the preview image, click the Set Poster Frame button ▣ (**Figure 4.37**).

   The current frame of the preview becomes the poster frame—the image used to represent the clip when you view thumbnail images of clips in the Project window (**Figure 4.38**).

## ✔ Tips

■ In previous versions of Premiere, setting the poster frame set the zero marker for a clip. In Premiere Pro, the poster frame and the zero marker are independent of each other.

■ If you have not set a poster frame for a clip by clicking the Set Poster Frame button ▣, the poster frame will be the In point of the clip. If you have set the poster frame and it is before the In point, then it will be changed to the In point. If you set it after the In point, then it will remain where you set it.

**USING THE PREVIEW AREA**

# Organizing Clips in Bins

Premiere Pro allows you to manage clips in the project in much the same way that you manage files on your computer operating system. The Project window's clip area can list individual items, or you create folder-like containers known as *bins*. You can specify whether to list imported clips in the top-most level of the Project window's organizational hierarchy or nested inside a bin. Naturally, you can move clips in and out of bins at any time. But although moving clips and bins is analogous to moving files and folders, there are important differences.

### To create a bin:

1. In the Project window, click the Bin button ▢ (**Figure 4.39**).

   A bin appears in the Project window. By default, new bins are named Bin01, Bin02, and so on. However, the name is highlighted, ready for you to change it.

2. Enter a name for the bin (**Figure 4.40**).

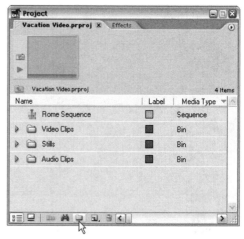

**Figure 4.39** In the Project window, click the Bin button.

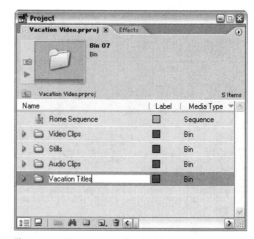

**Figure 4.40** Enter a name for the bin.

Figure 4.41 In list view, clicking the triangle next to the bin icon expands the bin and lets you view its contents in outline form.

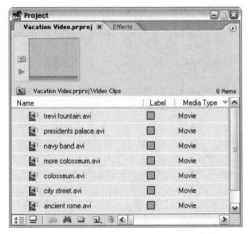

Figure 4.42 In list or icon view, double-click the bin to open it and view its contents in the main clip area of the Project window.

## To view the contents of a bin:

◆ *Do one of the following:*

▲ In list view, click the triangle next to the bin icon to expand the bin and view its contents in outline form (**Figure 4.41**).

▲ In list view or icon view, double-click the bin to open it and view its contents in the main clip area of the Project window (**Figure 4.42**).

## Clips and Bins (Not Files and Folders)

Premiere Pro often employs film-editing metaphors. Film editors use bins to store and organize their clips ("clipped" from reels of film). The film dangles from hangers into a bin until the editor pulls down a strip of film and adds it to the sequence. Premiere Pro's bins may be less tactile than film bins, but they're also a lot less messy.

If you've never seen a film bin, you may find it more useful to compare clips stored in bins with files stored in folders on a drive. In fact, bins were called folders in older versions of Premiere. If you import a folder of files, the folder appears in the project as a bin containing clips.

Unlike some other editing programs, Premiere Pro saves bins as part of the project file, not as separate files.

ORGANIZING CLIPS IN BINS

## To hide the contents of a bin:

◆ *Do one of the following:*

▲ In list view, click the triangle next to the bin icon so that the bin's contents are hidden.

▲ In list view or icon view, click the exit Bin button 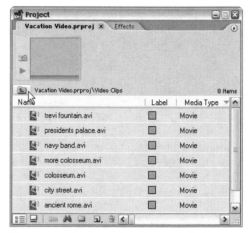 above the main clip area (**Figure 4.43**). The button looks and works like the Up One Level button in Windows XP.

## To move clips into a bin:

1. In list view or icon view, make sure the clips you want to move and the destination bin are both visible in the main clip area of the Project window.

2. Select one or more items.

3. Drag the selected items to another bin (**Figure 4.44**).

    The items are moved into the destination bin (**Figure 4.45**).

**Figure 4.43** In list view or icon view, click the bin navigation icon.

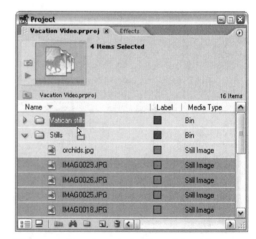

**Figure 4.44** Dragging selected items into a bin...

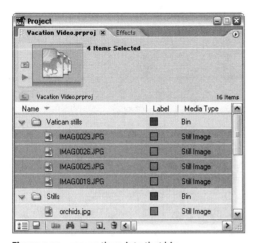

Figure 4.45 ...moves them into that bin.

## To move items out of a bin in list view:

1. Set the Project window to list view.

2. Click the triangle next to a bin to expand the bin and view its contents.

3. Select the items you want to remove from the bin.

4. Drag the selected items down to an empty part of the main clip area (**Figure 4.46**).

   When you release the mouse, the selected items are moved out of the folder and placed one level up in the bin hierarchy (**Figure 4.47**).

Figure 4.46 When you drag items to an empty part of the main clip area...

Figure 4.47 ...the selected items are moved out of the folder and placed one level up in the bin hierarchy.

# Duplicating and Copying Source Clips

You can duplicate any item in the Project window. A duplicate item appears alongside the original, with *Copy* appended to its name.

Alternatively, you can use the Cut, Copy, and Paste commands. This method is useful when you want to replicate a clip in a different bin. A pasted clip uses the same name as the original.

## To duplicate clips:

1. Select one or more clips.

2. Choose Edit > Duplicate (**Figure 4.48**).

   A duplicate clip appears in the Project window. It uses the name of the source clip with the word *Copy* appended to it (**Figure 4.49**).

**Figure 4.48** Choose Edit > Duplicate.

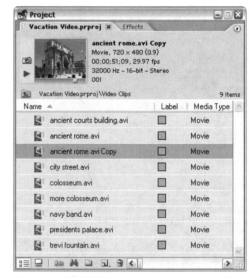

**Figure 4.49** The duplicate uses the same name with *Copy* appended to it.

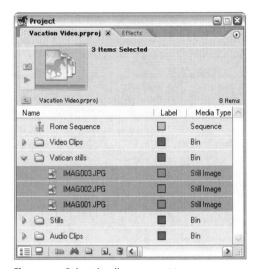

Figure 4.50 Select the clips you want to copy.

## To copy and paste clips:

1. Select one or more clips (**Figure 4.50**).

2. *Do one of the following:*
   ▲ Choose Edit > Cut.
   ▲ Choose Edit > Copy (**Figure 4.51**).

3. View the destination in the main clip area of the Project window.
   If necessary, open the destination bin.

4. Choose Edit > Paste (**Figure 4.52**).
   A duplicate of the clip appears in the selected destination. The clip uses exactly the same name as the original (**Figure 4.53**).

Figure 4.51 Choose Edit > Copy.

Figure 4.52 Navigate to a destination in the Project window and choose Edit > Paste.

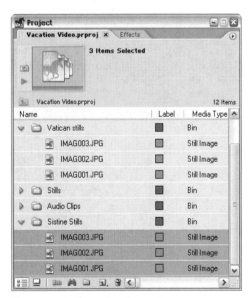

Figure 4.53 The pasted item uses the same name as the original.

## Duplicate Clips and Subclips

In most cases, there's no need to copy a clip; you can add the same clip to any sequence again and again (changing its In point and Out point each time, if you want). However, on some occasions you may want the same clip listed more than once. For example, you may want to interpret each copy of a clip differently, for instance ignoring the alpha channel for one and not the other (see "Interpreting Footage" later in this chapter). More commonly, you may want to make a copy for organizational purposes. For example, you might copy a long clip to make it easier to work with. Then you can give each copy its own name and keep them each cued to the appropriate section. In addition, copies let you use parts of the same clip more than once in a storyboard (see "Storyboard Editing" in Chapter 6).

Although you might think of clip copies as *subclips*, they are really full-fledged clips in their own right. Remember that each clip in the Project window refers to a media file. A duplicate clip refers to the same media file; it isn't dependent on another clip. So deleting one copy of a clip has no effect on other copies. (But, of course, deleting a source clip does delete any instance of that clip in a sequence.) In addition, clip copies access the same full range of source media; you can't limit a copy to a shorter segment.

If you really need subclips, you can edit a clip in a sequence, export the pieces as new media files, and then import each one as a clip. Otherwise, you can use the Project Manager discussed at the end of this chapter to trim all of the used media in the project, creating subclips from each section of the original footage.

DUPLICATING AND COPYING SOURCE CLIPS

**Figure 4.54** Choose Clip > Rename.

**Figure 4.55** Enter a new name for the clip.

# Renaming Clips

After you import a file as a clip, you shouldn't rename the file on your hard disk. Doing so will ruin your project's reference to the file, and Premiere Pro won't be able to locate the file the next time you open the project. Nevertheless, you may still need to identify a clip by another name. Fortunately, you can rename a clip in a project for the purposes of editing. Renaming the clip doesn't affect the source file's name or interfere with your project's references.

## To rename a clip:

1. Select a clip.

2. *Do one of the following:*
   ▲ Click the clip's name and then click it again (do not double-click).
   ▲ Choose Clip > Rename (**Figure 4.54**). The clip's name becomes highlighted.

3. Enter a new name (**Figure 4.55**).

4. Press Enter or click away from the clip. The clip takes another name in the project. The source file on the drive isn't renamed, however.

## ✔ Tip

■ If you want to know the original name of a renamed clip, you can right-click the clip and choose Properties from the menu. In the Properties window, look at the file path to discover the source media file's name, which is the default name of the clip.

# Finding Clips

Even the most organized editor can lose track of a clip, particularly when a project contains a lot of clips. Here's how to find one from the Project window.

### To find a clip:

1. In the Project window, click the Find button ![icon] (**Figure 4.56**).

   The Find dialog box appears. It contains two lines of search criteria (**Figure 4.57**).

2. From the Column pull-down menu, choose a category by which to search.

   Find options match the columns of the Project window's list view.

3. From the Operator pull-down menu, choose a limiting option.

4. In the Find What field, enter search content.

5. To narrow the search, specify another column, another operator, and more search content in the next line.

6. For Match, choose either All or Any.

7. To find only items that match the capitalization of the item you're searching for, select Case Sensitive.

8. Click Find.

   If a clip meets your criteria, it is selected in the Project window (**Figure 4.58**).

9. To search for other clips that meet the search criteria, click Find again.

   If an additional clip meets your criteria, it is selected in the Project window.

10. Repeat step 9 until you find the clip you're searching for or finish searching.

11. Click Done to close the Find dialog box.

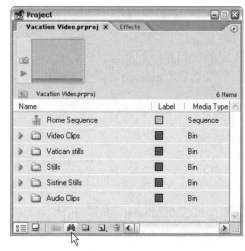

**Figure 4.56** In the Project window, click the Find button.

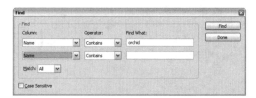

**Figure 4.57** In the Find dialog box, enter search criteria.

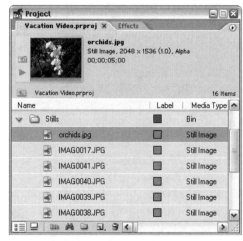

**Figure 4.58** If a clip meets your criteria, it is selected in the Project window.

# Interpreting Footage

In most cases, Premiere Pro correctly *interprets* imported clips, accurately processing characteristics such as frame rate, pixel aspect ratio, and alpha channel. Nevertheless, sometimes you must override Premiere Pro's assessment and specify how these characteristics should be interpreted. For example, a still image sequence may be designed to play at a particular frame rate that you need to set. Or an imported still image may appear distorted—a sure sign that its pixel aspect ratio has not been interpreted correctly. Finally, you may need to manually specify how to handle a clip's alpha channel. In these situations, use the Interpret Footage command to set things right. As usual, Premiere Pro doesn't alter the source media file; it just processes it differently.

**Figure 4.59** Select a clip and choose File > Interpret Footage.

**Figure 4.60** To use a frame rate different from that of the file, select Assume This Frame Rate and enter the rate, expressed in frames per second.

### To set the frame rate of a clip:

1. Select a clip and choose File > Interpret Footage (**Figure 4.59**).

   The Interpret Footage dialog box appears.

2. In the Interpret Footage dialog box, select an option:

   **Use Frame Rate from File:** Uses the file's inherent frame rate.

   **Assume This Frame Rate:** Uses the frame rate that you enter here (**Figure 4.60**).

INTERPRETING FOOTAGE

## To set the pixel aspect ratio of a clip:

1. Select a clip and choose File > Interpret Footage.

   The Interpret Footage dialog box appears.

2. In the Pixel Aspect Ratio area of the Interpret Footage dialog box, select an option:

   **Use Pixel Aspect Ratio from File:** Uses the pixel aspect ratio Premiere Pro assumed.

   **Conform To:** Uses the alternative pixel aspect ratio you select from the drop-down menu (**Figure 4.61**).

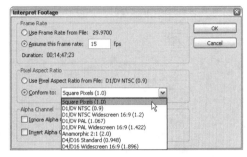

**Figure 4.61** To change the pixel aspect ratio, select Conform To and select an option from the drop-down menu.

## To ignore or invert a clip's alpha channel:

1. Select a clip and choose File > Interpret Footage.

   The Interpret Footage dialog box appears.

2. In the Alpha Channel area of the Interpret Footage dialog box, select the options you want (**Figure 4.62**):

   **Ignore Alpha Channel:** Disregards the clip's alpha channel so that it doesn't define transparent areas when the clip is added to video track 2 and higher.

   **Invert Alpha Channel:** Reverses the transparent and opaque areas defined by the clip's alpha channel.

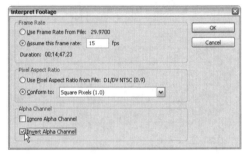

**Figure 4.62** In the Interpret Footage dialog box, specify whether to ignore or invert the clip's alpha channel.

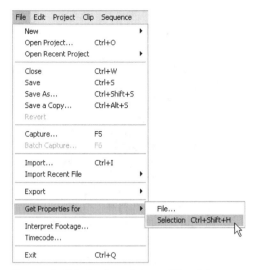

Figure 4.63 Select a clip and choose File > Get Properties For > Selection.

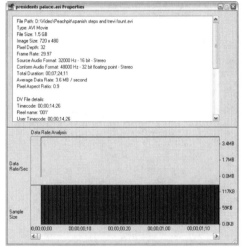

Figure 4.64 The Properties dialog box contains detailed information about the clip, including an analysis of its data rate.

# Viewing Clip Properties

If you need more information about a clip than the Project window provides, you can view detailed information by using the Get Properties For command. You can also view the properties for any media file on a disk. When you select a movie file, the Properties window provides an analysis of the movie's data rate, which can help you troubleshoot a file that isn't playing back properly. For an explanation of data rates, see Chapter 16, "Video and Audio Settings."

## To view properties for a file or clip:

◆ *Do one of the following:*

  ▲ Choose File > Get Properties For > File and choose a file in the Get Properties dialog box.

  ▲ Select a clip and choose File > Get Properties For > Selection (**Figure 4.63**).

  A Properties dialog box appears listing the properties of the selected item (**Figure 4.64**).

# Unlinking and Relinking Media

By now, you should appreciate the relationship between clips and media. You should know, for example, that a clip you log remains offline until you batch-capture the actual media to which it refers. Moreover, you should understand that deleting a clip doesn't remove the media from the hard disk, and conversely, that deleting media results in clips with missing references. To truly manage your assets, however, you need control over the connection, or *link*, between clip and media.

Premiere Pro allows you to unlink a clip from its corresponding media file and relink the two again. Suppose you've been editing with low-quality proxy versions of your media (what some would call *offline quality*). You can unlink the clips from the proxies and then link them to the high-quality versions (*online quality*, if you like). Alternatively, you can unlink media and remove it from the hard disk. This allows you to free up storage space and still retain the clip information in the form of an offline clip—ensuring that you can recapture the media if you decide you need it later.

## To unlink clips from media:

1. In the Project window, select one or more clips (**Figure 4.65**).

2. Choose Project > Unlink Media (**Figure 4.66**).

   The Unlink Media dialog box appears.

**Figure 4.65** Select one or more clips.

**Figure 4.66** Choose Project > Unlink Media.

**Figure 4.67** In the Unlink Media dialog box, select the appropriate option.

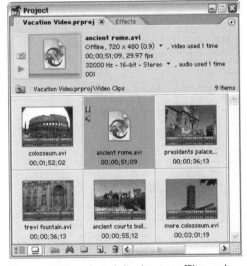

**Figure 4.68** The selected clips become offline, and the corresponding media files are either retained or deleted, depending on your choice.

**3.** In the Unlink Media dialog box, *select one of the following* (**Figure 4.67**):

   ▲ **Media Files Remain on Disk:** Breaks the clip's reference to the media file without deleting the file.

   ▲ **Media Files Are Deleted:** Breaks the clip's reference to the media file and deletes the file.

The selected clips' icons change to indicate that they are offline, unrelated to media on the hard drive (**Figure 4.68**).

## To link clips with media:

1. In the Project window, select one or more offline clips.

2. Choose Project > Link Media (**Figure 4.69**).

   The Attach Which Media to *clipname* dialog box appears.

3. In the Attach Which Media to *clipname* dialog box, find and select the media file you want to attach to the clip and click Select (**Figure 4.70**).

   If you selected more than one clip, Premiere Pro automatically relinks the other clips to matching media files in the same location.

4. Repeat step 3 for clips with media in other locations on the hard disk.

   When you're finished relinking clips and media, the dialog box closes. In the Project window, the selected clip's icon indicates that it's linked to media.

**Figure 4.69** Select offline clips and choose Project > Link Media.

**Figure 4.70** Locate the correct media file and click Select to link the clip to the file.

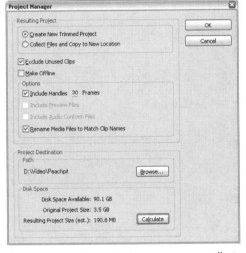

**Figure 4.71** Choose Project > Project Manager to open the Project Manager.

**Figure 4.72** With the Project Manager, you can collect and trim your project.

# Using the Project Manager

Because video files can consume large amounts of precious storage space, it's particularly important to manage them efficiently. You can organize your media and reduce storage requirements with the *Project Manager*. With the Project Manager, you can *collect* and *trim* your project.

*Collecting* a project moves all the project's media to a single location. This is useful when it's time to archive your project or move it to another editing system—especially if your assets aren't well organized and are scattered over one or more hard disks.

*Trimming* a project identifies the clips you actually used in sequences and creates a duplicate project that includes only those clips. Moreover, their corresponding media files are trimmed, or shortened, to the range of footage actually present in sequences. This way, the footage you used consumes less storage space, and you can more easily delete the footage you didn't use.

Whether you collect or trim a project, note that Premiere Pro saves a new project separately, leaving the original version untouched. This is consistent with the idea of nonde-structive editing, explained in Chapter 2, "Starting a Project."

## To use the Project Manager:

1. Choose Project > Project Manager (**Figure 4.71**).

   The Project Manager dialog box appears (**Figure 4.72**).

   *continues on next page*

**USING THE PROJECT MANAGER**

2. In the Project Manager dialog box, *do one of the following:*

   ▲ To create a new trimmed project, select Create New Trimmed Project

   ▲ To collect all of the project's assets into a common location, select Collect Files and Copy to New Location.

3. In the Project Manager dialog box, specify other options.

   These options are explained in detail in the section "Choosing Project Manager Options" on the next page.

4. In the Disk Space area of the Project Manager, click Calculate to calculate the disk space required to store the new files.

   The Calculate Progress window appears briefly while the required disk space is being calculated (**Figure 4.73**).

5. In the Project Destination area, click the Browse button and specify a destination.

   The Browse for Folder dialog box appears (**Figure 4.74**).

6. In the Browse for Folder dialog box, specify the location for the collected or trimmed files.

7. Click OK to create the new files.

   The Project Manager Progress window appears, indicating that the project is being trimmed (**Figure 4.75**) or copied (**Figure 4.76**). When processing is complete, the original project is still open. To use the new project, close the original project and open the new project.

**Figure 4.73** The Calculate Progress window appears briefly while Premiere Pro calculates the required disk space.

**Figure 4.74** Use the Browse for Folder dialog box to select a destination.

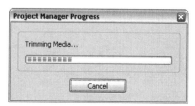

**Figure 4.75** The Project Manager Progress window shows the project being trimmed...

**Figure 4.76** ...or copied.

# Choosing Project Manager Options

The Project Manager includes a number of options, depending on whether you trim or collect your project.

**Exclude Unused Clips:** Excludes media from the new project that you did not use in the original project.

**Make Offline:** Marks as offline any footage that you can recapture later. Select this option when you want the Project Manager to retain reel names and timecode to facilitate quick batch capture. This option is available only if Create New Trimmed Project is selected.

**Include Handles:** Specifies the number of frames retained before the In point and after the Out point of each trimmed clip.

**Include Preview Files:** Specifies that effects you rendered in the original project stay rendered in the new project. When this option is selected, the new project requires more disk space, so unless the footage requires extensive rendering, leave this option unchecked when backing up projects. This option is available only if you select Collect Files and Copy to New Location.

**Include Audio Conform Files:** Specifies that the audio you conformed in the original project remains conformed in the new project. When this option is selected, the new project requires more disk space, but the audio does not need to be conformed again when you open the project. This option is available only if you select Collect Files and Copy to New Location.

**Rename Media Files to Match Clip Names:** Renames the copied clips with the same names as the captured clips. Select this option if you rename your captured clips in the Project window and want the copied footage files to have the same names.

## ✔ Tips

- Handles are extra frames that allow you to make additional small adjustments to the edits in a new project.

- In cases where multiple clips use segments from the same captured footage file and you rename each project, the Project Manager renames the footage file using the name of the first clip in the project.

- If you select the Make Offline option and then rename captured clips, the copied project retains and displays the original file name, not the new name.

# VIEWING CLIPS IN THE MONITOR WINDOW

As its name implies, the Monitor window lets you see your footage much as you would on the video monitors in a traditional video editing suite or the screens on a flatbed film editing table. In fact, the Monitor window is modeled after an *entire* editing station, complete with editing controls to play back your clips and assemble them into a sequence. Not that the Monitor window merely emulates its predecessors—it has features and advantages you can find only in a digital, nonlinear editing program.

This chapter focuses on using the Monitor window to view clips. First, you'll learn to customize the Monitor window to suit your personal preference or the task at hand. You'll also learn to open and play clips and specify a number of viewing options. With these features under your belt, you'll be prepared to use the Monitor window's editing features, covered in the next chapter.

# Using the Monitor Window

Depending on your needs or preferences, the Monitor window can appear in two incarnations: dual view or single view. In *dual view,* the left side of the Monitor window is the *source view,* where you view individual clips; the right side is the *program view,* where you view the edited sequence (**Figure 5.1**). Most editors prefer this layout not only because it's familiar, but also because it enables them to see the source and sequence side by side, which helps them make editing decisions. You can even *gang* the two views, so that the source and sequence play synchronously. This feature is invaluable when you need to preview the timing of certain edits or see other editing relationships.

Once you've assembled a rough cut, however, dual view becomes less useful. At this point, you may opt to switch to *single view*. In single view, the Monitor window shows either the source view or the program view only (**Figure 5.2**). By setting the Monitor window to show the program view only, you can use the extra screen space for controls you'll need to fine-tune the sequence, such as the Effect Controls window or the Audio Mixer window.

**Figure 5.1** When set to dual view, the left side of the Monitor window is the source view, where you view individual clips; the right side is the program view, where you view the edited sequence.

**Figure 5.2** When set to single view, the Monitor window includes either the source view or, more commonly, the program view (shown here).

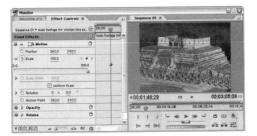

**Figure 5.3** You can add the Effect Controls window to the source view side of the Monitor window and switch between them by clicking a tab.

Alternatively, you can leave the Monitor window set to dual view and use the source view side for the Effect Controls window (**Figure 5.3**).

In much the same way, each sequence in your project appears as a tab in the program view. Clicking a sequence tab switches the sequence visible in the Monitor window, as well as the corresponding sequence in the Timeline window. Although it was pointed out in Chapter 1, "Premiere Pro Basics," it's worth reiterating that the program view and Timeline window depict the same sequence in different ways. The video frame displayed in the program view corresponds to a vertical line in the Timeline window called the *current time indicator (CTI)*.

# Modifying the Monitor Window

As you saw in Chapter 1, you can choose from among several preset workspace options to arrange the windows for your preferred work method or to optimize them for a particular editing task. Some layouts alter the way the Monitor window looks, but you can change the way this window looks at any time.

### To set the Monitor window to single view:

◆ *Do one of the following:*

  ▲ To include the source view only, choose Single View from the source view's drop-down menu.

  ▲ To include the program side only, choose Single View from the program view's drop-down menu (**Figure 5.4**).

### To set the Monitor window to dual view:

◆ Choose Dual View from either view's drop-down menu (**Figure 5.5**).

  The Monitor window includes both a source and a program view.

### ✔ Tips

■ You can view source clips and a sequence in separate windows, but this "view" is not functionally equivalent to dual view. Create a reference monitor for the sequence and gang (synchronize) it to the program monitor (see "Using a Reference Monitor" later in this chapter). Then set the source view to single view. You get two separate windows, but the reference monitor lacks the program view's editing controls.

■ Unlike in past versions of Premiere, the video images in the Monitor window aren't restricted to a handful of standard sizes. Instead, they scale to fit in the available space of each view, no matter how you resize the Monitor window.

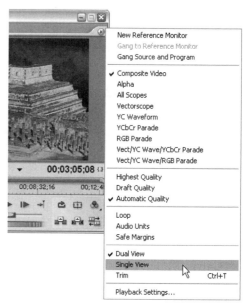

**Figure 5.4** Choose Single View from the source or program view's drop-down menu.

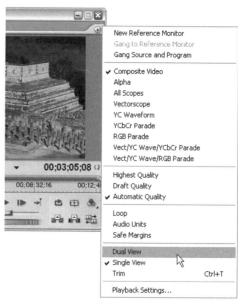

**Figure 5.5** To switch the Monitor window back to dual view, choose Dual View from the drop-down menu.

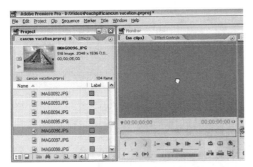

**Figure 5.6** Double-click a clip or drag it to the source view of the Monitor window, as shown here.

**Figure 5.7** The clip opens in the source view, and its name appears on the source tab.

# Viewing Clips

When you open any kind of clip—a movie, a still image, or audio—it appears in the source view of the Monitor window, where you can play it and mark frames for editing. The name of the open clip appears in a tab at the top of the source view, the *source tab*. Clicking the small triangle on the source tab reveals a *source menu*; this menu lists all the clips you've opened, in order starting with the most recent. You can quickly reopen a clip by selecting it from the source menu. When the menu becomes unwieldy, you can clear items from the list.

### To open a clip in the source view:

◆ *Do one of the following:*

▲ Double-click a clip in the Project window, the preview image, or the Timeline window.

▲ Drag a clip from the Project window or the preview image into the source view of the Monitor window (**Figure 5.6**).

The clip's image or audio waveform appears in the source view, and its name appears on the source tab (**Figure 5.7**).

## To load several clips into the source menu at once:

1. In the Project window, select one or more clips (**Figure 5.8**).

2. Drag the selected clips to the source view of the Monitor window (**Figure 5.9**).

   The clips appear in the source menu in order, so that the last clip selected is first and its video or audio waveform appears in the source view.

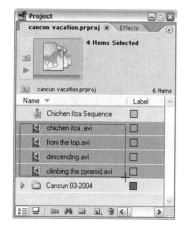

**Figure 5.8** In the Project window, select one or more clips...

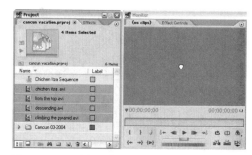

**Figure 5.9** ...and drag them to the source view to load them into the source menu.

## Opening Source Clips and Clip Instances

When you open a clip from the Project window, you're opening a *source* clip. As you'll learn in the next chapter, you open a source clip to view and edit it before adding it to a sequence.

Each time you add a source clip to a sequence, you create a new *instance* of the source clip, also called a *sequence clip*. Opening a clip instance allows you to view that particular use of the clip in the source view, and any edits you make are instantly reflected in the Timeline window (although once the clip is in a sequence, there are numerous other ways to edit it).

For now, note that the source menu lists source clips by name. It lists clip instances by a kind of path name that includes the sequence name, the clip name, and the clip's current In point in the sequence.

VIEWING CLIPS

**Figure 5.10** From the source menu, choose the name of the clip you want to view.

**Figure 5.11** To remove all clips from the source menu, choose Close All.

## To view clips using the source menu:

◆ In the source menu, choose the name of a clip (**Figure 5.10**).

The selected clip appears in the image area of the source view.

## To remove clips from the source menu:

◆ *Do one of the following:*

▲ To close the open clip and clear it from the source menu, click the Close button ⊠ on the source tab or choose Close from the source menu.

▲ To clear all the clips from the source menu, choose Close All from the source menu (**Figure 5.11**).

Depending on your choice, one or more clips are removed from the source menu. However, closed clips remain listed in the Project window.

## ✔ Tips

■ You can also open nested sequences in the source view for editing. See Chapter 6, "Creating a Sequence," for details.

■ Double-clicking a selection of multiple clips won't load all the selected clips into the source menu, just the one you double-click.

■ If the sequence's CTI is cued to a frame of the clip instance, when you double-click the clip it will open in the source view cued to the same frame, or *match frame.*

# Opening Audio Clips

The source view works the same for audio clips as for movie clips, except that instead of showing the current frame of the video, it depicts the audio as a *waveform*—a kind of graph of the audio's power over time. A monophonic track appears as a single waveform; a stereophonic track appears as two waveforms (**Figures 5.12** and **5.13**). Often, you can identify particular sounds by examining the audio waveform. Powerful beats in a song are depicted as spikes in the waveform; silence or pauses between lines of dialogue result in flat horizontal lines in the waveform.

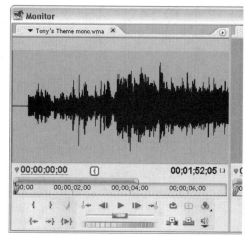

**Figure 5.12** In the source view, monophonic audio clips appear as a single waveform...

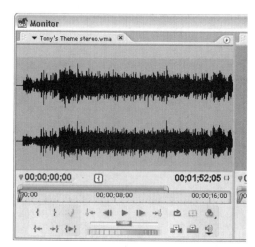

**Figure 5.13** ...whereas stereophonic clips appear as a dual waveform.

In point icon · Clip marker icon · Current time indicator · Out point icon

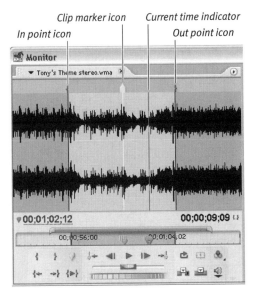

**Figure 5.14** In addition to a waveform, the source view shows other information for audio clips differently than it does for video.

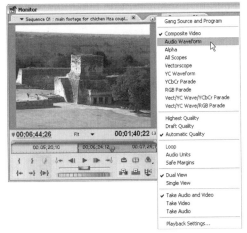

**Figure 5.15** In the source view's drop-down menu, choose Audio Waveform.

Because the waveform depicts audio over a span of time (as opposed to a single video frame), the source view can display other information as well. A vertical line indicates the current time—the position of the playback head, if you will. In addition, icons for clip markers and In and Out points appear at the top of the source view, with vertical lines extending from them to help you see their positions in terms of the waveform. Furthermore, the area between the current In and Out points is shaded lighter so you can see your selection as well as hear it (**Figure 5.14**). For more about markers and In and Out points, see Chapter 6.

## To view the audio portion of a video:

◆ In the source view's pull-down menu, choose Audio Waveform (**Figure 5.15**). The audio waveform linked to the video file appears in the image area of the source view.

## ✔ Tips

- You can switch the source view's time ruler to show audio samples rather than video frames. See Chapter 6 for details.

- As you will see in Chapter 6, audio clips can be added to a sequence only in a track of the same channel type. In other words, mono audio clips can be added only to a mono track in the sequence, and stereo clips can be added only to a stereo track.

- You can separate, or break out, the mono channels from a stereo track. See Chapter 11, "Mixing Audio," for more information.

# Using Playback Controls

Whether you're playing a clip in the source view or an edited sequence in the program view, the basic playback controls work the same.

Most playback controls also have preset keyboard shortcuts, which are well worth learning. Before you use keyboard playback controls, however, make sure that you select the proper view of the Monitor window. When you select a view, blue bars appear above and below the image (or waveform) in the view.

Also bear in mind that the program view of the Monitor window corresponds to the sequence in the Timeline window. As you change the current time in the program view, watch how it affects the current time indicator in the Timeline window (and vice versa). The same keyboard playback commands that work in the program view also work when the Timeline window is selected.

## To use the playback controls:

◆ Below the image in the source view and program view, click the appropriate playback control (**Figure 5.16**):

**Play/Stop:** Plays the clip or program until it reaches the last frame. Click the control again to stop playback. The icon toggles accordingly.

**Frame Advance:** Moves the current view one frame forward in time (or forward by the timebase division you selected for the time display).

**Frame Back:** Moves the current view one frame back (or backward by the timebase division you selected for the time display).

**Loop:** Repeats a playback operation (play or play In to Out) until you click Stop.

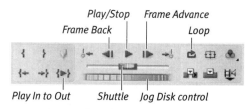

**Figure 5.16** Most playback controls work the same in the source and program views.

**Table 5.1**

| Default Keyboard Shortcuts for Playback | |
|---|---|
| ACTION | RESULT |
| Press L | Play. |
| Press K | Pause. |
| Press J | Play in reverse. |
| Press J or L repeatedly | Increase speed. (Most media plays at 2x, 3x, and then 4x normal speed.) |
| Press Shift-J or Shift-L repeatedly | Play slowly. (Most media plays at 0.1x and then 0.2x normal speed.) |
| Spacebar | Toggle between play and stop. |

**Play In to Out:** Plays the portion of the clip or program between the selected In and Out points.

**Jog Disk control:** Advances or reverses the clip by small amounts as you drag and release the control. The Jog Disk control is comparable to a jog wheel on a video deck.

**Shuttle:** Scans the clip more quickly the farther you drag the control from its center position; drag left to scan in reverse, and drag right to scan forward. Releasing the control returns it to its center position and stops playback.

### To use keyboard shortcuts to control playback:

1. Make sure the appropriate view is active.

2. *Do one of the following* (see **Table 5.1**):
   - ▲ To play in reverse, press J.
   - ▲ To stop playback, press K.
   - ▲ To play forward, press L.
   - ▲ To increase playback speed, press J or L again. For most media types, speed increases by increments of 1x, 2x, 3x, and 4x normal speed.
   - ▲ To play forward slowly, press Shift-L.
   - ▲ To play in reverse slowly, press Shift-J. For most media types, clips play at 0.1x and 0.2x normal speed.
   - ▲ To toggle between play and stop, press the spacebar.

### ✔ Tips

- ■ The J-K-L keyboard combination is worth getting used to. In the next chapter, you'll see how you can use J-K-L along with other keyboard shortcuts for speedy keyboard-based editing. This keyboard combination has become standard in several popular editing programs. You can think of J-K-L as the home keys of nonlinear editing.

- ■ Pressing Alt toggles the Play In to Out button to the Play Around button. Play Around plays frames just before and after the current time indicator. The number of frames are defined by the preroll and postroll values you specify in the Preferences.

- ■ If you use a mouse with a scroll wheel, you can use the wheel as a jog disk control for the active view of the Monitor window.

USING PLAYBACK CONTROLS

# Cuing Clips Numerically

You can use the time displays to cue the source and program views to a particular frame number, or *absolute time*. Or you can cue to a *relative time*—in other words, add frames to or subtract frames from the current time. Like most user-defined values in Premiere Pro and other Adobe products, the time display is *scrubbable hot text*—that is, you can adjust the value by dragging the number.

### To cue the view to an absolute time:

1. Click the current time display for a view to highlight the number (**Figure 5.17**).

2. Enter the number of the frame that you want to view and press Enter (**Figure 5.18**).

   As long as the frame number that you entered exists, the view displays that frame (**Figure 5.19**).

**Figure 5.17** Click a view's current time display to highlight the number.

**Figure 5.18** Type a valid timecode and press Enter...

## Entering Frame Values

Any duration value that you enter in Premiere Pro has a *threshold* of 100. That is, numbers 99 and below are interpreted as frames; numbers 100 and above are expressed in the units of the selected time display. In a project that uses a timecode display, for example, the number 99 is interpreted as 99 frames, or 3 seconds and 9 frames; the number 100 is interpreted as seconds and frames, or 1 second and 00 frames.

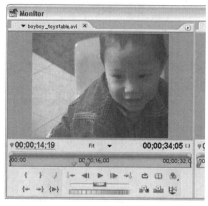

**Figure 5.19** ...and the view cues to that frame.

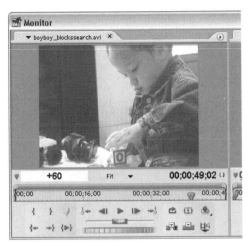

**Figure 5.20** Here, the time display is set to cue the current time 60 frames forward.

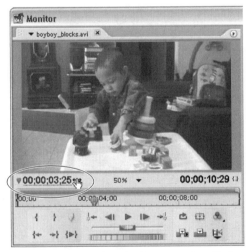

**Figure 5.21** You can also drag the current time display to change its value. This is true for underlined values in all Adobe programs.

## To cue the view to a relative time:

1. Click the current time display for a view to highlight the number.

2. Type a plus (+) or a minus (−) sign and a number (**Figure 5.20**).

   To cue the clip 30 frames after the current frame, for example, type +30. To cue the view 60 frames before the current frame, type −60.

## To cue the view by scrubbing the current time:

◆ *Do one of the following:*

   ▲ Drag the current time display to the right to increase the number and advance the current time (**Figure 5.21**).

   ▲ Drag the current time display to the left to decrease the number and reverse the current time.

## ✔ Tips

■ You can highlight individual numbers in the current-time readout and change them to cue the current frame of the view.

■ If the time that you enter in the current-time readout does not exist, the view is cued to the nearest available frame: either the first or the last frame of the clip or program.

■ The frame-counting method displayed in the time readout is determined by the Project settings (see Chapter 2, "Starting a Project"). For most users (and for most screenshots in this book) the readout displays drop-frame timecode. For more about timecode, see Chapter 16, "Video and Audio Settings."

# Using the Monitor Window's Time Ruler Controls

A *time ruler* in each view of the Monitor window provides another way to navigate through a clip or sequence (**Figure 5.22**). The full width of the ruler represents the entire length of the clip in the source view or the entire length of a sequence in the program view. Tick marks and numbers measure time using the unit of measure you specified in the project settings, although you can toggle the ruler to measure audio samples as well. The frame displayed in the view corresponds to a blue triangular marker in the ruler, called the *current time indicator (CTI)*. Each time ruler also displays icons for its corresponding view's markers and In and Out points. You can move the current time, markers, and In and Out points by dragging the appropriate icon in the time ruler.

Just above each time ruler is a thin bar with curved ends, called the *viewing area bar*. By changing the width of the viewing area bar, you can control the scale area of the time ruler. Expanding the bar to its maximum width reveals the entire span of its time ruler, and contracting the bar zooms into the ruler for a more detailed view. Dragging the center of the bar scrolls through the time ruler without changing its scale.

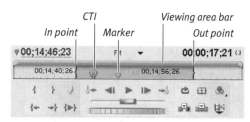

**Figure 5.22** A *time ruler* in each view provides another way to navigate through a clip or sequence.

**Figure 5.23** Here, the viewing area bar is set to show the full span of time. Note how the tick marks and icons appear at the current scale.

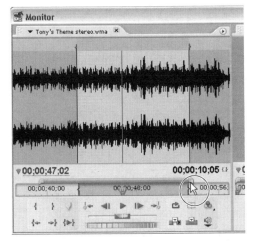

**Figure 5.24** To view the ruler in more detail, drag the ends of the viewing area bar closer together. Again, note how the tick marks and icons look at the new scale.

## To view the time ruler in more or less detail:

◆ *Do one of the following:*

▲ To show the view's time ruler in more detail, drag the ends of the viewing area bar closer together (**Figures 5.23** and **5.24**).

▲ To show more of the view's time ruler, drag the ends of the viewing area bar farther apart.

Dragging one end of the viewing area bar scales the bar from its center.

## To change the visible area of a view's time ruler:

◆ Drag the center of the viewing area bar to the left to see an earlier part of the time ruler, or to the right to see a later part (**Figure 5.25**).

## To set the current time in a time ruler:

◆ *Do one of the following:*

　▲ Click the time ruler to cue the current time.

　▲ Drag the blue CTI (**Figure 5.26**).

## ✔ Tip

■ Because the program view and Timeline window correspond to the same sequence, they show the same current time, markers, and In and Out points. However, their viewing area bars operate independently; the part of the time ruler you view in the program view can be different than the part you see in the Timeline window.

**Figure 5.25** Drag the viewing area bar from the center to view a different part of the time ruler.

**Figure 5.26** To set the current time, click the time ruler or drag the CTI.

**Figure 5.27** In the source or program view, click the Safe Margins button.

Action safe (90 percent)
Title safe (80 percent)

**Figure 5.28** Safe-zone guides appear in the view.

# Viewing Video Safe Zones

The Monitor window displays the entire video frame, but television monitors are likely to crop off the outer edges of the image. If your program is destined for full-screen display on a video monitor, you may need to check whether certain parts of the image fall within the video *safe zones*.

In video, the inner 90 percent of the complete image is considered to be *action safe*—that is, everything within that area is likely to appear on most television screens. The inner 80 percent is considered to be *title safe*. Because you can't afford to let any of the title's content be lost, the title-safe area defines a necessary safety margin. The safe-zone guides are for your reference only; they aren't added to the source image and don't appear in the program output.

### To view safe zones:

◆ In the source or program view of the Monitor window, click the Safe Margins button ⊞ (**Figure 5.27**).

Safe-zone guides appear in the corresponding view of the Monitor window (**Figure 5.28**). Deselect the button to hide the safe-zone guides.

### ✔ Tips

■ As you might guess, safe zones are particularly useful when you're creating titles or moving images through the screen. See Chapter 12, "Creating Titles," or Chapter 13, "Working with Effects," for more information.

■ You can change the position of the safe-margin guides in the General panel of the Project settings, but 10 percent and 20 percent margins (to demarcate the 90 percent and 80 percent zones) are standard.

# Choosing a Quality Setting

You can set the relative quality of the video image in each view of the Monitor window. Even though you may prefer the highest quality—which displays all the pixels in each frame of video—using a lower quality setting can be useful. By reducing a view's resolution, you reduce the processing demands on your computer and make it easier for your system to play video at the proper frame rate. This is particularly useful in the program view; lowering its quality setting enables your system to play effects or other processing-intensive parts of a sequence right away, without pausing to render (see Chapter 10, "Previewing a Sequence").

But even at the highest quality setting, the methods used to process images in the Monitor window are inferior to those used to export the final video. All of the quality settings use a bi-linear pixel resampling method to resize the video image, and none of them process interlaced fields. When it's exporting a sequence, on the other hand, Premiere Pro processes interlaced fields and uses a cubic resampling method, which is superior to bi-linear.

### To set a view's quality:

◆ In the source or program view, click the output button ⚙, and choose a quality option from the menu (**Figure 5.29**):

**Highest Quality:** Displays video in the Monitor window at full resolution.

**Draft Quality:** Displays video in the Monitor window at one-half resolution.

**Automatic Quality:** Measures playback performance and dynamically adjusts the video quality.

**Figure 5.29** In the source or program view, click the output button and choose a quality setting from the drop-down menu.

**Figure 5.30** To magnify a view, choose a magnification setting from the drop-down menu.

**Figure 5.31** Here, the image is reduced so that motion effects can be adjusted more easily.

**Figure 5.32** Scrollbars appear when you magnify the view over 100 percent.

# Changing the Magnification

Whatever size you make the Monitor window, the video in each view automatically scales to fit in the available space. However, you can see the video in more detail by increasing a view's *magnification setting*. Alternatively, you can decrease the magnification setting to reduce the image relative to the pasteboard area around it, so you can adjust motion effects more easily, for example. The magnification setting is for viewing purposes only; it doesn't alter the video's appearance for output or change the source file in any way.

## To set the view's magnification:

◆ Under the source or program view's video image, click the Magnification button and choose an option from the drop-down menu:

▲ To fit in the available area of the view, choose Fit.

▲ To magnify the view, choose a percentage value (**Figure 5.30**).

Increasing the magnification setting zooms into the video image; using a lower magnification setting reduces the image relative to the view's pasteboard area (**Figure 5.31**).

Scrollbars will appear when you magnify the view over 100 percent. You can navigate around the view using the scrollbars, or you can use the cursor (or the Hand tool) to grab in the middle of the view to move the image (**Figure 5.32**).

# Choosing a Display Mode

Ordinarily, the video in each view of the Monitor window appears as it would on any television screen. However, you can set a view's *display mode* to show the video's *alpha channel*—its transparency information as represented by a grayscale image. In addition, you can set the display mode to show several iterations of a *waveform monitor* and *vectorscope*, tools that precisely measure the video's luminance and chrominance values. The waveform monitor and vectorscope (often collectively referred to as *scopes*) are invaluable for color correction and for ensuring that your video meets broadcast specifications.

### To set the display mode:

◆ In the source or program view of the Monitor window, click the Display Mode button, and choose an option from the menu (**Figure 5.33**):

**Composite Video:** Displays the normal video image, sometimes referred to as the *composite* of the luminance (grayscale) and chrominance (color) components of the video.

**Alpha:** Displays the image's transparency information (called the *alpha channel* in digital formats) as a grayscale image, so that the range of black to white corresponds to the range of transparency to opacity (**Figure 5.34**).

**All Scopes:** Displays all four measurement devices—YC Waveform monitor, vectorscope, YCbCr Parade, and RGB Parade—one in each corner of the view.

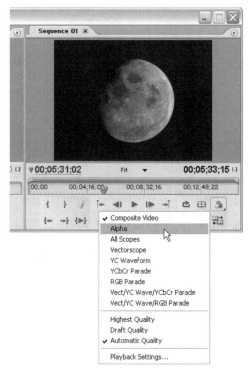

**Figure 5.33** In the source or program view, click the Display Mode button and choose an option.

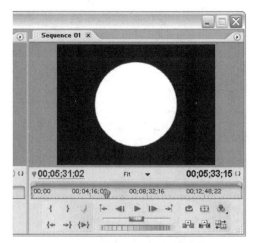

**Figure 5.34** The Alpha option shows transparency information as a grayscale image in which white represents opaque areas and black represents transparent areas.

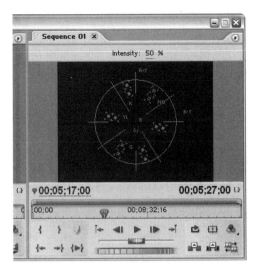

**Figure 5.35** A vectorscope measures the video's chrominance.

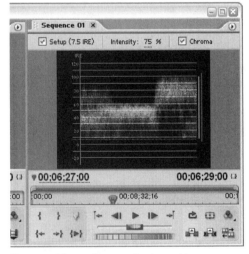

**Figure 5.36** A waveform monitor is used to measure the video's luminance levels.

**Vectorscope:** Displays a standard vectorscope, a device used to measure the video's chrominance levels, which include hue and saturation (**Figure 5.35**).

**YC Waveform:** Displays a standard waveform monitor, a device used to measure the video's luminance levels in units called IRE (**Figure 5.36**).

**YCbCr Parade:** Displays a variation of the waveform monitor that charts the components of the video image separately, in terms of a YCbCr color model.

**RGB Parade:** Displays a variation of the waveform monitor that charts the components of the video image separately, in terms of an RGB color model.

**Vect/YC Wave/YCbCr Parade:** Displays three scopes: a standard waveform monitor and vectorscope in the top half of the view and YCbCr Parade in the bottom half.

**Vect/YC Wave/RGB Parade:** Displays three scopes: a standard waveform monitor and vectorscope in the top half of the view and RGB Parade in the bottom half.

# Setting Waveform and Vectorscope Display Options

You can use the display mode options in the source window to modify your view of the YC Waveform and Vectorscope displays (**Figure 5.37**). These options appear in the Vectorscope, YC Waveform, and All Scopes display modes.

**Setup** pins black to 7.5 IRE or 0 IRE. Setup specifies the voltage level for pure black. In the United States, NTSC standards place the setup (also known as *pedestal*) at 7.5 IRE; Japan's implementation of NTSC standards place the setup at 0 IRE. This setting is for the monitor only. It does not affect the actual footage. If you are using an analog output device, it may add a pedestal of 7.5 IRE, so this option gives you a similar view. This setting applies to the YC Waveform display only.

**Intensity** duplicates the function of the Intensity slider on external waveform monitors. The default setting is 50 percent. This setting applies to both the YC Waveform and Vectorscope displays.

**Chroma** turns off the display of chroma information. Because the waveform monitor displays chroma information (blue) over the luminance waveform (green), it can be difficult to accurately measure luminance. Turning off the chroma display filters out the chroma information so that you can easily identify the luminance values. This setting applies to the YC Waveform display only.

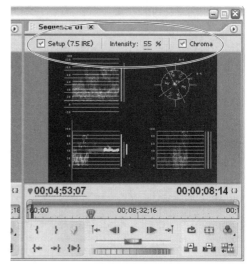

**Figure 5.37** The All Scopes mode has all three display mode options.

## To set the Vectorscope or YC Waveform intensity:

◆ In the Vectorscope display mode (Figure 5.35) or YC Waveform display mode (Figure 5.36), *do one of the following:*

▲ Drag the Intensity value down or to the left to decrease the intensity; drag up or to the right to increase the intensity.

▲ Click the Intensity value, type a new value, and press Enter.

## To set the YC Waveform setup:

◆ In the YC Waveform display mode (Figure 5.36), *do one of the following:*

▲ Click the Setup check box to uncheck it. This sets the IRE to 0.

▲ Click the Setup check box to select it. This sets the IRE to 7.5.

## To modify the YC Waveform chroma display:

◆ In the YC Waveform display mode (Figure 5.36), *do one of the following:*

▲ Click the Chroma check box to uncheck it. This turns off the blue chroma display and enhances visibility of the green luminance display.

▲ Click the Chroma check box to select it. This turns on the blue chroma display.

**WAVEFORM AND VECTORSCOPE DISPLAY**

## Using a Waveform Monitor

You can use a waveform monitor to measure the video's brightness, or more precisely, its luminance component. You can read the waveform monitor just as you would read a graph. Horizontally, the graph corresponds to the video image; vertically, it measures luminance in units called IRE (pronounced letter by letter and named for the Institute of Radio Engineers). The video produces a waveform pattern (bright green areas) on the graph, so that bright objects produce a waveform near the top of the graph, and darker areas produce a waveform near the bottom (**Figure 5.38**).

For NTSC video in the United States, luminance levels should range from 7.5 to 100 IRE. Japan's implementation of NTSC standards permits a luminance range from 0 to 100 IRE. Allowing video levels to stray outside these limits, or *NTSC-safe* levels, may ruin more than the video's appearance; it could interfere with parts of the signal that keep the picture stable and make it ineligible for broadcast.

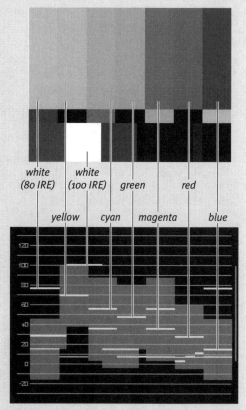

**Figure 5.38** The top image shows a standard color bars pattern in a view set to the composite display mode. The bottom image shows the same color bars as seen in a waveform monitor. Note how the bars and the pattern in the waveform monitor correspond.

## The Waveform Monitor and Vectorscope Are Not Surf Reports

In Chapter 3, "Capturing and Importing Footage," you learned that a *leader* (the boilerplate information on the first few minutes of a master tape) always includes a color-bars test pattern. Video technicians use the color bars as a reference to faithfully reproduce your video's color and brightness levels (in much the same way that a service bureau uses a color-chip chart or PANTONE colors to reproduce printed material). To accurately calibrate their equipment to the color bars, technicians use hardware devices known as a *waveform monitor* and a *vectorscope*. The *scopes*, as they are sometimes called, accurately measure the video's brightness and color (in technical terms, its luminance and chrominance). Using a waveform monitor and vectorscope ensures that the bars—and the rest of the video program—are copied exactly.

Similarly, you can use Premiere Pro's software waveform monitor and vectorscope to accurately judge video levels and make precise adjustments, such as color correction. Because the scopes measure the video signal itself, they provide more accurate information than does judging the video by eye. Even the keenest eye is subjective; even the best monitor can be poorly calibrated and inaccurate.

If you've never used scopes to evaluate video, see the previous sidebar, "Using a Waveform Monitor," and "Using a Vectorscope" on the next page.

## I Love a Parade: RGB and YCbCr

Even those familiar with the waveform monitor may be confused by two of the viewing mode options: RGB Parade and YCbCr Parade. In short, these describe the components of video using two different color models: one native to most computer applications, the other native to digital video. For many users, the basic waveform and vectorscope will suffice, and the parade options will be of little interest. For the rest of you—well, you asked for it. Here's a brief explanation.

Most computer programs process and display video using the RGB color space. However, video is often processed using a YUV model (which itself is derived from another model). When converted into the digital realm, YUV becomes YCbCr. For this reason, YUV and YCbCr are sometimes used interchangeably, though the results are not entirely accurate.

In most cases, video must be translated from its native tongue, YCbCr, to the local dialect, RGB. And as with spoken languages, there's always something lost in the translation. In literal terms, one system must be mathematically scaled and converted into the other, losing a degree of precision in the process.

Premiere Pro can process video using YCbCr—provided that everything in your project uses it, including all your footage and effects. Otherwise, Premiere Pro processes everything in RGB. But you probably shouldn't worry about this too much. Only the most demanding applications (or finicky users) will suffer from the conversion to RGB. Your energy will be better spent maintaining image quality at other points in the production and post-production process.

## Using a Vectorscope

You can use a vectorscope to measure a video signal's color, or, more precisely, its *chrominance*. A vectorscope maps chrominance to a circular chart according to chrominance's two components: saturation and hue (**Figures 5.39** and **5.40**).

*Saturation* is measured from the center of the chart outward, so that more saturated, vivid colors produce a pattern near the edges of the chart, whereas a grayscale image produces only a dot at the center of the chart. The particular color, or *hue*, in the image determines the angle of the pattern in the vectorscope.

Fully saturated magenta, blue, cyan, green, yellow, and red—all present in a color-bars test pattern—should each register in a corresponding box on the vectorscope. In NTSC video, chrominance levels should never overshoot these target areas, the *NTSC-safe* color range. In video, oversaturated colors tend to *bleed*. That is, colors actually shift horizontally, so that the video resembles pictures in a coloring book belonging to a kid who doesn't color within the lines.

**Figure 5.39** This video of a campfire contains bright yellows and reds.

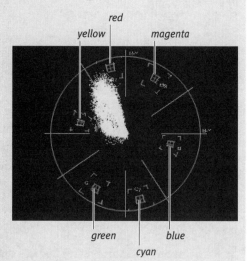

**Figure 5.40** Here is the same video in a vectorscope. Hue is indicated by the angle of the pattern, whereas saturation is measured from the center outward. Target boxes show where fully saturated colors (as in color bars) should produce a pattern.

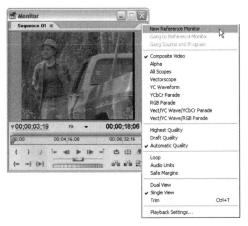

**Figure 5.41** In the program view's drop-down menu, choose New Reference Monitor.

**Figure 5.42** Here, the reference monitor is set to a different frame of the sequence for purposes of comparison.

# Using a Reference Monitor

A *reference monitor* acts much like a secondary program view that opens in a separate window or can be dragged to the source view side of the Monitor window. You can use the program view and reference monitor to compare different frames of a sequence side by side or to view the same frame of a sequence using different display modes.

For example, by cuing the program view and reference monitor to different clips in the sequence, you can correct the scenes using the color-matching filter. On the other hand, you can *gang* the program view and reference monitor, so that their playback controls are locked together and always show the same frame. This allows you to set the program view to a composite display mode and the reference monitor to a waveform monitor or vectorscope—the ideal setup for using the color-correction filter.

The reference monitor has many of the same controls as the source and program views, but because it's used as a reference, it lacks editing controls. You can open only one reference monitor, and it always displays the same sequence as the program view.

### To open a reference monitor:

1. In the program view, select the sequence from which you want to create a reference monitor.

2. In the program view's drop-down menu, choose New Reference Monitor (**Figure 5.41**).

   A reference monitor appears for the current sequence (**Figure 5.42**).

## To gang a reference monitor to a sequence:

◆ *Do one of the following:*

▲ In the reference monitor, click the Gang to Program Monitor button  to select it (**Figure 5.43**).

▲ In the reference monitor's drop-down menu, choose Gang to Program Monitor.

▲ In the program view's drop-down menu, choose Gang to Reference Monitor.

The reference monitor and program view are linked so that the playback controls used in one affect the other (**Figure 5.44**).

**Figure 5.43** Click the reference monitor's Gang to Program Monitor button to synchronize the monitor with the program view.

**Figure 5.44** Here, the reference monitor is ganged to the program view, and its display mode is set to All Scopes for the purposes of color correction.

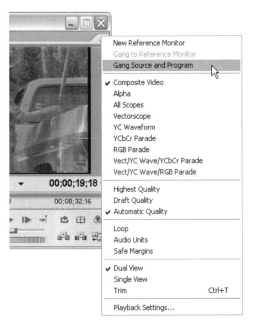

**Figure 5.45** In the program view's drop-down menu, choose Gang Source and Program.

**Figure 5.46** When you jog or shuttle either view, they move together in a synchronized relationship.

# Ganging the Source and Program Views

In some circumstances, you need to preview the relationship between a source clip and the program visually. You may want to preview to see which frames will be replaced by an overlay edit, for example, before you perform the edit.

For these situations, you can calculate durations, or you can simply gang the source and program views. *Ganging* the source and program views synchronizes them, so that playing one plays the other. This way, you can see how the frames of the source view correspond to those of the program view to help you decide where to set editing marks.

## To gang the source and program views:

1. In the Monitor window, cue each view to the frame from which you want to synchronize. For example, cue the views to the In points you're considering for the next edit.

2. In the source or program view's drop-down menu, select Gang Source and Program (**Figure 5.45**).

3. Use the playback controls in either the source or program view.

   The views move in sync (**Figure 5.46**). To make each view work independently, deselect Gang Source and Program in either view's drop-down menu.

# CREATING A SEQUENCE

You may have heard film editing referred to as *cutting*. This, of course, refers to the fact that you literally cut the work print of a film. In some circles, however, editing is called *joining*, which refers to the process of splicing film segments together. The term you prefer might say something about your attitude toward editing—emphasizing either the elimination or the union of footage. Literally speaking, of course, editing involves both cutting and joining clips. You select portions of the source footage and arrange them into one or more sequences.

The basic editing methods covered in this chapter fall into three categories: drag-and-drop editing, editing with the controls in the Monitor window, and an automated process sometimes called *storyboard editing*. The number of choices can make the process seem more complex than it really is. Editing can always be reduced to two simple tasks: defining the part of the clip you want to use and adding that part to a particular point in the sequence.

This chapter takes you through the rough cut; the following two chapters cover fine-tuning the sequence. Although each chapter tends to emphasize a particular part of the interface, the divisions are really based on the general editing tasks: cutting and joining, rearranging, and trimming clips. The tools and techniques you use to accomplish these tasks are varied, flexible, and tightly integrated. When you've mastered the material in these chapters, you'll be able to integrate all the techniques smoothly.

# Comparing Editing Methods

You can add clips to a sequence in three ways. You can drag them to the Timeline window and assemble a sequence in a manner akin to splicing film (albeit much faster). Or you can use the Monitor window's editing controls, which is comparable to using an editing controller in a traditional video-editing suite (only much easier). Alternatively, you can use the Project window to plan the sequence in storyboard fashion and have Premiere Pro execute your plan automatically. Each method has its advantages, so it's to your benefit to learn them all.

## Drag-and-drop

The drag-and-drop method takes advantage of the computer's ability to display clips as objects that you can move and place using the mouse (**Figure 6.1**). Most users find this technique the most intuitive and reassuringly similar to the way that the operating system works. In fact, we could argue that Premiere Pro's design encourages this method—especially because you can apply the same techniques to refine and rearrange clips in the Timeline window (fully explained in Chapter 8, "Refining the Sequence").

## Monitor window controls

Although this method is not as intuitive as dragging and dropping clips into the timeline, using the Monitor window enables you to employ a traditional editing technique called *three-point editing* (**Figure 6.2**). You can also perform four-point edits. (For more information on both techniques, see "Editing with Monitor Window Controls" later in this chapter.) Because the Monitor

**Figure 6.1** Using the drag-and-drop method, you drag a clip from the Project window or the source view (shown here) to a sequence in the Timeline window.

**Figure 6.2** Use the Monitor window's editing controls to perform traditional three-point and four-point edits. Here, the Insert button (circled) was used to add the clip to the sequence.

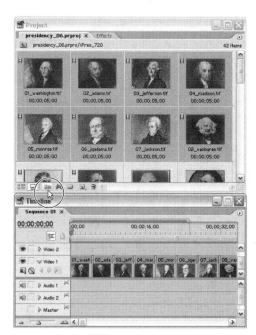

**Figure 6.3** In the Project window, you can arrange clips in storyboard fashion and use the Automate to Sequence feature (circled) to quickly assemble them into a sequence.

window's editing controls have single-stroke keyboard shortcuts, some editors find they can edit more quickly than when they drag with the mouse. Other editors prefer editing this way because it is similar to using traditional edit controllers or other nonlinear editing interfaces.

## Automate to sequence

Instead of building a sequence shot by shot, you can assemble an entire sequence automatically, according to how you've arranged the clips in the Project window—a technique often called *storyboard editing*. With the Project window set to icon view, you can arrange the clips in storyboard fashion and use the Automate to Sequence command to assemble them into a sequence (**Figure 6.3**). You can even have Premiere Pro apply a default transition between video and audio clips. If your footage lends itself to storyboarding, this method provides a fast way to generate a rough cut. It's also well suited to editors who prefer a storyboard's visual layout or who are working with a client who does.

### ✔ Tip

■ Actually, there's yet another method you can use to add a clip to a sequence. You can drag clips from the source view or Project window to the program view. The clips are overlayed or inserted at the sequence's current time. In a way, this method combines the drag-and-drop method with the monitor editing controls—but it is less elegant than either of those approaches.

COMPARING EDITING METHODS

# Setting In and Out Points

Setting In points and Out points is central to all editing. An *In point* is where you want the clip to start playing, and an *Out point* is where you want the clip to stop playing. The length of time between the In and Out points is called the *duration*.

When you edit, you can set In and Out points for both individual clips and a sequence. In Premiere Pro, you can accomplish this essential editing task in many ways. This section focuses on setting In and Out points for clips using controls in the source view—a technique used in all three editing approaches. However, you apply the same techniques to setting In and Out points for the sequence using the program view—required for three-point and four-point edits, as well as lift and extract edits.

You can open a clip that's already in the sequence in the source view, to adjust its In and Out points. Any changes you make to the clip are instantly reflected in the Timeline window. However, adjacent clips may prevent you from extending a clip in this way. When you open a clip this way, you can simultaneously view the In and Out points in the source window.

In the chapters to follow, you'll learn many other ways to change the In and Out points of clips already in a sequence.

## To mark In and Out points in the Monitor window:

1. *Do one of the following:*
   ▲ To set edit points in a clip, open a clip in the source view.
   ▲ To set edit points in the sequence, activate the program view or the Timeline window.

**Figure 6.4** Cue to the starting frame and click the Set In Point button.

**Figure 6.5** Cue to the ending frame and click the Set Out Point button.

**Figure 6.6** Drag the textured area between the In and Out points. Both frames appear in the source view.

**Figure 6.7** To clear an In or Out point, Alt-click the Set In Point or Set Out Point button (shown here).

2. Cue the current time to the frame where you want the clip to start and click the Set In Point button ⁅ or press I (**Figure 6.4**).

An In point icon ⁅ appears at the current time indicator (CTI) in the view's time ruler.

3. Cue the current time to the frame where you want the clip to end and click the Set Out Point button ⁆ or press O (**Figure 6.5**).

An Out point icon ⁆ appears at the CTI in the view's time ruler. In the view's time ruler, the area between the In point and Out point is shaded.

## To view both the In point and Out point in the source view:

1. Double-click a clip in the sequence to put it into the source view.

2. Set the In point and the Out point.

3. Drag the textured area between the In and Out points.

   The In point and the Out point frames appear in the source view (**Figure 6.6**).

## To clear an In or Out point in the Monitor window:

◆ *Do one of the following:*

   ▲ To clear an In point, Alt-click the Set In Point button ⁅.

   ▲ To clear an Out point, Alt-click the Set Out Point button ⁆ (**Figure 6.7**).

   ▲ To clear both the In and the Out points, select the appropriate view and press G.

## To change In and Out points in a view's time ruler:

◆ In a view's time ruler, *do one of the following*:

▲ To change the In point, drag the In point icon (the mouse pointer becomes a trim head icon +⊢.

▲ To change the Out point, drag the Out point icon (the mouse pointer becomes a trim tail icon ⊣+ ) (**Figure 6.8**).

▲ To change both the In and the Out points without changing the duration, drag the textured area between the In and Out points (**Figure 6.9**). (When the mouse is over the textured area, the hand tool 🖑 appears; otherwise, clicking cues the CTI.)

## ✔ Tips

■ When you use the source view to change the In or Out point of a clip that's already in the sequence, adjacent clips may prevent you from extending the duration. In this case, adjust the clip directly in the Timeline window or by using the Trimming window (see Chapter 8).

■ The In and Out points you set in the program view are also reflected in the Timeline window's time ruler. For more about using the Timeline window, see Chapter 7, "Editing in the Timeline."

■ To set In and Out points around selected clips in the Timeline window, select one or more contiguous clips and choose Marker > Set Sequence Marker > In and Out Around Selection.

**Figure 6.8** You can change an In or Out point by dragging the appropriate icon directly in the view's time ruler. Here, the Out point is being dragged to a different time. Note how the mouse pointer changes.

**Figure 6.9** To change both the In and Out points without changing the duration, drag the textured area between the In and Out points.

**SETTING IN AND OUT POINTS**

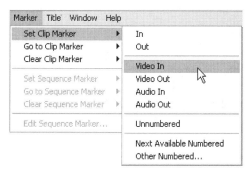

**Figure 6.10** Cue the clip to the frame you want, choose Marker > Set Clip Marker, and select the edit point you want to set.

Video Out    Audio Out

**Figure 6.11** Video edit points appear in the top half of the view's time ruler, and audio edit points appear in the bottom half.

**Figure 6.12** The split edit is apparent when the clip is added to the sequence in the Timeline window.

# Setting Split Edit Points

When you set In and Out points for a *linked clip*—a clip that contains both video and audio—both tracks share the same In point and Out point. Most editors wait until after they've assembled a rough cut to create *split edits* (also known as *L-cuts* and *J-cuts*), in which the audio and video use different In or Out points. (You'll learn a number of ways to create split edits in the following chapters.) However, you can mark audio and video In and Out points separately using the source view's editing controls. The clip will then have a split edit when you first add it to a sequence. (See "Adding Clips by Dragging" later in this chapter.)

## To set source In and Out points for a split edit:

1. Open a clip in the source view of the Monitor window.

2. Cue the clip to the frame you want to mark as an edit point and choose the appropriate command (**Figure 6.10**):
   ▲ Marker > Set Clip Marker > Video In
   ▲ Marker > Set Clip Marker > Video Out
   ▲ Marker > Set Clip Marker > Audio In
   ▲ Marker > Set Clip Marker > Audio Out
   Icons for the edit mark you set appear in the source view time ruler.

3. Repeat step 2 until you've set In and Out points for the audio and video.

   The split edit marks appear as icons in the view's time ruler. Video edit points appear in the top half of the view's time ruler; audio edit points appear in the bottom half (**Figure 6.11**).

   When you add the clip to a sequence, it has a split edit (**Figure 6.12**).

# Setting Precise Audio In and Out Points

Setting an In or Out point can be compared with cutting film between image frames. In Premiere Pro, frame divisions are set by the timebase of the project, which is based on one of several standard frame rates: 24 fps film, 25 fps PAL video, 29.97 fps NTSC video, or 30 fps video. Naturally, you would never cut through the middle of a picture frame.

Digital audio, however, isn't based on video frame rates, but on audio *sample rates*. A CD-quality sample rate is 44.1 kHz, or approximately 44,100 samples per second. Therefore, it's possible to cut audio much more finely than video.

In Premiere Pro, you can take advantage of audio's more-precise time divisions by setting audio In points based on samples rather than frames.

### To toggle the time ruler between frames and audio units:

◆ In the source view or program view drop-down menu, choose Audio Units (**Figure 6.13**).

   The time ruler's scale changes to audio samples, permitting you to navigate and set edit marks based on audio timebase divisions (**Figures 6.14** and **6.15**).

### ✔ Tip

■ As you'll see in the next chapter, you can set the Timeline window's time ruler to audio units as well. And although the program view and Timeline window are related, you can set one time ruler to video frames while the other is set to audio units.

**Figure 6.13** In the source view or program view drop-down menu, choose Audio Units.

**Figure 6.14** The time ruler's scale changes to audio samples, as indicated by the time display and musical note icon.

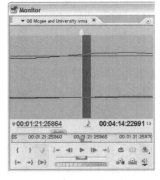

**Figure 6.15** You can zoom the time ruler to the sample level.

**Figure 6.16** In the Monitor window, clip markers appear in the source view's time ruler; sequence markers appear in the program view's time ruler.

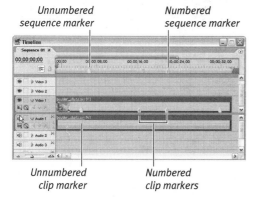

**Figure 6.17** In the Timeline window, clip markers appear in each clip; sequence markers appear in the sequence's time ruler.

# Setting Clip Markers

During the editing process, you often need a way to mark important points in time. *Markers* allow you to visibly stamp these points both in individual clips and in a sequence's time ruler in the Timeline window (**Figures 6.16** and **6.17**). Markers help you visually identify beats in a song, synchronize video with a sound effect, or note where a title should fade up.

In each clip and in each sequence, you can add up to 100 numbered and any number of unnumbered markers. You can cue the CTI to markers in the source view, program view, or Timeline window.

When you add markers to a source clip, its markers are included with the clip when you add it to a sequence. The markers aren't added to instances of the clip that are already in sequences. This means that each instance of the clip has a unique set of markers that aren't subject to unintentional changes.

This section concentrates on using the source view to add clip markers. You'll use similar controls in the program view and Timeline window to add sequence markers. But because sequence markers appear in a sequence's time ruler and have a few special features, they're discussed in the next chapter.

## To add an unnumbered clip marker in the source view:

1. Open a clip in the source view.

2. Cue the current frame to the point where you want to add a marker.

3. In the Monitor window, click the Marker button (**Figure 6.18**).

   An unnumbered marker appears in the source view's time ruler. When the clip is added to a sequence, the marker also appears in the clip in the Timeline window (provided that the marker is between the clip's In and Out points).

## To add numbered clip markers:

1. *Do one of the following:*
   - ▲ Open a clip in the source view.
   - ▲ Select a clip in the Timeline window.

2. *Do one of the following:*
   - ▲ For a clip in the source view, cue the CTI to the frame you want to mark.
   - ▲ For a selected clip in the Timeline window, cue the CTI in the program view or Timeline window.

3. Choose Marker > Set Clip Marker and *do one of the following* (**Figure 6.19**):
   - ▲ To mark the frame with the next consecutive number not already present in the clip, choose Next Available Numbered.
   - ▲ To mark the frame with the number of your choice, choose Other Numbered.

4. Enter the number for the marker in the Set Numbered Marker dialog box and click OK (**Figure 6.20**).

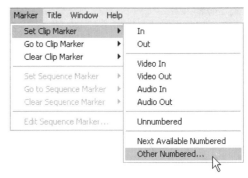

**Figure 6.18** In the Monitor window, click the Marker button.

**Figure 6.19** Choose Marker > Set Clip Marker and choose an option. Here, Other Numbered is selected.

**Figure 6.20** If you chose Other Numbered, a Set Numbered Marker dialog box appears. Enter a number and click OK.

SETTING CLIP MARKERS

Marker

**Figure 6.21** The marker you specified appears at the current time in the view's time ruler (here, the CTI has been moved aside so you can see the marker).

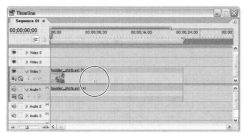

**Figure 6.22** The clip marker appears with a number when added to the sequence in the Timeline window.

**Figure 6.23** Each time you press the asterisk key (on the numeric keypad), an unnumbered marker appears. Here, the technique is being used to mark the beats of a music clip.

The marker you specified appears at the current time in the view's time ruler (**Figure 6.21**). In the Timeline window, the clip marker's number is visible (**Figure 6.22**).

## To add unnumbered clip markers on the fly:

1. Open a clip in the source view.

2. Play the clip.

3. Press the asterisk key (*) on the numeric keypad (not Shift-8 on the main keyboard).

   Each time you press the asterisk key, a marker appears in the source view's time ruler (**Figure 6.23**). If you opened a clip instance from a sequence, markers also appear in the clip as it appears in the Timeline window.

## ✔ Tips

- Applying a numbered marker to a different frame eliminates its original position.

- You can't set a marker on the same frame as an existing marker (the option will appear dimmed in the menu). You'll have to clear the marker first and then set the new marker.

- Markers are helpful for marking where lines of dialogue or voice-over begin and end. Try using a numbered marker at the beginning of a line and an unnumbered marker at the end of a line. This technique makes it easy to identify pauses between lines (which often need to be cut).

- The 0 marker also has a special use with the Frame-Hold command (see "Creating a Freeze Frame" in Chapter 7). You may want to reserve the 0 marker for this purpose.

# Cuing to and Clearing Clip Markers

You can cue the current time indicator to consecutive markers by using buttons in the source view. (Note that the corresponding buttons in the program view have a different purpose: they cue the sequence's CTI to cuts in a sequence.) Clearing markers is best accomplished via a command on the menu bar (unless you use the keyboard customization feature to map the command to a keyboard shortcut).

### To cue the source view to clip markers:

1. Open a clip in the source view.

2. In the source view, *click one of the following buttons:*

   ▲ ↓← Go to Previous Marker

   ▲ →↓ Go to Next Marker (**Figure 6.24**)

   The source view's CTI moves to the previous or next marker, depending on your choice.

### To clear clip markers:

1. Open a clip in the source view.

2. *Do one of the following:*

   ▲ To clear a particular marker, cue the clip to a marker and choose Marker > Clear Clip Marker > Current Marker.

   ▲ To clear all markers in the clip, choose Marker > Clear Clip Marker > All Markers (**Figure 6.25**).

   The clip markers you cleared disappear from the source view's time ruler (and from the Timeline window, if the clip is in a sequence).

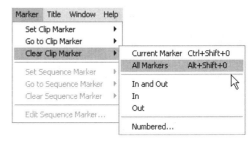

**Figure 6.24** Cue to clip markers by clicking the Go to Previous Marker button or Go to Next Marker button (shown here).

**Figure 6.25** To clear all markers in the clip, choose Marker > Clear Clip Marker > All Markers.

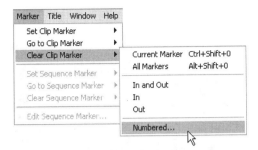

**Figure 6.26** To clear a particular numbered marker, choose Marker > Clear Clip Marker > Numbered.

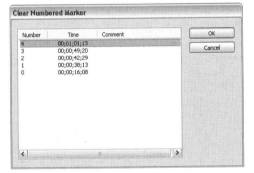

**Figure 6.27** In the Clear Numbered Marker dialog box, select the marker you want to clear and click OK.

## To clear specific numbered markers:

1. Open a clip in the source view.

2. Choose Marker > Clear Clip Marker > Numbered (**Figure 6.26**).

   The Clear Numbered Marker dialog box appears.

3. Select the marker you want to clear and click OK (**Figure 6.27**).

   You can select only one marker at a time. The selected numbered marker disappears from the source view's time ruler (and from the Timeline window, if the clip is in a sequence).

# Specifying Source and Target Tracks

Video and audio materials are often described as discrete tracks of information due to the way they are physically stored on traditional media, such as magnetic tape. Digital files don't encode video and audio the same way tape does, of course. Nevertheless, it's helpful to think of video and audio as occupying tracks that you can manipulate separately.

By selecting source and target tracks, you can add video, audio, or both to any appropriate track in the sequence.

Whatever editing method you use, you choose the source tracks by clicking the source view's Take Audio and Video toggle button (**Figure 6.28**) (as explained in the following task, "To specify source tracks"). How you choose the destination, or *target,* tracks depends on the editing method you use.

In drag-and-drop editing, you determine the target track *as* you perform the edit, by dragging the clip to an appropriate track in the Timeline window. When you edit with the Monitor window's editing controls, however, you must specify target tracks *before* you perform an edit, by selecting the track in the Timeline window (**Figure 6.29**). After all, you can choose any of several tracks in the sequence, and Premiere Pro can't make this decision for you.

Note that you can neither target nor drag a clip to a locked track (see "Locking and Unlocking Tracks" in Chapter 7). Also, remember that source and target audio tracks must be of the same channel type.

**Figure 6.28** You choose the source tracks by clicking the source view's Take Audio and Video toggle button.

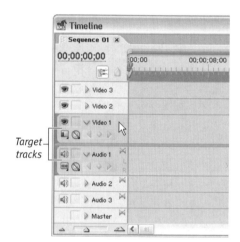

**Figure 6.29** To perform edits with the Monitor window editing controls, you must specify target tracks by clicking them in the Timeline window.

**Figure 6.30** In the source view, click the Take Audio and Video toggle button to specify whether you want to use both video and audio...

**Figure 6.31** ...video only...

**Figure 6.32** ...or audio only.

## To specify source tracks:

◆ In the source view, click the Take Audio and Video toggle button until it displays the icon corresponding to the tracks you want (**Figures 6.30**, **6.31**, and **6.32**):

  ▲ 🎬 Video and audio

  ▲ 🎬 Video only

  ▲ 🔊 Audio only

If the source clip doesn't contain a track, the corresponding icon will not appear when you toggle the button.

## To specify target tracks:

◆ In the Timeline window, *do one of the following:*

  ▲ Click the track you want to target in the track's header area, near the track name.

  ▲ Click a targeted track's header area to deselect it.

The selected track's header area is shaded darker than other tracks and has rounded corners.

# Comparing Overlay and Insert Edits

Whenever you add a clip to a sequence, you must determine how the new clip affects the clips already in the sequence. Specifically, you must specify whether to replace material with an overlay edit or shift material with an insert edit.

An *overlay edit* works like adding a clip using videotape, recording the new clip over any existing material on the master tape. When you *overlay* a clip, the source clip is added at the designated point in the timeline, replacing any material that was already there (**Figures 6.33** and **6.34**).

An *insert edit* works much like adding a clip using film, inserting the new clip without removing material that is already on the program reel. When you *insert* a clip, the source clip is added at the designated point in the timeline, and subsequent clips are shifted later in time to make room for the new clip. If the insertion point in the sequence occurs at a point where clips already occupy the timeline, the clips in the timeline are split, and the portions after the edit are shifted later in time. Depending on your choice, an insert edit can shift clips in all tracks or just in the target tracks (the tracks to which you add the new clip) (**Figures 6.35** and **6.36**).

## ✔ Tip

■ In versions of Premiere prior to Premiere Pro, overlay edits were not the default. In fact, you weren't permitted to perform an overlay edit by dragging a clip to the timeline; you had to use the Monitor window editing controls. If you're a longtime Premiere user, the new method will take some getting used to, but in the end you'll find it to be far superior to the old one.

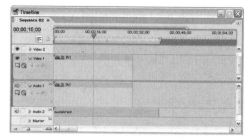

**Figure 6.33** This figure shows a clip in a sequence. A new clip will be added, starting at the current time indicator (the vertical line).

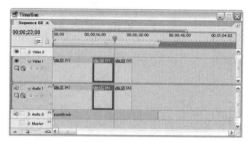

**Figure 6.34** In an overlay edit, the new material replaces the old material.

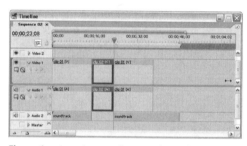

**Figure 6.35** In an insert edit, everything after the edit point shifts forward in time to make room for the new material. If necessary, clips are split at the edit point.

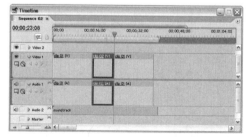

**Figure 6.36** Alternatively, you can perform an insert edit that shifts material in the target tracks only.

# Adding Clips by Dragging

You can add a source clip to a sequence by dragging it to the appropriate track in the Timeline window. Drag the clip from the source view if you want to set its edit marks before adding it to a sequence. If you want to use the clip's most recent edit marks, you can drag it directly from the Project window.

You can drag a linked clip (a clip containing both audio and video) to either a video or audio track. When you do, the video or audio components appear in a corresponding track. For example, dragging a clip to video 1 makes the linked audio appear in audio 1.

However, you can add an audio clip only to a compatible audio track. In other words, the clip and the target track must be of the same channel type: mono, stereo, or 5.1. If the audio doesn't match the channel type of the target track, the audio appears in the next compatible track, or a compatible track is created automatically. (The default tracks are determined by the project settings, covered in Chapter 2, "Starting a Project." See Chapter 7, "Editing in the Timeline," for more about adding tracks to a sequence.)

## To add a clip to a sequence by dragging:

1. Open a clip in the source view.

2. Set the In point and Out point in the source clip.

   You may also want to set numbered or unnumbered markers. See "Setting Clip Markers" earlier in this chapter.

3. Click the Take Audio and Video toggle button so that it shows the icon for the source tracks you want (**Figure 6.37**).

4. Drag the clip from the source view to the appropriate track of the sequence in the Timeline window, using one of the following methods:

   ▲ To perform an overlay edit, drag the clip to so that the pointer appears with the overlay icon ⬚ (**Figure 6.38**).

*In point*     *Out point*     *Take Audio and Video*

**Figure 6.37** In the source view, set a clip's edit marks and specify the source tracks.

*Frame before new clip*     *Frame after new clip*

*Overlay icon*

**Figure 6.38** To perform an overlay edit, drag the clip to the track you want. Note that visual feedback in the program view shows the frames before and after the new clip.

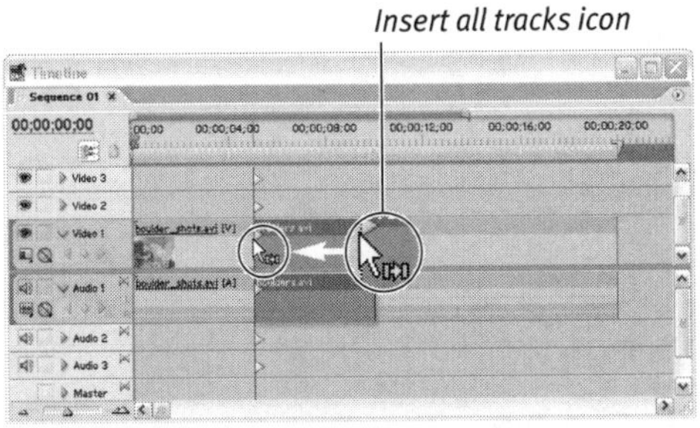

*Insert all tracks icon*

**Figure 6.39** To perform an insert edit that shifts material in all tracks, Ctrl-drag the clip to the track you want.

*Insert target tracks icon*

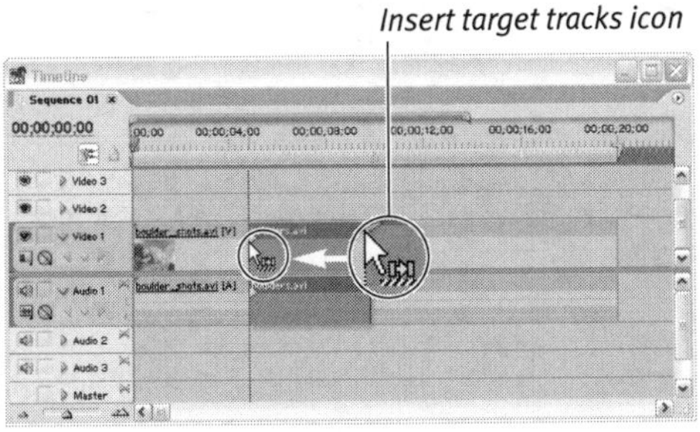

**Figure 6.40** To perform an insert edit that shifts target tracks only, Alt-Ctrl-drag the clip to the track you want.

▲ To perform an insert edit that shifts all tracks, Ctrl-drag the clip so that the mouse pointer appears with the insert icon ⟲ and arrows appear at the edit point in all tracks (**Figure 6.39**).

▲ To perform an insert edit that shifts target tracks only, Alt-Ctrl-drag the clip so that the mouse pointer appears with the insert target icon ⟲ and arrows appear at the edit point in the target tracks (**Figure 6.40**).

A shaded area indicates where the clip will appear when you release the mouse.

## ✔ Tips

■ When you drag and drop a linked clip, be sure you're not inadvertently overwriting material in one of the corresponding tracks. For example, if you pay attention only to where you're dragging the video, you might end up overwriting something in the audio track.

■ To precisely align clips as you drag them, make sure the Timeline window's Snap button ▦ is selected. As you drag a clip with snap on, a vertical line appears whenever In points, Out points, or markers align. For more about the snap feature, see Chapter 7.

■ To zoom in or out on a clip when you drag it to the timeline, continue to hold down the mouse button and press the + key to zoom in or the – key to zoom out until you have zoomed in or out as far as you want.

## To add clips to the program from the Project window:

1. Select one or more clips in the Project window.

2. Drag the selection from the Project window to the appropriate track of the sequence in the Timeline window, using one of the following methods:

   ▲ To perform an overlay edit, drag the clip to so that the pointer appears with the overlay icon 📎 (**Figure 6.41**).

   ▲ To perform an insert edit that shifts all tracks, Ctrl-drag the clip so that the mouse pointer appears with the insert icon 📎 and arrows appear at the edit point in all tracks.

   ▲ To perform an insert edit that shifts target tracks only, Alt-Ctrl-drag the clip so that the mouse pointer appears with the insert target icon 📎 and arrows appear at the edit point in the target tracks.

   A shaded area indicates where the selected clips will appear when you release the mouse. Multiple clips are added to the sequence in the order in which you selected them in the Project window.

## ✔ Tip

■ You can drag clips to the source view, the program view, or the timeline directly from the thumbnail viewer at the top of the Project window just like you can from the list view or icon view. This procedure is useful if you are in the habit of using the thumbnail viewer to look at clips before using them in your project.

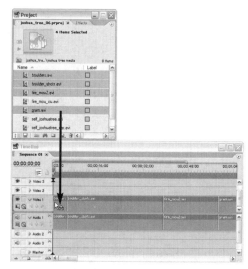

**Figure 6.41** You can drag one or more clips from the Project window to the Timeline window to perform overlay and insert edits.

## Overlay and Insert Keyboard Modifiers and Icons

As you gain experience editing in Premiere Pro, you'll notice a pattern in how you perform overlay and insert edits using the mouse: overlay edits are the default and never require a keyboard modifier; insert edits are accomplished by pressing the Ctrl key. This is true not only when you add a new clip to a sequence, but also when you rearrange clips already in a sequence (see Chapter 8).

Ordinarily, insert edits shift material in all tracks. This is usually the desired behavior, because it tends to keep everything in sync. However, there are times when you want an insert edit to shift only the target tracks. In this case, add another keyboard modifier: the Alt key. When you edit clips already in a sequence by manipulating them in the Timeline window, the Alt key modifier serves another purpose: it allows you to select and trim one track of a linked clip.

The editing conventions for overlay and insert edits are reinforced by visual feedback in the Timeline window. When you perform overlay edits and insert edits with the mouse, a corresponding icon appears next to the mouse pointer. See **Table 6.1** for an overview.

And while we're on the subject, similar icons are invoked when you move and rearrange clips by dragging them in the Timeline window. But you'll learn about that in Chapter 8.

**Table 6.1**

| Overlay and Insert Icons | | |
| --- | --- | --- |
| EDIT | MODIFIER | ICON |
| Overlay | None | |
| Insert (all tracks) | Ctrl | |
| Insert (target tracks) | Alt-Ctrl | |

# Editing with Monitor Window Controls

As suggested earlier in this chapter, editing with the Monitor window controls isn't as intuitive as editing using the drag-and-drop method. However, the Monitor window's editing controls use a paradigm familiar to those who have used traditional video edit controllers or other nonlinear systems. In addition, this method lets you rely less on the mouse and more on single-stroke keyboard shortcuts, which could mean faster editing.

Before you proceed, however, you need to understand a few basic concepts:

**Insert and overlay:** Methods for determining how a three-point or four-point edit affects the clips in the sequence. You're already familiar with these concepts from the previous sections.

**Three-point and four-point editing:** Methods for determining where clips begin and end in both the source and the sequence.

**Lift and extract:** Methods for removing frames from the program; roughly the reverse of the insert and overlay methods.

The following sections explain these concepts and then put them into practice. Don't worry— these ideas are as easy to grasp as they are essential. Taking a moment to learn them will be well worth the effort. If you prefer, you can skip ahead to the editing tasks and then turn back to see the full explanations.

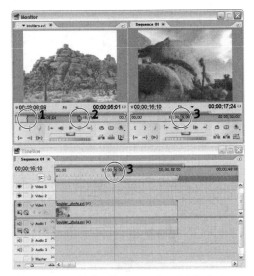

**Figure 6.42** Typically, the three edit points include two In points and an Out point—in this example, the source In, source Out, and sequence In points. Note the shading after the program In point.

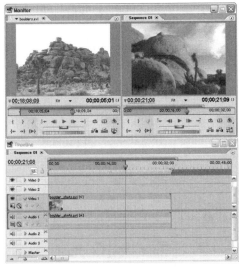

**Figure 6.43** Sometimes where the clip ends is more important than where it begins. In this case, you can set two Out points and one In point. Note the shading before the program Out point.

# Three-Point Editing

The *point* in the term *three-point editing* refers to In points and Out points. In points and Out points in a clip define where the clip starts and ends. Similarly, In and Out points in a sequence define where a clip starts and ends in the sequence.

In drag-and-drop editing, you set the source In and Out points in the source view, but the sequence's In and Out points were implied by where you dragged the clip into the Timeline window (see "Drag-and-drop" earlier in this chapter). In the following sections, you mark both the source and sequence editing points in the Monitor window.

Technically, every edit has four points: source In, source Out, sequence In, and sequence Out. To add a clip to the sequence, you must define at least three of these four points in the source and program views. If you provide three points, Premiere Pro figures out the fourth. Hence the term *three-point editing*.

Most often, this means that you mark two In points and one Out point. **Figure 6.42** shows a typical edit, in which the source In point and source Out point define a portion of the clip, and the sequence In point defines where the clip starts in the sequence. The sequence Out point is implied by the duration of the clip.

Sometimes, however, it's more important to set where the clip ends than to set where it begins. In such a case, you mark two Out points and only one In point. In **Figure 6.43**, the next shot will follow the last clip in the program: a typical program In point. However, a particular frame of the new shot (the source Out point) must coincide with a particular cue in the sound track, at marker 1 (the sequence Out point). That defines three edit points: sequence In point, source Out point, and sequence Out point. The editor doesn't need to mark the source In point, because it's determined by the other three points.

# Four-Point Editing

As you have seen, every edit uses four
points, but you need to set only three of
them. Premiere Pro always figures out the
missing variable to balance out the editing
equation. Actively marking all four points
forces Premiere Pro to balance the equation
in another way. If the source duration differs
from the program duration, Premiere Pro
asks whether you want to shorten the
source clip, change the speed of the source
clip to fit, or ignore one of the sequence edit
points and perform a three-point edit.

Typically, you use a four-point edit to
change the speed of the source to match the
duration defined by the sequence's In and
Out points. This technique is frequently
called *fit to fill*, because you *fit*, or change,
the speed (and duration) of the source to *fill*
the duration you specified in the sequence.

Suppose that you require a two-second cut-
away or reaction shot, but your source clip
includes only one second of footage. A four-
point edit can stretch the one second of
source footage to fill two seconds in the
program. In the sequence, the clip plays in
slow motion—in this case, at half normal
speed (**Figure 6.44**).

## ✔ Tip

- You can change the speed of a clip after
  it's in the timeline by using the
  Speed/Duration command or the Rate
  Stretch tool. For more information about
  using editing techniques in the timeline,
  see Chapter 7.

**Figure 6.44** Here, the editor defined all four edit
points. Because the durations differ, you have to
resolve the difference. Usually, this means changing
the speed of the clip.

**Figure 6.45** In the source view, set the edit marks and specify source tracks.

**Figure 6.46** In the Timeline window, specify target tracks.

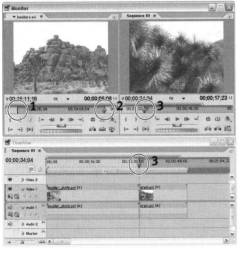

**Figure 6.47** Set any combination of three edit points.

# Performing an Edit Using Monitor Window Controls

Now that you understand the essential concepts behind an edit, it's time to put them into practice.

### To perform a three-point edit:

1. Open a clip in the source view.

2. Click the Take Audio and Video toggle button so that it shows the icon for the source tracks you want (**Figure 6.45**).

3. Specify the target tracks in the sequence by clicking in the track header area, near the track's name in the Timeline window (**Figure 6.46**).

   The track header area of the targeted tracks appears darker than that of the other tracks.

4. Set any combination of three In and Out points in the source and program views (**Figure 6.47**).

   Sequence In and Out points appear both in the program view's time ruler and in the sequence's time ruler in the Timeline window.

*continues on next page*

**5.** In the source view, *do one of the following:*

▲ To replace material in the specified area of the sequence, click the Overlay button .

▲ To shift subsequent clips in all tracks, click the Insert button **(Figure 6.48)**.

▲ To shift subsequent clips in target tracks only, Alt-click the Insert button .

The clip appears in the timeline in the position and tracks you specified (**Figure 6.49**). Premiere Pro cues the sequence's current time to the end of the new clip and clears the sequence's In and Out points.

## ✔ Tips

■ If you don't specify an In or Out point in the program view, the current time in the program view (and in the Timeline window) serves as the In point. After an edit, Premiere Pro cues the current program time to the end of the new clip in the program and clears any sequence In and Out points. You can save time by using the program's current time as the In point, especially when you want to assemble clips into a sequence quickly.

■ You can quickly set the In and Out points around the area you have selected in the timeline by pressing the forward slash (/) key.

■ When you perform an insert edit that shifts material in target tracks only, use caution: it is easy to inadvertently shift linked video and audio out of sync this way.

■ You've lost sync between linked video and audio when a number appears before the clip's name in the Timeline window. For now, use the Undo command to restore sync. To learn more about linked clips and sync, see Chapter 7.

**Figure 6.48** In the source view, click the Overlay or Insert button (circled).

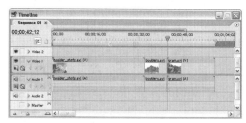

**Figure 6.49** The clip appears in the sequence in the position and tracks you specified.

2) Source Out point   3) Sequence In point
1) Source In point               4) Sequence Out point

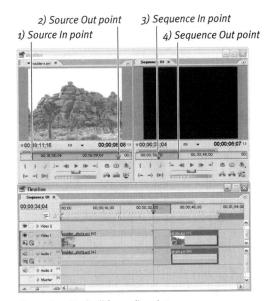

**Figure 6.50** Mark all four edit points.

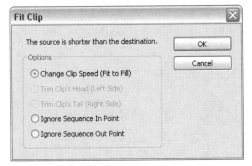

**Figure 6.51** If the source duration and sequence duration differ, Premiere Pro prompts you to resolve the discrepancy.

## To perform a four-point edit:

1. Mark all four edit points in the source and program views (**Figure 6.50**).

2. Select the source tracks by clicking the source view's Take Audio and Video toggle button.

3. Specify the target tracks in the sequence by clicking the tracks in the track header area in the Timeline window.

    The track header area of the targeted tracks appears darker than that of the other tracks.

4. Click the Insert or Overlay button.

5. If the source duration and sequence duration differ, Premiere Pro prompts you to choose one of the following options (**Figure 6.51**):

*continues on next page*

**Change Clip Speed (Fit to Fill):** Changes the speed of the source clip to fit the specified duration in the sequence. Only the speed changes; the In and Out points stay the same. In **Figure 6.52**, the source clip has been slowed, making its duration long enough to fit in the range defined by the program In and program Out points. If the source clip were too long, its speed would increase so that its duration would match the program duration. You can learn the clip's exact speed by selecting the clip and viewing its information on the Info palette (**Figure 6.53**) or by hovering the cursor over the clip until a tool tip appears.

**Trim Clip's Head (Left Side):** Changes the source In point to fit the specified duration in the program. The Out point and the speed of the clip are unaffected. (In other words, this option ignores the source Out point and works like a three-point edit.)

**Trim Clip's Tail (Right Side):** Changes the source Out point to fit the specified duration in the program. The In point and the speed of the clip are unaffected.

**Ignore Sequence In Point:** Disregards the sequence In point and performs a three-point edit.

**Ignore Sequence Out Point:** Disregards the sequence Out point and performs a three-point edit.

The clip is added to the sequence according to your selection.

## ✔ Tip

■ You can set a sequence edit point beyond the last frame of the last clip by using the arrow keys to move the CTI later in time. Press Shift-arrow to move in increments of five frames.

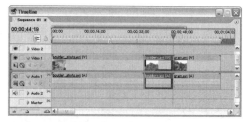

**Figure 6.52** Change Clip Speed alters the speed of the clip so that it matches the sequence's duration.

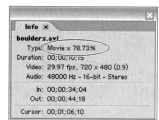

**Figure 6.53** You can learn the clip's exact speed by selecting the clip and viewing its information on the Info palette.

**Figure 6.54** Set sequence In and Out points. Here, sequence In and Out marks surround the second clip, but you can remove any range of frames, including portions of clips.

# Lift and Extract

Just as the source view has two buttons for adding frames to the program, the program view has two buttons for removing frames from the program: Lift and Extract. You can think of lift and extract edits as being the opposite of insert and overlay edits, respectively:

**Lift:** Removes the defined range from the timeline, leaving a gap in the timeline

**Extract:** Removes the defined range from the timeline and shifts all the later clips earlier in the timeline, closing the gap

But unfortunately, an extract edit isn't the perfect opposite of an insert edit: it won't shift linked audio and video out of sync. Suppose you try to extract frames of video from the beginning or middle of a clip and leave the audio track untargeted. Extracting the video should shift it and subsequent material in that track back to close the gap—and out of sync with any linked audio. Instead, extract works just like lift in this case. Some would argue that Premiere Pro helps prevent you from inadvertently losing sync; others complain that the extract functions inconsistently. If you want to shift material out of sync, you'll have to drag in the Timeline window using techniques covered in Chapter 8.

## To lift a segment from a sequence:

1. Set an In point and an Out point in the program view to define the range to be removed from the sequence.

   You can see the editing marks in both the program view's time ruler and the Timeline window (**Figure 6.54**).

   *continues on next page*

**2.** *Do one of the following:*

▲ To remove material from particular tracks in the defined range, target the tracks by clicking in the track header area in the Timeline window (**Figure 6.55**).

▲ To remove material from all tracks in the defined range, deselect all tracks so none are targeted.

**3.** In the program view, click the Lift button ⬚ (**Figure 6.56**).

The frames between the In and Out points in the selected tracks of the program are removed, leaving an empty space (**Figure 6.57**).

**Figure 6.55** Deselect all tracks to remove frames from all tracks, or select particular tracks. Here, only the video 1 track is targeted.

**Figure 6.56** In the program view, click the Lift button.

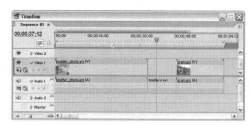

**Figure 6.57** The frames between the In and Out points in the selected tracks of the program are removed, leaving an empty space.

**Figure 6.58** Set sequence In and Out points.

**Figure 6.59** To remove material from all tracks in the defined range, deselect all tracks so none are targeted.

**Figure 6.60** In the program view, click the Extract button.

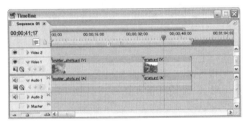

**Figure 6.61** The frames between the In and Out points are removed, shifting subsequent material in target tracks to close the gap.

## To extract a segment from a sequence:

1. Set an In point and an Out point in the program view to define the range to be removed from the sequence (**Figure 6.58**).

2. *Do one of the following:*
   - ▲ To remove material from particular tracks in the defined range, target the tracks by clicking in the track header area in the Timeline window.
   - ▲ To remove material from all tracks in the defined range, deselect all tracks so none are targeted (**Figure 6.59**).

3. Click the Extract button ▨ in the program view (**Figure 6.60**).

   The frames between the In and Out points are removed, shifting subsequent material in the target tracks to close the gap (**Figure 6.61**). If no tracks are targeted, material in all tracks shifts. If shifting material would move linked clips out of sync, then a lift edit is performed instead.

## ✔ Tip

- ■ Until Adobe modifies the extract and track targeting functions in Premiere Pro, it is probably best to use extract to remove material from all tracks. See the sidebar "Extraction Exception" in Chapter 8.

---

## Editing with the Home Keys, or Three-Finger Editing

As any typist will tell you, the basis for touch-typing is learning to keep your fingers over the home keys. Well, desktop editing programs have developed their own version of home keys: J, K, and L (**Figure 6.62**). Keeping one hand on your editing home keys and the other on the mouse is the secret to blazing-fast Monitor window editing. This technique works in other popular editing programs as well. Learning it can produce joy and speed akin to typing 60 words per minute. But if you insist, you can just use onscreen buttons for the equivalent of hunt-and-peck editing.

**Figure 6.62** You can think of the J-K-L combo as the home keys of nonlinear editing. They give you quick three-finger control over the main playback and editing features.

# Storyboard Editing

Before shooting any footage, filmmakers usually create a *storyboard*—a series of sketches that depicts each shot in the finished program. Planning each shot in a storyboard can save you enormous amounts of time, money, and energy in production. In postproduction, you can use a similar storyboarding technique to plan a rough cut and instantly assemble it into a sequence, again saving time and energy.

As you learned in Chapter 3, "Capturing and Importing Footage," setting the Project window to icon view allows you to arrange clips in a storyboard fashion. If you want, you can open the clips in the source view to set In and Out points as well. Once your storyboard is complete, use the Automate to Sequence command to assemble the selected clips into a sequence. Premiere Pro can even add the default video and audio transitions between clips.

Although the Automate to Sequence feature is best suited to storyboard editing, you can also use it to add clips to a sequence according to the order in which you select clips in the Project window. Also, note that it ignores target tracks and always adds clips to video track 1 and audio track 1.

## To add clips using the Automate to Sequence command:

1. In the Project window, *do one of the following:*

   ▲ Sort the clips in the order you want them to appear in the sequence (from left to right and top to bottom in icon view, or from top to bottom in list view) and select them (**Figure 6.63**).

   ▲ Select the clips in the order you want them to appear in the sequence.

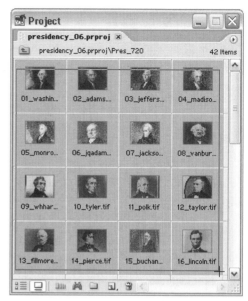

**Figure 6.63** With the Project window set to icon view, arrange the clips as on a storyboard and select the ones you want to add to the sequence.

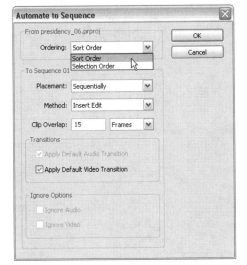

**Figure 6.64** Click the Automate to Sequence button.

**Figure 6.65** If you've arranged the clips in storyboard fashion, select Sort Order from the Sort Order drop-down menu.

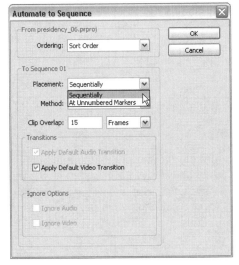

**Figure 6.66** In most cases, you'll choose Sequentially from the Placement drop-down menu.

2. In the Project window, click the Automate to Sequence button (**Figure 6.64**).

An Automate to Sequence dialog box appears.

3. Choose an option from the Ordering drop-down menu (**Figure 6.65**):

**Sort Order:** Arranges clips in the order in which they are sorted in the Project window.

**Selection Order:** Arranges clips in the order in which they are selected in the Project window.

4. Specify how the clips are added to the program by making a choice from the Placement drop-down menu (**Figure 6.66**):

**Sequentially:** Adds the clips in the timeline one after the other.

**At Unnumbered Markers:** Adds the clips in the timeline at unnumbered program markers.

*continues on next page*

**5.** Specify the editing method used to add each clip to the sequence by choosing an option in the Method drop-down menu (**Figure 6.67**):

**Insert Edit:** Adds the selected clips to the sequence beginning at the current time, using insert edits.

**Overlay Edit:** Adds the selected clips to the sequence beginning at the current time, using overlay edits.

**6.** Make a choice from the Clip Overlap drop-down menu to specify the length of transitions between clips and the time unit:

**Frames:** Interprets the value you enter as frames, at the frame rate you set in the project settings.

**Seconds:** Interprets the value you enter as seconds.

If you want only cuts between clips, with no overlap, enter 0.

**7.** In the Transitions area of the dialog box, select the options you want:

**Apply Default Audio Transition:** Applies the default transition between audio clips if you specified a positive value for Clip Overlap in step 6.

**Apply Default Video Transition:** Applies the default transition between video clips if you specified a positive value for Clip Overlap in step 6.

**8.** In the Ignore Options area of the dialog box, select the options you want:

**Ignore Audio:** Excludes audio from being added to the sequence.

**Ignore Video:** Excludes video from being added to the program.

**9.** Click OK.

The selected clips are added to the sequence beginning at the sequence's current time according to the options you specified (**Figure 6.68**).

**Figure 6.67** In the Method drop-down menu, choose whether to add the clips using insert or overlay edits. Then specify the other options you want.

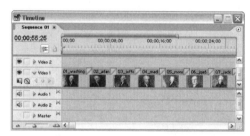

**Figure 6.68** The selected clips are added to the sequence beginning at the sequence's current time according to the options you specified.

## ✔ Tip

■ Automate to Sequence ignores target tracks and always adds clips to video track 1 and audio track 1 (unless they are locked). But, as usual, if the audio clips don't match the audio 1 track's channel type (mono, stereo, or 5.1), they will be added to the next compatible track, or a compatible track will be created automatically.

# About Multiple and Nested Sequences

So far, you've assembled clips into a single configuration, called a sequence. But Premiere Pro allows you to create any number of sequences in a single project. The obvious implication is that you can edit multiple versions of your masterpiece—to try out ideas, cater to different audiences, or meet various presentation requirements.

But even more important, you can edit an entire sequence into another sequence, a process called *nesting*. This doesn't mean copying and pasting the *contents* of one sequence into another (which you can do); it means adding the sequence as a *single item*, just like any other clip. The concept of nesting is simple, but its practical implications are powerful and far reaching.

# Using Multiple Sequences

As discussed previously, each sequence appears as an item in the Project window. When you open a sequence, it appears as a tab in the program view of the Monitor window and in the Timeline window. Clicking a sequence's tab in either the Timeline or the program view makes it the active sequence in both windows; clicking a tab's Close button removes it from both windows. You can also tear away a sequence tab from the Timeline window to open it in a separate Timeline window. In this case, selecting the Timeline window activates the sequence, and vice versa.

You can create any number of sequences, each with any number and type of tracks. But as you learned in Chapter 2, "Starting a Project," all the sequences in a project must use the same timebase, which cannot be changed.

### To create a new sequence:

1. *Do one of the following:*
   ▲ Choose File > New > Sequence.
   ▲ In the Project window, click the New Item button ▣, and choose Sequence (**Figure 6.69**).
   The New Sequence dialog box appears, using the default settings for the number and type of the master audio tracks.

2. In the New Sequence dialog box, name the sequence (**Figure 6.70**).

3. In the Tracks area of the dialog box, *do any of the following:*
   ▲ Enter the number of video tracks.
   ▲ Enter the number of each type of audio track, including audio submix tracks.
   ▲ In the Master drop-down menu, specify the type of master audio track.

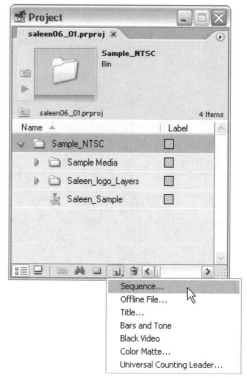

**Figure 6.69** Click the New Item button and choose Sequence.

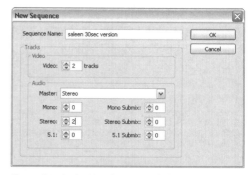

**Figure 6.70** In the New Sequence dialog box, enter a name for the sequence and specify the number and type of tracks.

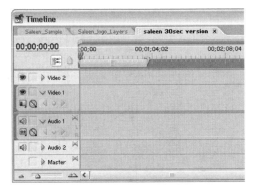

**Figure 6.71** The new sequence appears as the active tab in the Timeline window.

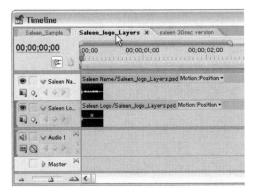

**Figure 6.72** Click a tab to view that sequence.

**4.** Click OK.

The new sequence appears as a tab in the program view and in the Timeline window (**Figure 6.71**).

## To view different sequences:

◆ *Do one of the following:*

▲ To open a sequence as a tab, double-click the sequence in the Project window.

▲ To switch sequences, click the sequence's tab in the program view or in the Timeline window (**Figure 6.72**).

## To view a sequence in a separate Timeline window:

◆ In the Timeline window, drag a sequence's tab out of the window and into an empty part of the workspace (**Figure 6.73**).

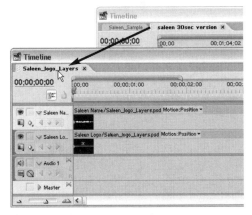

**Figure 6.73** Drag a sequence's tab to an empty area to open it in a new Timeline window.

**USING MULTIPLE SEQUENCES**

## To move tabs between windows:

◆ Drag a sequence's tab from one Timeline window to another Timeline window (**Figure 6.74**).

The tab appears in the window to which you drag it. Dragging the last sequence's tab from a Timeline window closes the window.

## To duplicate a sequence:

1. In the Project window, context-click a sequence and choose Duplicate (**Figure 6.75**).

A duplicate of the sequence appears in the Project window. It uses the original sequence's name with the word *Copy* appended to it (**Figure 6.76**).

**Figure 6.74** Dragging a sequence's tab to another Timeline window opens it in that window.

**Figure 6.75** In the Project window, context-click a sequence and choose Duplicate.

USING MULTIPLE SEQUENCES

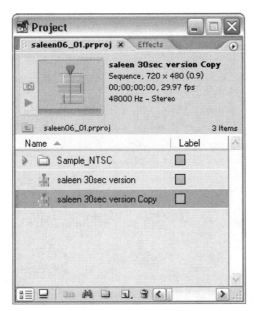

**Figure 6.76** The duplicate appears with the word *Copy* appended to its name.

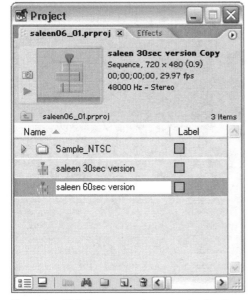

**Figure 6.77** Click the sequence's name twice (don't double-click) to highlight it and enter a new name.

**2.** To give the copied sequence a unique name, *do one of the following:*

▲ Click the sequence and then click it again to highlight its name.

▲ Context-click the sequence and choose Rename.

Type a new name and press Enter (**Figure 6.77**).

### ✔ Tip

■ You can specify the default settings for a sequence by choosing Project > Project Settings > Default Sequence. This command determines the initial settings in the New Sequence dialog box.

# Nesting Sequences

You use the same techniques to nest a sequence as you use to add a clip to a sequence. You can drag and drop the sequence from the Project window or open the sequence in the source view and add it from there. No matter how many clips and tracks a sequence contains, it appears as a single linked clip when you nest it in another sequence. Once it's nested, you can edit the sequence like any other clip; you can move and trim it, apply speed changes and filters, adjust its audio and transparency levels, apply motion settings, and so on. Any alterations you make to the content of the source sequence are instantly reflected in its related nested sequences. Not only can you nest a sequence as many times and in as many sequences as you want, but you can also nest them to any *depth*, like Russian dolls. Nesting lets you group elements and create hierarchies to get effects you couldn't achieve any other way.

If you nest a sequence with sequence markers in a new sequence, the markers appear as clip markers with a slightly different color than the other clip markers in the new sequence. To adjust the location of the markers, display the original sequence and drag the markers to adjust them.

See the sidebar "Crowing about Nesting" for some examples; see the sidebar "Nesting Rules" for a list of restrictions.

## To open a sequence in the source view:

◆ *Do one of the following:*

- ▲ Ctrl-double-click the sequence in the Project window (**Figure 6.78**).

- ▲ Ctrl-double-click a nested sequence in a Timeline window.

The sequence opens in the source view of the Monitor window and functions like a single clip (**Figure 6.79**).

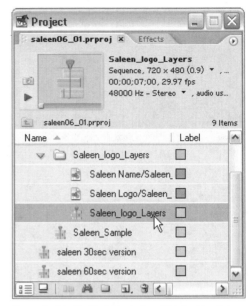

**Figure 6.78** In the Project window, Ctrl-double-click a sequence. You can also Ctrl-double-click a nested sequence in a Timeline window.

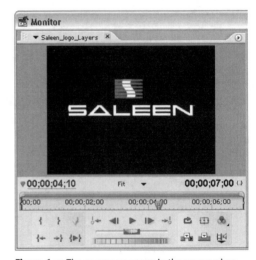

**Figure 6.79** The sequence opens in the source view.

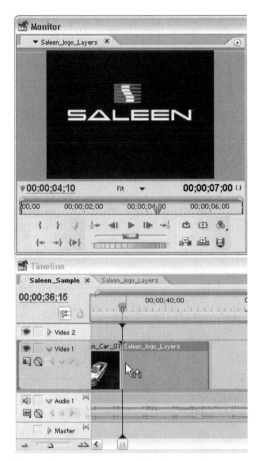

**Figure 6.80** You nest a sequence the same way you add a clip to a sequence. Here, a title sequence is being dragged from the source view into the main sequence.

## To nest a sequence:

◆ Add a sequence from the Program window or source view to the active sequence using any of the editing methods you learned in this chapter (**Figure 6.80**).

You can use the same editing controls and drag-and-drop methods with a sequence as you would use with a single clip. Although a nested sequence acts like any other sequence clip, it refers to its source sequence.

## To open the source of a nested sequence:

◆ *Do one of the following:*

▲ In the Timeline window, double-click a nested sequence (**Figure 6.81**). The source of the nested sequence becomes the active sequence. Any changes you make to the source sequence are reflected in all of its instances nested in other sequences (**Figure 6.82**).

*continues on next page*

**NESTING SEQUENCES**

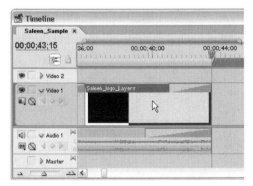

**Figure 6.81** Double-clicking a nested sequence...

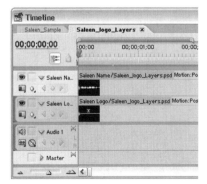

**Figure 6.82** ...makes it the active sequence.

▲ In the Timeline window, position the CTI on the frame that you want to show in its original sequence (**Figure 6.83**). Press Shift-T to open the original sequence cued to the same frame (**Figure 6.84**).

## ✔ Tips

■ If you're familiar with Premiere Pro's sibling, After Effects, you'll instantly recognize the nesting concept and appreciate what it means for your project. Conversely, knowing how nesting works in Premiere Pro will give you a head start when you learn After Effects.

■ Nesting makes the virtual clip feature found in versions of Premiere prior to Premiere Pro obsolete.

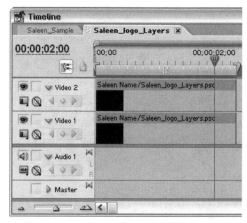

**Figure 6.83** Position the CTI and press Shift-T...

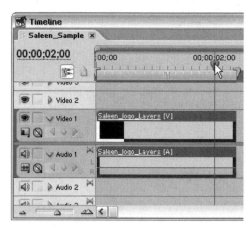

**Figure 6.84** ...and the original sequence displays the same frame.

NESTING SEQUENCES

## Crowing about Nesting

Essentially, nesting lets you group sequences and arrange them into hierarchies. With nesting, you can streamline a workflow that otherwise would be elaborate and create effects that otherwise would be impossible. Nesting lets you do the following:

◆ Break a complex or long project into manageable sequences and then bring them together into a single sequence.

◆ Easily repeat material in a sequence, such as a complex transition.

◆ Reuse material in several sequences, such as an opener or other boilerplate elements.

◆ Easily update multiple instances of the nested material by changing the content of its source sequence.

◆ Apply an effect to a sequence, thus altering all the clips within it, such as letterboxing the entire program or applying a speed adjustment to the sequence as a whole.

◆ Apply different effects to each instance of the nested sequence.

◆ Reduce a complex sequence to a single clip. This both streamlines the timeline and prevents you from making inadvertent changes or shifting elements out of sync.

◆ Create complex hierarchies and layering of effects. You can create transitions within transitions or use motion and transparency settings to show multiple nested sequences onscreen at once, as in a split-screen or picture-in-picture effect (**Figure 6.85**).

**Figure 6.85** In this example, three sequences have been nested into a main sequence and then resized and composited together.

## Nesting Rules

Here are a few things to keep in mind when you use nesting:

◆ You can't nest a sequence within itself (think about it; it doesn't work).

◆ Nesting can increase processing demands on your system, and thereby the time it takes to see certain effects at the full frame rate.

◆ A nested sequence includes empty space at the beginning of its source sequence but not at the end.

◆ Whereas a nested sequence reflects changes you make to its source sequence, it does not reflect changes to duration. Therefore, you must use standard trimming methods to lengthen a nested sequence and reveal material added to its source sequence. Conversely, trim back the Out point of the nested sequence to remove black video and silent audio resulting from the shortening of its source sequence.

# Editing in
# the Timeline

7

As you saw in Chapter 6, "Creating a Sequence," you can view an edited sequence in two ways: in the Monitor window's program view or in the Timeline window. The program view shows the frame at the current time, much as it would appear on a television display; the Timeline window graphically represents all of the program's clips arranged in time.

In the timeline, the program looks a lot like edited film. Like film, the timeline lays out the instances of clips before you. Unlike film, however, the timeline allows you to view any segment of the program instantly or to view the entire program. Yet the timeline doesn't provide simply another way to look at or navigate through the program; it also gives you a way to edit. Editing in the timeline can feel almost as tactile as editing film but can be far more flexible and efficient than using razors and tape.

This chapter discusses how to use the Timeline window and how to manipulate clips in this window to perform a number of basic editing tasks. For now, you'll concentrate on manipulating clips as discrete objects in the timeline. You'll learn how to select and group clips; disable and delete them; split, copy, and paste them; and alter their playback speed. You'll discover ways to make more subtle changes in Chapter 8, "Refining the Sequence."

# Customizing the Time Ruler

As in any other timeline, the Timeline window measures time horizontally, along a *time ruler*. By default, the time ruler starts at zero, but you can set the ruler to start at any number you choose. The time ruler uses the counting system you specified in the project settings—which for most DV projects is drop-frame timecode. However, you can toggle the ruler between video frames and audio units. In Chapter 6, you learned that changing the source view's timeline to audio units enables you to set more precise audio In and Out points. In the same way, you can set the Timeline window's time ruler to audio units to view audio clips in greater detail and make precise, sample-based adjustments.

### To set a sequence's starting time:

1. In the Timeline window menu, choose Sequence Zero Point (**Figure 7.1**).

   The Sequence Zero Point dialog box appears.

2. In the Sequence Zero Point dialog box, set the time at which the sequence's time ruler starts (**Figure 7.2**).

   You can change the number by dragging it or clicking the number and entering a new value.

3. Click OK.

   The number you set becomes the sequence's starting time, as reflected in the program view and Timeline window time rulers and time displays (**Figure 7.3**).

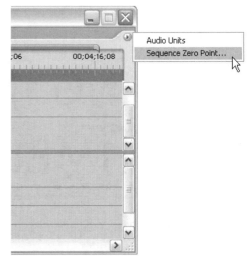

**Figure 7.1** In the Timeline window menu, choose Sequence Zero Point.

**Figure 7.2** In the Sequence Zero Point dialog box, enter a starting time for the sequence's time ruler.

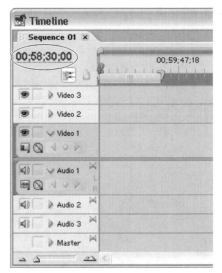

**Figure 7.3** The number you enter becomes the sequence's starting time.

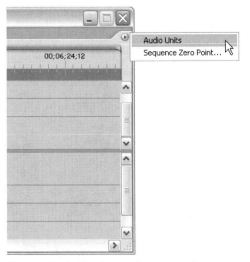

**Figure 7.4** In the Timeline window menu, select Audio Units.

## To toggle the timeline time ruler between video frames and audio samples:

◆ In the Timeline window menu, select Audio Units (**Figure 7.4**).

The Timeline window time ruler changes to audio units (**Figure 7.5**). Deselect Audio Units to change the time ruler's scale to video frames.

## ✔ Tip

■ A typical two-minute leader starts at 00;58;00;02, so that the actual program content starts at 01;00;00;00. (See the sidebar "Creating a Leader" in Chapter 3.)

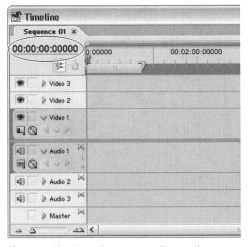

**Figure 7.5** The time ruler counts audio samples.

# Customizing Track Views

You can view the contents of each track in a sequence in more or less detail, according to your preferences or the task at hand. *Collapsed* tracks show the least information, displaying each clip as a relatively narrow band of color containing only the clip's name. Collapsed tracks also consume the least vertical space, allowing you to view the greatest number of tracks at once and providing a clean interface that updates and scrolls quickly.

Expanding a track makes the track and the clips it contains wider, revealing options for viewing additional clip information. An *expanded* video track can display *thumbnails* (small images taken from each clip's video content). The clips in an expanded audio track can display a *waveform*, a visual representation of the audio. Expanded tracks also reveal controls for viewing and navigating keyframes, which you can use to control video and audio effects such as filters, transparency, and audio fades. For more about keyframes, see Chapter 13, "Working with Effects."

### To expand or collapse a track:

◆ Click the triangle to the left of a track's name to toggle it between expanded and collapsed states (**Figures 7.6** and **7.7**).

Additional display options appear in the track header area of expanded tracks.

**Figure 7.6** Clicking the triangle to the left of a track's name toggles it from a more compact collapsed state...

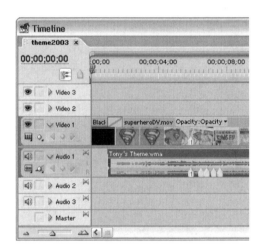

**Figure 7.7** ...to an expanded state, which reveals additional controls and information about the clips in the track.

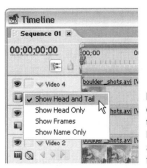

Figure 7.8 In an expanded video track, click the Set Display Style button and choose an option from the menu.

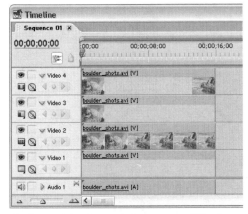

Figure 7.9 Each video track shown uses a different display style: (from top to bottom) Head and Tail, Head Only, Show Frames, and Show Name Only.

## To set a video track's display style:

1. If necessary, expand the track.

   Additional buttons, including the Set Display Style button, appear in the track's header area.

2. Click the Set Display Style button (under the track's eye icon) and choose an option from the drop-down menu (**Figure 7.8**):

   **Show Head and Tail:** Displays a thumbnail image at the beginning and end of each clip in the expanded track.

   **Show Head Only:** Displays a thumbnail image at the beginning of each clip in the expanded track.

   **Show Frames:** Displays thumbnail images for each time unit in the clips in the expanded track.

   **Show Name Only:** Displays the name of the clips in the expanded track without thumbnail images.

   The Set Display Style button's icon reflects your choice. The clips in the expanded track use the display style you specify (**Figure 7.9**).

CUSTOMIZING TRACK VIEWS

## To show and hide audio waveforms in an audio track:

1. If necessary, expand the track.

   Additional buttons, including the Set Display Style button, appear in the track's header area.

2. Click the audio track's Set Display Style button and choose an option from the drop-down menu (**Figure 7.10**):

   **Show Waveform:** Displays an audio waveform in each clip in the expanded track.

   **Show Name Only:** Displays the audio clip's name only in the expanded track, without a waveform.

   The Set Display Style button's icon reflects your choice. The clips in the expanded audio track use the display style you specify (**Figure 7.11**).

**Figure 7.10** In an expanded audio track, click the Set Display Style button and choose an option from the menu.

**Figure 7.11** The clip in audio track 1 is set to Show Waveform; the clip in audio track 2 is set to Show Name Only.

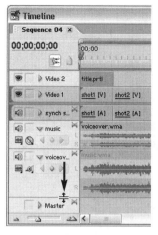

**Figure 7.12** Drag the top of an expanded video track or the bottom of an audio track (shown here) to change its height.

**Figure 7.13** Dragging the right side of the track header area...

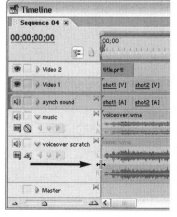

**Figure 7.14** ...widens the track header area and makes room for longer track names.

# Resizing Tracks

You can resize the height of each track to aid in the use of keyframes or other controls, or just to aid your eyesight. You can also resize the track header area to minimize its width or, more likely, to accommodate longer custom track names. When there are more tracks than the Timeline window can show at once, you can adjust the border between the video and audio tracks to favor the tracks you need the most.

## To resize the height of an expanded track:

1. If necessary, expand the track.

2. Position the mouse pointer at the top edge of a video track's header area or the bottom edge of an audio track's header area so that the height adjustment icon ‡ appears. Drag up or down to change the track's height (**Figure 7.12**).

   Press Shift while resizing to adjust the height of all of the expanded tracks simultaneously.

## To resize the track header area:

◆ Position the mouse pointer over the right edge of the track header area so that the width adjustment icon ‖‖ appears. Drag right or left to change the track header width (**Figures 7.13** and **7.14**).

## To change the proportion of video and audio tracks:

◆ Position the mouse pointer between the vertical scroll bars between the video and audio tracks (at the right of the Timeline window) so the height adjustment icon appears. Drag up or down to change the proportion of video and audio tracks visible in the Timeline window (**Figure 7.15**).

## ✔ Tip

■ To maximize both screen space and performance, display only the information that you need. Large icons, detailed track formats, and waveforms not only use up valuable screen space, but also take longer to appear on the screen. Excessive detail can result in an overcrowded screen and slow scrolling in the timeline.

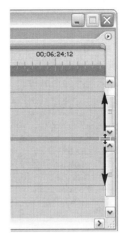

**Figure 7.15** Change the proportion of video and audio tracks visible in the Timeline window by dragging between the scroll bars for video and audio.

RESIZING TRACKS

Figure 7.16 Choose Sequence > Add Tracks.

Figure 7.17 In the Add Tracks dialog box, enter the number of video, audio, and audio submix tracks you want to add.

Figure 7.18 For each type of track you add, choose an option in the Placement drop-down menu.

# Adding, Deleting, and Renaming Tracks

As you learned in Chapter 2, "Starting a Project," the Default Sequence settings determine the initial number of tracks in a sequence. For many projects, you'll need only a modest number of tracks: video tracks for the main content and for super-imposed images; audio tracks for dialogue, soundtrack, and sound effects. However, Premiere Pro permits you to have as many as 99 video and 99 audio tracks in the time-line. What's more, you can name all those tracks, so you can easily distinguish the sound-effects track from the music and dialogue tracks, for example.

Similarly, you can remove either a particular track (and all the clips it contains) or empty tracks only. You can't remove the master audio track, however.

## To add tracks:

1. Choose Sequence > Add Tracks (**Figure 7.16**).

   The Add Tracks dialog box appears (**Figure 7.17**).

2. In the Add Tracks dialog box, specify the number of video, audio, and audio submix tracks you want to add.

3. For each type of track you add, specify an option in the Placement drop-down menu: Before First Track, After Target Track, or After Last Track (**Figure 7.18**).

*continues on next page*

ADDING, DELETING, AND RENAMING TRACKS

**4.** For audio tracks, choose an option in the Track Type drop-down menu: Mono, Stereo, or 5.1 (**Figure 7.19**).

**5.** When you've finished specifying the track options, click OK.

The number and type of tracks you specified appear in the sequence (**Figure 7.20**).

## To delete tracks:

**1.** To delete a particular video or audio track, target the track by clicking the track's header area (near the track's name).

You can target one video and one audio track, including audio submix tracks. You can't target the master audio track.

**2.** Choose Sequence > Delete Tracks (**Figure 7.21**).

**Figure 7.19** In the Track Type drop-down menu, choose the type of audio track you want to add.

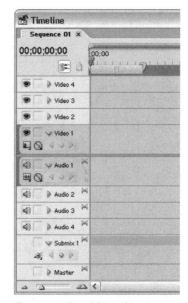

**Figure 7.20** The additional tracks appear in the positions you specified.

**Figure 7.21** Choose Sequence > Delete Tracks.

**Figure 7.22** In the Delete Tracks dialog box, choose the types of tracks you want to delete.

**Figure 7.23** For each type of track you want to delete, specify whether you want to delete all empty tracks or only the targeted track.

The Delete Tracks dialog box appears (**Figure 7.22**).

3. Choose the types of tracks you want to delete by checking the appropriate boxes.

4. For selected video or audio tracks, choose an option from the corresponding drop-down menu (**Figure 7.23**):

   **Target Track:** Removes the currently targeted track (and any clips it contains).

   **All Empty Tracks:** Removes all video or audio tracks that don't contain clips.

   If you selected audio submix tracks, then all unassigned submix tracks will be removed.

5. Click OK.

   The tracks you specified are removed from the sequence.

## To rename a track:

1. Context-click the track's name and choose Rename from the menu (**Figure 7.24**).

   The track's name is highlighted with a text-insertion cursor.

2. Type a new name for the track and press Enter (**Figure 7.25**).

   The track uses the name you entered.

### ✔ Tips

- You can also access the Add Tracks and Remove Tracks dialog boxes by context-clicking the track header area.

- If none of the available audio tracks matches a new clip's audio channel type, Premiere Pro adds a compatible audio track automatically. See Chapter 6 for details.

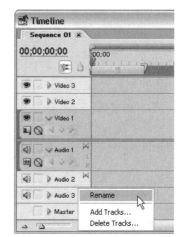

**Figure 7.24**
Context-click the track's header area and choose Rename from the menu.

**Figure 7.25**
Type a new name for the track and press Enter.

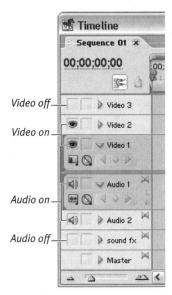

Video off
Video on
Audio on
Audio off

**Figure 7.26** Tracks with the eye icon are visible during playback, and tracks with the speaker icon can be heard.

■ The Audio Mixer window includes switches for monitoring audio tracks during mixing. For more information, see Chapter 11, "Mixing Audio."

# Monitoring Tracks

When used as a noun, the term *monitor* can refer to a video screen or an audio speaker. It's also used as a verb, meaning to see or hear, as in "to monitor the video and audio." In Premiere Pro, you can monitor any combination of the tracks in the timeline. Only monitored tracks are included during playback and when you preview or export the program. Though you usually monitor all the tracks, at times you may want to monitor only certain tracks. You may want to hear the dialogue track without the music and effects tracks, for example.

## To monitor tracks:

◆ In the Timeline window, *do one of the following:*

▲ Click a video track's Track Output toggle button to hide or reveal the eye icon 👁.

▲ Click an audio track's Track Output toggle button to hide or reveal the speaker icon 🔊.

The Track Output toggle button is the first box in the track's header area. When a track output icon (eye or speaker) is visible, you can see or hear the clips in the corresponding track; when the icon is hidden, clips in the track are excluded from playback (**Figure 7.26**).

## ✔ Tips

■ Shift-click next to the track name in the timeline to reveal or hide all the speaker icons or all the eye icons.

■ Isolating a single audio monitor can be especially helpful when you're synching sound effects to video. (On an audio mixer, this procedure is called *soloing* the track.) The other sound tracks often prevent you from hearing whether a sound effect is synched properly.

# Locking and Unlocking Tracks

Locking a track protects the clips in the track from accidental changes. You can't add clips to a locked track, and you can't move or modify the clips that are already in the locked track. Moreover, clips in locked tracks don't shift in time after an insert edit is performed. Locking a track makes a lock icon appear in the track's header area and marks the track under the time ruler with a pattern of slashes.

Although you can't alter the clips in a locked track, you can still monitor those clips, and the track is included when you preview or export the program.

## To lock and unlock tracks:

◆ Click the track's Track Lock toggle button (the second square in the track's header area) to show or hide the lock icon 🔒 (**Figure 7.27**).

This icon indicates that the corresponding track is locked and can't be modified. Locked tracks also appear with a pattern of slashes. If no icon appears, the track is unlocked.

**Figure 7.27** Click to make the lock icon appear and lock the track. The contents of the track appear with a pattern of slashes. Click the lock icon to make it disappear and unlock the track.

# Getting Around the Timeline

You can navigate the sequence in the timeline in several ways. You can zoom in, zoom out, and scroll through the timeline. In addition to using the standard zoom tools and scroll bars, you can take advantage of the Timeline window's *viewing area bar*.

You're already familiar with the source and program view's viewing area bar from Chapter 5, "Viewing Clips in the Monitor Window." The Timeline window's viewing area bar works just like its counterparts: The width of the viewing area bar corresponds with the area of the sequence visible in the Timeline window. Drag the ends of the viewing area bar to view the sequence in more detail; drag them farther apart to see more of the sequence. Dragging the center of the bar left or right scrolls the visible area.

Whereas the Zoom tool magnifies the part of the timeline you click or drag, the time unit slider, zoom buttons, and viewing area bar use the current time indicator (CTI) as the center of changes in scale. In other words, using these controls zooms into the CTI or out from the CTI. Note how the time ruler zooms smoothly, rather than by large, discrete increments.

## To view part of the sequence in more detail:

◆ *Do one of the following:*

▲ Above the Timeline window's time ruler, drag the ends of the viewing area bar closer together (**Figure 7.28**).

▲ In the Tools window, select the Zoom tool 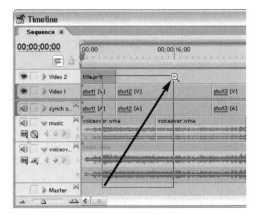 and then click the part of the timeline that you want to see in more detail.

▲ In the Tools window, select the Zoom tool and then drag a marquee around the area of the timeline that you want to see in detail (**Figure 7.29**).

▲ At the bottom left of the Timeline window, drag the zoom slider to the right (**Figure 7.30**).

▲ To the right of the zoom slider, click the Zoom In button.

**Figure 7.28** To view the sequence in more detail, you can drag the ends of the viewing area bar closer together...

**Figure 7.29** ...click or drag a marquee (shown here) with the Zoom tool...

**Figure 7.30** ...or drag the zoom slider to the right (shown here) or click the Zoom In button.

**Figure 7.31** To view more of the sequence, you can drag the ends of the viewing area bar farther apart...

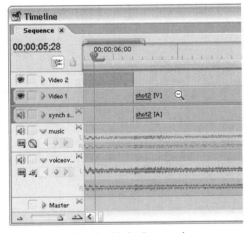

**Figure 7.32** ...Alt-click with the Zoom tool...

**Figure 7.33** ...or drag the zoom slider to the left (shown here) or click the Zoom Out button.

## To view more of the sequence in the timeline:

◆ *Do one of the following:*

▲ Above the Timeline window's time ruler, drag the ends of the viewing area bar farther apart (**Figure 7.31**).

▲ In the Tools window, select the Zoom tool 🔍 and then Alt-click the part of the timeline that you want to center in the wider view (**Figure 7.32**).

When you press Alt, the Zoom tool icon appears with a minus sign to indicate that it will zoom out.

▲ At the bottom left of the Timeline window, drag the zoom slider to the left (**Figure 7.33**).

▲ To the left of the zoom slider, click the Zoom Out button.

## ✔ Tips

■ To zoom out quickly to view the entire program in the timeline, press the back-slash key (\).

■ To select the Zoom tool quickly, press Z.

■ When you zoom into the time ruler closely enough for the ruler to measure video frames, a short blue line extends from the right side of the CTI. This represents the duration of the frame.

## To scroll through the timeline:

♦ *Do one of the following:*

▲ At the bottom of the Timeline window, click either the left or right scroll arrow to gradually move across a close view of the program.

▲ Drag the scroll box right or left to view a different part of the program.

▲ Click the scroll bar next to the scroll handle to shift the view one width of the timeline.

▲ Above the Timeline window's time ruler, drag the center of the viewing area bar to the right or left (**Figure 7.34**).

▲ In the Tools window, select the Hand tool 🖐 and then drag the sequence (grab the clip content area) to the right or left (**Figure 7.35**).

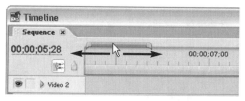

**Figure 7.34** To scroll the visible area of the timeline, grab the center of the viewing area bar and drag left or right...

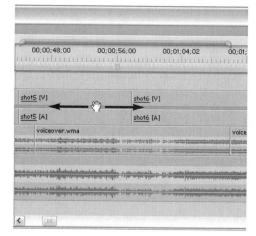

**Figure 7.35** ...or select the Hand tool and drag the sequence to the left or right.

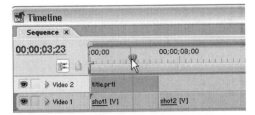

**Figure 7.36** Click the Timeline window's time ruler to cue the CTI to that point.

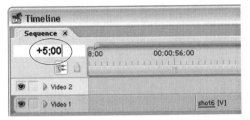

**Figure 7.37** Select the Timeline window's time display and enter an absolute time or a number relative to the current time. You can also drag the time display to change the number.

# Playing the Sequence in the Timeline

In Chapter 4, "Managing Clips," you learned to use playback controls in the Monitor window to cue the current frame of the program. In the Timeline window, a small blue triangle in the time ruler, the CTI, looks and works like its counterpart in the program view. However, a vertical line extends from the Timeline window's CTI through the tracks of the sequence. This makes it easy to see the current frame in relationship to the clips in the sequence. Furthermore, the vertical line makes it even easier to align clips with the CTI, and vice versa. You can cue the Timeline window's CTI by clicking or dragging the time ruler or by using the Timeline window's time display.

You can also snap the Timeline window's CTI to an edit point by pressing Shift while dragging the CTI.

Remember that the Timeline window's CTI and the program view's CTI show the same frame of the sequence and move in tandem; however, their time rulers can show different parts of the same sequence at different scales and using different time units.

## To cue the Timeline window CTI:

◆ *Do one of the following:*

▲ In the Timeline window, click the time ruler to move the CTI to that point in the sequence (**Figure 7.36**).

▲ In the Timeline window, click the current time display to select it and then type a relative or absolute time and press Enter (**Figure 7.37**).

▲ In the Timeline window, drag the current time display to change the number.

▲ In the program view, use the playback controls (or a keyboard shortcut) to cue the current program frame. (See "Using Playback Controls" in Chapter 5.)

## To snap the Timeline window CTI to an edit point:

◆ In the Timeline window, press Shift and drag the CTI to an edit point in the sequence. Edit points can be clip edges or markers.

When you drag to the edge of a clip, the CTI snaps to the edge and an indicator ▼ appears at the corner of the clip.

When you drag to a marker or the edge of the work area bar, an indicator ▲ appears under the timeline ruler.

When the edge of a clip and the edge of the timeline ruler (or marker) coincide, both indicators appear (**Figure 7.38**).

### ✔ Tip

■ You can also drag the vertical line extending from the Timeline window's CTI, as long as there are no clips at the point where you grab the CTI.

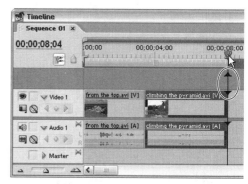

**Figure 7.38** Hold down the Shift key and drag the CTI to an edit point in the sequence.

**Figure 7.39** Select the tracks containing the edits to which you want to cue the CTI.

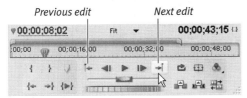

**Figure 7.40** In the program view, click the Previous Edit or Next Edit button.

# Cuing to Edits

An *edit* is the point between two clips or the point directly before or after a clip in a selected track. By cueing the CTI by clicking the Previous Edit and Next Edit buttons, you can easily insert a clip before, after, or between clips in the timeline.

## To cue to the next or previous edit:

1. Target the tracks containing the edits to which you want to cue the CTI (**Figure 7.39**).

2. In the Monitor window's program view, click one of these buttons (**Figure 7.40**):

   **Previous Edit:** Cues the edit line to the previous edit in a selected track.

   **Next Edit:** Cues the edit line to the next edit in a selected track.

## ✔ Tip

- You can also use the playback controls in the program view to cue the edit line to an absolute or relative time position or to an In point, Out point, or sequence marker. See "Using Playback Controls" in Chapter 5 for details.

# Using Sequence Markers

Just as clip markers can help you identify important frames in the source clips, you can use *sequence markers* to specify important points in the timeline.

In most respects, sequence markers work exactly the same way as clip markers. The commands you use to set, delete, and cue to sequence markers are equivalent to the commands you use for source clip markers. However, sequence markers appear in a sequence's time ruler, rather than in clips. Apart from these minor differences, the methods you learned in Chapter 6 can be applied to sequence markers.

However, sequence markers do have a few unique features that merit separate explanations. First, a sequence marker can include a text message. Comments are for your reference only and can be accessed only through the Marker dialog box; they don't appear during playback, nor are they exported.

In addition, a sequence marker can contain a Web link or chapter link that's embedded in the exported movie file. When the movie reaches a Web link marker, it automatically opens a Web page in your browser. A chapter link specifies points to which you can cue the movie when you author a DVD or QuickTime movie.

### To add a comment to a sequence marker:

**1.** To access the Marker dialog box, *do one of the following*:

- ▲ In the Timeline window's time ruler, double-click a sequence marker (**Figure 7.41**).

- ▲ With the CTI cued to an existing marker, double-click the Set Unnumbered Marker button on the left side of the timeline ruler (**Figure 7.42**).

A dialog box for the marker appears.

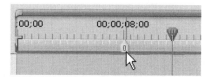

**Figure 7.41** Double-click a sequence marker.

**Figure 7.42**
Double-click the Set Unnumbered Marker button.

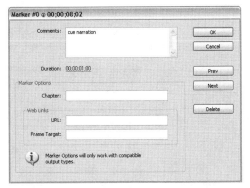

Figure 7.43 In the Marker dialog box, enter a comment and duration.

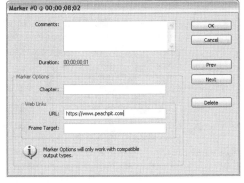

Figure 7.44 To set a chapter link, enter the name of the chapter in the Chapter field. To set a Web link, enter a URL (circled) and, if you want, a file name for the frame target.

## ✔ Tips

- DVD authoring guidelines restrict the proximity of chapter links. When you set markers for use as chapter links, make sure they are spaced at least 15 frames apart or by the number of frames your authoring software requires.

- Double-clicking the Set Unnumbered Marker button on the left side of the timeline ruler allows you to set a marker and add a comment and/or Web link in one step.

2. In the Marker dialog box, enter information in the following fields (**Figure 7.43**):

    **Comments:** A text message that will appear in the Monitor window's program view.

    **Duration:** The amount of time the marker lasts, beginning at the marked time in the program.

3. Click OK to close the Marker dialog box.

    In the time ruler, a line extending from the marker indicates the comment duration you specified.

## To add a Web or chapter link to a sequence marker:

1. To access the Marker dialog box, *do one of the following:*

    ▲ In the Timeline window's time ruler, double-click a sequence marker.

    ▲ With the CTI cued to an existing marker, double-click the Set Unnumbered Marker button.

2. In the Marker Options section of the dialog box, *do one of the following* (**Figure 7.44**):

    ▲ To set a chapter link, enter the name of the chapter in the Chapter field.

    ▲ To set a Web link, enter the Web address in the URL field.

    ▲ To activate a particular frame of the site in a Web link, enter the file name of the frame in the Frame Target field.

3. Click OK to close the Marker dialog box.

USING SEQUENCE MARKERS

# Viewing Clip Information

When you are working in the Timeline window you need to be able to easily see a clip's properties, including its name and duration. And when you drag a clip, you need to be able to see the timecode offset (the number of frames you are dragging the clip). Premiere Pro supplies this useful information in the form of a tool tip.

### To view clip properties in a tool tip:

◆ Position the mouse pointer over a clip in the Timeline window.

A tool tip displays the clip name, starting and ending points in the sequence, and duration (**Figure 7.45**).

The tool tip also lists any speed changes you have made to the clip, and if you have applied a frame hold, the tool tip displays the type of frame hold.

### To view the timecode offset while dragging a clip:

◆ Drag the clip you want to reposition in the timeline.

A tool tip appears listing the number of frames the clip has traveled from its original position. Positive numbers appear as you drag to the right of the original position, and negative numbers appear as you drag to the left (**Figure 7.46**).

### ✔ Tip

■ Tool tips also pop up when you trim a clip. See "Trimming Clips in the Timeline" in Chapter 8.

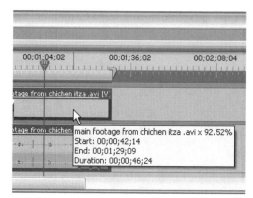

**Figure 7.45** Position the cursor over a clip in the Timeline window to display information about the clip.

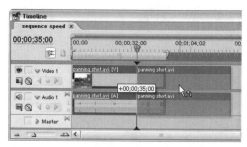

**Figure 7.46** Drag the clip you want to reposition on the timeline. A tool tip lists the number of frames the clip has traveled from its original position.

# Using Linked Clips

When a clip contains both video and audio material, it's known as a *linked clip*. When you move a linked clip in the timeline, the video and audio portions of the clip move together. Similarly, when you change a linked clip's edit marks, the video and audio tracks both change—unless you deliberately treat them separately.

The link helps you keep the video and audio synchronized. Even if your video and audio were recorded separately (as in a film shoot), you can create an artificial link between them. If you've ever edited film and magnetic tape, you know how convenient linked clips are.

Nevertheless, it's possible to lose sync between the tracks of a linked clip. Fortunately, Premiere Pro alerts you to the loss of sync by tagging the affected clips in the timeline. Premiere Pro even tells you by exactly how much the clips are out of sync and provides easy ways to restore sync.

Although the link is usually an advantage, Premiere Pro permits you to override the link if necessary. You can even break the link if you want.

To perform the tasks described in this chapter, you need to understand how linked clips behave in the timeline. In the next chapter, you'll learn to tackle more advanced tasks related to sync and links.

# Selecting Clips in the Timeline

Not surprisingly, whenever you want to manipulate or affect a program clip in any way, you have to select it first.

Clicking a linked clip selects both the video and audio portions of the clip. To select or otherwise manipulate only the video or audio portion of a linked clip, use the Alt keyboard modifier.

### To select clips in the Timeline window:

◆ *Do any of the following:*

▲ To select a clip, click the clip in the timeline (**Figure 7.47**).

▲ To add or subtract from the selection, Ctrl-click clips.

▲ To select a range of clips, drag a marquee around a range of clips (**Figure 7.48**).

▲ To select only the video or audio portion of a linked clip, Alt-click the clip (**Figure 7.49**).

When a clip is selected, its border is highlighted.

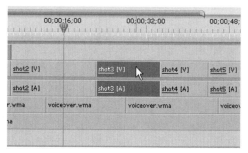

**Figure 7.47** To select clips in the Timeline window, click a clip...

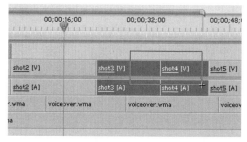

**Figure 7.48** ...or drag a marquee around multiple clips. Make sure to start dragging in an empty track; otherwise, you could move a clip.

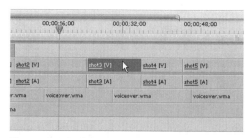

**Figure 7.49** Alt-click to select only the video or audio portion of a linked clip.

**Figure 7.50** In the Tools window, select the Track tool.

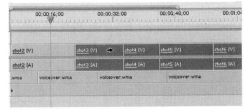

**Figure 7.51** Click a clip with the Track tool to select that clip and all subsequent clips in that track (including their linked counterparts in unlocked tracks).

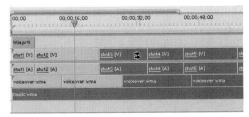

**Figure 7.52** Pressing Shift toggles the Track tool to the Multitrack tool, which selects a clip and all subsequent clips in all tracks.

■ Because selecting a track of clips also selects any linked audio or video, keep an eye on the clips in linked tracks when you move a selection. Otherwise, you may overwrite other clips without noticing.

## To select all the clips in one or more tracks:

1. In the Tools window, choose the track tool ⊡ (**Figure 7.50**).

2. *Do one of the following:*

   ▲ To select all clips in the track from a particular clip forward, including the linked audio or video in other tracks, click the clip (**Figure 7.51**).

   ▲ To select all clips in the track from a particular clip forward, not including the linked audio or video in other tracks, Alt-click the clip.

   ▲ To select all clips in all tracks from a particular clip forward, Shift-click the clip (**Figure 7.52**).

   Pressing Shift changes the Track tool into the Multitrack tool ⊞.

## ✔ Tips

■ You can't select clips in locked tracks. This isn't a restriction, but an advantage. Lock tracks to protect the clips in a track from inadvertent changes.

■ Although it looks the same, the Track tool doesn't function as it did in previous versions of Premiere. In Premiere Pro, Shift-clicking with the Track tool toggles to the Multitrack tool. Therefore, you can select either one track or all tracks. And unlike in past versions, selecting a track of clips also selects any linked audio or video unless you press the Alt modifier key.

■ When you select multiple contiguous clips in the timeline, the Info window indicates the number of clips selected and the total duration of the clips. If you select noncontiguous clips, the duration is calculated from the In point of the first clip to the Out point of the last clip.

# Grouping Clips

Even though you can select and move any number of clips (even a noncontiguous range of clips), at times it may be more convenient to group clips. *Grouping* clips allows you to select and move the clips as a single clip.

You can adjust the outer edges—the In point of the first clip or the Out point of the last clip—of the group, but not the interior In and Out points. Unlike with individual clips, you can't apply clip-based commands (such as speed changes) or effects to a group. However, you can select individual members of the group and apply effects to them without ungrouping the clips. And, of course, you can ungroup the clips at any time.

### To group clips:

1. Select more than one clip in the Timeline window (**Figure 7.53**).

2. Choose Clip > Group (**Figure 7.54**).

   The clips are grouped together. Clicking any member of the group selects the entire group.

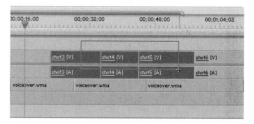

**Figure 7.53** Select more than one clip in a sequence for your group.

**Figure 7.54** Choose Clip > Group.

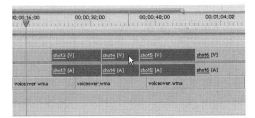

**Figure 7.55** Select a grouped clip.

**Figure 7.56** Choose Clip > Ungroup.

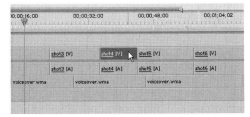

**Figure 7.57** Alt-click to select members of a group clip without ungrouping them.

## To ungroup clips:

1. Select a grouped clip in the Timeline window (**Figure 7.55**).

2. Choose Clip > Ungroup (**Figure 7.56**).

   The clips are ungrouped so that you can select and manipulate each clip independently.

## To select individual clips in a group:

◆ *Do one of the following:*

   ▲ Alt-click individual clips in a group (**Figure 7.57**).

   ▲ Shift+Alt-click to add to or subtract from the selection.

## ✔ Tip

■ You can't apply an effect to a group clip, but you can apply an effect to a nested sequence. For more about nested sequences, see Chapter 6.

# Deleting Clips and Gaps from the Timeline

Whatever you can select, you can delete. That includes both clips and gaps between clips. Delete commands work much like the lift and extract edits you learned about in Chapter 6. When you delete a clip, the result is like a lift edit, leaving an empty space behind and leaving surrounding clips unaffected. The result of a Ripple Delete command is comparable to an extract edit. Ripple deleting a clip removes the clip and closes the gap, shifting all subsequent clips back in time by the duration of the clip. You can also select and ripple delete a gap between clips. However, you can't select a gap and a clip simultaneously. Also, the Ripple Delete command always shifts clips in all tracks. To limit the ripple effect to the tracks containing the deleted clip, you'll need to lock the other tracks or use a variation of an extract edit, explained in Chapter 6.

### To delete clips from the timeline:

1. Select one or more clips in the timeline (**Figure 7.58**).

2. Press Backspace (or Delete, on an extended keyboard).

   The selected clips are removed from the timeline (**Figure 7.59**).

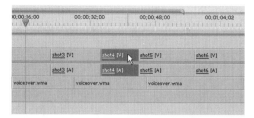

**Figure 7.58** Select one or more clips in the Timeline window.

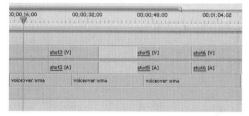

**Figure 7.59** Pressing Backspace (or Delete) is like performing a lift edit, removing the selection and leaving empty space.

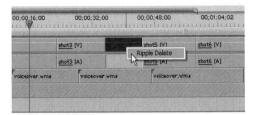

**Figure 7.60** Context-click selected clips (or a gap between clips) and choose Ripple Delete. Because a ripple delete won't split clips in other tracks to perform the ripple edit, other tracks must be locked.

**Figure 7.61** The selection or gap is extracted, and subsequent material in the sequence shifts back in time by the number of frames that were removed.

## To ripple delete a clip or a gap between clips:

◆ Context-click a clip or gap in the timeline and choose Ripple Delete from the menu (**Figure 7.60**).

The subsequent clips shift back in the timeline to close the gap (**Figure 7.61**). The command won't split clips in other tracks to perform the ripple edit, and if other clips are unlocked, the command will appear dimmed. Lock tracks containing other clips to enable the command.

## ✔ Tips

■ Delete and Ripple Delete are great for removing entire clips or gaps. To remove portions of clips or to remove frames from several clips and tracks, perform a lift or extract edit. See "Lift and Extract" in Chapter 6.

■ You can Alt-click to select only the video or audio portion of a linked clip and then delete or ripple delete just that part.

DELETING CLIPS AND GAPS FROM THE TIMELINE

# Enabling and Disabling Clips

Disabling a clip in the sequence prevents it from appearing during playback and when you preview or export the program. Disabling a clip is useful if you want to keep the clip in the program but exclude it temporarily. You might want to disable a single audio clip to hear what the program sounds like without it, for example. You can still move and make other changes to a disabled clip.

## To disable or enable clips:

1. Select one or more clips in the timeline (**Figure 7.62**).

2. Choose Clip > Enable (**Figure 7.63**).

   A check mark indicates that the clip is enabled. If no check mark appears, the clip is disabled. Disabled clips appear dimmed in the Timeline window (**Figure 7.64**).

**Figure 7.62** Select one or more clips in the Timeline window.

**Figure 7.63** Choose Clip > Enable to uncheck the option.

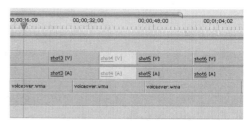

**Figure 7.64** Disabled clips appear dimmed in the Timeline window and don't appear in the program view or in exported movies.

**ENABLING AND DISABLING CLIPS**

**Figure 7.65** Select the Razor tool.

# Splitting Clips

Sometimes you need to cut a clip in the timeline into two or more pieces. You may want to apply an effect to one part of a shot but not to another, for example. When you split a clip, each piece becomes an independent sequence clip or clip instance. When you split a linked clip, both the video and audio tracks are split.

### To split a clip with the razor:

1. In the Tools window, select the Razor tool ⬚ (**Figure 7.65**).

2. Click a clip in the timeline at the point where you want to split it (**Figure 7.66**). The clip is split into two individual clips at that point (**Figure 7.67**).

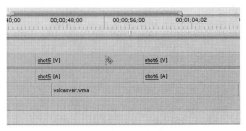

**Figure 7.66** Clicking a clip with the Razor tool...

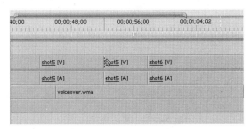

**Figure 7.67** ...splits it into two clips at the point you click.

## To split clips in multiple tracks:

1. In the Tools window, select the Razor tool 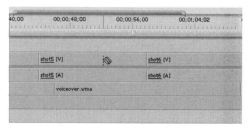.

2. Shift-click the point in the timeline where you want to split the clips in all tracks (**Figure 7.68**).

   Pressing Shift changes the Razor tool to the Multirazor tool ✎. Shift-clicking splits all clips in all unlocked tracks at the same point in time (**Figure 7.69**).

**Figure 7.68** Pressing Shift toggles the Razor tool to the Multirazor tool. Clicking with the Multirazor tool...

**Figure 7.69** ...splits clips in all tracks.

**Figure 7.70** Position the CTI at the point you want to split clips. The program view displays the frame after the cut point.

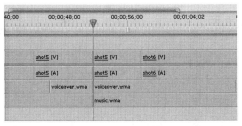

**Figure 7.71** Choose Sequence > Razor at Current Time Indicator.

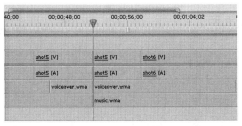

**Figure 7.72** Clips in all unlocked tracks are split at the CTI.

## To split clips at the CTI:

1. Position the CTI at the point where you want to split the clips (**Figure 7.70**).

2. Choose Sequence > Razor at Current Time Indicator (**Figure 7.71**).

   All unlocked clips in all unlocked tracks are split at the same point in the timeline (**Figure 7.72**).

### Match-Frame Edits

Splitting a clip creates a cut that is visible in the Timeline window but invisible during playback. This kind of cut is called a *match-frame edit*. In traditional tape-based editing, match-frame edits are essential to A/B roll editing. In Premiere Pro, match-frame edits can be useful if you want to add an effect or speed change in one part of a shot but not another. Because the viewer can't detect a match-frame edit, the effect appears to be seamless.

# Cutting, Copying, and Pasting Clips

As you would expect of any computer program, Premiere Pro offers copy and paste functions. You may be pleasantly surprised by Premiere Pro's powerful paste commands. You can paste any number of clips in any number of tracks within the same sequence or from one sequence to another. The standard Paste command works like an overlay edit, whereas the Paste Insert command works like an insert edit. (For more about overlay and insert edits, see Chapter 6.)

In this section, you'll learn how to copy and paste the contents of a clip.

### To paste clips:

1. Select one or more clips in a sequence (**Figure 7.73**).

2. *Do one of the following:*
   ▲ Choose Edit > Cut.
   ▲ Choose Edit > Copy (**Figure 7.74**).

3. Open the sequence in which you want to paste the selection and position the CTI where you want the pasted clips to begin (**Figure 7.75**).

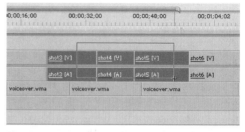

**Figure 7.73** Select one or more clips in the Timeline window.

**Figure 7.74** Choose Edit > Cut or Edit > Copy (shown here).

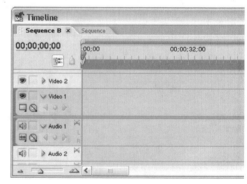

**Figure 7.75** Position the destination sequence's CTI where you want the pasted selection to start.

**Figure 7.76** Choose Edit > Paste (shown here) or Edit > Paste Insert.

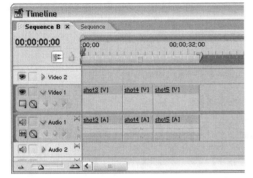

**Figure 7.77** The selection appears in the sequence, starting at the CTI. In this example, the selection was pasted into a different sequence.

**4.** *Do one of the following* (**Figure 7.76**):

▲ Choose Edit > Paste.

▲ Choose Edit > Paste Insert.

The selection appears in corresponding tracks beginning at the CTI (**Figure 7.77**). If there are not enough tracks or not the appropriate type of audio tracks to accommodate the pasted selection, Premiere Pro creates the necessary tracks automatically.

## ✔ Tip

■ Versions of Premiere prior to Premiere Pro offered various tools and procedures for copying and pasting multiple clips. Premiere Pro's streamlined paste procedure makes the old methods unnecessary.

## Copying and Pasting between Premiere Pro and Adobe After Effects

Beginning with Premiere Pro 1.5 and After Effects 6.5, you can copy and paste clips and sequences—called layers and compositions in After Effects—between the two applications' Timeline windows. Not all of the effects available in one application are available in the other. While both applications have some similar attributes, there are considerable differences. With some minor limitations, everything in Premiere Pro can be copied to After Effects. However, After Effects has 3D layers, masks, text layers, and transfer modes that are not available in Premiere Pro, and therefore cannot be pasted into the Premiere Pro Timeline window.

**Tables 7.1** and **7.2** summarize the effects on the various settings and features when you copy and paste between the two Adobe applications. Table 7.1 lists what happens when you copy from After Effects and paste into Premiere Pro. Table 7.2 lists what happens when you copy from Premiere Pro and paste into After Effects.

Note: It is important that you start Premiere Pro before copying an item in After Effects.

**Table 7.1**

### Copying from After Effects to Premiere Pro

| COPIED ITEM | RESULT |
| --- | --- |
| Adobe Photoshop layers | Imported into an active track in the Timeline window and added to the Project window. |
| Alpha channels | Alpha channels are imported with other media data. |
| Audio layers | Imported as an audio track. |
| Effects with keyframes | Imported as an effect with keyframes if the effect exists in Adobe Premiere Pro; imported as an offline effect if the effect doesn't exist in Adobe Premiere Pro. |
| Keyframe interpolations (for example, Bézier and Auto Bézier) | Imported with copied media. |
| Layer with a footage item | The layer is imported as a track item (inserted into an active track in the Timeline window), and the footage item is added to the Project window. |
| Solids | Imported as a color matte. |
| Speed options | 200% Stretch is imported as 50% Speed. |
| Transform properties with keyframes | Transform settings are applied to the Motion effect. |

# Copying and Pasting between Premiere Pro and Adobe After Effects
## *(continued)*

Table 7.2

## Copying from Premiere Pro to After Effects

| Copied Item | Result |
| --- | --- |
| Adobe Photoshop layers | Imported as a Photoshop layer. |
| Alpha channels | Alpha channels are imported with other media data. |
| Audio effects (limited) | Only the Channel Volume effect can be copied. The Channel Volume effect is imported as the Stereo Mixer effect. All other audio effects are ignored. |
| Audio tracks (limited) | Audio tracks that are either 5.1 surround or greater than 16-bit aren't supported. Mono and stereo audio tracks that are 16-bit or less are imported as one or more layers. |
| Clip markers | Imported as layer-time markers. |
| Color matte | Imported as solid. |
| Fixed effects (for example, Motion and Opacity) | Imported as transform properties that are mapped with keyframes. |
| Keyframe interpolations (for example, Bézier and Auto Bézier) | Auto Bézier is imported as Continuous Bézier. |
| Offline files | Imported as missing files. |
| Nested sequence | Imported as a nested composition. |
| Sequence markers (limited) | Imported as markers on a new solid layer. Note: To copy sequence markers, you must either copy the sequence itself or import the entire Adobe Premiere project as a composition. |
| Speed options | 50% Speed is imported as 200% Stretch. Frame Hold is imported as Time Remap. |
| Offline files | Imported as missing files. |
| Stills | Imported as a layer. |
| Titles | Imported as a solid. |
| Track item (audio) | Track items with 5.1 surround audio aren't supported. All other track items are imported as a layer. |
| Track item (linked audio and video) | Track items with linked 5.1 surround audio aren't supported. All other track items are imported as one video layer. |
| Track item (video) | Imported as layer. |
| Transitions (video and audio) | Cross Dissolve is imported as Opacity. All other transitions are imported as a solid. |
| Video effects | Imported with keyframe data only if the effect exists in After Effects. The Crop effect is imported as a mask. |

# Playing Clips at a Different Speed or in Reverse

In Premiere Pro, you can change the speed of a clip by choosing a menu command or by dragging directly in the timeline. A clip's speed correlates inversely with duration: increasing speed reduces duration; decreasing speed increases duration. The clip's In and Out points, however, remain intact. In other words, if the clip shows a 10-second countdown, increasing the speed won't cut out any of the shot. You'll still see all 10 numbers—they'll just go by in less than 10 seconds. You can also use the Speed/Duration command to reverse playback at the specified speed, which would make the 10-second countdown in the example count *up*.

Note that a speed change applies to the entire clip. If you want to affect only part of a clip, split the clip and apply the speed change to one part only. If you want the speed to change over the course of the clip—making its playback accelerate or decelerate—you'll need to use a program like Adobe After Effects.

Unlike some editing programs, Premiere Pro doesn't create a new media file at the new speed; it merely plays back the clip at the specified speed in the project. The source media is unaffected. (If you do want a new media file, you can change the clip's speed and then export it as a new movie file. See Chapter 16, "Video and Audio Settings," to learn about exporting movie files.)

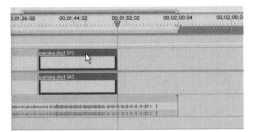

**Figure 7.78** Select a source clip in the Project window or a sequence clip in the Timeline window (shown here).

**Figure 7.79** Choose Clip > Speed/Duration.

**Figure 7.80** In the Speed / Duration dialog box, make sure the chain icon shows that speed and duration values are linked. Enter a value for the speed and check the other options you want.

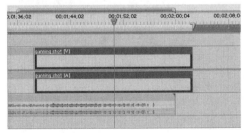

**Figure 7.81** The clip's speed (and consequently, its duration) changes according to your choices. In this example, the clip's speed is 50 percent, and therefore the clip is twice as long as it was in Figure 7.78.

## To change the speed of a clip using the Speed/Duration command:

1. Select a source clip in the Project window or a sequence clip in the Timeline window (**Figure 7.78**).

2. Choose Clip > Speed/Duration (**Figure 7.79**).

   The Clip Speed / Duration dialog box appears (**Figure 7.80**).

3. In the Clip Speed / Duration dialog box, click the chain icon so that speed and duration values are linked.

   A link icon 🔗 indicates that speed and duration are linked; an unlink icon ⛓ indicates that speed and duration values operate independently.

4. Enter a value for either of the following:

   **Speed:** Enter a speed for the clip, expressed as a percentage of the normal speed. A value less than 100 percent decreases the clip's speed; a value greater than 100 percent increases the clip's speed.

   **Duration:** Enter a total duration for the clip. Durations shorter than the original increase the clip's speed; durations longer than the original decrease the clip's speed.

5. Select the options you want:

   **Reverse Speed:** Plays the clip in reverse at the speed you specify.

   **Maintain Audio Pitch:** Shifts an audio clip's pitch to compensate for pitch changes caused by speed adjustments.

6. Click OK to close the Clip Speed / Duration dialog box.

   In the timeline, the clip's speed—and therefore its duration—change according to the values you specified (**Figure 7.81**). The source In and Out points are not changed, only the speed of the clip.

## To change the speed of a clip using the Rate Stretch tool:

1. In the Tools window, select the Rate Stretch tool  (**Figure 7.82**).

2. Position the Rate Stretch tool at the edge of a clip in the timeline and drag the edge (**Figure 7.83**).

   Dragging the edge to shorten the clip increases its speed; dragging the clip to lengthen it decreases its speed. The clip's In and Out points are not changed, only its speed. You can view the clip's speed by hovering the mouse over the clip until a tool tip appears (**Figure 7.84**).

**Figure 7.82** Select the Rate Stretch tool.

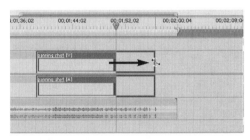

**Figure 7.83** With the Rate Stretch tool, drag the edge of a clip in the Timeline window.

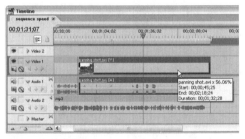

**Figure 7.84** In this example, the clip's duration is stretched to match the Out point of the music clip. Hover the mouse over the clip to view the speed in a tool tip.

## ✔ Tips

- You can unlink the speed and duration values to change the clip's speed or duration independent of each other. However, changing the speed independently can yield unpredictable results.

- You can also use the Speed/Duration command to change a clip's duration without affecting its speed. Doing so changes the clip's Out point so that the clip becomes the length you specify. Because there are numerous (and better) ways to change a clip's duration, this section doesn't cover this option.

- You can change the speed of an entire sequence by nesting the sequence in another sequence. Because a nested sequence appears as a single linked clip, you can apply the Speed command to it, just as you would to any other clip. You can use this technique to make a program meet a specified running time, provided the speed change isn't too drastic. For more on nesting sequences, see Chapter 6.

- Premiere Pro displays speed changes only when you select the clip and open the Speed / Duration dialog box or view the clip's information on the Info palette. Speed information appears neither in the Project window (for source clips) nor in the Timeline window (for sequence clips).

### Slow-Mo Mojo

The quality of a slow-motion effect is limited by your source material. When shooting film, you can create a slow-motion effect in the camera by *overcranking*. Overcranking sets the frame rate higher than the film's standard frame rate, thereby capturing more images per second. When the film is played back at the normal frame rate, the image appears to move in slow motion. On most video cameras, however, you can't increase their frame rate; instead, you must use a program such as Premiere Pro to create a slow-motion effect by repeating the existing frames. Because overcranked film captures a greater number of unique frames, the slow-motion image appears to be much smoother than a similar image created using a video effect, which merely duplicates frames.

PLAYING CLIPS AT A DIFFERENT SPEED

# Creating a Freeze Frame

Using the Frame Hold command, you can make any frame of a clip appear for the entire duration of the clip. Because the held frame is based on the clip's current In point, Out point, or zero marker, you can easily change the held frame. However, you have to be careful not to change the held frame inadvertently.

When you use Frame Hold, you may need to take extra steps to achieve certain effects. For example, if you want the frame to remain longer than the clip's full duration, you'll have to use more than one copy of the clip with the same Frame Hold effect applied. Creating what is commonly known as a *freeze frame*—playing the video at normal speed and then halting the motion and holding on that frame—also requires two copies of the clip. The Out point of the first clip must match the held frame of the second clip. Because a match-frame edit is undetectable, it appears as though a single clip plays and freezes on a frame.

If you find the way the Frame Hold command works too cumbersome, you can use a still image instead. Just export a frame as a still image file and import the still. See Chapter 15, "Creating Output," for more about exporting a frame of a sequence as a still image file.

## To use the Frame Hold command:

1. Select a clip in the Timeline window (**Figure 7.85**).

2. Choose Clip > Video Options > Frame Hold (**Figure 7.86**).

   The Frame Hold Options dialog box appears.

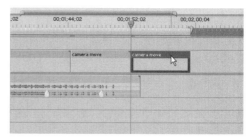

**Figure 7.85** Select a clip.

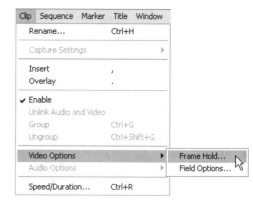

**Figure 7.86** Choose Clip > Video Options > Frame Hold.

CREATING A FREEZE FRAME

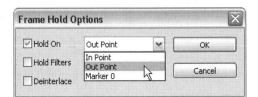

**Figure 7.87** In the Frame Hold Options dialog box, select Hold On and choose the frame you want to hold. Specify other options you want and click OK.

3. In the Frame Hold Options dialog box, select Hold On and choose an option from the drop-down menu (**Figure 7.87**):

   **In Point:** Displays the clip's current In point frame.

   **Out Point:** Displays the clip's current Out point frame.

   **Marker 0:** Displays the frame with marker 0, if present.

4. In the Frame Hold Options dialog box, select other options you want:

   **Hold Filters:** Uses any effect settings at the held frame; otherwise, keyframed effects animate.

   **Deinterlace:** Removes one field from an interlaced video frame and doubles the remaining field, to remove interlace artifacts (such as combing).

5. Click OK to close the dialog box.

   The specified frame appears for the duration of the clip. Changing the specified frame (In point, Out point, or zero marker) changes the held frame.

## ✔ Tips

- Speed changes, freeze frames, and other effects can sometimes result in *field artifacts*—defects in the image caused by the way that video fields (the alternating lines of every frame) are processed. For more about fields and field artifacts and how to solve field-related problems, see Chapter 16.

- If the freeze frame you want consists of more than one clip—the result of transparency and compositing techniques—you must either export the frame of the sequence as a still image or nest the sequence and apply the Frame Hold command to it.

# REFINING
# THE SEQUENCE

After you assemble a rough cut, you can refine it by making adjustments to the In and Out points of the clips in the sequence—a process known as *trimming*. Although you already know several ways to trim clips in the sequence, the techniques in this chapter will expand your repertoire.

Just as you assembled the sequence using a combination of overlay, insert, lift, and extract edits, you can rearrange and refine the clips in a sequence using comparable techniques, this time by dragging the sequence's clips in the Timeline window. You'll also learn various other ways to fine-tune edit points in the sequence, both by manipulating clips directly in the Timeline and by using a window optimized for trimming edits, called (appropriately enough) the Trim window. In addition, this chapter covers techniques that deal with the connection between the audio and video components of linked clips. You'll learn how to trim linked audio and video separately to accomplish a common editing technique known as a *split edit*, or *L cut*. You'll also find out how to break the link between video and audio so you can handle each component separately and, conversely, how to create a link between previously unrelated video and audio clips. And should linked video and audio inadvertently shift out of their synchronized relationship, you'll be able to detect and correct the problem.

# Using the Snapping Feature

When you move clips in the timeline, you usually want to align them precisely. In a sequence of clips in a single track, alignment generally isn't a problem: You can easily drag clips to butt up against one another without overlaying another clip or leaving a gap. At times, however, aligning clips isn't as straightforward. You may want a title in video track 2 to start right after the clip in track 1 ends, for example. When you're placing a sound effect, you may want to align a marker in a video clip with a marker in an audio clip. Or you may want to move a clip to exactly where you placed the CTI.

The timeline provides an easy way to align clips through a feature called *snapping*. When you activate snapping, clips behave as though they're magnetized; they tend to snap to the edge of another clip, to a marker, and to the CTI. A vertical line with black arrows, or *snap line*, confirms that elements are flush (**Figure 8.1**).

A red snap line indicates that the audio portions of the clips aren't flush. This can occur when the audio has been edited based on its sample rate but the timeline is set to count frames (see "Customizing the Time Ruler" in Chapter 7). For example, when the timeline is set to *audio units*, it's possible to cut or trim an audio clip to a point that doesn't coincide with a frame boundary. If you then attempt to snap one audio clip to another while the ruler is set to show frame divisions, the clip aligns with the frame boundary instead of the sample boundary—and leaves a gap in the audio track. The red snap line may also appear when you drag clips to the work area In and Out points, sequence markers, and sequence In and Out points (**Figure 8.2**).

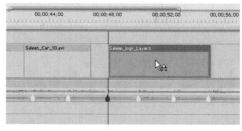

**Figure 8.1** When snapping is on, a vertical line appears when clips are aligned with edges, markers, or the CTI.

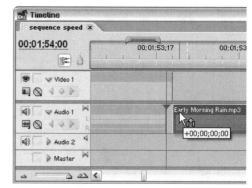

**Figure 8.2** A gap occurs in the audio track if the clip is dropped while the red snap line is displayed.

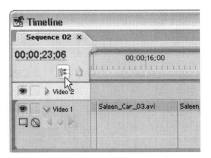

**Figure 8.3** In the Timeline window, click the Snap button (with the magnet icon) to toggle it on and off.

Snapping also works when you're trimming clips in the timeline. When snapping is off, clips move smoothly past one another as you drag them in the timeline. Because snapping is so convenient, you'll probably leave it on most of the time.

## To toggle snapping on and off:

◆ At the top left of the Timeline window, click the Snap button ▦ to toggle snapping on and off (**Figure 8.3**).

## ✔ Tips

■ When snapping is on, it's easy to use clip markers to cut video to the beat of music or to sync sound effects to video.

■ Occasionally, several edges may be so close together that snapping makes it difficult to place the clip properly. In these infrequent cases, you should zoom in to the timeline so that competing edges appear farther apart. Alternatively, you can turn off snapping and disable its magnetic effect.

■ By default, you can toggle snapping by pressing the S key. This feature works even while you're dragging a clip.

**USING THE SNAPPING FEATURE**

# Editing by Dragging

You can move clips in the timeline much as you rearrange clips of film: you can drag and move each clip almost as though it were a physical object. But, obviously, clips aren't bits of celluloid, so they aren't constrained by the laws of the physical world. In Premiere Pro, you aren't limited to rearranging clips like so many building blocks. Moving a clip from its current position performs a lift or extract edit; placing it somewhere new performs an overlay or insert edit. (For an explanation of overlay, insert, lift, and extract edits, see Chapter 6, "Creating a Sequence.")

To perform edits by dragging, you need to learn a simple set of *keyboard modifiers*, keys you press to toggle editing functions. You'll find that these modifiers work consistently throughout Premiere Pro—in fact, you've already applied them in earlier chapters.

Lift and overlay edits are accomplished by dragging and dropping. Add the Ctrl key to perform an extract or insert edit (**Figures 8.4** through **8.8**). Add Ctrl+Alt to perform an insert edit that shifts only clips in the destination tracks. The Ctrl+Alt combination is also called a *rearrange edit* or *recycle edit*; it offers a quick and easy way to swap the position of clips in a sequence.

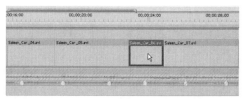

**Figure 8.4** This figure shows the sequence before the edit. The selected clip (Saleen_car_06) will be moved back in time.

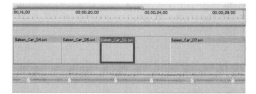

**Figure 8.5** The selection you made in Figure 8.4 has been lifted and dropped into its new position using an overlay edit.

**Figure 8.6** Here the selection has been extracted and overlayed...

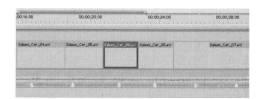

**Figure 8.7** ...lifted and inserted...

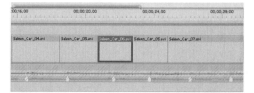

**Figure 8.8** ...and finally, extracted and inserted. In these examples, the audio track containing the soundtrack is locked to make extract edits possible (see the sidebar "Extraction Exception").

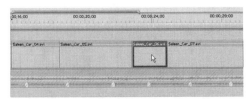

**Figure 8.9** Select the clips you want to move. You must make a selection first if you want to move multiple clips at once.

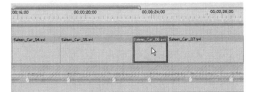

**Figure 8.10** Click and then drag a selection to lift it from its original position.

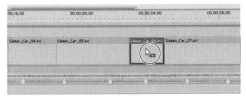

**Figure 8.11** Ctrl-click and then drag a selection to extract it. Note the extract icon and the pattern of slashes in audio 1, indicating that it is locked.

**Table 8.1**

### Editing by Dragging

| Function | Action | Icon |
|---|---|---|
| Lift | Drag | No icon |
| Extract | Ctrl-click+drag | |
| Overlay | Drop | |
| Insert | Ctrl-drop | |
| Rearrange/Recycle | Ctrl-Alt-drop | |

As you discovered in Chapter 6, an icon associated with each type of edit accompanies the mouse pointer, confirming that you're pressing the correct keys for the edit you want (**Table 8.1**). In addition, the Monitor window's program view provides helpful visual feedback, displaying the frames involved in the edit as you make it. And when you drag a clip in the timeline, a tool tip tells you how many frames the clip has traveled from its starting point.

As usual, if you want to limit the edit to either the video or audio portion of a linked clip, first Alt-click either the video or audio portion to select it; then perform the edit. Also, make sure you lock any tracks you don't want to shift as a result of an insert edit (or, to limit shifting to the destination tracks, use the Ctrl+Alt combo described earlier). Finally, there's one caveat when it comes to extracting; see the sidebar "Extraction Exception" later in this chapter.

## To perform an edit by dragging:

1. In the Timeline window, select one or more clips that you want to move (**Figure 8.9**).

   Alt-click the video or audio portion of a linked clip to affect only that part of the clip.

2. *Do one of the following:*
   - ▲ To lift the selection, click it and drag (**Figure 8.10**).
   - ▲ To extract the selection, Ctrl-click the selection before dragging it (**Figure 8.11**).

*continues on next page*

EDITING BY DRAGGING

**3.** Drag the clip to its new position, using the visual feedback in the program view as a reference (**Figure 8.12**).

You don't have to hold down any modifier keys as you drag.

**4.** *Do one of the following:*

▲ To overlay the selection, drop the clip at any point in an appropriate track (**Figure 8.13**).

▲ To insert the selection, Ctrl-drop the clip at any point in an appropriate track (**Figure 8.14**).

The selection is repositioned according to the methods you used. Insert edits shift all material in unlocked tracks by the duration of the selection, splitting clips if necessary (refer to Figures 8.4 through 8.8).

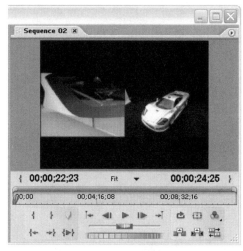

**Figure 8.12** The program view helps you position the clip by showing the frame preceding the selection on the left and the frame after the selection on the right.

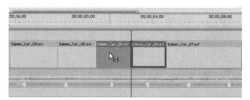

**Figure 8.13** Dropping the selection overlays it, as the icon indicates.

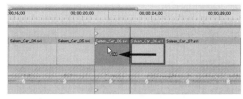

**Figure 8.14** Pressing Ctrl as you drop the selection inserts it in the new location. Again, note the icon and the pattern of slashes in the audio track, indicating that it is locked to prevent it from being split at the edit point.

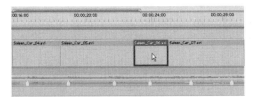

**Figure 8.15** Select the clips you want to move.

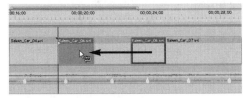

**Figure 8.16** Press Ctrl+Alt as you drop the selection in its new location. Note the icon.

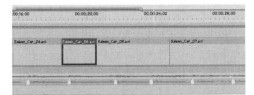

**Figure 8.17** The selection is extracted from its original position and inserted into its new position. Clips in other tracks are not affected, even in unlocked tracks. This figure illustrates how you can use a recycle edit to quickly exchange the order of clips—in this case, shots 5 and 6.

## To perform a recycle edit:

1. In the Timeline window, select one or more clips that you want to move (**Figure 8.15**).

    Alt-click the video or audio portion of a linked clip to affect only that part of the clip.

2. Click and drag the selection to its new position, using the visual feedback in the program view as a reference.

    You don't have to use a keyboard modifier until you're ready to drop the selection.

3. Press Ctrl+Alt so that the recycle icon appears and then drop the selection (**Figure 8.16**).

    The selection is extracted from its original position and inserted into its new position (**Figure 8.17**). The edit affects only material in the destination tracks. Because the extracted material and the inserted material are of equal duration, the total duration of the sequence remains the same.

## ✔ Tips

- You can change keyboard modifiers as you drag; just make sure you have the correct combination before you drop the clip.

- Versions of Premiere prior to Premiere Pro permitted much more limited building-block editing in the timeline. Users upgrading to Premiere Pro will quickly discover that its full-featured drag-and-drop editing model is superior to the older editing model.

**EDITING BY DRAGGING**

**241**

## Extraction Exception

Whereas inserting a clip splits clips in all unlocked tracks and shifts subsequent material forward, extracting a clip *won't* extract material in other tracks and shift subsequent material back.

A rearrange edit lets you extract insert in the destination tracks only. Similarly, you can extract overlay, but only if other tracks are empty, or if you first lock other tracks—otherwise, the edit will work like a lift overlay (**Figures 8.18** through **8.20**). To extract material from all tracks, you must perform additional edits, use different editing methods, or both.

The corollary to this behavior is that locking other tracks enables an extract edit but disables an insert edit from shifting clips in all tracks. Conversely, leaving other tracks unlocked disables an extract edit but enables insert edits to shift clips in all tracks.

Because there are plenty of ways to edit the clips in a sequence, this idiosyncrasy doesn't pose an unsolvable problem. Even so, many editors expect extract edits to work like the inverse of insert edits and would welcome more consistent behavior in a future release of Premiere Pro.

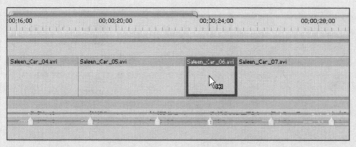

**Figure 8.18** This example is similar to the extract-overlay edit shown in Figures 8.4 and 8.6 except that in this figure, the audio track is left unlocked, which prevents an extract edit from working.

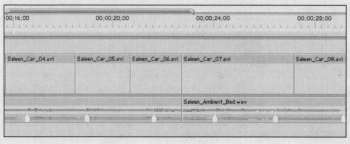

**Figure 8.19** If you could drag extract across all tracks, the edit would look like this.

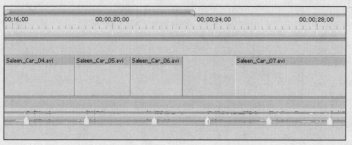

**Figure 8.20** Instead, the audio clip prevents the extract edit from working, resulting in a lift edit.

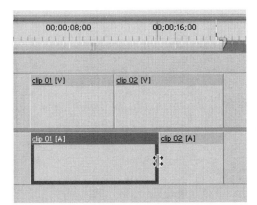

**Figure 8.21** You can trim clips in the timeline by dragging with the mouse...

**Figure 8.22** ...or you can trim clips using the Trim window.

## ✔ Tips

- Extending the duration of a clip is often referred to as *trimming out* the In or Out point; reducing the clip's duration is called *trimming in*.

- Because the Timeline window represents clips graphically, a clip's In and Out points are also called *edges*. The beginning of a clip is also known as the *head*, and the end is also known as the *tail*.

# Choosing a Trimming Method

Making an adjustment to a clip's In or Out point—particularly a small adjustment—is called *trimming*. You can trim a clip by manipulating it directly in the timeline or by using the Trim window. Although you can use either method to perform some editing tasks, each has unique features.

Trimming in the timeline relies on the mouse to move the edges of a program's clips, thereby changing their In or Out point (**Figure 8.21**). By selecting various tools, you can perform specialized trimming tasks known as ripple edits, rolling edits, and simple trimming. You can also slip or slide clips—something you can't accomplish in the Trim window.

Like all timeline editing, trimming in the timeline is graphically clear and intuitive. The precision of the edit, however, depends partly on the detail of your view of the timeline. Also, this kind of trimming doesn't permit you to preview the changes before you make them final.

Alternatively, you can open the Trim window, a specialized window designed for trimming clips in the sequence (**Figure 8.22**). Like trimming in the timeline, trimming in the Trim window lets you perform ripple edits and rolling edits. Although using the Trim window isn't as intuitive as editing directly in the timeline, the Trim window always gives you precise control. Trim view also provides a large view of the edit as you make adjustments and allows you to preview the changes.

Whether you trim in the timeline or in the Trim window, you can't extend a clip beyond the limits of its source media. When a clip's edge reaches the end of the source media, the top corner of that edge appears curved.

The following sections explain trimming techniques, first in the timeline and then in the Trim window.

# Trimming Clips in the Timeline

To perform simple trimming in the timeline, you don't need to select a special tool. The default tool, the Selection tool, automatically switches to a trim tool when you position it at a clip edge in the timeline.

Simple trimming affects only one edge of a single clip and won't affect adjacent clips. Trimming a clip in this way won't shift subsequent clips in time, nor will it allow you to extend the clip to overlay an adjacent clip. (You'll learn other techniques to accomplish these tasks later in this chapter.) In other words, shortening a clip leaves empty space behind; you can extend a clip only up to the edge of an adjacent clip (or to the beginning of the time ruler, or to the limit of the clip's source media).

The Monitor window's program view displays the edge frame as you trim. To gain more precise control, you can zoom in to the sequence before you start trimming.

### To trim a clip in the timeline:

1. Using the Selection tool ▶, *do one of the following:*
   - ▲ To trim the In point, position the pointer on the left edge of a clip in the timeline.

   The pointer becomes the Trim Head tool ⊹ (**Figure 8.23**).
   - ▲ To trim the Out point, position the pointer on the right edge of a clip in the timeline.

   The pointer becomes the Trim Tail tool ⊹ (**Figure 8.24**).

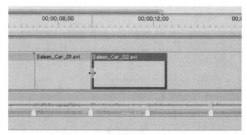

**Figure 8.23** Position the mouse at the left edge of the clip to trim its In point, or head...

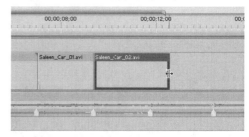

**Figure 8.24** ...or position the mouse at the right edge to trim the Out point, or tail.

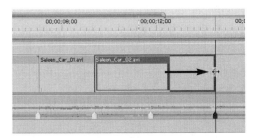

**Figure 8.25** Drag to shorten (trim in) or lengthen (trim out) the clip. In this figure, the clip's Out point is being dragged to the right to extend the clip's duration.

**2.** Drag to the left or right to change the clip's In or Out point (**Figure 8.25**).

The program view displays the edge frame (In point or Out point) as you adjust it.

When you release the mouse button, the clip's In or Out point changes.

## ✔ Tips

■ If snapping is on, edges snap to other edges, markers, or the CTI as you trim. This setting is often advantageous, but if it prevents you from trimming to the frame you want, turn off snapping. (See "Using the Snapping Feature" earlier in this chapter.)

■ When you place the mouse pointer near the edge of short clips that do not have adjacent clips in the timeline, the pointer changes to the trim icon. This makes it easier to work with short clips without zooming in on the timeline.

■ If you've internalized the pattern of keyboard modifiers, you've already guessed that pressing Ctrl changes the trimming tool to a ripple edit tool, which makes trimming work like an extract or insert edit (depending on which way you're trimming). Ripple editing is covered in the next section.

# Making Ripple and Rolling Edits

Whereas the basic trimming method affects only a single clip, ripple edits and rolling edits affect the cut point between clips. You might think of ripple and rolling edits as the trimming equivalents of insert and overlay edits, respectively. You can make rolling edits or ripple edits by using tools in the Timeline window or by using the Trim window.

In a *ripple edit,* you change the duration of one clip but don't affect the duration of the adjacent clips. After you ripple edit the edge of a clip, all subsequent clips shift in the timeline to compensate for the change, in a ripple effect. Therefore, the total length of the sequence changes.

In a *rolling edit,* you change the Out point of one clip while you change the In point of the adjacent clip. Put another way, you make one clip shorter while you make the adjacent clip longer; one clip rolls out while the other rolls in. Because both edges are trimmed by the same amount, the total length of the sequence remains the same.

The program view displays the frames of the changed cut as you perform a ripple or rolling edit.

## ✔ Tip

■ Because overlay edits are the default (and don't require a keyboard modifier), earlier sections covered overlay edits first and then insert edits. Technically, rolling edits and slide edits are derived from overlay edits; ripple edits and slip edits are descended from insert edits. Even so, the following sections cover the insert family first and then the overlay family— *ripple and roll* and *slip and slide* are catchier and easier to remember than saying them the other way around.

**Figure 8.26** Select the Ripple Edit tool.

## To perform a ripple edit in the timeline:

1. In the Tools window, select the Ripple Edit tool ⬌ (**Figure 8.26**).

2. *Do one of the following:*
   ▲ To ripple edit an In point, position the mouse over the left edge (In point) of a clip in the timeline.

   The pointer becomes the Ripple Edit In tool ⬌ (**Figure 8.27**).

   ▲ To ripple edit an Out point, position the mouse over the right edge (Out point) of a clip in the timeline.

   The pointer becomes the Ripple Edit Out tool ⬌ (**Figure 8.28**).

3. Drag to the left or right to trim the clip's edge.

   The subsequent clips shift in the timeline by the number of frames you trimmed (**Figure 8.29**).

**Figure 8.27** Position the mouse over a clip's left edge to ripple edit its In point...

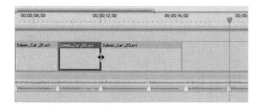

**Figure 8.28** ...or position the mouse over a clip's right edge to ripple edit its Out point.

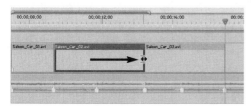

**Figure 8.29** In this example, a ripple edit has been used to extend the duration of the clip and shift subsequent clips later in time.

MAKING RIPPLE AND ROLLING EDITS

## To perform a rolling edit in the timeline:

1. In the Tools window, select the Rolling Edit tool ⊞ (**Figure 8.30**).

2. Position the pointer between the two adjacent clips you want to change.

   The pointer becomes the Rolling Edit tool ⊞ (**Figure 8.31**). Blank space in the track can also act as one of the clips, but this method is then functionally equivalent to using the basic trimming method.

3. Drag to the left or right to trim the Out point of the first clip and the In point of the second clip by the same number of frames (**Figure 8.32**).

   The program view displays the edge frames as you perform the rolling edit.

### ✔ Tips

- You can use a rolling edit to adjust the point at which you split a clip with the razor. If you weren't precise when you split the clip, use the Rolling Edit tool to move the cut point to the left or right.

- You can make a rolling or ripple edit between a clip and an empty space (or gap) in the track. The gap will function like another clip.

**Figure 8.30** Select the Rolling Edit tool.

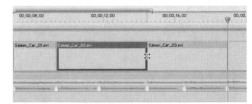

**Figure 8.31** Position the mouse between two clips so that the rolling edit icon appears.

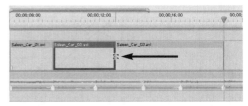

**Figure 8.32** A rolling edit trims the Out point of the first clip and the In point of the second clip by the same amount, effectively moving the edit point. In this example, the cut from Figure 8.31 has been moved back in time.

**Figure 8.33** Notice how the frames of the center clip look before a slip edit. This figure uses numbers to represent image frames and better illustrate the effect.

**Figure 8.34** Dragging the center clip with the Slip Edit tool changes its In and Out points simultaneously, maintaining its duration.

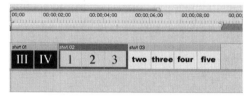

**Figure 8.35** A slide edit retains the In and Out points of the center clip while changing the In point of the preceding clip and the In point of the following clip.

# Making Slip and Slide Edits

When you have three clips side by side in the timeline, you can perform specialized editing techniques called slip edits and slide edits. Slip and slide edits could be described as ways to adjust two edit points simultaneously, but they're much easier to understand visually, by watching them in action in the Timeline window. This may explain why these edits can be accomplished only in the Timeline window and not in the Trim window.

In a *slip edit,* you change both the In point and the Out point of a clip at the same time without altering the adjacent clips. It's as if you're viewing part of the clip through a space between the two other clips; when you slip the center clip back and forth, you get to see a different part (**Figures 8.33** and **8.34**).

In a *slide edit,* the clip's In and Out points remain the same as you shift the clip in the timeline. When you drag, or slide, the clip to the left, the preceding clip gets shorter, and the following clip gets longer. When you slide the clip to the right, the preceding clip gets longer, and the following clip gets shorter (**Figure 8.35**).

## To slip a clip:

1. In the Tools window, select the Slip Edit tool  (**Figure 8.36**).

2. Position the pointer on a clip that's between two other clips in a track of the timeline.

   The mouse pointer changes to the slip edit icon.

3. Drag left or right to change the clip's In and Out points without changing the clip's duration or position in the timeline (**Figure 8.37**).

   The program view displays the frames at the edit points of the slip edit and reports the number of frames by which you're shifting the clip (**Figure 8.38**).

**Figure 8.36** Select the Slip Edit tool.

**Figure 8.37** Drag a clip positioned between two clips to perform a slide edit.

**Figure 8.38** The program view displays the frames affected by the slip edit.

**Figure 8.39** Select the Slide Edit tool.

## To slide a clip:

1. In the Tools window, select the Slide Edit tool ⊕ (**Figure 8.39**).

2. Position the pointer on a clip that's between two other clips in the timeline.

   The pointer changes to the slide edit icon ⟷.

3. Drag right or left to shift the clip in the timeline (**Figure 8.40**).

   The program view displays the frames at the edit points of the slide edit and reports the number of frames by which you're shifting the clip (**Figure 8.41**).

**Figure 8.40** Drag a clip positioned between two clips to perform a slide edit.

**Figure 8.41** The program view displays the frames affected by the slide edit.

# Using the Trim Window

To some extent, the current scale of the time ruler determines the precision of the edits you make in the Timeline window: the closer you're zoomed in, the easier it is to make precise adjustments. When your work is focused on fine-tuning edits, however, you should take advantage of a window optimized for trimming tasks: the aptly named Trim window. Like the Monitor window, the Trim window has two views. But instead of a source view and a program view, the Trim window shows two adjacent clips in the sequence. The Out point of the first clip appears on the left; the In point of the second clip appears on the right. An array of controls allows you to perform precise ripple and rolling edits.

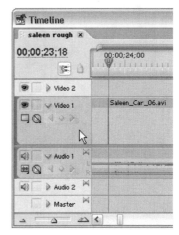

**Figure 8.42** Target the tracks containing the clips you want to trim.

Although you can perform the same edits in the timeline, the Trim window has several unique advantages. In the Trim window, you can see both sides of the edit in a large window and trim them with numerical precision. Also, the Trim window lets you play back the adjusted edit before you finalize it.

## To prepare to edit in the Trim window:

1. In the Timeline window, specify the target tracks by clicking the tracks' header areas.

   The header areas of targeted tracks appear darker than those of other tracks (**Figure 8.42**).

2. Cue the CTI to an edit point by *doing one of the following*:

   ▲ In the Timeline window, position the edit line (the program's current time) on or before the cut you want to trim and open the Trim window.

   If the edit line isn't positioned on a cut point, trim mode cues to the next cut in the timeline.

**Figure 8.43** In the Monitor window, click the Trim button.

*Outgoing Out point (first clip's Out point)*    *Incoming In point (second clip's In point)*

**Figure 8.44** The Trim window opens. The frame to the left of the edit point appears on the left; the frame to the right of the edit point appears on the right.

*Blue bar indicates active view*    *Ripple Out point icon*

*Out Shift time display*    *Out point icon*

*Outgoing Out point time*    *Left Jog Disk control*

**Figure 8.45** Click a view's image to make it active for ripple editing with numerical trim buttons, or drag its image or other controls to apply a ripple edit. This figure shows a ripple edit being applied to the left view (Out point of the first clip); use corresponding controls to ripple edit the right view (In point of the second clip).

▲ In the Trim window, click the Previous Edit button ⊩ or the Next Edit button ⊪.

If you alter an edit in the Trim window, the changes are finalized by cueing to another cut point.

3. To open the Trim window, *do one of the following:*

   ▲ In the program view controls, click the Trim button ⊞ (**Figure 8.43**).

   ▲ Press Ctrl+T.

   The Trim window opens (**Figure 8.44**). In a typical editing workspace, the Trim window opens directly over the Monitor window.

## To perform a ripple edit numerically in the Trim window:

1. In the Trim window, *do one of the following:*

   ▲ To trim the first clip's Out point, click the image on the left (**Figure 8.45**).

   ▲ To trim the In point of the second clip, click the image on the right.

   Blue bars appear above the active image.

2. To trim frames in the active view, *do one of the following:*

   ▲ Click the Trim Back One Frame button -1 to trim one frame to the left (earlier in time).

   ▲ Click the Trim Back by Large Trim Offset button -5 to trim several frames to the left (earlier in time).

   ▲ Click the Trim Forward One Frame button +1 to trim one frame to the right (later in time).

   ▲ Click the Trim Forward by Large Trim Offset button +5 to trim several frames to the right (later in time).

   ▲ Click the Out Shift or In Shift time display, type a relative or absolute time to trim that view, and press Enter.

*continues on next page*

**USING THE TRIM WINDOW**

As you trim frames, the number of trimmed frames appears in the Out Shift field or the In Shift field. Trimming to the left subtracts from an Out point or adds to an In point. Trimming to the right adds to an Out point or subtracts from an In point. You can see the effects in the timeline.

### To perform a ripple edit in the Trim window by dragging:

◆ In the Trim window, *do one of the following:*

▲ Position the mouse pointer in the view you want to trim so that a ripple edit icon (◀▌ or ▐▶) appears; then drag left or right.

▲ Drag the Jog Disk control below the view you want to trim.

▲ Drag the Out point icon in the left view's time ruler or the In point icon in the right view's time ruler.

▲ Drag the Out Shift or In Shift time display left or right.

As you trim frames, the number of trimmed frames appears in the Out Shift field or the In Shift field. Trimming to the left subtracts from an Out point or adds to an In point. Trimming to the right adds to an Out point or subtracts from an In point. You can see the effects in the timeline.

### To perform a rolling edit numerically in the Trim window:

1. In the Trim window, click between the two views.

   Blue bars appear above and below both views.

2. To trim frames in both views, *do one of the following:*

   ▲ Click the Trim Back One Frame button ◄-1 to trim one frame to the left.

_Rolling edit icon_

_Edit point position_          _Center Jog Disk control_

**Figure 8.46** Click between the images to activate both views and apply a rolling edit using numerical trim buttons. You can also drag between the views or use the center trimming controls to apply a rolling edit.

▲ Click the Trim Back by Large Trim Offset button `-5` to trim several frames to the left.

▲ Click the Trim Forward One Frame button `+1` to trim one frame to the right.

▲ Click the Trim Forward by Large Trim Offset button `+5` to trim several frames to the right.

▲ Highlight the roll edit display, type a positive number to move the edit forward in time or a negative number to move the edit back in time, and then press Enter.

▲ Click the Edit Point Position time display (the center time display), type a relative or absolute time to move the edit in time, and then press Enter.

As you trim frames, the number of trimmed frames appears in the Out Shift and In Shift fields. A rolling edit moves both the In Shift and Out Shift values by the same amount (**Figure 8.46**). Trimming to the left moves the cut earlier in time; trimming to the right moves the cut later in time. You can see your changes in the timeline.

## To perform a rolling edit in the Trim window by dragging:

◆ In the Trim window, *do one of the following:*

▲ Place the pointer between the two views so that the pointer becomes the rolling edit icon ⟷ and then drag left or right.

▲ Drag the Edit Point Position time display to the left or right.

▲ Drag the center Jog Disk control left or right.

As you trim frames, the number of trimmed frames appears in the Out Shift and In Shift fields. A rolling edit moves both the In Shift and Out Shift values by the same amount. Trimming to the left moves the cut earlier in time; trimming to the right moves the cut later in time. You can see your changes in the timeline.

## ✔ Tips

■ By default, the multiframe trim buttons ( -5 and +5 ) trim 5 frames or 100 audio samples. However, you can change this amount by choosing Edit > Preferences > Trim and entering a new value for the large trim offset.

■ In the Trim window, you can switch between ripple and rolling edits before you apply the edit.

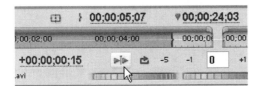

**Figure 8.47** Clicking the Play button plays the edit.

# Previewing and Applying Edits in the Trim Window

After you've made your adjustments in the Trim window, you can play them back—complete with audio and transitions—before you finalize your changes. After you look at your handiwork, you can use the Previous Edit or Next Edit button to trim other edits, or you can close the Trim window and resume other editing tasks. If you don't like what you've done, you can undo your actions as usual. Using the Undo command closes the Trim window and cancels the most recent trim. Choose Undo again or use the History palette to cancel previous edits.

### To preview the edit in the Trim window:

◆ *Do one of the following:*
   ▲ Click the Play Edit button ▶▏▶ (**Figure 8.47**).
   ▲ Press the spacebar.
   To loop the edit, click the Loop button 🔁 and click the Play Edit button or press the spacebar.
   The Trim window shows a single image and plays a short segment of the sequence that includes the edit. The preroll and postroll times (specified on the General panel of the Preferences dialog box) determine the duration of the segment.

### To apply the trimmed edit and trim other edits:

◆ In the Trim window, *do one of the following:*
   ▲ To trim the next edit in a selected track of the timeline, click the Next Edit button.
   ▲ To trim the previous cut in a selected track of the timeline, click the Previous Edit button.
   The current frame of the program (CTI) is cued to the next or previous cut, which is displayed in the Trim window. Trim the cut as usual.

# Working with Links

As you learned in earlier chapters, a linked clip contains both video and audio. Although the video and audio portions of the clip appear in different tracks of the timeline, a link between the two portions of the clip helps maintain their synchronized relationship. (See "Using Linked Clips" in Chapter 7.)

At times, however, you want to manipulate the two parts of a linked clip separately. For example, you may want to employ a traditional editing technique called the split edit (also known as L-cuts and J-cuts). Or you may want to break the link altogether, so you can manipulate the video and audio independently. Sometimes you may want to create a link between audio and video clips that weren't captured together—in film production, for example, the image and sound are recorded separately; after they're digitized, you can create a link to synchronize the two elements in the timeline.

The following sections describe how to manipulate linked clips in the timeline.

**Figure 8.48** Select the Rolling Edit tool.

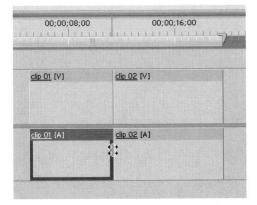

**Figure 8.49** Alt-click and then drag with the Rolling Edit tool...

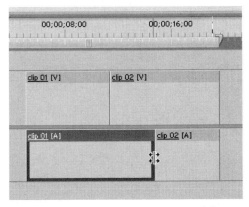

**Figure 8.50** ...to create a split edit with linked clips.

# Creating Split Edits

In a split edit, or L-cut, the video and audio have different In points or Out points. A dialogue scene serves as a good example. First you see and hear a person talking, with the video and audio in sync. Then you hear the person's voice but see the person being addressed; in this case, the video Out point occurs earlier than the audio Out point, and in the timeline, the video and audio form an L shape—hence the name *L-cut.* (When the situation is reversed, it's sometimes called a *J-cut.*) Split edits are a great way to make your edits feel much smoother. Watch a movie closely, and you'll find that split edits far outnumber *straight cuts,* in which the video and audio share the same In and Out points.

By now, you know numerous ways to create a split edit. The following tasks outline a few ways to create a split edit from a straight cut in the timeline.

### To split edit clips in the timeline:

1. In the Tools window, select the Rolling Edit tool ⁕ (**Figure 8.48**).

2. Position the Rolling Edit tool between two clips in the timeline in either the video or audio track and Alt-click (**Figure 8.49**).

3. Drag to perform a rolling edit in the audio without editing the corresponding video, or vice versa.

   The In and Out points in the video track now differ from those in the audio track (**Figure 8.50**).

## To split edit clips using the Trim window:

1. In the Timeline window, target either a video or an audio track.

2. In the Timeline window, lock the linked track you don't want to affect (**Figure 8.51**).

   If you targeted video, lock the audio track that contains the linked audio; if you targeted audio, lock the video track that contains the linked video.

3. In the Trim window, cue the CTI to the cut you want to trim.

4. To use the numerical trim buttons, make sure both views are active by clicking between the views.

   Blue bars appear above and below both views.

5. In the Trim window, *do one of the following:*

   ▲ Click the Trim Back One Frame button `-1` to trim one frame to the left (earlier in time).

   ▲ Click the Trim Back by Large Trim Offset button `-5` to trim several frames to the left (earlier in time).

   ▲ Click the Trim Forward One Frame button `+1` to trim one frame to the right (later in time).

   ▲ Click the Trim Forward by Large Trim Offset `+5` to trim several frames to the right (later in time).

   ▲ Click the Out Shift or In Shift time display, type a relative or absolute time to trim that view, and press Enter.

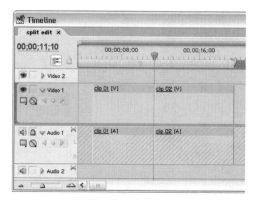

**Figure 8.51** In the Timeline window, target the track that contains the clip you want to trim and lock the track that contains the linked counterpart.

**Figure 8.52** In the Trim window, perform a rolling edit. This figure shows a rolling edit performed by dragging between the two views.

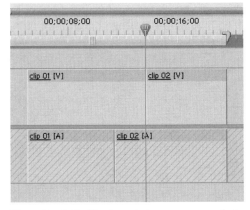

**Figure 8.53** In the Timeline window, you can see that the cut point in the target track changes while the cut point in the locked track remains fixed—creating a split edit.

▲ Place the pointer between the two views so that the pointer becomes the rolling edit icon ⁇ and then drag left or right (**Figure 8.52**).

▲ Drag the Edit Point Position time display to the left or right.

▲ Drag the center Jog Disk control left or right.

The cut point in the unlocked track changes while the cut point in the locked track remains fixed, creating a split edit (**Figure 8.53**).

## ✔ Tips

■ Unless you're sure you know what you're doing, don't use a ripple edit to create a split edit. Ripple edits cause clips to shift, and only the selected tracks will shift, causing linked clips to lose sync.

■ As you've seen, using the Trim window to create split edits in linked clips requires what seems to be an unnecessary extra step: locking the track you don't want to trim. Perhaps in future versions, Adobe will streamline the procedure so that specifying a single target track will be sufficient to limit trimming to that track.

# Breaking and Creating Links

You can break or create links in the timeline, but the links of the source clips and their associated media files on the drive remain unaffected.

## To unlink audio and video:

1. In the timeline, select a linked clip.

   Both the video and audio tracks of the linked clip are selected (**Figure 8.54**).

2. Choose Clip > Unlink Audio and Video (**Figure 8.55**).

   The video and audio portions unlink, becoming two independent clips. In the Timeline window, the names of the clips are no longer underlined, and they don't include *[V]* or *[A]* (**Figure 8.56**).

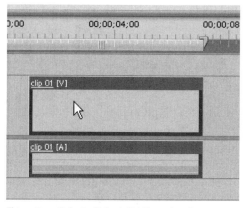

**Figure 8.54** Select a linked clip. Note that the name of the video portion contains *[V]* and the name of the audio portion contains *[A]*, and that both names are underlined.

**Figure 8.55** Choose Clip > Unlink Audio and Video.

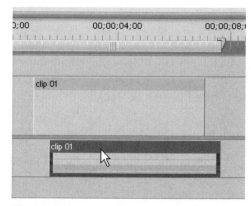

**Figure 8.56** The video and audio are unlinked. The names are no longer underlined and don't contain *[V]* or *[A]*.

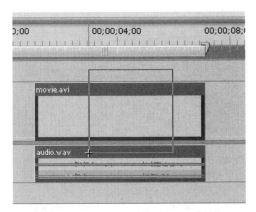

**Figure 8.57** Arrange a video clip and an audio clip to establish their synchronized relationship and then select them.

**Figure 8.58** Choose Clip > Link Audio and Video.

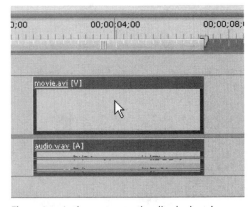

**Figure 8.59** In the sequence, the clips look and behave like a single linked clip.

## To link a video clip and an audio clip:

**1.** In the Timeline window, arrange a video clip and an audio clip to establish their relative positions in time.

**2.** Select the video clip and the audio clip (**Figure 8.57**).

**3.** Choose Clip > Link Audio and Video (**Figure 8.58**).

The video and audio clips behave like a linked clip. In the Timeline window, the names of the video and audio portions are underlined; *[V]* is appended to the name of the video portion, and *[A]* is appended to the name of the audio portion (**Figure 8.59**).

## ✔ Tip

■ You can use the Link Audio and Video command to sync film footage with audio. Mark the frame in the video where the slate (clapper board) closes, mark the sound of the slate mark in the audio, align the marks, and link the clips. If the shot doesn't contain a slate, you can use some other visible source of a hard, percussive sound as the sync point.

# Keeping Sync

During the course of editing, you may inadvertently lose sync between linked video and audio. Fortunately, Premiere Pro alerts you when linked clips are out of sync, and it provides a simple way to correct the problem.

### To detect loss of sync:

◆ Look at the left edge of linked video and audio.

A timecode number appears at the left edge of linked video and audio that are out of sync (**Figure 8.60**).

### To restore sync automatically:

◆ Context-click the out-of-sync time display in either the video or audio portion of the clip and choose an option (**Figure 8.61**):

**Move into Sync:** Shifts the selected portion of the clip in time to restore sync, overwriting other clips if necessary (**Figure 8.62**).

**Slip into Sync:** Performs a slip edit on the selected portion of the clip to restore sync (**Figure 8.63**).

If the track has space available, the clip shifts in the timeline to resynchronize with the linked portion. If it doesn't, you'll have to create space in the track before resynching the clips.

For more information about slip edits, see "Making Slip and Slide Edits" earlier in this chapter.

### ✔ Tip

■ Avoid loss of sync by locking tracks that shouldn't be moved, creating a link between clips that require a synchronized relationship and using clip markers as sync marks that you can use to check alignment visually. Finally, when you're creating a split edit, use a rolling edit rather than a ripple edit.

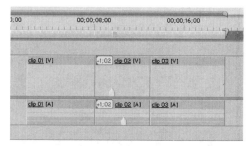

**Figure 8.60** A number indicates the amount that linked video and audio have shifted out of sync.

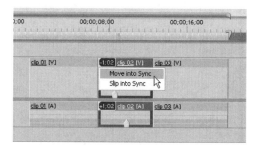

**Figure 8.61** Context-click the number and choose an option.

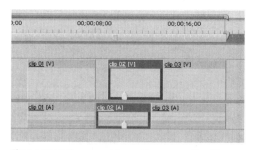

**Figure 8.62** When you release the mouse, the clips move into sync.

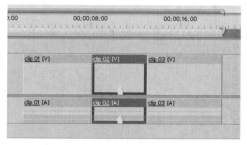

**Figure 8.63** When you release the mouse, the clips slip into sync.

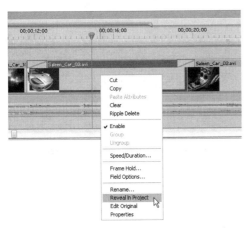

**Figure 8.64** Context-click a clip and choose Reveal in Project.

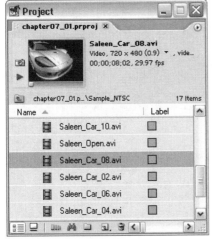

**Figure 8.65** The sequence clip's associated source clip appears highlighted in the Project window.

# Finding Source Clips

As you edit in the timeline, you may want to reexamine the source of a clip in a sequence. The source clip may contain another take of the shot or other footage you want to use, for example. But as you know, trimming the clip in the timeline would disturb your current edit, and double-clicking the clip in question would allow you to view only the clip instance in the source view, not the source clip. Fortunately, you can view the source clip associated with a sequence clip quickly and easily, without having to search through your project.

### To find a sequence clip's source:

◆ Context-click a clip in the timeline and choose Reveal in Project from the menu (**Figure 8.64**).

The sequence clip's associated source clip is highlighted in the Project window (**Figure 8.65**).

# Finding the Match Frame

Experienced editors may wonder whether Premiere Pro has a *match-frame* feature. This feature not only opens a program clip's associated source clip but also cues the source view's CTI to the identical frame in the sequence. In other words, by cueing the CTI in the program, you can find the matching frame in the appropriate master clip.

**Figure 8.66** Cue the sequence's CTI to the frame you want to match.

## To find a sequence clip's match frame:

1. Cue the sequence to the frame for which you want to find a match frame (**Figure 8.66**).

2. Press T.

   The master clip appears in the source view (**Figure 8.67**) and is cued to the match frame.

## ✔ Tip

■ After you find the match frame, you can keep the source clip and the sequence synchronized by ganging them together. See "Ganging the Source and Program Views" in Chapter 5.

**Figure 8.67** Pressing T opens the source clip to the matching frame in the source view.

---

## Syncing Up

If clicking the out-of-sync time display isn't a practical way to resynchronize your clips, you can use many other techniques to solve the problem:

◆ Alt-click to select the video or audio only and then move it into sync.

◆ Alt-click the video or audio portion of a linked clip with the Slip or Slide tool and then drag it into sync.

◆ Use the Track tool to shift all the clips in a track back into sync.

◆ Insert edit the proper number of frames, making sure to shift only the out-of-sync track.

◆ Open the source clip and edit it into the sequence again.

# Adding
# Transitions

In editing, *transition* refers to the way one clip replaces another. Although the cut is the most basic transition, the term *transition* usually refers to a more gradual change from one clip to another. Adobe Premiere Pro ships with 74 customizable video transitions, including an array of dissolves, wipes, and special effects. You can also transition between audio clips using two types of cross-fade.

You select the transition you want from the *Effects palette*, which lists not only video and audio transitions, but also video and audio filters (including transparency keys) in categorized folders.

Adding a transition is as simple as dragging it to a cut in the Timeline window. You can even make adjustments to a transition's duration and placement by dragging the transition in the Timeline window, in much the same way you can move and trim a clip. But to really fine-tune a transition, you use the *Effect Controls palette*. The main area of the Effect Controls palette describes the effect and includes an animated thumbnail demonstration. It also lets you control attributes common to all transitions—duration and placement—as well as settings specific to the particular transition. The Effect Controls palette may also include an area that illustrates the selected transition in an *A/B roll* style of timeline, which depicts the transition between two overlapping clips. This alternative view of a transition can be easier to understand and adjust than the Timeline window's version.

As you may have guessed, you also use both the Effects palette and Effect Controls palette to add and adjust other types of effects—including motion, transparency, and filters. These techniques are covered in upcoming chapters. This chapter explains how to create and modify transitions, and Chapter 10, "Previewing a Sequence," describes how to render them for playback.

# Using the Effects Palette

The Effects palette lists and organizes all effects, including audio and video transitions. You can open the Effects palette in a separate window, or it can share the Project window as a tab.

By default, the Effects palette contains five folders: Presets, Audio Effects, Audio Transitions, Video Effects, and Video Transitions. You can't rename these folders or remove items from them. However, you can add and name custom folders, which can contain copies of your favorite items. You can expand a folder to reveal its contents, but you can't open a folder the way you can open a bin in the Project window. The Video Transitions folder includes 10 subfolders; the Audio Transitions folder contains 1 subfolder. Video transitions appear as ◼ icons; audio transitions appear as ◼ icons.

The number and type of effects and transitions available on the Effects palette are determined by the contents of Premiere Pro's Plug-Ins folder. You can add effects and filters from Adobe and third-party developers by adding plug-in files to the Plug-Ins folder.

### To open the Effects palette:

◆ Choose Window > Effects (**Figure 9.1**).

The Effects palette either appears in a separate window or becomes the frontmost tab in the Project window (**Figure 9.2**).

### To use the Effects palette as a tab:

◆ Drag the Effects palette to the Project window to add the palette to the window (**Figure 9.3**).

Click the Effects tab to bring the Effects palette to the front of the window.

**Figure 9.1** Choose Window > Effects.

**Figure 9.2** The Effects palette can appear in its own window...

**Figure 9.3** ...or you can drag it into the Project window.

**Figure 9.4** Click the triangle to expand or collapse a folder.

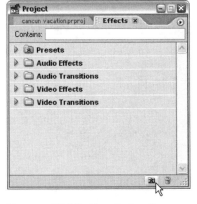

**Figure 9.5** Click the New Custom Bin button.

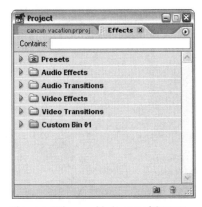

**Figure 9.6** The new bin is named Custom Bin 01 by default.

## To expand and collapse folders:

◆ On the Effects palette, click the triangle next to a folder to expand or collapse it (**Figure 9.4**).

A folder expands to reveal subfolders; a subfolder expands to reveal individual effects or transitions. Double-clicking a folder has no effect.

## To create a custom folder:

◆ On the Effects palette, click the New Custom Bin button 🗔 (**Figure 9.5**).

A new custom folder appears on the Effects palette; the folder is named Custom Bin 01 by default (**Figure 9.6**).

**USING THE EFFECTS PALETTE**

## To rename a custom folder:

1. Click the name of the custom folder and then click again (don't double-click) to highlight the name.

2. Type the name you want (**Figure 9.7**) and press Enter.

   You can rename only custom folders.

## To add items to a custom folder:

1. Expand the folders containing the items you want to copy into a custom folder.

2. Select the items you want to copy *by doing one of the following:*

   ▲ Click to select an item.

   ▲ Ctrl-click to add to or subtract from the selection.

   You can't drag a marquee to select items on the Effects palette.

3. Drag the selected items to the custom folder (**Figures 9.8** and **9.9**).

   The selected items appear in the custom folder. Dragging a folder into the custom folder copies all of the folder's contents into the custom folder. A custom folder can contain other custom folders.

**Figure 9.7** Click the custom folder's name twice to highlight it and then enter a new name.

**Figure 9.8** Dragging items into a custom folder...

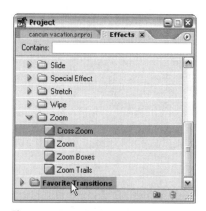

**Figure 9.9** ...copies them into the folder.

Figure 9.10 Select the items you want to remove from a custom folder and click the Effect palette's trashcan icon...

Figure 9.11 ...to remove the items from the list.

Figure 9.12 As you type the name of the item you're looking for in the Contains field, the list is sifted to show only matching items.

## To delete custom items:

1. *Do one of the following:*
   - ▲ Click to select a custom folder or an item contained in a custom folder.
   - ▲ Ctrl-click to add items to or subtract items from your selection.

2. Click the Effects palette's Delete Custom Items button ⬛ (**Figure 9.10**).

   The selected custom items are removed from the Effects palette (**Figure 9.11**).

## Finding an item on the Effects palette:

- ◆ On the Effects palette, in the Contains field, type the name of the item you're looking for (**Figure 9.12**).

   As you type, the palette displays items that match what you type and hides other items. To unsift the list, clear the Contains field.

## ✔ Tip

- ◼ Even though icons for folders on the Effects palette look like the icons for bins in the Project window (and the palette includes a Create Custom Bin button), this book refers to effect folders as *folders* rather than *bins*.

# Understanding Transitions

If you're an experienced editor and already know the concepts behind transitions, feel free to skip ahead to the tasks (cut to the chase, as the old editing expression goes). But if you're new to editing—or new to the single-track transition model used in Premiere Pro—the inner workings of transitions can seem a little mysterious at first.

When you cut from one clip to another, the transition is instantaneous. The Out point of the first clip is immediately followed by the In point of the second clip. To switch from one clip to another more gradually, however, transitions must use frames *beyond* the cut point. In other words, the transition must mix some of the frames you previously trimmed away: frames after the first clip's Out point, before the second clip's In point, or, most often, a combination of both. (Remember: because editing in Premiere Pro is nondestructive, the frames you trimmed away are always available for use.)

But in the Timeline window, these frames are hidden from view. When the track is collapsed, you can see only when the transition begins and ends (**Figure 9.13**). When the track is expanded, you can see the former cut point between the clips and thereby the transition's position relative to the cut (**Figure 9.14**), but you can't tell how much footage lies beyond the cut transition, and therefore how much footage is available for making adjustments. For many editors, this layout makes it difficult to plan for the transition beforehand and to adjust it afterward.

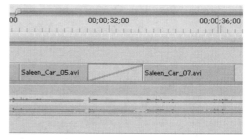

**Figure 9.13** In a collapsed track, you can see only the transition's duration...

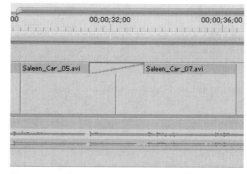

**Figure 9.14** ...but in an expanded track, you can also see the transition's position relative to the cut. Neither view shows how much footage each clip has beyond the cut point.

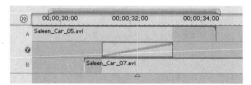

**Figure 9.15** Here's the same transition in the Effect Controls window's timeline view. The A/B roll layout lets you see the footage hidden in the Timeline window's single-track layout.

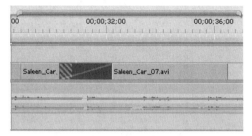

**Figure 9.16** When there isn't enough footage for the transition, Premiere Pro repeats the edge frames. Premiere Pro marks the area with a pattern of slashes on the transition in the Timeline window...

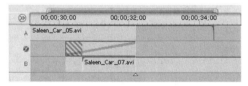

**Figure 9.17** ...and in the Effect Controls window's timeline view.

Transitions are depicted more explicitly on the Effect Controls palette. In the Effect Controls palette's Timeline view, each clip occupies a separate track—the first in track A, the second in track B. The transition appears between the two clips in its own track (labeled with an effect icon). As usual, the area where the transition overlaps the clips represents the duration of the transition's effect. A vertical line represents the cut point before the transition was applied. But because this view shows each clip in its own track, you can see the otherwise hidden material beyond the cut point—all the available material beyond the first clip's Out point and before the second clip's In point. This view allows you to adjust the transition not only relative to the cut point, but also in terms of the footage available in each clip (**Figure 9.15**).

If there isn't enough footage to create the transition, Premiere Pro repeats the first clip's Out point frame or the second clip's In point frame. Of course, repeating frames results in a freeze-frame effect that you may find unacceptable. You can adjust the transition or trim the clips to avoid repeating frames, which are marked with a pattern of slashes (**Figures 9.16** and **9.17**). (See "Adjusting a Transition's Duration and Alignment" later in this chapter.)

## ✔ Tip

- Beginning with Premiere Pro 1.5, a Dip to Black transition is provided in the Dissolve subfolder. It is no longer necessary to fade a black video clip in and out to achieve a simple dip to black (dissolve to black and dissolve from black). You can place this transition in between two clips or use it at the edge of a clip to fade in or fade out.

UNDERSTANDING TRANSITIONS

# Understanding Transition Duration and Alignment

In the Timeline window, transitions appear as clip-like objects whose width and position correspond with their duration and alignment (relative to the cut point). Once you add a transition, you can adjust its duration and alignment freely. However, its initial settings are more limited. A transition's initial duration is determined by a default setting you specify; its initial alignment is limited to three options, depending on where you drop it relative to the cut: Center of Cut, Start of Cut, or End of Cut. Understanding these options makes it easier to plan for a transition beforehand and to adjust it afterward:

**Center of Cut:** Centers the transition over the cut so that an equal number of hidden frames on both sides of the edit are used to create the transition. A one-second transition centered on the cut would use 15 frames of footage after the Out point of footage of the first clip and 15 frames before the In point of the second clip (**Figure 9.18**).

**Start of Cut:** Starts the transition at the cut, so that the hidden frames of the first clip are combined with the frames of the second clip that were visible before the transition was applied. Using the same example as before, the transition would combine 30 frames of footage after the first clip's Out point (hidden frames) with the first 30 frames of the second clip (**Figure 9.19**).

**End of Cut:** Ends the transition at the cut, so that the hidden frames of the second clip are combined with the frames of the first clip that were visible before you added the transition. Continuing the same example, the transition would combine the last 30 frames of the first clip with 30 frames of the footage before the second clip's In point (hidden frames) (**Figure 9.20**).

**Figure 9.18** When a one-second transition is centered on the cut, it looks like this in the Effect Controls window.

**Figure 9.19** Here's the same transition as in the previous figure, except that it starts on the cut.

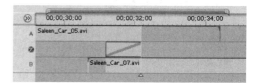

**Figure 9.20** And here, the transition ends on the cut.

## ✔ Tip

■ In a typical workflow, transitions and other effects are applied after the main editing tasks are complete. When this is the case, it's a good idea to customize the workspace for the task at hand. Consider rearranging the windows of the interface to emphasize the program view, Timeline window, Effects palette, and Effect Controls palette. De-emphasize the source view and Project window.

Figure 9.21 Choose Default Transition Duration.

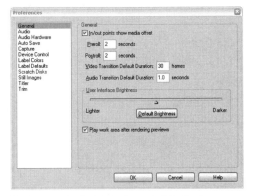

Figure 9.22 On the General panel of the Preferences dialog box, enter a duration for video transitions in frames, and a duration for audio transitions in seconds (to two decimal points).

# Setting the Default Transition Duration

Initially, transitions are one second in duration. However, you can specify any default duration for video and audio transitions.

## To specify the default duration for transitions:

1. On the Effects palette's menu, choose Default Transition Duration (**Figure 9.21**).

   The General panel of the Preferences dialog box opens.

2. In the Preferences dialog box, *do the following* (**Figure 9.22**):

   ▲ For Video Transition Default Duration, enter a value in frames.

   ▲ For Audio Transition Default Duration, enter a value in seconds.

   For audio, you can enter a value to two decimal points.

3. Click OK to close the dialog box.

   From this point on, video and audio transitions will use the durations you specified.

# Specifying a Default Transition

If you use a transition frequently, you can set it as the default transition to apply it quickly without having to go to the Transitions palette. For more about adding a transition, see the next section, "Applying a Transition."

## To specify the default transition:

1. On the Effects palette, select the transition you want to set as the default.

2. On the Effects palette's menu, choose Set Selected as Default Transition (**Figure 9.23**).

   The selected transition becomes the default transition.

**Figure 9.23** Select the transition that you want as the default and choose Set Selected as Default Transition.

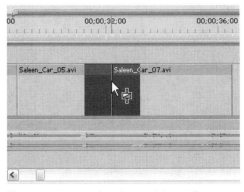

**Figure 9.24** You can drop the transition on the center of the cut, as indicated by the icon...

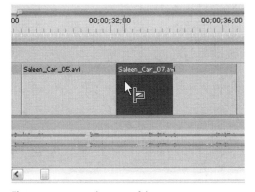

**Figure 9.25** ...or at the start of the cut...

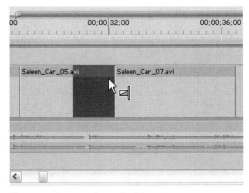

**Figure 9.26** ...or at the end of the cut.

# Applying a Transition

You can apply a video transition to any cut in a video track, and you can apply any audio transition to any cut in an audio track. Furthermore, video transitions aren't limited to video track 1. Thus, it's possible to layer and composite video tracks, complete with transitions. (See Chapter 13, "Working with Effects," for more about transparency and Chapter 14, "Effects in Action," for more about compositing.)

In addition to adding transitions between clips, you can add a transition to the end of a clip adjacent to an empty area in the track. Doing so automatically aligns the clip using End of Cut and is useful when you want to create an audio fade-out or a video fade-to-black (the empty track acts as silence or black video).

## To add a transition:

◆ Drag a transition from the Effects palette to a cut point in the Timeline window and position the mouse so that its icon indicates the alignment option you want:

**Center at Cut** ⌖: Centers the transition on the cut so that an equal number of hidden frames from each clip are used (**Figure 9.24**).

**Start at Cut** ⌖: Aligns the beginning of the transition with the cut (**Figure 9.25**).

**End at Cut** ⌖: Aligns the end of the transition with the cut (**Figure 9.26**).

*continues on next page*

When you release the mouse, the transition appears over the clips. It uses the alignment you specified and the default duration (**Figure 9.27**).

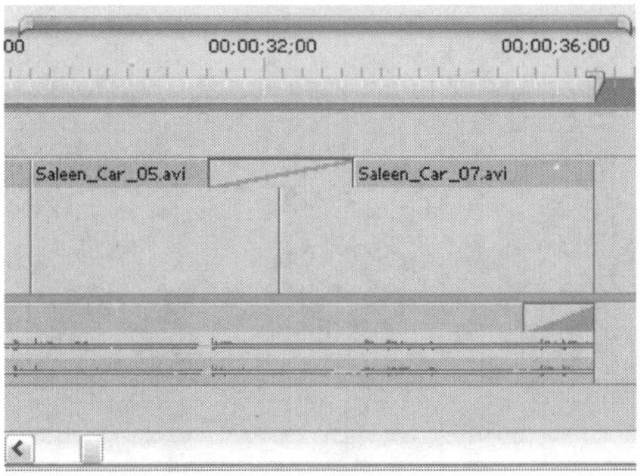


**Figure 9.27** In this figure, the new transition is centered on the cut. The cross-dissolve on the audio clip ends on the cut; because the clip is followed by an empty area, the transition functions as an audio fade-out.

## To force a Start at Cut or End at Cut transition:

- Ctrl-drag a transition from the Effects palette to a cut point in the Timeline window.

  Depending on which side of the cut you drag the transition to, the icon indicates either of two alignment options: Start at Cut or End at Cut.

## To add the default transition:

1. Cue the sequence CTI to a cut point.

   The program view's Go to Previous Edit Point and Go to Next Edit Point buttons usually offer the quickest way to cue the CTI.

2. With the Monitor window or the Timeline window active, press Ctrl+D.

   The transition appears over the clips. It uses the alignment you specified and the default duration.

## ✔ Tips

- You can replace a transition by dropping a new transition on top of the old one.
- The default duration can be applied automatically to a sequence created with the Automate to Timeline feature (explained in Chapter 6, "Creating a Sequence").
- Unlike a clip, a transition in the Timeline window doesn't include a name, just a diagonal line. Hovering the mouse over a transition reveals the transition's name in a tool tip.

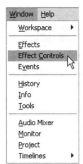

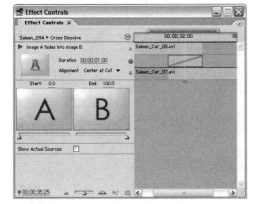

**Figure 9.28** Choose Window > Effect Controls.

**Figure 9.29** The Effect Controls palette can appear in its own window.

# Using the Effect Controls Palette with Transitions

Although you can adjust a transition directly in the Timeline window, you'll need to use the Effect Controls palette to adjust the transition in an A/B layout or to customize the transition's settings. You can view the Effect Controls palette in its own window, or you can add it to the Monitor window's source view or the Project window and select its tab. However, because the Effect Controls window serves many purposes, you must select the transition in the Timeline window to make its controls appear on the palette.

The Effect Controls palette's main panel contains information about the transition, a thumbnail preview, and controls for adjusting the transition's duration, alignment, and various custom settings. You can also reveal a timeline view, which lets you view and adjust the selected transition in its own timeline using an A/B roll layout. The timeline view's CTI and viewing area bar work just like those in the Monitor window and the Timeline window.

### To open the Effect Controls palette:

◆ *Do one of the following*:
  ▲ Choose Window > Effect Controls (**Figure 9.28**).
  ▲ Click the Effect Controls palette's tab to bring it to the front of the Monitor window's source view.

  The Effect Controls palette becomes visible (**Figure 9.29**). Select a clip with an effect or a transition to view its controls on the palette.

## To add the Effect Controls palette to the source view:

◆ Drag the Effect Controls palette's tab to the Monitor window's source view.

The palette's tab appears in the source view (**Figure 9.30**). Switch between the source view and the Effect Controls palette by clicking the appropriate tab.

## To add the Effect Controls palette to the Project window:

◆ Drag the Effect Controls palette's tab to the Project window.

The palette's tab appears in the Project window (**Figure 9.31**). Switch between the Project tab and the Effect Controls palette by clicking the appropriate tab.

## To show or hide the Effect Controls palette's timeline view:

◆ In the upper-right corner of the Effect Controls palette's main panel, click the Show/Hide Timeline View button.

When the button's chevrons point left, the timeline view is concealed (**Figure 9.32**); when the chevrons point right, the timeline view is visible (**Figure 9.33**).

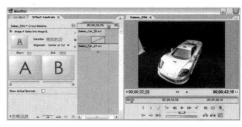

**Figure 9.30** The Effect Controls palette also can share the source view as a tab.

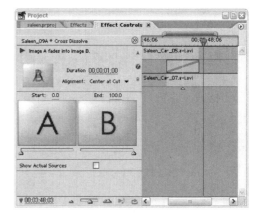

**Figure 9.31** And the Effect Controls palette can share the Project window as a tab.

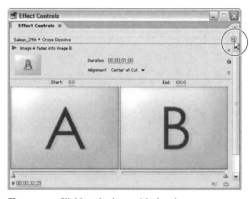

**Figure 9.32** Clicking the icon with the chevrons...

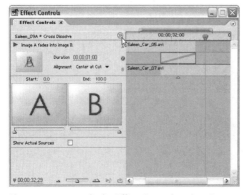

**Figure 9.33** ...reveals the Effect Controls palette's timeline view.

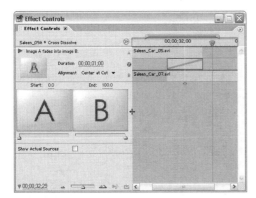

**Figure 9.34** Drag the border between the two panels to change their relative sizes.

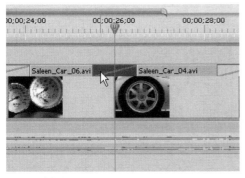

**Figure 9.35** Selecting a transition in the Timeline window...

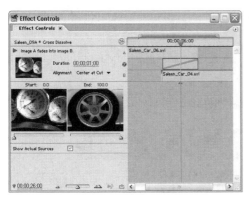

**Figure 9.36** ...makes its settings appear on the Effect Controls palette.

## To change the relative size of the timeline view:

◆ Position the mouse pointer between the Effect Controls palette's main panel and timeline view so that the pointer changes to the Width Adjustment tool ⬌ and then drag left or right to change the relative widths of the two areas (**Figure 9.34**).

## To view a transition on the Effect Controls palette:

1. Click a transition in the Timeline window to select it (**Figure 9.35**).

   The Effect Controls palette displays settings for the selected transition (**Figure 9.36**).

2. Adjust the transition *by doing one of the following:*

   ▲ Use controls on the Effect Controls palette's main panel to adjust the transition's settings.

   ▲ Use the Effect Controls palette's timeline view to adjust the transition's duration and placement manually or to adjust the cut point between clips.

## To show actual sources in thumbnail images:

◆ On the main panel of the Effect Controls palette, select Show Actual Sources (**Figure 9.37**).

When the check box is selected, the A and B sample images are replaced by the clips of the transition, which play back normally (**Figure 9.38**).

## To play a thumbnail preview of a transition:

◆ Click the Play button ▶ in the upper-left corner of the Effect Controls palette (next to the transition's description; (**Figure 9.39**).

The Play button toggles to a Stop button. The small thumbnail image demonstrates the transition, including any adjustments you make to the transition's settings. If Show Actual Sources is selected, the A and B sample images are replaced by the clip images.

## ✔ Tip

■ When all of a transition's customizable settings don't fit in the available vertical space of the Effect Controls palette, a scrollbar appears. But when the timeline view is visible, the scrollbar appears to the right of the timeline view, not the main panel. If some settings seem to be missing, look for the scrollbar at the far right.

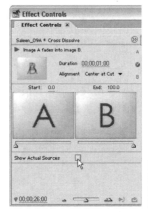

**Figure 9.37** Click Show Actual Sources to replace the A and B sample images...

**Figure 9.38** ...with the actual footage, including playback.

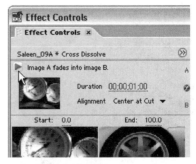

**Figure 9.39** Click the Play button to preview the transition.

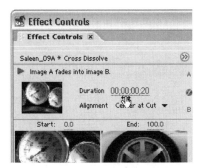

**Figure 9.40** You can adjust the transition's duration by changing the Duration value on the Effect Controls palette's main panel.

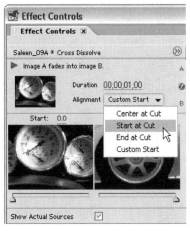

**Figure 9.41** You can move the transition by choosing an option from the Alignment drop-down menu.

# Adjusting a Transition's Duration and Alignment

Sometimes, a transition's initial duration and alignment work perfectly, and you can move on to other edits. But chances are, you'll want to make small adjustments. You may even need to trim the clips involved in the transition. You can make these adjustments using controls on the Effect Controls palette's main panel. Or you can make manual adjustments by dragging in either the Timeline window or the Effect Controls palette's timeline view.

### To adjust a transition's duration numerically:

◆ On the main panel of the Effect Controls window, *do one of the following:*

▲ Drag the Duration display to change the value (**Figure 9.40**).

▲ Click the Duration display, type a new duration, and press Enter.

The selected transition reflects the duration you specify in the Timeline window and in the timeline view of the Effect Controls palette.

### To adjust a transition's alignment automatically:

◆ On the main panel of the Effect Controls palette, choose an option from the Alignment drop-down menu (**Figure 9.41**):

**Center at Cut:** Centers the transition on the cut.

**Start at Cut:** Aligns the beginning of the transition with the cut.

**End at Cut:** Aligns the end of the transition with the cut.

Custom Start is dimmed, unless the transition is already positioned at a custom alignment.

ADJUSTING DURATION AND ALIGNMENT

## To adjust a transition manually:

1. In either the Timeline window or the Effect Controls palette's timeline view, *do one of the following:*

   ▲ To change the alignment of the transition without changing its duration, position the mouse pointer on the center of the transition, so that the pointer changes into a move transition icon 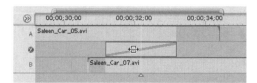 (**Figure 9.42**).

   ▲ To change the duration of the transition by changing its starting point, position the mouse on the transition's left edge, so that the pointer changes into the Trim Head tool ⊹ (**Figure 9.43**).

   ▲ To change the duration of the transition by changing where it ends, position the mouse pointer on the transition's right edge, so that the pointer changes into the Trim Tail tool ⊹ (**Figure 9.44**).

   The Trim Head or Trim Tail tool also appears if you position the mouse at the transition's edge in track A or track B.

2. Drag left or right to move or trim the transition.

**Figure 9.42** Drag the transition from the center to change its position relative to the cut.

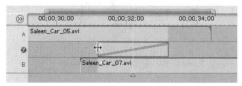

**Figure 9.43** You can change the transition's duration by trimming its left edge...

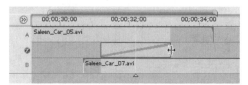

**Figure 9.44** ...or by trimming its right edge.

ADJUSTING DURATION AND ALIGNMENT

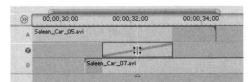

**Figure 9.45** You can perform standard edits to the cut point of a transition in the Timeline window and on the Effect Controls palette. On the Effect Controls palette, drag the white vertical line to apply a rolling edit...

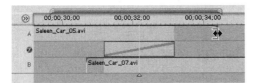

**Figure 9.46** ...drag the clip in the A track to ripple edit its Out point...

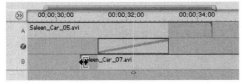

**Figure 9.47** ...or drag the clip in the B track to ripple edit its In point.

## To trim clips of a transition in the timeline view:

1. In the Effect Controls palette's timeline view, *do one of the following:*

   ▲ To perform a rolling edit, position the mouse pointer on the white vertical line (that indicates the cut point), so that the pointer becomes the Rolling Edit tool ⁑ (**Figure 9.45**).

   ▲ To ripple edit the first clip's Out point, position the mouse pointer on the clip in the A track, so that the pointer becomes the Ripple Tail tool ╬ (**Figure 9.46**).

   ▲ To ripple edit the first clip's In point, position the mouse pointer on the clip in the B track, so that the pointer becomes the Ripple Head tool ╬ (**Figure 9.47**).

   If you position the mouse pointer at the edge of the transition, the pointer changes to the Trim Head or Trim Tail tool, which changes the duration of the transition.

2. Drag left or right to trim the clip.

## ✔ Tip

■ As you make adjustments to a transition, the Monitor window's program view displays the frames that are affected.

**ADJUSTING DURATION AND ALIGNMENT**

# Customizing Transition Settings

Each transition has its own collection of customizable settings. The options available depend on the transition you're modifying. By modifying these settings, you can effectively expand your list of 74 video transitions. You can, for example, set the Wipe transition to wipe in any of eight directions; you can make it hard-edged or soft-edged; and you can add a border of any color or thickness.

As usual, you have to add the transition to a cut first and then select it to modify its settings on the Effect Controls palette.

### To set the direction of the transition:

◆ On the Effect Controls palette, click the small arrows, or *edge selectors*, around the transition thumbnail to select the orientation of the transition (**Figure 9.48**).

The movement of the transition, such as the direction of a wipe, progresses in the direction you specify (**Figure 9.49**).

**Figure 9.48** Click one of the small arrows to set the direction of a transition. Here, a wipe is set to progress from the top-left corner of the image.

**Figure 9.49** Here, the wipe is set to begin from the right side.

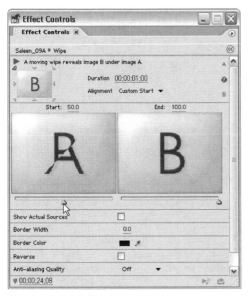

**Figure 9.50** Adjust the Start value or drag the corresponding slider to define the initial appearance of the transition.

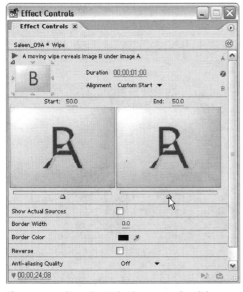

**Figure 9.51** Adjust the End value or use the slider to define the transition's final appearance. Instead of wiping from shot A to shot B, this transition is set to show a mix of the two shots for the duration of the transition.

## To adjust the start and end of the transition:

◆ On the Effect Controls palette, *do one of the following:*

▲ Adjust the Start and End values by dragging or by entering a value between 0 and 100.

▲ Drag the Start and End sliders under the A and B thumbnail images, respectively (**Figures 9.50** and **9.51**).

▲ Shift-drag either slider to set the start and end to the same value.

A standard transition starts at 0 and ends at 100.

CUSTOMIZING TRANSITION SETTINGS

## To reverse a transition:

◆ On the Effect Controls palette, select Reverse.

The transition is reversed. For example, reversing an Iris Round transition makes the iris close to reveal the next shot rather than open (**Figure 9.52**).

## ✔ Tips

■ You can use the sliders to get a preview of a transition, but make sure you reset the transition to the position you want before you finish.

■ You can't keyframe a transition; you can only set a start state and an end state.

## To set the center point of the transition:

◆ On the Effect Controls palette, drag the handle in the Start (A) or End (B) image to set the center point of the transition (**Figures 9.53** and **9.54**).

The handle represents the center of an iris transition, for example.

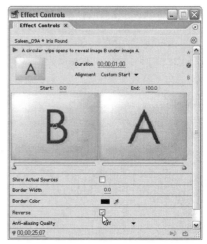

**Figure 9.52** Clicking Reverse makes the transition progress in the opposite way. For example, reversing an Iris Round transition makes the iris close to reveal the second shot, rather than open to reveal it.

**Figure 9.53** Drag the round handle in the start thumbnail image to set the center point of transitions, such as iris transitions.

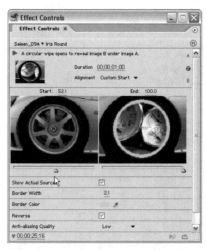

**Figure 9.54** Here, the center point, or origin, has been moved slightly to match the center of the wheel. To better illustrate the effect, the Start slider has been moved and a border has been added.

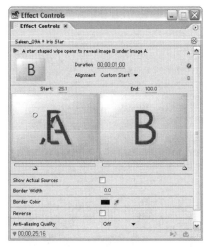

**Figure 9.55** When the border width is set to 0, no border appears at the transition's edge (the Start setting has been increased so you can see the edge).

**Figure 9.56** Increasing the value adds a border to the transition's edge.

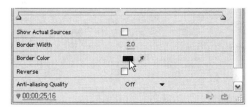

**Figure 9.57** Change the color of the border by clicking the color swatch or using the Eyedropper tool.

## To set the border thickness:

◆ On the Effect Controls palette, drag the underlined number in the Border Width field or click it and enter a new value (**Figure 9.55**).

The edges of the transition appear with a border of the thickness you specified (**Figure 9.56**).

## To set the border color:

◆ On the Effect Controls palette, in the Border Color field, *do one of the following:*

▲ Click the color swatch to select a color using the color picker (**Figure 9.57**).

▲ Click the Eyedropper tool and, holding down the mouse button, position the tool over any color on the screen. Release the mouse to set the current color.

The edges of the transition use the border color you specified.

## To specify the smoothness of edges:

◆ On the Effect Controls palette, choose an option from the Anti-aliasing Quality, drop-down menu (**Figure 9.58**).

Settings range from Off to High. Off applies no anti-aliasing; High applies the maximum amount of smoothing (**Figures 9.59** and **9.60**).

## ✔ Tips

■ To see the border, you have to play the thumbnail preview or the actual transition. You can also set the Start slider to a higher number (such as 50) to help you adjust the border. Make sure you set the Start slider back to 0, though.

■ Border thickness and anti-aliasing can only be approximated in the thumbnail images. The program view and output monitor give an accurate representation.

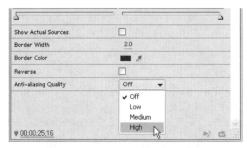

**Figure 9.58** Choose an option from the Anti-aliasing Quality drop-down menu.

**Figure 9.59** Compare the edge of the transition with Anti-aliasing Quality set to Off...

**Figure 9.60** ...to the same edge when the setting is High. The difference is slight in the Program view, even when seen in the magnified area (circled). The effect is more apparent in the video output, however.

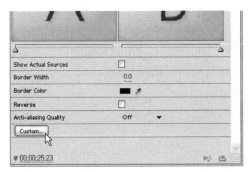

**Figure 9.61** Some transitions have additional settings you can access by clicking the Custom button.

**Figure 9.62** The Custom button opens a dialog box for the transition's special settings, such as the number of slices in the Slash Slide transition.

## To specify custom settings:

◆ On the Effect Controls palette, click the Custom button to define settings specific to that transition (**Figure 9.61**).

You can define the number of slices in the Slash Slide transition, for example (**Figure 9.62**).

# Using Special Transitions

Most transitions included with Premiere Pro operate along the same lines and use similar settings. However, a few transitions work a little differently from the rest. Because these transitions can't all be covered in the limited scope of this book, the following list describes a few to which you should give special attention:

**Channel Map:** Manipulates the image's red, green, blue, and alpha channels.

**Luminance Map:** Manipulates the image's luminance values.

**Displace:** Shifts pixels in an image based on the luminance values of a clip or other image.

**Gradient Wipe** and **Image Mask:** Transitions between clips using a separate image as a matte or mask.

These transitions are explained in detail in the *Adobe Premiere Pro User Guide.*

## ✔ Tip

■ Although a cross-dissolve transition is the best tool for creating a simple transition from one clip to the next, blending images for longer periods or blending multiple clips is best achieved by using the video fade controls on a superimposed clip. See Chapter 13, "Working with Effects," for more information.

# Previewing a Sequence

As you know, you can watch a sequence in the program view by just clicking its Play button (or the keyboard equivalent). But for the most accurate view, you need to output the video to a television monitor via a DV camera or deck.

Premiere Pro uses your system's resources to render the frames of a sequence on the fly. Naturally, segments with transitions and other effects require more processing than those without. That's because effects force Premiere Pro to generate new material. To create a cross-dissolve transition, for example, the system must digitally combine the first shot with the next. But with the proper system configuration, Premiere Pro can play back even layered clips, transitions, and other effects in *real time*—that is, right away and at the full frame rate. Even when a complex segment exceeds your system's ability to deliver the effect at the full frame rate, Premiere Pro can still display the effect by reducing the image quality, the frame rate, or both.

To see these segments at the full frame rate, you'll have to forego on-the-fly processing and create a *render file* instead. Initially, rendering takes time—how much time depends on the complexity of the effect and your system's processing speed. But once rendered, the area should play back as easily as any other clip, and at the full frame rate.

In the past, the need to render effects was the Achilles' heel of nonlinear editing systems (NLEs). But technical developments—such as DV's ability to encode high-quality video at modest data rates and ever-increasing storage and processing power—have made real-time editing accessible without the need for special hardware. Even so, special hardware may be required if you want to work with a lot of effects in real time or use formats that have higher data rates.

# Using Real-Time Rendering

If your system meets the minimum requirements for DV (listed in the book's introduction), it should be able to render many transitions and effects on the fly and still play them back at the project's full frame rate.

When an effect is too complex for your system to deliver frames at the project's frame rate, you may be able to see the effect in real time by lowering the program view's Quality setting. Alternatively, you can set the Quality setting to automatically degrade the program view's image quality as needed.

### To set the program view's image quality:

◆ Click the program view's Output button and choose a quality option (**Figure 10.1**):

**Highest Quality:** Displays video in the Monitor window at full resolution.

**Draft Quality:** Displays video in the Monitor window at one-half resolution.

**Automatic Quality:** Measures playback performance and dynamically adjusts the video quality.

### ✔ Tips

■ Although it's an odd turn of phrase, the term *real time* makes sense to digital video editors, who are necessarily obsessed with rendering times. Rendering times are often measured in multiples of real time. For example, if compressing a movie file to a particular codec on a particular system takes seven times real time, then a 10-second clip will take 70 seconds to compress.

■ If you're considering investing in real-time hardware, make sure you understand what you're getting. Some hardware is designed to process DV footage in real time, and other equipment can handle uncompressed video. And the ability to see real-time previews doesn't necessarily mean you'll get real-time output.

**Figure 10.1** Setting the program view to Automatic Quality lets Premiere Pro dynamically adjust the quality of the image as needed.

**Figure 10.2** Click the Output button and choose Playback Settings from the menu.

**Figure 10.3** In the DV Playback Settings dialog box, select Play Video on DV Hardware.

# Viewing a Sequence via a DV Device

Even at the Highest Quality setting, the image in the program view is inferior to video output to an actual television monitor. When you're editing DV, you can output the video signal through your DV camera or deck to a television monitor. This allows you to see (and evaluate) the video as your audience will see it.

The DV playback settings let you specify whether to play video and audio through your DV device. You can also specify whether you want real-time playback in the program view, on a television monitor, or both.

To use these options, your IEEE 1394 interface must be connected to a DV camcorder (set to VTR mode) or DV deck, which in turn must be connected to an NTSC (television) monitor.

## To play back via a DV device:

1. Make sure a DV camera or deck is connected to your computer's Premiere Pro–certified IEEE 1394 controller card and to a television monitor. Also make sure the DV device is on and set to receive a signal.

2. Click either view's Output button and choose Playback Settings (**Figure 10.2**). The DV Playback Settings dialog box appears.

3. In the DV Playback Settings dialog box, select Play Video on DV Hardware (**Figure 10.3**).

   Other options become highlighted and available. Leaving the option unselected prevents the signal from being sent to the DV device for playback.

   *continues on next page*

VIEWING A SEQUENCE VIA A DV DEVICE

**4.** Choose a Real-Time Playback option (**Figure 10.4**):

**Playback on Desktop Only:** Plays back sequences in the program view.

**Playback on DV Hardware Only:** Plays back sequences on a television, via a DV device.

**Playback on DV Hardware and Desktop:** Plays back sequences in the program view and on a television. This option requires the most processing power from your system.

If you choose a DV option, the Audio Playback options become available.

**5.** Choose an Audio Playback option:

**Play Audio on DV Hardware:** Plays audio through your DV device.

**Play Audio on Audio Hardware:** Plays audio through your computer's sound card.

The Export to Tape options let you specify audio output during export. See Chapter 15, "Creating Output," for details.

**6.** Click OK to close the dialog box.

The video and audio play back according to your selections. If you choose Playback on DV Hardware Only, the program view displays a "playing on DV hardware" message during playback (**Figure 10.5**).

**Figure 10.4** For Real-Time Playback, specify where you want real-time rendering to appear. For Audio Playback, choose the device you want to use to play the audio.

**Figure 10.5** When you play back through the DV device only, the program view displays this message instead of video.

VIEWING A SEQUENCE VIA A DV DEVICE

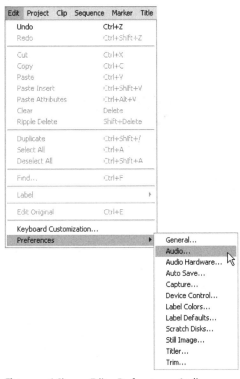

Figure 10.6 Choose Edit > Preferences > Audio.

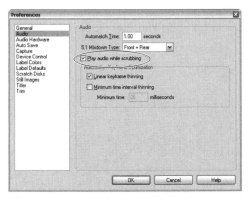

Figure 10.7 On the Audio panel of the Preferences dialog box, select Play Audio While Scrubbing.

## To play audio while scrubbing:

1. Choose Edit > Preferences > Audio (**Figure 10.6**).

   The Audio panel of the Preferences dialog box appears.

2. Select Play Audio While Scrubbing (**Figure 10.7**).

   When this option is selected, you can hear audio as you drag the CTI in the time ruler of the source view, program view, or Timeline window.

## ✔ Tip

■ You can also access the Playback Settings dialog box by choosing Project > Project Settings > General and then clicking the Playback Settings button.

# Rendering the Work Area

At the bottom of the Timeline window's time ruler, a thin red line appears above any frame that requires additional processing, such as the frames involved in a transition or a clip with effects (**Figure 10.8**). Premiere Pro's real-time rendering feature can process and play back most of these areas on the fly at the project's full frame rate, assuming that your system meets the minimum requirements to do so. Otherwise, you can render these areas, creating new media on your hard drive called *render files* or *preview files*.

You specify the area you want to render, called the *work area*, with (appropriately) the *work area bar*. The work area bar is the adjustable bar located near the bottom of the Timeline window's time ruler (**Figure 10.9**). Premiere Pro automatically sets the work area bar over all the clips in the project, extending it as clips are added. However, you can reset the work area bar manually.

When you render the work area, Premiere Pro generates new media for all the transitions and effects under the work area bar and places them in a Preview Files folder on your hard disk. Once the frames have been rendered, the thin red line indicators become green. By default, Premiere Pro plays back the work area after the render is complete. This setting can be changed to not play the work area, leaving the CTI in place.

When you make changes to a previewed area, Premiere Pro tries to use the rendered file as much as possible. However, significant changes will make the preview file obsolete; the green line will turn red, and you will have to re-render the area or use the standard playback method, which may not be able to play complex effects at the full frame rate (see "Using Real-Time Rendering" earlier in this chapter).

*Red line indicates a frame that requires rendering*

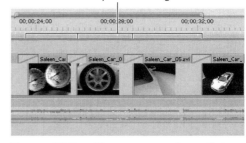

**Figure 10.8** Thin red lines appear over frames that require additional processing. Here, a line appears over each transition (the lines are highlighted to make them more visible).

*Work area bar*

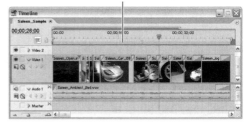

**Figure 10.9** The work area bar defines the part of a sequence you can render. In this figure, the work area spans the entire sequence.

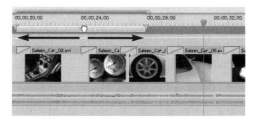

**Figure 10.10** Drag the work area bar from the center to move it over the area you want to render...

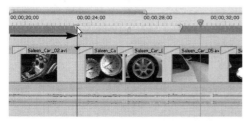

**Figure 10.11** ...or drag either end to resize the work area bar. In this figure, snapping is on, so the start of the work area easily aligns with the beginning of the transition.

**Figure 10.12**
Choose Sequence >
Render Work Area.

This section explains how to set the work area bar and preview the part of the sequence it includes. However, you can also export the work area as explained in Chapter 15.

## To preview the work area:

1. To set the work area bar over the part of the program that you want to preview, *do one of the following:*

   ▲ Drag the textured area at the center of the work area bar to move the bar without resizing it (**Figure 10.10**).

   ▲ Drag either end of the work area bar to shorten or lengthen it (**Figure 10.11**).

   ▲ Double-click the dark gray area at the bottom of the Timeline window's time ruler to resize the work area bar over a contiguous series of clips or the current visible area of the time ruler, whichever is shorter.

2. *Do one of the following:*

   ▲ Choose Sequence > Render Work Area (**Figure 10.12**).

   ▲ Press Enter.

*continues on next page*

**RENDERING THE WORK AREA**

The Rendering window appears; a progress bar indicates the approximate time required to process the effects, based on the current operation (**Figure 10.13**). Click the triangle to expand the Render Details section to see additional information (**Figure 10.14**). When processing is complete, the red lines under the work area bar turn green, and the audio and video under the work area bar play back.

## ✔ Tips

- If snapping is on, the work area bar snaps to clip and transition edges, markers, and the CTI.

- Hover the mouse pointer over the work area bar to see a tool tip showing the bar's start, end, and duration.

**Figure 10.13** A Rendering window estimates the approximate processing time.

**Figure 10.14** Clicking the triangle expands the window and provides additional details.

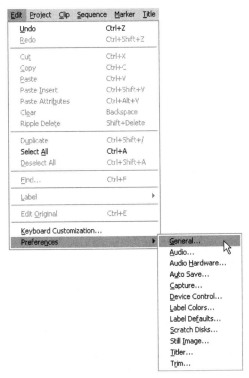

**Figure 10.15** Choose Edit > Preferences > General.

## To specify whether the work area plays after rendering:

1. Choose Edit > Preferences > General (**Figure 10.15**).

   The General panel of the Preferences dialog box appears.

2. Select or deselect Play Work Area after Rendering Previews (**Figure 10.16**).

   When the option is selected, the part of the sequence under the work area bar plays after rendering. When the option is not selected, the CTI remains where it was when rendering commenced.

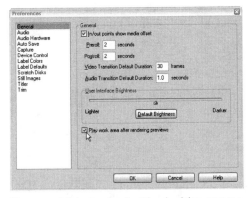

**Figure 10.16** Select or deselect the check box next to Play Work Area after Rendering Previews.

# Storing Preview Files

By default, Premiere Pro stores rendered effects in a folder called Adobe Premiere Pro Preview Files. You can find this file by following the path: My Documents > Adobe > Premiere Pro > 1.5 > Adobe Premiere Pro Preview Files. In this main folder, Premiere Pro stores each project's preview files in separate subfolders; the files use the naming convention *projectname*.prv.

However, by specifying a scratch disk, you can designate any location for the video and audio preview files. This way, you can take a more active role in managing your files or ensure they're being played from a disk with adequate space and speed.

### To choose scratch disks for preview files:

1. Choose Edit > Preferences > Scratch Disks (**Figure 10.17**).

    The Scratch Disks panel of the Preferences dialog box appears (**Figure 10.18**).

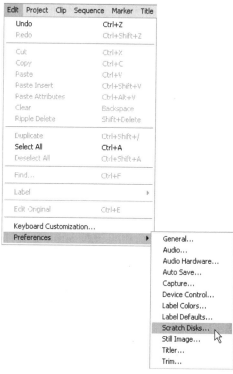

**Figure 10.17** Choose Edit > Preferences > Scratch Disks.

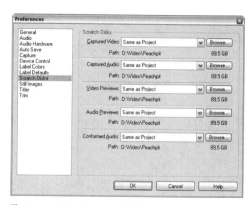

**Figure 10.18** The Scratch Disks panel of the Preferences dialog box appears.

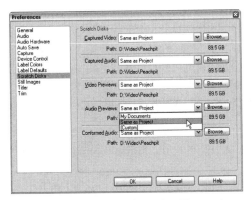

**Figure 10.19** Choose a location for the video previews and audio previews from the appropriate drop-down menus, or choose a custom location by clicking the Browse buttons.

2. For the Video Previews and Audio Previews settings, *do one of the following* (**Figure 10.19**):

   ▲ To store preview files in the My Documents folder, choose My Documents from the drop-down menu.

   ▲ To store preview files in the same folder as the current project, choose Same as Project from the drop-down menu.

   ▲ To specify a location for the Preview Files folder, click Browse.

   The path for the folder appears for each type of scratch disk.

3. Click OK to close the Preferences dialog box.

### ✔ Tips

■ Because the scratch disk plays back audio and video files, it should be a relatively large, fast disk. If you have several volumes, consider putting the Premiere Pro application, media files, and preview files on separate volumes.

■ By default, the Premiere Pro Preview Files folder resides in the user's My Documents folder under \Adobe\Premiere Pro\1.5\.

**STORING PREVIEW FILES**

## Audio Conform Files

To get the best possible real-time speed and maintain full quality, Premiere Pro converts all audio into CFA files, known as audio conform files. The audio is converted to the current audio sample rate for the project at 32-bit quality (usually 48KHz or 32KHz) and stored in a folder named Conformed Audio Files inside the My Documents\Adobe\Premiere Pro\1.5\ folder. You can change where the files are stored by choosing Edit > Preferences > Scratch Disks and then specifying a location for Conformed Audio. Except to set up this scratch disk location, you don't have to do anything with the conformed audio files.

Because it has been made consistent with all other audio in the project, conformed audio plays back instantly at high quality. Moreover, conformance allows Premiere Pro to display the audio waveform at the sample rate instead of just the frame rate. This allows much finer detail while editing audio clips.

When audio is being conformed, you can see a progress bar in the lower-right corner of the Adobe Premiere Pro application window. Beginning with Premiere Pro 1.5, you can hear uncompressed audio (including DV) play back before the conform operation is finished. Highly compressed audio files, on the other hand, must be conformed completely before you can hear the audio in the Project window or timeline. But for most users, processing time is unnoticeable.

Once the audio has been conformed, it does not need to be conformed again unless you delete the corresponding conformed audio files in the Conformed Audio folder. If you delete conformed audio files, Premiere Pro conforms the audio the next time you open a project that requires those audio files. Therefore, you don't need to archive CFA files with the project. Premiere Pro regenerates them automatically when you reopen the project.

## 32-Bit Floats (Your Boat)

Premiere Pro processes all internal audio using 32-bit floating-point numbers (32-bit *floats*). In contrast to integers, which are limited in their ability to represent a large range of numbers with precision, 32-bit floating point calculations are capable of representing very small and very large values with great precision. More precise calculations means less error accumulation with each succeeding calculation. In terms of audio, this precision introduces less noise and error with each audio adjustment you make. Put simply, 32-bit float audio processes faster and sounds better than, say, audio that uses 16-bit integer processing.

Consequently, audio mixing in Premiere Pro is far superior to that in previous versions of Premiere. Because previous versions worked entirely in 16- (or 8!) bit audio, any audio adjustments (including simple volume changes) were likely to reduce the effective signal-to-noise ratio. The more you tweaked the signal, the more noise you added. In Premiere Pro, all audio is maintained at 32-bit float, from import to export.

The cost for all of this is some disk space. For DV footage, the ratio of original video file size to CFA size is about 10:1 for stereo audio in a 48 KHz project. For a 32 KHz project, the ratio is about 15:1. It's a small price to pay to make audio a little bit sweeter.

**Figure 10.20** Choose Sequence > Delete Render Files.

**Figure 10.21** Click OK to confirm that you want to delete all preview files for the project.

# Deleting Preview Files

You can delete preview files to free up drive space or for housekeeping purposes (to save a project just prior to archiving it, for example). In contrast to deleting the preview files by using the operating system, using Premiere Pro's Delete Render Files command ensures that the project no longer refers to the preview files and doesn't prompt you for them the next time you open the project.

Note that Premiere Pro can't distinguish between preview files made obsolete by editing changes and preview files that are still in use. You can try to work around this limitation, though; see the sidebar "Managing Preview Files Manually," on the next page.

## To delete preview files:

1. Choose Sequence > Delete Render Files (**Figure 10.20**).

   A dialog box prompts you to confirm your choice and warns you that the operation can't be undone.

2. In the Confirm Delete dialog box, click OK (**Figure 10.21**).

   The preview files associated with the current project are deleted from the hard disk. In the Timeline window, the green lines indicating rendered areas turn red.

## ✔ Tips

- Premiere Pro keeps track of preview files in much the same way it references source media files. If you move or delete preview files using the operating system instead of from within Premiere Pro, you're prompted to locate the files the next time you open the project. In this case, direct Premiere Pro to the preview file's new location. Or if you deleted the preview files, choose Skip Preview Files when prompted. See Chapter 2, "Starting a Project," for more about locating missing files.

- Premiere Pro uses the terms *render files* and *preview files* interchangeably.

**DELETING PREVIEW FILES**

## Managing Preview Files Manually

As you learned in this chapter, making significant changes to a rendered area of a sequence makes the corresponding preview file obsolete. But even though the project no longer references it, the obsolete preview file remains on the hard disk. Unfortunately, Premiere Pro doesn't provide a way to delete the obsolete preview files while retaining the preview files that are still in effect. You can accomplish this task manually, using your operating system rather than Premiere Pro, but doing so can be tricky.

The preview files' long, cryptic names don't indicate whether the files are obsolete or still referenced by a project. However, you may be able to identify a rendered file by its thumbnail icon or creation date or by playing it back in Premiere Pro or Windows Media Player. If you manage to separate the wheat from the chaff, you can send the unwanted preview files to the Recycle Bin, thereby freeing up storage space. If you end up removing preview files that are in use, no problem—just render new ones.

Ultimately, managing your files this way is probably more trouble than it's worth. Storage space is more affordable than ever, so most editors have ample drive space, even for obsolete preview files.

Or you can use the Project Manager (see Chapter 4, "Managing Clips") to collect your project. The Project Manager collects only the most current video preview files. Unfortunately, it collects all of the conformed audio files, even when Exclude Unused Clips is selected and the audio clip is not included in the collected project. Adobe will most likely correct this in a future version of Premiere Pro.

# MIXING AUDIO

Whether you use numerous audio tracks or just a few, you'll probably need to make subtle adjustments to them to achieve the best overall effect. This process, known as audio mixing, can be accomplished by employing the Audio Mixer window.

The Audio Mixer window resembles a physical audio mixing board, complete with fade and pan controls and VU meters that display audio power in decibels. But unlike a physical mixing board, Premiere Pro's audio mixer includes a set of controls for every audio track in your program. To create complex mixes, you can route the audio using submixes and sends. You can also apply a wide range of audio effects to correct or enhance the tracks—a process some call audio sweetening—right from the audio mixer. With the proper hardware, you can even use the mixer to record audio directly into a track of a sequence.

The audio mixer works like an automated mixing console. As you mix a track, the audio mixer records your adjustments. When you play back the mix, the audio mixer reproduces your adjustments, moving the pan and fade controls just as you did.

In the Timeline window, these adjustments are depicted as specified values, or keyframes, in property graphs. Whereas you use the audio mixer to control tracks of audio, you can manipulate keyframes to adjust both tracks and individual clips in the tracks. But because keyframes work the same for audio properties as they do for other effects—transparency, motion, and filters—a full discussion of keyframes is reserved for Chapter 13, "Working with Effects." This chapter focuses on the use of the audio mixer to make track-based audio adjustments.

If you're already familiar with audio mixing principles and practices, feel free to skip to the end of the chapter to start mixing with the audio mixer. If there's a step you don't understand, you can turn back to the pertinent section. Otherwise, proceed from the beginning for a detailed explanation of each part of the process.

# Planning an Audio Mix

As a rule, you mix a sequence's audio only after you're satisfied with the editing, a stage sometimes referred to as picture lock. This workflow helps ensure that you don't waste time and effort repeatedly revising a carefully crafted mix. However, this approach is only part of your overall audio editing strategy. It's possible to make adjustments on several levels: to clips, to the track containing the clips, to a submix track that includes several tracks. By nesting the sequence, you allow the cycle to start over. To avoid making redundant or conflicting adjustments, it's important to understand your choices at each step in the process.

## Specifying the track type

As always, tailor your plans to your output goal. Make sure your final sequence's master track matches the type of audio you want to output: mono, stereo, or 5.1. The master track's channel type is fixed when you create the sequence—so if you need a different type of master track, you'll have to create a new sequence. In contrast, you can add or delete the type of standard or submix tracks you need at will.

## Clip-based vs. track-based editing

You can pan, fade, and apply effects both to individual clips and to entire tracks. In general, adjust individual clips first and then mix the tracks. However, don't adjust a clip when it would make more sense to make the same adjustment to the entire track. Similarly, be careful not to let a clip's setting contradict the track's setting, and vice versa. Adjust clips in the Timeline window and Effect Controls window (see Chapter 13). Adjust tracks in the Timeline window or the audio mixer.

### Audio Processing Order

When you're planning a mix or troubleshooting problems, it's helpful to know the order in which audio adjustments are processed. Premiere Pro processes audio data in the following order:

1. Gain adjustments using the Audio Gain command

2. Effects applied to individual clips

3. Track settings in this order: pre-fader effects, pre-fader sends, mute, fader, meter, post-fader effects, post-fader sends, pan/balance

4. Track output volume, from left to right in the audio mixer (or top to bottom in the Timeline window)

## Automation vs. keyframing

In the audio mixer, you use automation to adjust a track's pan, fade, and effect values as the audio plays; in the Timeline window, you directly manipulate the values, called keyframes, on a graph. Both methods affect the same set of audio track property values. The audio mixer offers real-time audio response, whereas keyframing favors graphical control. You can also view and adjust keyframes for individual audio clips (as well as other effects, such as transparency, motion, and filters) in the Timeline window and the Effect Controls window.

## Routing and nesting

Complex mixes involving multiple tracks can be grouped into submix tracks and output, or routed, to other submix tracks or to the master track. You can also use sends to blend processed or wet versions of a track or submix with its unprocessed or dry signal. And, as you learned in Chapter 6, "Creating a Sequence," you can nest one sequence within another, so that the combined tracks of one sequence appear as a single linked clip in another sequence. This means that you mix a sequence's tracks and then make adjustments to the audio track of its nested instance.

## Subtractive Mixing

When you adjust audio levels, follow the principle of subtractive mixing. In subtractive mixing, you favor reducing (subtracting) levels over increasing them. First, establish a strong, representative audio level for the sequence (such as the standard level for dialogue). Then, if necessary, decrease the gain of a clip in relation to others. Increasing a level in relation to other clips often leads to successive increases. Adding volume not only increases the signal (the sounds you want), but also the noise (the sounds you don't want, such as buzz and hiss) and can introduce distortion.

PLANNING AN AUDIO MIX

# Specifying Audio Hardware Options

To record, process, and output audio, Premiere Pro uses your system's audio hardware. Although a run-of-the-mill audio card is adequate for stereo input and output, multi-channel recording and output require an ASIO-compliant audio device. ASIO is a widely accepted audio transfer protocol that allows software like Premiere Pro to use the multichannel recording and output capabilities of more powerful sound cards. With the proper hardware, you can use the audio mixer to record multiple tracks simultaneously and to mix and output audio in 5.1 surround.

You can specify the way that Premiere Pro uses your particular device on the Audio panel of the Preferences dialog box. The panel includes various options:

◆ **Input/Output Device** specifies which connected audio hardware device Premiere Pro uses for input and output.

◆ **Output Channel Mappings** describes how your device's output channels correspond to a sequence's master track output. The column marked with a stereo icon ⋈ shows the correspondence between each channel of your device and a stereo or mono mix: left speaker ⋈ and right speaker ⋈. (Mono mixes are output to a left and right speaker.) The column labeled 5.1 shows the correspondence between each channel of your device and the channels in a 5.1 surround mix: left ▢, right ▢, center ▢, surround left ▢, and surround right ▢.

◆ **Latency** refers to the delay, or the time it takes the audio signal to be processed and output. A short latency is best for live recording; a longer latency can process effects more efficiently.

**Figure 11.1** Choose Edit > Preferences > Audio Hardware.

## ASIO

ASIO stands for Audio Stream Input/Output, a multichannel audio transfer protocol developed by Steinberg (the company that produces audio products such as Cubase).

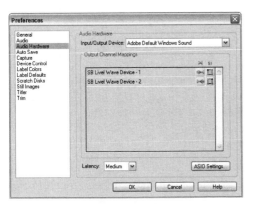

**Figure 11.2** The Audio Hardware panel of the Preferences dialog box appears.

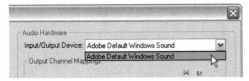

**Figure 11.3** For Input/Output Device, choose an option.

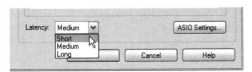

**Figure 11.4** For Latency, specify the option best suited for the task at hand.

◆ **ASIO Settings** accesses a separate dialog box for configuring your particular audio device.

## To specify audio hardware preferences:

1. Choose Edit > Preferences > Audio Hardware (**Figure 11.1**).

   The Audio Hardware panel of the Preferences dialog box appears (**Figure 11.2**).

2. Select the audio hardware you want to use from the Input/Output Device drop-down menu (**Figure 11.3**).

3. Choose an option in the Latency drop-down menu (**Figure 11.4**).

4. If it's available, click ASIO Settings to access options specific to your particular sound card.

**SPECIFYING AUDIO HARDWARE OPTIONS**

# Understanding Audio Tracks and Channel Types

Recall from Chapter 6, that a sequence can contain any number of standard audio tracks, but it must contain a single master audio track that controls the combined output of all the other tracks in the sequence.

You can also create submix tracks, which you can use to redirect the output of standard tracks and other submix tracks before it reaches the master track. Routing with submix tracks helps you group tracks and control the processing of effects.

You must specify the number of channels each track supports: mono, stereo, or 5.1 surround:

◆ **Mono**, or monophonic, tracks contain a single channel of audio data, which is output equally by all the output speakers.

◆ **Stereo**, or stereophonic, tracks contain two discrete channels of audio. When reproduced on a stereo speaker system, a sound's relative strength in each channel, or balance, gives it an apparent location between stereo speakers.

◆ **5.1**, or 5.1 surround, tracks contain five discrete channels of information, plus a low-frequency effects (LFE) channel that may be decoded either by the main speakers or a separate subwoofer. A surround-sound system uses five or more speakers placed around the listener to give sounds an apparent location anywhere in a 360-degree lateral range.

Standard audio tracks contain audio clips of the same audio type, including audio you record using the audio mixer. Once a track is created, you can't change its channel type.

## ✔ Tip

■ Once you create a sequence, its master track's channel type is fixed. However, you can easily create a new sequence with the type of master track you want. Then you can either paste the contents of the original sequence in the new one or nest the original sequence in the new one.

Figure 11.5 Selecting a mono clip and choosing Clip > Audio Options > Treat as Stereo lets you use the clip in stereo tracks.

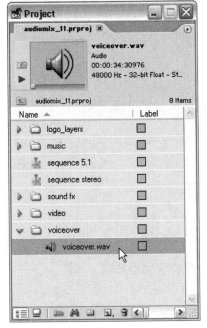

Figure 11.6 Select a stereo clip.

# Converting Mono and Stereo Clips

As discussed previously, audio tracks can contain only clips that use the same channel type. However, you can easily work around this limitation. A few simple commands allow you to treat a mono clip as a stereo clip or, conversely, extract a stereo clip's channels as two mono clips.

## To treat a mono clip as stereo:

1. In the Project window, select a mono audio clip.

2. Choose Clip > Audio Options > Treat as Stereo (**Figure 11.5**).

   The information area of the Project window describes the clip as a stereo clip, and you can add the clip to any stereo audio track. To treat the clip as mono, choose the command again.

## To break out mono clips from a stereo clip:

1. In the Project window, select a stereo audio clip (**Figure 11.6**).

*continues on next page*

**2.** Choose Clip > Audio Options > Breakout to Mono Clips (**Figure 11.7**).

Each of the clip's stereo channels becomes a mono clip in the Project window. Left is appended to one clip's name, and Right is appended to the other (**Figure 11.8**).

### ✔ Tips

■ Make sure your audio cabling is correct. It's surprisingly common for the left and right channels to be reversed.

■ On stereo equipment, the left channel is synonymous with audio channel 1 and a white connector. The right channel is synonymous with audio channel 2 and a red connector.

**Figure 11.7** Choose Clip > Audio Options > Breakout to Mono Clips.

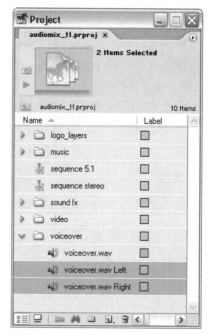

**Figure 11.8** The clip's stereo channels appear as two mono clips in the Project window.

# Adjusting a Clip's Gain

You can adjust the overall volume, or gain, of a clip in the timeline by using a menu command. You can think of gain as the clip's input levels—the volume the clip starts with. The Audio Gain command provides a good way to bring a clip's levels in line with those of other clips before making adjustments to the output levels, either for the individual clip or for all the clips in the track. Adjusting gain doesn't affect the initial position of a clip's volume value graph. See "Viewing Audio Data in the Timeline" later in this chapter. To learn about adjusting a value graph, see Chapter 13.

## Decibels

A decibel (dB) is the standard measure of acoustical power used by audio professionals everywhere. To double the volume, increase the level by +6 dB.

Technically speaking, a decibel is one-tenth of a bel, which measures the ratio of two audio power levels, usually, an audio signal and a reference (such as the threshold of hearing). And yes, it's bel as in Alexander Graham Bell, the telephone guy.

## To adjust a clip's gain:

1. In the Timeline window, select an audio clip (**Figure 11.9**).

2. Choose Clip > Audio Options > Audio Gain (**Figure 11.10**).

   The Clip Gain dialog box appears (**Figure 11.11**).

3. To adjust the gain, *do one of the following*:

   ▲ Enter a value for the gain, in decibels.

   A value of more than 0 amplifies the audio; a value of less than 0 attenuates the audio, making it quieter.

   ▲ Click Normalize to have Premiere Pro calculate the gain value automatically.

   Normalizing audio boosts the volume where it's too quiet and limits it where it's too loud.

4. Click OK.

   The audio clip's overall gain is adjusted by the amount you specified.

## ✔ Tips

- Certain audio effects let you boost or attenuate gain in particular frequencies.

- You can't see changes you make using the Audio Gain command by looking at the clip, its waveform, or its keyframes. You can see the amount of gain applied only in the Clip Gain dialog box itself.

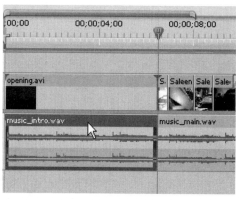

Figure 11.9 In the Timeline window, select an audio clip.

Figure 11.10 Choose Clip > Audio Options > Audio Gain.

Figure 11.11 In the Clip Gain dialog box, either enter a gain value in dB or click Normalize to have Premiere Pro calculate the gain automatically.

Figure 11.12 On the Effects palette, open the Audio Transitions folder and drag either Constant Gain or Constant Power...

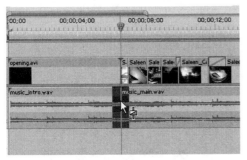

Figure 11.13 ...and drop it at an audio cut in the Timeline window, aligning it so it starts at the cut, ends at the cut, or is centered on the cut (shown here).

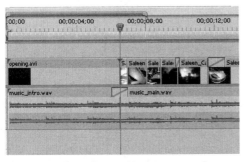

Figure 11.14 The audio transition appears on the cut using the alignment you specified, at the default duration.

# Creating Cross-Fades with Audio Transitions

A cross-fade occurs when one audio clip fades out (grows silent) while another audio clip fades in (becomes audible). In Premiere Pro, you can fade up, fade out, and cross-fade audio using an audio transition. Although transitions were covered in Chapter 9, "Adding Transitions," it's useful to review them in the context of audio.

## To create a cross-fade transition:

1. On the Effects palette, open the Audio Transitions folder to reveal the audio transitions. Select one of the following (**Figure 11.12**):

   **Constant Gain:** Changes the volume using a linear scale, which nonetheless may not sound like a linear, constant change.

   **Constant Power:** Changes the volume using a logarithmic scale, which emulates the way the human ear perceives volume changes.

2. Drag the audio transition to a cut between audio clips in a track, so that the mouse icon indicates the alignment you want.

   Alignment options include Start at Cut, Centered at Cut, and End at Cut (**Figure 11.13**).

3. Release the mouse to drop the transition.

   The transition appears at the edit using the alignment you specified and the default transition duration (**Figure 11.14**). You can adjust the audio transition's alignment or duration using any of the techniques you learned in Chapter 9.

## To create a fade-up or fade-out:

1. On the Effects palette, open the Audio Transitions folder to reveal the audio transitions. Select one of the following:

   **Constant Gain:** Changes the volume using a linear scale, which nonetheless may not sound like a linear, constant change.

   **Constant Power:** Changes the volume using a logarithmic scale, which emulates the way the human ear perceives volume changes.

2. *Do one of the following:*

   ▲ Drag the transition to the head of an audio clip so that the Start at Cut icon appears (**Figure 11.15**).

   ▲ Drag the transition to the tail of an audio clip so that the End at Cut icon appears.

   Release the mouse to drop the transition in place.

   The transition appears at the edit, using the default transition duration (**Figure 11.16**). You can adjust the transition's duration using any of the techniques explained in Chapter 9.

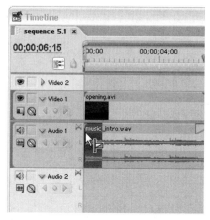

**Figure 11.15** To fade in audio, drag an audio transition to start at the cut.

**Figure 11.16** The transition appears at the beginning of the clip and uses the default duration.

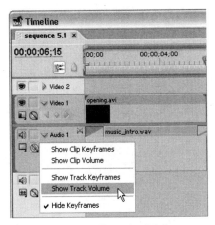

Figure 11.17 In an audio track, click the Show/Hide Keyframes button and choose Show Track Volume.

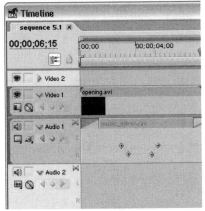

Figure 11.18 A yellow line graphs the audio levels. In this figure, the line reflects the results of automation as keyframes in the graph. Waveforms are hidden so the line is easier to see.

# Viewing Audio Data in the Timeline

In Chapter 7, "Editing in the Timeline," you learned that you can view audio waveforms for clips in a track by expanding the track and setting its display style to Show Waveforms. An expanded audio track can also display other information, including controls for manipulating levels, panning, balancing, and effects. Each parameter's values appear as a graph, which you can keyframe; that is, you can specify values for particular points in time, thereby changing the graph and altering the values over time. You can view one graph at a time for individual clips in the track or for the entire track.

For now, you'll learn how to view parameter values for tracks, to get visual feedback for adjustments you make using the audio mixer. Turn to Chapter 13 to find out how to view audio data for clips and how to make adjustments by manipulating the graph directly in the Timeline window.

## To show track volume in the Timeline window:

1. If necessary, expand an audio track by clicking the triangle next to the track's name.

2. In the audio track, click the Show/Hide Keyframes button (next to the Show Waveforms button) and choose Show Track Volume (**Figure 11.17**).

    The track display includes a yellow line that graphs the track's volume values over time (**Figure 11.18**). When the line is at the center of the track, the volume is unadjusted; when the line is at the top of the track, the volume is doubled, or +6 dB; when the line is at the bottom of the track, the track is silent, or −∞dB.

## To show track panning values in the Timeline window:

1. If necessary, expand an audio track by clicking the triangle next to the track's name.

2. In the audio track, click the Show/Hide Keyframes button and choose Show Track Keyframes from the menu (**Figure 11.19**).

   A drop-down menu appears in the track, at the beginning of the visible area of the timeline.

3. In the track's drop-down menu, choose Panner and then choose an option from the submenu (**Figure 11.20**):

   **Balance:** Shows the balance between left and right channels when outputting to a stereo track.

   **Left–Right:** Shows the balance between left and right channels when outputting to a 5.1 track.

   **Front–Rear:** Shows the balance between front and rear channels when outputting to a 5.1 track.

   **Center:** Shows the percentage value output to the center channel in a 5.1 track.

   **LFE:** Shows the volume, in dB, output to the LFE (low-frequency effects) channel in a 5.1 track.

   A yellow line in the track graphs the selected value over time (**Figure 11.21**). When the line is at the center of the track, the track is distributed evenly between the channels represented by the graph. When Center or LFE is selected, the line is initially at the bottom of the track, which represents silence (0% when Center is selected or –∞dB when LFE is selected).

**Figure 11.19** In the audio track, click the Show/Hide Keyframes button and choose Show Track Keyframes.

**Figure 11.20** In the track's drop-down menu, choose the parameter for which you want to view a value graph—in this case, Balance.

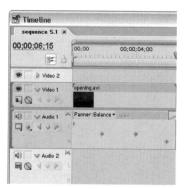

**Figure 11.21** A yellow line graphs the selected panning values. In this figure, the line reflects the results of adjusting balance values as keyframes in the graph. Again, waveforms are hidden.

# Using the Audio Mixer

The audio mixer resembles a conventional mixing board in both form and function (**Figure 11.22**). Just as each channel of a mixing board contains controls to adjust and monitor each audio source, each track in the audio mixer corresponds to a track in the sequence. Unlike its physical counterpart, however, the audio mixer adds tracks for each track you add to the sequence.

Faders (or fade controls) control the audio levels, expressed in decibels (dB). Alternatively, you can enter a numeric value for the level. Similarly, you can pan audio using the audio mixer's pan knobs or by entering a numerical value.

You make these adjustments in each track as the video and audio play back. As you do, Premiere Pro creates keyframes in the corresponding track's fade and pan lines in the timeline.

To help you evaluate the levels, a VU (volume unit) meter graphically represents the levels of each channel, as well as the overall combined, or master, level. An indicator light at the top of the VU meter warns you if your levels are too high and clipping (causing distortion).

Each channel of the audio mixer also contains standard buttons for selectively monitoring (listening to) each track. You can monitor all the channels, mute a channel to exclude it from output, or solo a channel to monitor it without the others. Each channel also includes a Record button, which you can use to record live audio directly to the track.

As in the program view and Timeline window, each sequence of the project can appear as a tab in the audio mixer. Clicking a sequence's tab in any window makes it the current sequence in all windows.

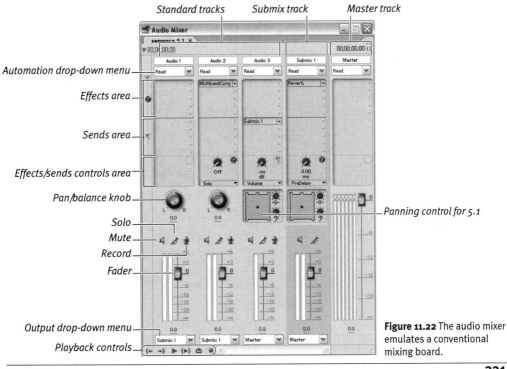

Standard tracks    Submix track    Master track

Automation drop-down menu

Effects area

Sends area

Effects/sends controls area

Pan/balance knob

Solo

Mute

Record

Fader

Output drop-down menu

Playback controls

Panning control for 5.1

**Figure 11.22** The audio mixer emulates a conventional mixing board.

**321**

## To open the audio mixer:

◆ Choose Window > Audio Mixer
(**Figure 11.23**).

The Audio Mixer window appears.

## To optimize the workspace for audio mixing:

◆ Choose Window > Workspace > Audio
(**Figure 11.24**).

The arrangement of windows is optimized for audio mixing. You can use the arrangement as a starting point for customizing your workspace (**Figure 11.25**).

## ✔ Tips

■ You may find that the preset audio workspace is a good start, but it probably needs a little tweaking to get the right arrangement for your screen and personal style. Ideally, you'll have a secondary monitor so you can spread out the windows. Also, consider closing and minimizing the windows and palettes you don't need.

■ You may hear audio engineers refer to a knob on a mixing console as a *pot*, which is short for potentiometer (it affects electrical potential). In other words, like most volume knobs, a pot controls the amount of electrical current that flows through a circuit.

■ Ordinarily, each source on a mixer is referred to as a channel. (*Channel* also refers to the way audio data is recorded, as in mono, stereo, and 5.1 channels.) But for the sake of convenience, and to remain consistent with the terminology used in the Premiere Pro interface, this book refers to *tracks* in the timeline and in the audio mixer.

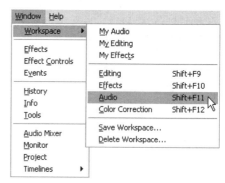

**Figure 11.23** To open the Audio Mixer window, choose Window > Audio Mixer.

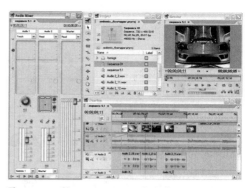

**Figure 11.24** Choose Window > Workspace > Audio.

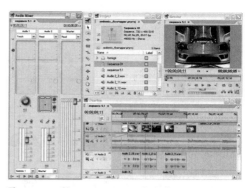

**Figure 11.25** The arrangement of windows is optimized for audio mixing. Here, the preset has been modified slightly. For example, the Monitor window has been set to single view.

USING THE AUDIO MIXER

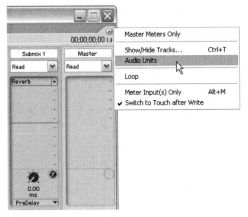

**Figure 11.26** In the audio mixer's drop-down menu, choose Audio Units.

# Customizing the Audio Mixer

Like the program view and the Timeline window, the audio mixer lets you toggle the current sequence's time ruler between frames and audio samples. Depending on whether your mix requires effects, you can expand or collapse an area that includes effects and sends (later sections explain how to use effects and sends). When the number of tracks in a complex mix makes the audio mixer consume too much screen space, you can hide the tracks you're not using. On the other hand, when you're concentrating on video editing, you can reduce the audio mixer to show only the master meters, so you can keep an eye on the output levels.

## To toggle between frames and audio units:

◆ In the audio mixer's drop-down menu, choose Audio Units (**Figure 11.26**).

The time displays in the audio mixer and in the Timeline window switch to audio samples. Select the option again to switch the time displays back to frames. The audio mixer and the Timeline window always display the same units, and you can toggle between frames and samples from either window's drop-down menu.

## To show or hide effects and sends:

◆ Click the triangle at the upper left in the audio mixer to expand and collapse the audio mixer's effects and sends area (**Figures 11.27** and **11.28**).

Effects and sends are explained in detail later in this chapter.

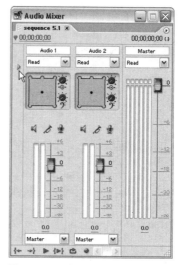

**Figure 11.27** Clicking the triangle toggles between hiding the effects and sends...

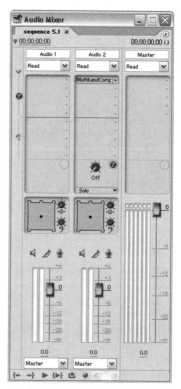

**Figure 11.28** ...and revealing the effects and sends.

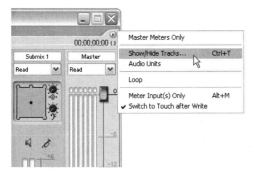

**Figure 11.29** In the audio mixer's drop-down menu, choose Show/Hide Tracks.

**Figure 11.30** In the Show/Hide Tracks dialog box, select the tracks you want to appear in the audio mixer.

## To show or hide tracks in the audio mixer:

1. In the audio mixer's drop-down menu, choose Show/Hide Tracks (**Figure 11.29**). The Show/Hide Tracks dialog box appears.

2. In the Show/Hide Tracks dialog box, *do one of the following* (**Figure 11.30**):

   ▲ Select a track to make a check appear next to its name and to include the track's controls in the Audio Mixer window.

   ▲ Deselect a track to make the check mark disappear and exclude the track's controls from the audio mixer.

   ▲ Click Show All to include all tracks' controls in the audio mixer.

   ▲ Click Hide All to exclude all tracks' controls from the audio mixer (leaving only the master track's controls visible).

3. Click OK.

   Only the tracks you selected appear in the audio mixer. The tracks still appear in the Timeline window, and their clip contents continue to play (provided the tracks aren't muted).

CUSTOMIZING THE AUDIO MIXER

## To show master meters only:

◆ In the audio mixer's menu, choose Master Meters Only (**Figure 11.31**).

The Audio Mixer window is reduced to show only the meters for the master track output (**Figure 11.32**).

## To switch from the master meters to the audio mixer:

◆ In the master meter's drop-down menu, choose Audio Mixer (**Figure 11.33**).

The window becomes the full audio mixer.

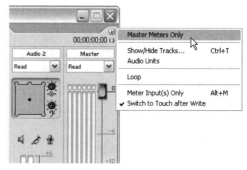

**Figure 11.31** Choosing Master Meters Only in the audio mixer's menu...

**Figure 11.32** ...reduces the window to show only the master track's VU meters.

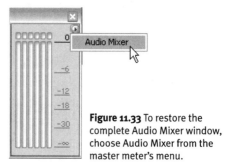

**Figure 11.33** To restore the complete Audio Mixer window, choose Audio Mixer from the master meter's menu.

Figure 11.34 Click a track's Mute button to exclude its output from playback.

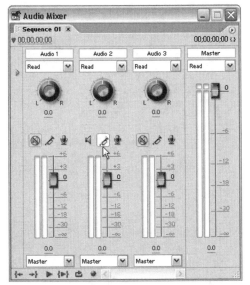

Figure 11.35 Clicking a track's Solo button mutes all other tracks, letting you listen to the track in isolation.

# Monitoring Tracks in the Audio Mixer

Although mixing audio is about making all the tracks sound good together, one way to do this is to listen to them separately. Buttons above each track's fader allow you to control which one you listen to, or monitor. If you don't want to monitor a track, click the Mute button. Conversely, click the Solo button to monitor a track without hearing the others. Monitor buttons don't affect the levels—just whether you hear the audio during the mixing process.

## To mute a track:

◆ In the audio mixer, click the Mute button for the track you want to exclude from playback (**Figure 11.34**).

Deselect the Mute button to include the track's audio in playback.

## To solo a track:

◆ In the audio mixer, click the Solo button for the track you want to hear exclusively (**Figure 11.35**).

Deselect the Solo button to include the audio of other tracks in playback.

## ✔ Tip

■ Musicians who amplify their instruments use the term *monitor* to refer to a speaker directed toward the band. These monitors help the musicians hear (and therefore modulate) their own performance better.

## Reading the VU Meters

As you monitor audio, watch the levels in the VU meters. Your speaker volume can provide only a relative, changeable indication of levels. You can rely on the VU meters for a more objective measure. The loudest sounds should reach their highest levels, or peak, near the top of the meters, at 0 dB. If a sound is too loud to be accurately reproduced, it clips and will sound distorted. When clipping occurs, the indicator light above a VU meter comes on. Click the lights to turn them off. Readjust the levels to avoid clipping.

# Recording with the Audio Mixer

With the proper sound card, you can connect a microphone, instrument, or MIDI device to your system and record audio directly to a track of the sequence. The types of devices you can connect and the number of tracks you can record simultaneously depend on your sound card's features.

Submix tracks don't contain audio clips; they serve to route the audio of other tracks. Therefore, you can't record audio to a submix track, and in the audio mixer, submix tracks don't include a Record button.

## To record with the audio mixer:

1. Make sure your sound card is configured and that a microphone or other device is connected properly.

2. In the audio mixer, click the Enable Record button 🎤 for the tracks to which you want to record audio (**Figure 11.36**).

   A drop-down menu appears above the Mute, Solo, and Record buttons listing the recording devices (sound cards) connected to your system.

3. Choose the proper recording device from the track's drop-down menu (**Figure 11.37**).

4. Monitor the tracks you want to hear during recording, and mute tracks you don't want to hear.

   In some circumstances, it's best to monitor the audio using headphones instead of speakers. For example, you should prevent a microphone from picking up audio from the speakers. If a microphone picks up its own audio, the result will be audio feedback.

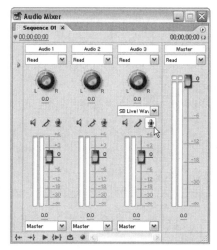

**Figure 11.36** Click the Enable Record button to enable the track for recording.

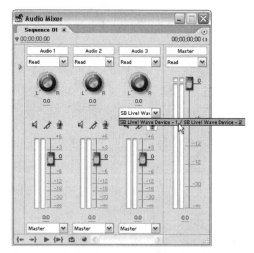

**Figure 11.37** In the drop-down menu, select the recording device you want to use.

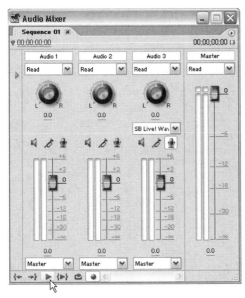

**Figure 11.38** Cue the sequence's CTI and then click the track's Record and Play buttons. When you've finished recording, click Stop or press the spacebar.

5. Cue the sequence's CTI to the point at which you want to start recording.

   If you want, set sequence In and Out points to more easily cue and repeat the section of the sequence you're recording.

6. In the audio mixer, click the Record button to activate record mode and then click the Play button to begin recording. When you've finished recording, click the audio mixer's Stop button (**Figure 11.38**).

7. To review your recording, make sure to monitor the tracks you want to hear. If necessary, repeat steps 5 and 6. When you're satisfied with your recording, deselect the Record button.

## ✔ Tip

■ Recording audio to a track is unrelated to its automation settings. Mixing automation options are for automating output settings, such as pan and fade adjustments.

## Controlling Audio Quality

You must maintain audio quality at every step of the production process: recording, digitizing, processing, and exporting. At each step, your goal is to capture and maintain a strong audio signal without distorting it. At the same time, you want to minimize noise: any extraneous sounds, including electronic hum and hiss. Audio engineers like to call achieving these goals maintaining a good signal-to-noise ratio; you might think of it as keeping the sound loud and clear.

If you use good recording and digitizing techniques, preserving audio quality in the editing and export process will be much easier.

RECORDING WITH THE AUDIO MIXER

# Fading, Panning, and Balancing

Two tasks are basic to audio mixing: fading and panning. Fading adjusts the volume, or level, that the track outputs. Over the course of a sequence, chances are you'll need to control the relative levels of the audio tracks. You may need to match the levels of dialogue recorded in different takes. Or you may need to gradually change the level of a sound effect track. For example, you might fade down the sound of a car to make it seem as though the car is driving away.

You can also control how a track's audio channels are distributed when they're output to a track with stereo or 5.1 channels. Distributing a mono track's single channel of audio between a stereo track's two channels or among a 5.1 track's multiple channels is called panning. When you output a stereo or 5.1 track to another stereo or 5.1 track, the process is called balancing. But because both methods are ways of controlling the distribution of audio output to channels in a submix or master track, it's common to refer to both as panning and to the control as a pan control, or panner. (For the sake of convenience, this book uses the term *pan* for both pan and balance, unless it's useful to make a distinction.)

Panning/balancing audio can imply an apparent position for a sound. Using the example of a car sound effect, panning can make a car sound as though it's moving from the listener's right to the left when played on a stereo system. Panning a 5.1 mix can make the car seem to drive right past or run circles around the listener (when reproduced on a 5.1 surround system).

With the audio mixer, you can adjust each track's fading and panning settings as the sequence plays, using controls that resembles those found on physical mixing consoles.

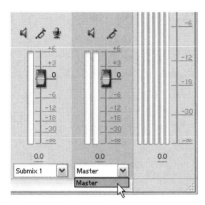

Figure 11.39 In the track's output drop-down menu, select a 5.1 submix or master track.

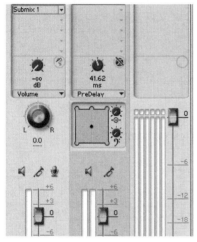

Figure 11.40 To distribute the track's audio among the five main channels, drag the black dot in the panning tray.

## ✔ Tip

■ Hovering the mouse pointer over the 5.1 tray reveals a tool tip describing the puck's position expressed as coordinates on a grid, where Left/Right axis and Front/Rear axis range from –100 to +100. Therefore, positioning the puck in the left channel places it at –100, –100; the right surround channel is at +100, +100.

# Mixing 5.1 Audio

Whereas a stereo track includes two discrete channels, a 5.1 audio track includes five discrete channels: left, right, center, surround left, and surround right. Just as sounds reproduced on a stereophonic system can seem to emanate from anywhere between the right and left speakers, sounds on a 5.1 audio system can seem to originate from anywhere in a 360-degree field created by (at least) five speakers.

The .1 in 5.1 refers to an optional LFE (low-frequency effects) channel. In contrast to the five main channels—which deliver a full range of frequencies—the LFE channel delivers bass information only.

## To balance audio in 5.1:

1. In a track's output drop-down menu, select a 5.1 audio track (**Figure 11.39**).

   A 5.1 control panel appears above the track's Mute, Solo, and Record buttons (in place of a pan/balance knob when the output is set to a stereo track).

2. To balance the audio, drag the black dot, or puck, to any position within a tray, which represents the 5.1 channels graphically (**Figure 11.40**).

   Rounded pockets along the edge of the tray correspond to the left, center, right, left surround, and right surround channels.

3. To adjust the center percentage value, drag the top-right knob in the 5.1 control panel, labeled with the icon ⊙.

4. To adjust the LFE volume, drag the lower-right knob in the 5.1 control panel, labeled with a bass clef icon 𝄢.

## To specify how 5.1 audio is mixed down:

**1.** Choose Edit > Preferences > Audio (**Figure 11.41**).

The Audio panel of the Preferences dialog box appears.

**2.** For 5.1 Mixdown Type, choose the channels you want mixed down from the drop-down menu (**Figure 11.42**).

### 5.1, 6.1, 7.1

When you're comparing sound cards and speaker systems that support 5.1 surround sound, you may find that some manufacturers boast that their equipment can support 6.1 and even 7.1 surround sound. All these systems decode 5.1 channels but can output them to different numbers of speakers: 6.1 outputs five main channels to six speakers, and 7.1 outputs five main channels to seven speakers. Plus, the optional LFE channel can be output to a subwoofer.

### The LFE Channel and Subwoofer Output

Although the LFE channel provides additional bass, it isn't necessarily output to a subwoofer speaker. The system used to decode the 5.1 signal may not output to a subwoofer if the main speakers are capable of reproducing the LFE signal instead. Conversely, if the main speakers can't reproduce the soundtrack's bass content, the system may output it to a subwoofer—even when an LFE channel isn't present.

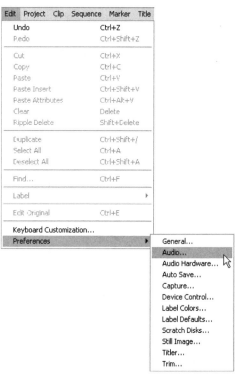

**Figure 11.41** Choose Edit > Preferences > Audio.

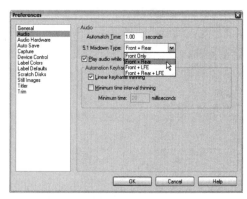

**Figure 11.42** In the drop-down menu, choose the channels you want mixed down.

MIXING 5.1 AUDIO

**Figure 11.43** Choose an option in each track's automation drop-down menu.

# Selecting an Automation Mode

Using the audio mixer is comparable to using a physical mixing console that can automate fade and pan adjustments. In other words, the audio mixer can record, or write, the adjustments you make as the sequence plays. Afterward, you can set the track to read, or play back, the adjustments you made—making the pan knobs and faders move as if controlled by some unseen hand. Alternatively, you can set the audio mixer to ignore the adjustments during playback, without deleting them.

Although only one automation option is called Write, three modes record your adjustments: Touch, Latch, and Write. Depending on the mode you choose, a track's pan knob and fader remain in place or snap back to the 0 position when you release the mouse during a mix, or when you stop playback and resume mixing. You can specify the amount of time it takes for a control to snap back to 0 during a mix by setting the automatch time. Switching between the automation modes allows you to make careful adjustments in multiple passes.

### To set a track's automation mode:

◆ For each track in the audio mixer, choose an option from the automation drop-down menu (under the track's name) (**Figure 11.43**):

**Off:** Ignores the adjustments you made to a track when using the audio mixer for playback but doesn't delete the settings (which appear as keyframes in the timeline).

**Read:** Reproduces the adjustments you made to a track during playback.

*continues on next page*

SELECTING AN AUTOMATION MODE

**Latch:** Releasing the mouse button leaves the fade/pan control at the current position. When playback is stopped and restarted, the fade/pan control resumes from 0.

**Touch:** Releasing the mouse button automatically returns the fade/pan control to 0. How quickly it returns to 0 is determined by the Automatch Time setting (see the task "To specify the automatch time").

**Write:** Releasing the mouse button leaves the fade/pan control at the current position. When playback is stopped and restarted, the fade/pan control resumes from the current position.

### To switch from Write to Touch automatically:

◆ In the audio mixer's menu, choose Switch to Touch after Write (**Figure 11.44**).

When this option is selected, tracks' automation mode switches from Write to Touch automatically. When the option is deselected, tracks remain in Write mode after a mixing pass.

### To specify the automatch time:

1. Choose Edit > Preferences > Audio (**Figure 11.45**).

   The Audio panel of the Preferences dialog box appears.

2. For Automatch Time, enter a value in seconds and click OK (**Figure 11.46**).

   The value you enter determines the time it takes for a track's controls to return to 0 when the track's automation mode is set to Touch.

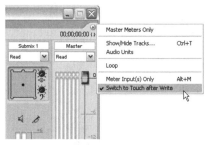

**Figure 11.44** In the audio mixer's menu, choose Switch to Touch after Write.

**Figure 11.45** Choose Edit > Preferences > Audio.

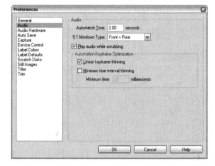

**Figure 11.46** On the Audio panel of the Preferences dialog box, enter a value for Automatch Time.

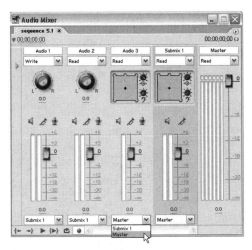

**Figure 11.47** Route each track's output by choosing an option from its output drop-down menu.

# Routing Track Output

By default, each audio track is output, or routed, to the master audio track. However, you can route any number of tracks to a submix track. The submix track combines the signals routed to it, enabling you to process multiple tracks together. In turn, the output of the submix can be routed to yet another submix track or to the master track.

Submixing allows you to work with multiple tracks more efficiently. For example, by applying an effect to a submix, you avoid applying the effect to each track separately, thereby sparing your system from processing the effect multiple times.

In the audio mixer, submix tracks always appear to the right of the standard audio tracks. To help further distinguish them from the standard tracks (which, unlike submix tracks, can contain audio clips), submix tracks appear slightly darker. To prevent feedback, a submix track can be routed only to a submix track to the right of it or to the master track.

### To route a track's output:

◆ At the bottom of a track's controls in the audio mixer, choose a track from the output drop-down menu (**Figure 11.47**):

**Master:** Outputs the track's audio to the sequence's master track.

**Submix:** Outputs the track's audio to the submix track you specify.

The track's audio is output to the track you specify. The output drop-down menu of a submix track contains only the names of submix tracks to the right and the master track.

# Working with Sends

Some mixes call for blending the processed version of an audio signal with its unprocessed signal. However, routing the signal to a submix track using the output drop-down menu won't retain an unprocessed signal. Instead, you need to use a send.

You assign a send by selecting an option from any of the five drop-down menus indicated by the sends icon 🎚 (grouped under the track effects). Each send includes a volume knob, which you use to control the volume of the processed (wet) signal produced by the submix relative to the unprocessed (dry) signal sent by the track. This process is known as adjusting the wet/dry mix.

In addition, you can specify whether the send is applied pre-fader or post-fader. A pre-fader send routes the audio before the track's fader settings are applied; a post-fader send routes the audio after. Therefore, a pre-fader send's output level isn't affected by adjustments you make to the track's fader. In contrast, a post-fader send's output changes according to the track's fader level.

Typically, you'll use a pre-fader send and set the wet/dry mix to maximize the wet signal. This allows you to control the dry signal with the track's fader and to control the wet signal with the submix's fader.

### To assign a send:

1. In the audio mixer, make sure the effects/sends area is visible.

2. In the sends area, click one of the five triangles and choose a track from the drop-down menu (**Figure 11.48**).

   The track's audio is output to the selected track, either pre-fader or post-fader, depending on your choice (see "To specify whether a send is pre-fader or post-fader" on the next page).

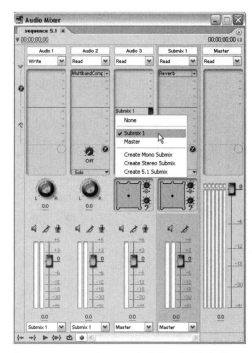

**Figure 11.48** To assign a send, click a triangle in the sends list and choose a track from the drop-down menu.

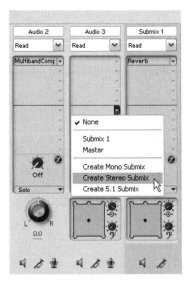

**Figure 11.49** You can also create a submix and send simultaneously by choosing the appropriate create option in the drop-down menu.

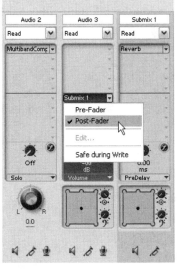

**Figure 11.50** Context-click a track's send and select either Pre-Fader or Post-Fader.

## To create a submix and assign a send simultaneously:

◆ In a track's sends area (indicated by a sends icon ), click one of the five triangles and choose an option from the drop-down menu (**Figure 11.49**).

A submix track of the channel type you specified is added to the sequence and appears in its timeline and its Audio Mixer window. Make sure to specify whether the send is pre-fader or post-fader (see the next task).

## To specify whether a send is pre-fader or post-fader:

◆ Context-click a track's send area and choose an option from the menu (**Figure 11.50**):

**Pre-Fader:** Sends the track's signal to the specified submix before the track's fade settings are applied.

**Post-Fader:** Sends the signal to the specified submix after the track's fade settings are applied.

## To view volume and panning controls for a send:

1. In a track of the audio mixer, select a send.

   Controls for one of the send's parameters appear at the bottom of the track's effects/sends area (**Figure 11.51**).

2. From the drop-down menu below the send's parameter controls, select the parameter you want to control (**Figure 11.52**).

   A control appears for the selected parameter.

## To mute a send:

1. In a track of the audio mixer, select a send.

   Controls for one of the send's parameters appear at the bottom of the track's effects/sends area.

2. In the send's controls, click the Sends button  to toggle it off, so that it appears crossed out  (**Figure 11.53**).

   When the send is off, it's excluded from output until you toggle it back on.

## ✔ Tips

- During automation, remember to protect effects and sends from inadvertent changes by context-clicking the effect or send and selecting Safe during Write.

- Older versions of Premiere allowed you to gang pan and fader controls. Submix tracks make that feature obsolete, and Premiere Pro doesn't include it.

**Figure 11.51** Selecting the name of a send makes its controls appear at the bottom of the effects/sends area.

**Figure 11.52** Choose the send parameter you want to view from the drop-down menu below the control.

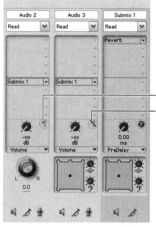

*Sends enabled*

*Sends disabled*

**Figure 11.53** Click the Sends button to toggle it on and off. A crossed-out icon means the send is disabled, or muted.

WORKING WITH SENDS

# Adding Track Effects

You can apply up to five effects to each track and submix track. There are 17 effects to choose from, but you can add VST plug-ins to expand your choices. (See the sidebar "What Is VST?") You can specify whether each effect is pre-fader or post-fader—that is, whether the effect is applied before or after the track's volume settings take effect.

As is the case with other settings, you can automate effect settings to change them over time. As with fade and pan controls, you can protect effect settings during mixing by choosing Safe during Write from the effect's context menu. And as with other effects, your automated changes can be viewed as keyframed values in the Timeline window.

When an effect has multiple parameters, you can view and adjust each parameter's values by selecting it from the effect's drop-down menu. Some effects also allow you to view the effect's controls in a separate window, which often contains special graphical controls to help you visualize the adjustments you're making.

You can also add effects to individual audio clips. Effects for audio clips, like those for video clips, are listed on the Effects palette. You adjust their settings over time by manipulating keyframes in the Timeline window and Effect Controls window. These techniques are covered in Chapter 13.

## What Is VST?

VST stands for Virtual Studio Technology and generally refers to a widely accepted audio plug-in format developed by Steinberg (the same company that introduced the ASIO standard). Third-party VST plug-ins often include controls in a dialog box separate from the audio mixer.

## To apply a track effect:

1. If the effects/sends area of the audio mixer isn't visible, click the triangle at the upper left of the window (below and to the left of the first track's automation drop-down menu) to make the area visible.

2. At the right side of the effects area, indicated by an effects icon **⊘**, click one of the five triangles and choose an effect from the drop-down menu (**Figure 11.54**).

   The effect's name appears in the list of effects, and the effect is applied to the track at the default settings. If the effect has adjustable parameter values, the first parameter's controls appears at the bottom of the track's effect/sends area.

3. Specify whether the effect is applied before or after the track's volume settings by context-clicking the effect's name and choosing one of the following (**Figure 11.55**):

   **Pre-Fader:** Applies the effect before volume adjustments.

   **Post-Fader:** Applies the effect after volume adjustments.

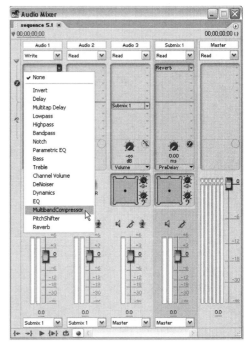

**Figure 11.54** Click one of the five triangles in the effects area and choose a track effect from the drop-down menu.

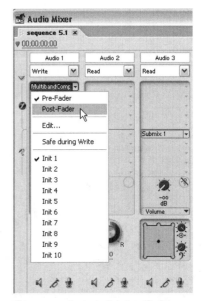

**Figure 11.55** Context-click the effect name and select either Pre-Fader or Post-Fader.

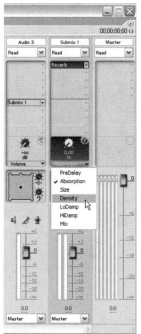

**Figure 11.56** Choose the parameter from the drop-down menu below the current control.

**Figure 11.57** To protect effect settings from being changed during automation, context-click the effect's name and choose Safe during Write.

## To view and adjust effect parameters:

1. Select a track effect.

   The controls for the effect's first parameter appear at the bottom of the track's effects/sends panel.

2. At the bottom of the track's effects/sends panel (below the parameter's value control), choose a parameter from the drop-down menu (**Figure 11.56**).

   The selected parameter's value control appears at the bottom of the track's effects/sends panel.

3. Adjust the selected parameter's values for the entire track, or during automation.

   To adjust effect parameters over time, follow the instructions in the task "To mix with automation" later in this chapter.

4. To protect the effect's parameters from changes during mixing, context-click the effect's name and choose Safe during Write (**Figure 11.57**).

## To select an effect preset:

◆ To select settings presets, context-click the effect's name and choose a parameter from the menu (**Figure 11.58**).

## To adjust a track effect's values using a separate dialog box:

1. *Do one of the following:*

   ▲ Double-click the effect's name.

   ▲ Context-click an effect's name and choose Edit from the menu (**Figure 11.59**).

   A dialog box for the effect's parameter controls opens. This option isn't available for all effects (**Figure 11.60**).

2. Adjust the effect's parameters in the dialog box either for the entire track or during automation. When you're finished, close the dialog box.

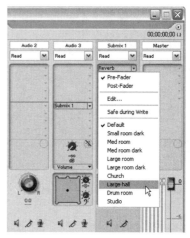

**Figure 11.58** If the effect has preset settings, you can context-click the effect and select the preset name from the drop-down menu.

**Figure 11.59** You can view the controls for many effects in a separate dialog box, which you access by double-clicking the effect's name or by context-clicking the effect and choosing Edit.

**Figure 11.60** This dialog box provides more graphical controls for the Reverb effect.

**Figure 11.61** To disable the selected effect, click its effect icon so that it appears crossed out. Click the icon again to re-enable the effect.

## To disable a track effect:

1. Select a track effect.

   The effect's parameter controls appear at the bottom of the track's effects/sends panel.

2. In the effect's parameter controls (at the bottom of the track's effects/sends panel), click the effect icon ● to toggle it off ● (**Figure 11.61**).

   The effect is disabled and won't alter the track's audio. Click the icon again to toggle it on and enable the effect.

## ✔ Tip

■ You can also apply effects to individual clips. To learn about clip-based effects and how to make a clip's effect parameters change over time, see Chapter 13.

**ADDING TRACK EFFECTS**

**343**

# Specifying Audio Keyframe Optimization

Using the audio mixer to automate audio changes can create many more keyframes than are needed in the audio track and so slow down the performance of your system. Also, an overabundance of keyframes makes it much more difficult to edit them individually.

To avoid creating too many keyframes, you can set the Automation Keyframe Optimization preference. You have a choice between Linear Keyframe Thinning and Minimal Time Interval Thinning.

◆ **Linear Keyframe Thinning:** Removes any superfluous keyframes between two perfectly straight keyframes so that only the start and end keyframes of the segment remain. This option is selected by default.

◆ **Minimal Time Interval Thinning:** Removes any keyframes within a specified time interval. The default is 20 milliseconds. Choosing this option can result in incremental keyframes of equal value. The slower the change in the effect, the more superfluous keyframes.

### To set the Automation Keyframe Optimization preference:

1. Choose Edit > Preferences > Audio (**Figure 11.62**).

   The Audio panel of the Preferences dialog box appears.

2. In the Automation Keyframe Optimization area, select one of the following and click OK (**Figure 11.63**):

   **Linear Keyframe Thinning:** Eliminates adjacent keyframes of identical value.

   **Minimal Time Interval Thinning:** Eliminates keyframes within a specified interval. Enter a time interval between 1 and 30 milliseconds (20 ms is the default).

**Figure 11.62** Choose Edit > Preferences > Audio.

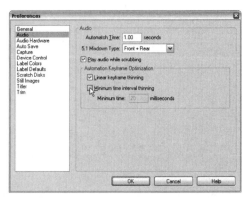

**Figure 11.63** In the Automation Keyframe Optimization area, set your preferences.

**SPECIFYING AUDIO KEYFRAME OPTIMIZATION**

**Figure 11.64** Set sequence In and Out points to define the area you want to mix. To see your adjustments in the timeline, set the tracks to show the appropriate audio data.

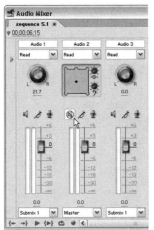

**Figure 11.65** In the audio mixer, monitor the tracks you want to hear during the mix and make sure the controls you need are visible. In this figure, Audio 2 is muted.

# Mixing with the Audio Mixer

Now that you understand all of your options, you're ready to mix.

Mixing can involve many tracks and encompass the entire length of a sequence. For this reason, you break the process into smaller, more manageable units by defining In and Out points in the sequence. Controls in the audio mixer let you play the selected area for mixing and evaluation.

Because your computer's mouse allows you to adjust only one thing at a time (and because doing so is an efficient strategy), you make adjustments to a single parameter in a single track and then adjust other parameters and tracks in separate passes.

## To prepare to mix:

1. To define the part of the sequence you want to mix, set sequence In and Out points (**Figure 11.64**).

2. To view the track volume or pan keyframes in the Timeline window, expand the audio tracks you want to adjust and then click the track's Show/Hide Keyframes button and *do one of the following:*
   ▲ Choose Show Track Keyframes > Panner; then choose the Panning option.
   ▲ Choose Show Track Volume.

3. In the audio mixer, choose monitoring options for each channel (**Figure 11.65**). You can monitor and mute any track or solo a track.

*continues on next page*

4. Make sure the controls for the parameters you want to adjust are visible.

Remember: you must select the effect or send parameter you want to adjust to view its controls.

5. Route each track's signal using its output drop-down menu and by assigning sends (**Figure 11.66**).

Routing doesn't affect automated settings directly, but it does influence the way the final mix sounds.

## To mix with automation:

1. In the audio mixer, set each channel's automation option (**Figure 11.67**).

Choose Touch, Latch, or Write for the channels you want to adjust. Generally, you adjust each channel in a separate pass.

2. To protect particular settings from being overwritten (in Touch, Latch, or Write mode), context-click the appropriate control and choose Safe during Write (**Figure 11.68**).

3. Cue the sequence's CTI to the point at which you want to start mixing and then play back the sequence.

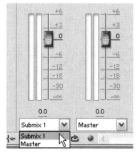

**Figure 11.66** Route each track's signal by choosing a destination in the output drop-down menu (shown here). You can also use sends to control signal flow and to blend wet and dry signals.

**Figure 11.67** In the audio mixer, use the automation drop-down menus to specify which tracks will write automated adjustments and which will read or ignore track settings.

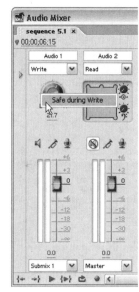

**Figure 11.68** To protect a setting from being affected during automation, context-click the setting's controls and choose Safe during Write. Here, the pan/balance control is being set to Safe during Write.

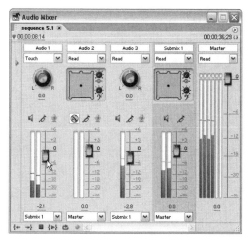

**Figure 11.69** Play the sequence and make adjustments to settings in tracks you set to an automation write mode (Latch, Touch, or Write). Here, the fader (output level) is being adjusted.

**Figure 11.70** Reset the tracks' automation mode to Read so you can review your changes.

4. As the sequence plays, make adjustments to any parameters of the tracks set to record automation (Latch, Touch, or Write) (**Figure 11.69**).

5. To stop playback and finish the mixing pass, click the Stop button in the audio mixer or program view or press the spacebar.

   In the Timeline window, changes appear as a value graph with keyframes (when the appropriate property is visible).

6. To review your adjustments, set all tracks' automation mode to Read (**Figure 11.70**) and then monitor and play back the mix.

# CREATING TITLES

Although Premiere Pro can accept graphic files created with other applications, no editing system would be complete without a title-creation tool of its own. At the very least, most videos require an opening title and end credits. But titles and graphics are far more pervasive than that. Titles can identify the onscreen speaker in a documentary, show the company logo in a commercial, list important concepts in a business presentation, or subtitle foreign-language footage. Even narrative projects may use titles within the program—for example, to identify a change of scene or time, like this: "Cape Kennedy. July 1969" or "35 Years Later."

Premiere Pro's title creation mode is called the Adobe Title Designer. The Title Designer includes tools for creating text and graphics, title rolls, and crawls. It also includes an extensive list of templates and preset styles, path text, pen tools, stroke and fill controls, and precise controls over a host of object attributes.

# The Title Designer Window

Whenever you create or change a title clip, you use the Title Designer window (**Figure 12.1**). The window is divided into several areas: a large drawing area that corresponds to the viewable screen; a toolbox for creating type and shapes, an Object Style area where you can control attributes such as font and fill color, a Transform area where you can control spatial attributes such as position and rotation, and a Styles area for storing frequently used style presets.

Beginning with Premiere Pro 1.5, new Align and Distribute buttons are located in the Title Designer's toolbox to make common tasks easier to access. A new Current Style swatch is provided next to the Object Style area. As you change text effects, the swatch is updated to reflect the changes. The revised Font menu makes accessing all of your fonts easier, and fonts are now grouped into categories.

When the window is active, a Title menu appears in the menu bar (**Figure 12.2**), and the Preferences dialog box includes Titler settings.

## ✔ Tips

- This chapter concentrates on the core features of the Title Designer. To find out how to convert titles created in older versions of Premiere, consult the online help and user guide.

- Technically, the Title Designer is a modal dialog box, not a window. In this way, titles are comparable to sequences; they're listed in the Window menu only when they're open, under Window > Titlers > *titlename*. And the Title menu is not in the Title Designer; rather, it is on the main Premiere Pro menu bar.

Toolbox          Drawing area          Object Style area

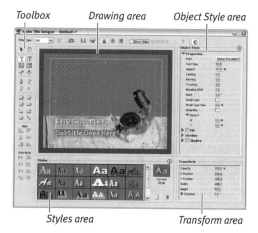

Styles area          Transform area

**Figure 12.1** The Title Designer window is divided into several sections.

**Figure 12.2** When the Title Designer window is active, so is a Title menu on the menu bar.

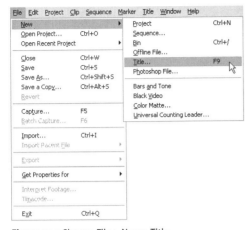

**Figure 12.3** Choose File > New > Title.

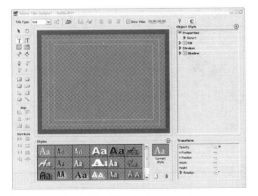

**Figure 12.4** Click the New Item button and choose Title from the menu.

**Figure 12.5** An untitled Title Designer window appears.

# Creating a Title

You can create a new title by choosing a menu command or by clicking the New Item button in the Project window. Don't forget that although you generate titles within Premiere Pro, you save them as independent files, separate from your project files. Make sure you back them up along with your other files.

### To create a new title with a menu command:

◆ Choose File > New > Title (**Figure 12.3**).

An untitled Title Designer window appears. Titles match the image size you selected in the project settings.

### To create a new title with the New Item button:

◆ In the Project window, click the New Item button 🔳 and choose Title from the menu (**Figure 12.4**).

An untitled Title Designer window appears (**Figure 12.5**). Titles match the image size you selected in the project settings.

## To save a new title:

1. With the Title Designer window active, choose File > Save As or press Ctrl+Shift +S (**Figure 12.6**).

   The Save As dialog box appears.

2. In the Save As dialog box, specify a location and name for the title and click Save.

   Premiere Pro titles use the file extension .prtl. The title appears as an item in the Project window.

## ✔ Tips

- If you make changes to a title and save it, you won't be prompted to specify a name and destination; the new version is saved over the old version. To save different versions, choose File > Save As again.

- You can use traditional keyboard short-cuts to copy and paste objects in the Title Designer: Ctrl+C to copy; Ctrl+V to paste.

**Figure 12.6** Choose File > Save As or press Ctrl+Shift+S.

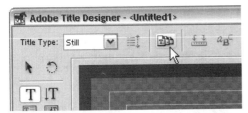

**Figure 12.7** Click the Templates button in the Title Designer window.

**Figure 12.8** A preview of the selected template appears in the dialog box.

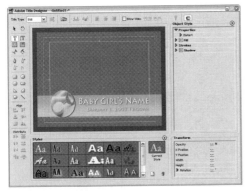

**Figure 12.9** The title template is loaded into the Title Designer window.

■ A *lower third* title is aligned with the bottom of the title-safe zone, where a title that identifies an onscreen subject is typically placed.

# Using Title Templates

The Title Designer comes with an extensive list of preset templates—ready-made designs with generic text that you can replace with your own. Templates are organized into categories, such as Celebrations, Sports, and Travel. Many contain photographic images that pertain to the topic at hand. There's also a long list of *lower third*, *upper third*, and *over the shoulder* titles (common designs in broadcast video). In addition, you'll find informational lists, which are perfect for business presentations on video.

## To load a title template:

1. In the Title Designer window, click the Templates button (**Figure 12.7**).

   The Templates dialog box appears.

2. In the Templates dialog box, select the title template you want to use.

   If necessary, click the triangle next to a folder or subfolder to reveal the templates it contains. A preview of the selected template appears in the Templates dialog box (**Figure 12.8**).

3. Click Apply.

   The title template is loaded into the Title Designer window (**Figure 12.9**). Modify the text or other objects (using methods described later in the chapter) and save the title.

## ✔ Tips

■ You can use options in the Templates dialog box to create, rename, or delete title templates.

■ A few templates don't include titles per se, but are designed to mask off areas of the video with black borders. You'll find them in the Mattes category of templates. For example, the *letterbox* template simulates a common motion-picture film aspect ratio.

# Viewing the Video Safe Zones

As you learned in Chapter 5 in the section "Viewing Video Safe Zones" standard television monitors *overscan* the image, cropping off the outer edges. For this reason, the Monitor window can display NTSC safe zones: reference marks indicating the areas of the screen that are considered to be action-safe and title-safe. It's only logical that the Title Designer window also displays guides to help you keep the titles you create within the safe zones (**Figure 12.10**). As you may recall, the inner 90 percent of the screen is considered action-safe; the inner 80 percent of the screen is considered title-safe.

### To view safe zones:

◆ With the Title Designer window selected, choose Title > View and select an option (**Figure 12.11**):

**Safe Title Margin:** Displays guides for the inner 80 percent of the title window.

**Safe Action Margin:** Displays guides for the inner 90 percent of the window.

Deselect an option to hide the safe-zone marks in the Title Designer window.

Title-safe zone          Action-safe zone

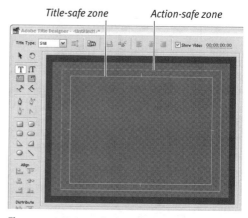

**Figure 12.10** You can display reference marks to indicate the action-safe and title-safe zones.

**Figure 12.11** With the Title Designer window active, choose Title > View and choose the safe zone you want to display.

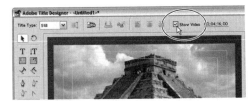

Figure 12.12 Click Show Video to display a frame of the program video as the background in the drawing area.

Figure 12.13 Change the background frame by scrubbing the current time display...

Figure 12.14 ...clicking the time display, and entering a frame number...

Figure 12.15 ...or clicking the Sync to Timeline button to show the current frame of the program view.

# Viewing the Video in the Background

Because most titles are keyed over video (see Chapter 13, "Working with Effects," and Chapter 14, "Effects in Action"), the background of a title is transparent. In the drawing area, a checkerboard pattern represents the transparent areas. However, you can fill the background with a representative frame of video from the program so you can adjust the colors and elements of the title to match.

The background frame isn't saved as part of the title; it's merely a helpful reference.

## To toggle background video:

◆ In the Title Designer window, click Show Video to display a frame of the program as the background of the drawing area (**Figure 12.12**).

Deselect Show Video to view a checkerboard background in the drawing area.

## To cue the background video frame:

◆ In the Title Designer window, *do one of the following:*

▲ Using the mouse, scrub the current frame display to change the frame number (**Figure 12.13**).

▲ Click the current frame display and enter a valid frame number (**Figure 12.14**).

▲ Click the Sync to Timeline button to cue the background video to the current position of the sequence's CTI (**Figure 12.15**).

The background video frame corresponds to the frame number you select.

## ✔ Tips

■ When you're selecting colors for objects you create in the Title Designer, you can use the Eyedropper tool to sample colors from the background video.

■ If the composition of the background video changes over the course of a title, make sure to spot-check the title against several representative frames.

# Adjusting Values

Each object you create has its own set of attributes—font, fill color, stroke color, opacity, drop shadow, and so on. Although many of an object's attributes (its position, for example) are apparent in the drawing area, you can view a display of their specific values in the Object Style and Transform areas of the Title Designer window.

To adjust the properties of any object, select it first; its properties will be listed in the Object Style area of the Title Designer. The operation of most property controls should be familiar to the experienced computer user. This chapter assumes that you know how to pick a color using a color picker or eyedropper, how to set an angle using a graphical control, and how to click a triangle to view hidden options. And by now you should be familiar with the ways to change a numerical value: either by clicking it and entering a number or by dragging it. As in other areas of Premiere Pro (and throughout Adobe programs), you can change a numerical value in the Title Designer by dragging, or *scrubbing*, the value.

This section explains how to temporarily disable certain properties of objects in a title. Later sections explain properties in greater detail: first the properties unique to each kind of object—text and graphics—and then the properties common to both text and graphics.

### To enable or disable an option:

1. Select an object in the Title Designer window.

2. *Do one of the following:*

   ▲ Click the box next to a property to enable it and the options associated with it (**Figure 12.16**).

   ▲ Deselect the box to temporarily disable the property.

   Reselecting a property restores the most recent settings associated with it.

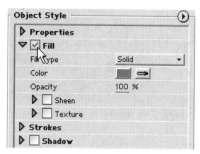

**Figure 12.16** Click the box next to a property value to enable it; deselect the box to disable the property.

### ✔ Tip

■ Although the Object Style section of the Title Designer has a Properties category, this book uses the term *properties* more generically, to refer to any attribute.

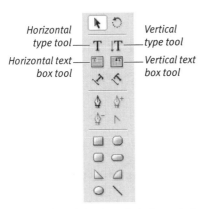

Horizontal type tool — Vertical type tool

Horizontal text box tool — Vertical text box tool

**Figure 12.17** The Title Designer includes tools for creating type bounded by the drawing area or by a text box.

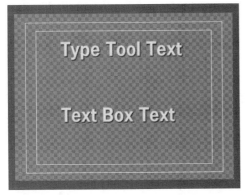

**Figure 12.18** At first glance, creating text with the type tools and the text box tools yields similar results.

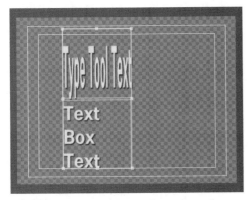

**Figure 12.19** Changing the size of a text box reflows the text it contains; changing the bounding box of text created with a type tool transforms the text.

# Creating Text Objects

The Title Designer includes tools for creating two types of text: text confined only by the drawing area, and text confined to a text box that you define. In each method, you can create either horizontally oriented or vertically oriented text (**Figure 12.17**).

At first glance, there seems to be little difference between using the type tools and using the text box tools (**Figure 12.18**). But a big practical difference emerges after you create the text. Whereas changing a text box reflows the text it contains, changing the bounding box of text created with a type tool transforms the text—that is, it resizes or stretches it (**Figure 12.19**). Therefore, it's best to use a text box to create larger blocks of text that may require tabs or margin changes. Use a type tool to create shorter messages that lend themselves to more expressive modifications such as distortion or rotation.

## To create text within the drawing area:

1. In the Title Designer window, select one of the type tools (**Figure 12.20**):

   **Horizontal Type tool T :** Creates horizontal text.

   **Vertical Type tool ₁T :** Creates vertical text.

2. Click the mouse pointer in the drawing area where you want to begin typing.

   A blinking insertion point appears.

3. Type the text you want (**Figure 12.21**).

4. When you've finished typing, click the Selection tool ▶ in the Title Designer toolbox.

5. With the title object still selected, modify any of its attributes, such as position, alignment, font, or color.

   You can use options on the Title menu or controls on the Properties panel, or you can select a style from the Style swatch panel (see the following sections).

**Figure 12.20** Select either the Horizontal (shown here) or Vertical Type tool.

**Figure 12.21** Click in the drawing area to set the insertion point and then type.

Figure 12.22 Select either the Horizontal (shown here) or Vertical Text Box tool.

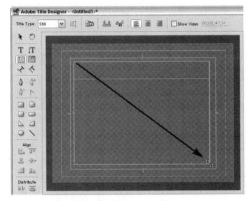

Figure 12.23 Drag diagonally in the drawing area to set the boundaries of the text box.

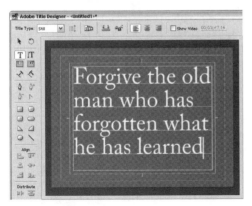

Figure 12.24 Type in the text box. If all the text doesn't fit in the box, you can resize the text later.

## To create text within a text box:

1. In the Title Designer toolbox, select one of the text box tools (**Figure 12.22**):

   **Horizontal Text Box** ▦**:** Creates horizontal text constrained by a text box.

   **Vertical Text Box** ▦**:** Creates vertical text constrained by a text box.

2. Drag the mouse pointer diagonally in the drawing area to define a text box (**Figure 12.23**).

   When you release the mouse, a text box appears, with a blinking insertion point in the upper-left corner.

3. Type the text you want (**Figure 12.24**).

   You can type more than the text box can contain. To view the hidden text, resize the text box after you've finished typing.

4. When you've finished typing, click the Selection tool ▸ in the Title Designer toolbox.

   With the title object still selected, modify any of its attributes, such as position, alignment, font, or color.

## ✔ Tip

■ Stretching type by changing the size of the bounding box doesn't affect the Distort values in the Properties section of the Title Designer window's Object Style panel.

# Setting Word Wrap

You can use the *word wrap* setting to control how text reflows within a text box. When word wrap is on, text automatically starts a new line when it reaches the edge of the text box or drawing area (depending on the kind of text you're using; see the previous sections). If you turn off word wrap, a line of text will continue offscreen if created with a type tool, and beyond the confines of its text box if created with a text box tool. To see the hidden text, reposition or resize the text, or resize the text box so that more text fits inside.

**Figure 12.25** Choose Title > Word Wrap.

## To toggle word wrap:

◆ With a text object selected, choose Title > Word Wrap (**Figure 12.25**).

Click Word Wrap to turn it on; deselect Word Wrap to turn it off. The word wrap setting you choose affects selected text objects.

## ✔ Tip

■ Resizing the bounding box reflows only lines of text created with soft returns—new lines created by word wrap. Hard returns—new lines created by pressing Enter—are not affected by resizing the bounding box.

SETTING WORD WRAP

**Figure 12.26** Choose Title > Tab Stops.

**Figure 12.27** Click the Tab Stops button.

**Figure 12.28** Select the kind of tab you want to use.

**Figure 12.29** Click above the ruler to set the tab's position.

# Setting Tabs

Larger blocks of text may also use tabs. You can set tab stops much as you would in a word processing program and view them in a text box.

### To set tabs:

1. Using a text box tool, create a text box.

2. *Do one of the following:*
   ▲ Choose Title > Tab Stops (**Figure 12.26**).
   ▲ In the Title Designer window, click the Tab Stops button (**Figure 12.27**).
   The Tab Stops dialog box opens.

3. In the Tab Stops dialog box, select the type of tab you want to set (**Figure 12.28**):
   **Left-aligned tab** ⬇
   **Center-aligned tab** ⬇
   **Right-aligned tab** ⬇

4. Click above the ruler where you want to set the tab (**Figure 12.29**).

5. To delete a tab stop, drag it away from the ruler.

6. Click OK to close the Tab Stops dialog box.

## To toggle tab reference marks:

1. Select a text box.

2. Choose Title > View > Tab Markers (**Figure 12.30**).

   A yellow line appears, corresponding to each tab (**Figure 12.31**). Deselect Tab Markers to hide the reference lines.

## ✔ Tip

■ Remember that it's hard to fit large amounts of text into the confines of a television screen—and still have it legible, that is. Consider cutting the amount of copy to the bare essentials or using a title roll instead (see "Creating Rolls and Crawls" later in this chapter).

Figure 12.30 Choose Title > View > Tab Markers.

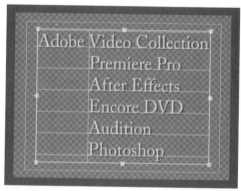

Figure 12.31 A yellow reference line corresponds to each tab you set.

SETTING TABS

**Figure 12.32** Select either the Vertical or Horizontal (shown here) Path Text tool.

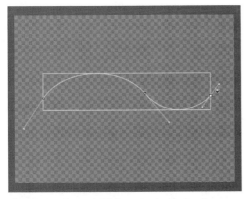

**Figure 12.33** Create a Bézier curve in the drawing area.

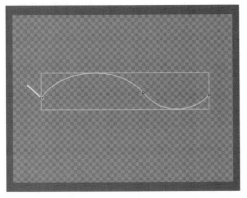

**Figure 12.34** Using the Selection tool, double-click the curve to make the insertion point appear.

# Creating Path Text

Rather than following a ramrod-straight baseline, path text follows a curved path that you create.

### To create path text:

1. In the Title Designer window, select one of the path text tools (**Figure 12.32**):

   **Horizontal Path Text** ⤳: Creates text horizontally aligned to the path.

   **Vertical Path Text** ⤳: Creates text vertically aligned to the path.

2. Create a Bézier curve in the drawing area (**Figure 12.33**).

   The mouse becomes the Pen tool. To learn more about creating Bézier curves, see "Using the Pen Tools" later in this chapter.

3. After you've finished creating the curve, choose the Selection tool.

   The Bézier curve's bounding box appears.

4. Double-click inside the curve's bounding box.

   A blinking insertion point appears at the beginning of the curve (**Figure 12.34**).

*continues on next page*

5. Type the text you want.

Each character's baseline is tangent to the curve (**Figure 12.35**).

### ✔ Tips

- Path text is prone to problems with *kerning*, the spacing between letters. Use the kerning controls as explained later in this chapter.

- You can edit path text just like you would text created with the type or text box tools.

- You can reshape the path text's curve at any time by double-clicking the path text object with the Selection tool and then clicking a control point.

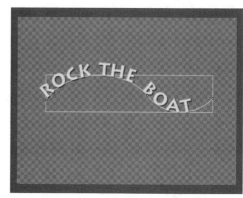

**Figure 12.35** The text follows the curve.

**Figure 12.36** To select an entire text object, click it with the Selection tool.

**Figure 12.37** Double-click to set a blinking insertion point.

**Figure 12.38** Drag the insertion-point cursor to select a contiguous range of text.

# Selecting Text

Whenever you want to edit or modify any of a text object's attributes, you must first select all or part of the object.

## To select text for editing:

1. *Do one of the following:*
   - ▲ To select the entire text object, click the text with the Selection tool (**Figure 12.36**).
   - ▲ To set an insertion point, double-click the text object with the Selection tool (**Figure 12.37**).
   - ▲ To select a range of text, drag across the text with the insertion-point cursor (**Figure 12.38**).

2. Type to change the selected text or to insert text at the insertion point.

   You can also adjust other attributes of selected text, such as font, size, or fill color. (See the following sections to find out more about adjusting text attributes.)

3. When you finish making changes to the text, choose the Selection tool.

   Click an empty part of the drawing area to deselect the text, or select another object-creation tool.

## ✔ Tip

- ■ You can use the arrow keys to move the insertion point.

# Setting Text Properties

You can assign numerous properties—color, drop shadow, and so on—to any object in the drawing area. However, some properties are exclusive to text. (See the next section, "Using the Font Browser," to learn how to select a font.)

**Figure 12.39** Edit the text as needed. Use the Object Style section of the Title Designer to adjust properties.

### To set text properties:

1. Select all or part of a text object.

2. In the Properties section of the Object Style area of the Title Designer window, set any of the following (**Figure 12.39**):

   **Font:** Lists fonts in a drop-down menu.

   **Font Size:** Sets the size of the text, in points.

   **Aspect:** Sets the horizontal ($x$) and vertical ($y$) scale of the selected font.

   **Leading:** Sets the spacing between lines of text.

   **Kerning:** Sets the spacing between character pairs; position the cursor between the characters you want to adjust.

   **Tracking:** Sets the spacing between a range of characters.

   **Baseline Shift:** Sets the distance of text characters from the baseline; use Baseline Shift to create superscripts and subscripts.

   **Slant:** Sets the slant of text, in degrees.

   **Small Caps:** When selected, makes selected characters appear as uppercase; all characters except the leading character (the first letter of each word) become small caps.

   **Small Caps Size:** When the All Caps check box is selected, sets the size of small caps as a percentage of the ordinary capital letter's height.

   **Underline:** When selected, underlines selected characters.

**Distort (*x, y*):** Distorts the selected characters; adjust the *x* value to distort the selection along its horizontal axis; adjust the *y* value to distort it along the vertical axis.

## ✔ Tips

- Starting with Premiere Pro 1.5, you can avoid scrolling through long lists of fonts, by simply selecting More from the font list. Fonts are now grouped in categories, such as Japanese fonts and Latin fonts.

- Like most text-editing or layout programs, the Title Designer allows you to *justify*, or align, the text within its text box. (There are positioning commands to move the box itself.) To align text within its text box, choose Title > Type Alignment and choose the alignment option you want: Left, Center, or Right. Better yet, use the corresponding alignment buttons at the top of the Title Designer window: ▤, ▤, ▤

- Premiere Pro 1.5 provides improved handling of Japanese characters. When you type Japanese characters while a roman font, such as Courier, is selected, Premiere Pro enters the characters using the system-default Japanese font. Premiere Pro automatically switches back to the roman font when you begin to type roman characters.

# Using the Font Browser

Choosing a font from a long drop-down menu works great if you're already familiar with the font you want. But if you could use a little help selecting a font, use the Font Browser feature. It not only lists fonts—it also shows what they look like and instantly changes the font of the selected text. This allows you to preview various fonts before you settle on one.

### To select a font using the Font Browser:

1. *Do one of the following:*
   - ▲ Select one or more text objects.
   - ▲ Select a range of text.
   - ▲ Set an insertion point using one of the text tools.

2. *Do one of the following:*
   - ▲ From the Title menu, choose Font > Browse (**Figure 12.40**).
   - ▲ In the Title Designer window, click the Browse button ᵃ𝐁ᶜ (**Figure 12.41**).

   The Font Browser dialog box appears.

**Figure 12.40** Choose Title > Font > Browse.

**Figure 12.41** In the Title Designer window, click the Browse button.

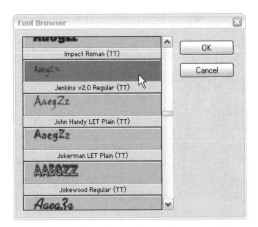

**Figure 12.42** Select a font in the Font Browser window.

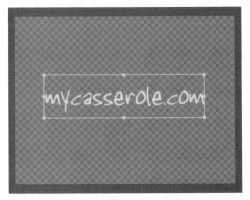

**Figure 12.43** The selected text reflects your choice.

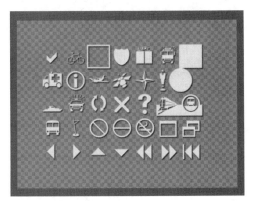

**Figure 12.44** The font Webdings creates symbols instead of letters.

**3.** In the Font Browser dialog box, select a font you want to consider (**Figure 12.42**). The selected text reflects the font you choose in the Font Browser (**Figure 12.43**).

**4.** When you find the font you want, click OK.

## ✔ Tips

■ Not all fonts look like letters. Special fonts—often called symbols, ornaments, and dingbats—let you create useful graphic elements easily (**Figure 12.44**). You use these fonts just like other fonts, and you don't have to draw a thing.

■ By default, the font browser presents a sample of each font consisting of six letters: *AaegZz*. You can change the letters by choosing Edit > Preferences > Titler and typing any other six letters you want.

USING THE FONT BROWSER

# Using Styles

Besides conveying raw information, titles also contribute to the overall look of a project. So, it's common for all the titles in a project to share similar characteristics. Using the Styles feature, you can reapply your favorite attributes quickly, without adjusting attributes time and time again.

The Current Style swatch always reflects the current style of the text. Any modifications you make to the style of the text updates the Current Style swatch.

### To assign a style to text:

1. Select a text object or a range of text (**Figure 12.45**).

2. In the Styles panel of the Title Designer, click a style swatch. (**Figure 12.46**).

   The selected text uses the style you selected (**Figure 12.47**).

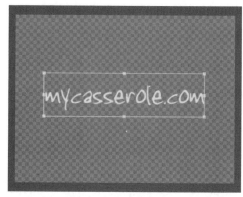

**Figure 12.45** Select a text object or range of text.

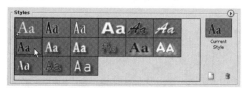

**Figure 12.46** Click a style swatch in the Styles area of the Title Designer window.

**Figure 12.47** The style is applied to the selection.

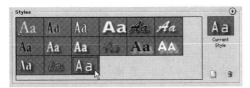

**Figure 12.48** Click a style swatch to select it. The swatch should display a thin square.

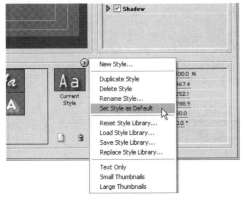

**Figure 12.49** Choose Set Style as Default in the Styles panel's menu.

**Figure 12.50** The default swatch always appears in the upper-left corner, with a small icon.

## To set a style as the default:

1. Make sure no text objects in the drawing area are selected and then click the style swatch you want to set as the default.

   A thin square outline indicates that the style is selected (**Figure 12.48**). If a text object is selected, it takes on the attributes of the style you choose.

2. From the Styles panel's menu, choose Set Style as Default (**Figure 12.49**). The swatch moves to the upper-left corner of the Styles panel. A small icon appears in the corner of the selected style swatch (**Figure 12.50**).

## To save a custom style:

1. Select a text object or range of text that has the attributes you want to save as a style (**Figure 12.51**).

2. In the Styles panel's menu, choose New Style (**Figure 12.52**).

   A New Style dialog box appears.

3. In the New Style dialog box, enter the name of the style and click OK (**Figure 12.53**).

   The style is added to the style swatches (**Figure 12.54**).

4. To view the styles by name, choose Text Only from the Styles panel's menu.

## ✔ Tips

- Commands in the Styles panel's menu also allow you to delete and rename styles and change the way the style swatches look.

- By default, style swatches show the way an uppercase and lowercase letter *A* look in the style. If you want to, you can choose Edit > Preferences > Titler and specify other letters.

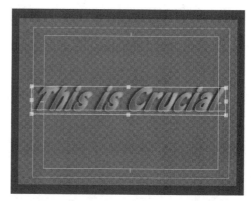

**Figure 12.51** Select text that uses the attributes you want to save as a style.

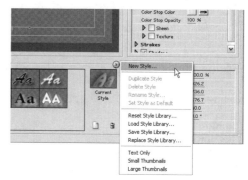

**Figure 12.52** From the Styles panel's menu, choose New Style.

**Figure 12.53** Name the style in the New Style dialog box and click OK.

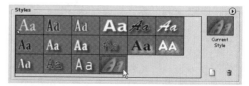

**Figure 12.54** The new style appears among the style swatches.

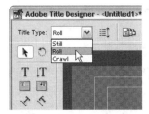

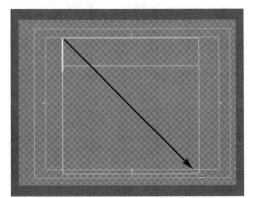

**Figure 12.55** Choose an option from the Title Type drop-down menu. Here, a title roll is selected.

**Figure 12.56** Using a text box tool (the Horizontal Text Box tool is selected here), drag in the drawing area to create a text box.

# Creating Rolls and Crawls

In a title roll, text appears to move from beyond the bottom of the screen to beyond the top of the screen. Title rolls are frequently used in a final credit sequence or to present lengthy text onscreen.

A title crawl moves across the screen horizontally, typically from right to left. An emergency news bulletin is a classic example of a title crawl.

## To create a roll or crawl:

1. In the Title Designer window, choose an option from the Title Type pull-down menu (**Figure 12.55**):
   **Still:** Creates stationary text.
   **Roll:** Creates rolling text.
   **Crawl:** Creates crawling text.

2. Select the Horizontal Text Box tool. To create vertically oriented text, choose the Vertical Text Box tool.

3. Drag in the drawing area to create a text box (**Figure 12.56**).
   You should drag beyond the bottom edge for a roll, or beyond the right edge for a crawl. Typically, you should keep title rolls between the left and right edges of the title-safe zone (see "Viewing the Video Safe Zones" earlier in this chapter).

*continues on next page*

CREATING ROLLS AND CRAWLS

4. Type the text you want (**Figure 12.57**).

5. *Do one of the following:*
   ▲ To make the text box larger, switch to the Selection tool and drag one of the text box's control handles to resize the box.
   ▲ To view other parts of the text box, drag the scrollbar (**Figure 12.58**).

6. Set the roll/crawl options, as explained in the next task.

7. Press Ctrl+S to save the title.

   When you add the title clip to the time-line, it rolls or crawls, according to your selections. The duration of the clip helps determine the speed of the roll or crawl.

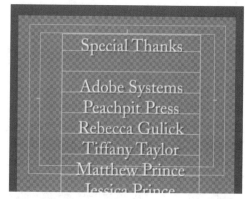

**Figure 12.57** Type the text you want to scroll or crawl. A scrollbar appears.

**Figure 12.58** To make the text box larger, resize it with the Selection tool; use the scrollbar to view different parts of the box.

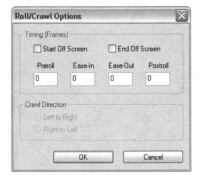

**Figure 12.59** With the rolling or crawling object selected, choose Title > Roll/Crawl Options.

**Figure 12.60** Choose the options you want in the Roll/Crawl Options dialog box.

## To set roll and crawl options:

1. With a rolling or crawling text object selected, choose Title > Roll/Crawl Options (**Figure 12.59**).

   The Roll/Crawl Options dialog box appears (**Figure 12.60**).

2. In the Roll/Crawl Options dialog box, choose one or more of the following options:

   **Start Off Screen:** Positions the text box offscreen at the beginning of the roll or crawl.

   **End Off Screen:** Positions the text box offscreen at the end of the roll or crawl.

   **Preroll:** Sets the number of frames to hold the title in its starting position before the roll or crawl begins (not available when Start Off Screen is selected).

   **Ease-In:** Sets the number of frames during which the roll or crawl slowly accelerates before reaching full speed.

   **Ease-Out:** Sets the number of frames during which the roll or crawl slowly decelerates before stopping.

   **Postroll:** Sets the number of frames to hold the title in its ending position after the roll or crawl ends (not available when End Off Screen is selected).

3. Click OK to close the dialog box.

   The roll or crawl obeys the settings you selected.

## ✔ Tip

■ Although you can hold a title roll in its ending position by setting a Postroll value, getting the last lines to stop where you want might take some practice. For example, to get the text *copyright 2004* to end up alone in the center of the screen, you may have to experiment with adding blank lines or resizing the text box.

CREATING ROLLS AND CRAWLS

# Creating Shape Objects

When you create a shape, you define its dimensions by defining the size of an invisible, rectangular box called a *bounding box.* Whereas a rectangle fits exactly inside its bounding box, other shapes are circumscribed within theirs. When you select a shape, its bounding box appears with six *handles,* small squares that you can grab and drag to change the dimensions of the box—and thereby the shape it contains.

You can also create open and closed polygons and Bézier shapes. These techniques are covered in later sections.

**Figure 12.61** Select one of the shape tools. In this example, the Ellipse tool is selected.

### To create a shape:

1. In the Title Designer window toolbox, select a shape tool (**Figure 12.61**):

   **Rectangle** □

   **Clipped-Corner Rectangle** ○

   **Rounded-Corner Rectangle** ○

   **Wedge** ◁

   **Arc** ◁

   **Ellipse** ○

2. *Do one of the following:*

   ▲ Drag in the drawing area to define the size of the shape (**Figure 12.62**).

   ▲ Shift-drag in the drawing area to make the shape's horizontal and vertical aspects the same (to create perfect circles and squares or wedges and arcs with two equal sides).

   ▲ Alt-drag in the drawing area to define the shape from its center rather than its corners.

### ✔ Tips

■ You can change the dimensions of a shape (or text created with a type tool) by selecting it and dragging a handle of its bounding box.

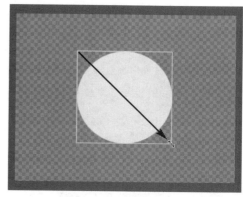

**Figure 12.62** Drag in the drawing area to define the size of the shape. Hold down Shift to constrain the aspect of the shape, and hold down Alt to draw the shape from its center.

■ You can change an existing shape into another shape with the same dimensions by selecting it and choosing an option from the Graphic Type drop-down menu.

■ Rounded-corner and clipped-corner rectangles have a Fillet Size setting, which specifies how much of the corner is rounded or clipped, respectively.

**Figure 12.63** Anchor points have no direction lines extending from them.

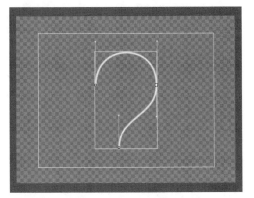

**Figure 12.64** Smooth points have two opposite direction lines.

# Understanding Control Points and Segments

You can use pen tools to create more complex shapes—the same kind of Bézier curves you can build in programs like Adobe Illustrator. But if you've never used a pen tool or heard of Bézier curves, it's time to review some basics.

Bézier paths consist of control points connected by line segments. *Control points* define each end of a segment; *direction lines* define the curve of the segment.

Direction lines and handles extend from control points to define and control the curve of a path segment. The length and angle of a direction line influence the shape of the curve. (Imagine that direction lines exert a gravitational pull on the line that enters and exits a control point.) Dragging the end of a direction line alters the line and thus its corresponding curve. When a point has two direction lines, the incoming direction line influences the preceding curve; the outgoing direction line influences the following curve.

It's helpful to categorize control points by how they use, or don't use, direction lines:

**Anchor point:** Click with the Pen tool to create an anchor point. Anchor points have no control handles extending from them (**Figure 12.63**).

**Smooth point:** Drag with the Pen tool to create a smooth point. Dragging extends two equal and opposite direction lines from a smooth point. Path segments connected by a smooth point result in a continuous curve (**Figure 12.64**).

*continues on next page*

**Corner point:** A corner point's direction lines operate independently. You can convert a smooth point into a corner point by dragging a direction handle with the Convert Point tool ⊾. Path segments connected by a corner point result in a discontinuous curve, or *cusp* (**Figure 12.65**).

### ✔ Tips

- Although the concepts that underlie the creation of Bézier curves are constant, terminology and practice differ slightly from one program to another. Even among well-integrated programs—Illustrator, Photoshop, After Effects, and Premiere Pro—the pen tools and keyboard shortcuts differ.

- You'll apply what you learn about Bézier curves to adjusting the spatial and temporal interpolation used when animating a clip's position and other effects. In other words, you can use Bézier curves to set a clip's motion path and to accelerate or decelerate changes in an animated effect. Learn all about it in Chapter 13.

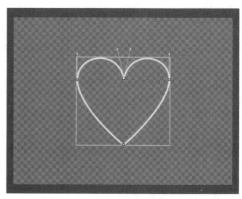

**Figure 12.65** Corner points, or cusps, result from two discontinuous direction lines.

### Qu'est-ce Que C'est Bézier? *Qui Est* Bézier?

In case your French is rusty, Bézier is pronounced *bez-ee-yay*, after the late Pierre Etienne Bézier, who developed the math behind his namesake curve in the 1970s for use in computer-aided design and manufacture. This same math became the basis for Adobe Postscript fonts, path-based drawing, and—yes—the interpolation methods used in computer animation. Bézier died in 1999. Merci, Monsieur Bézier.

**Figure 12.66** Select the Pen tool.

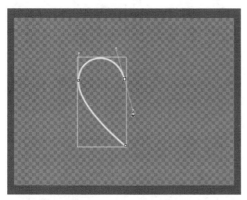

**Figure 12.67** Click to create an anchor point with no control handles...

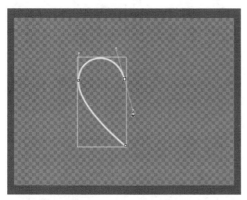

**Figure 12.68** ...or drag to create a smooth point and define its control handles.

# Using the Pen Tools

In contrast to the title feature found in older versions of Premiere, the Title Designer comes with the powerful Pen tool. Now the kinds of shapes you can create are practically limitless. You can create an open Bézier path—anything from a simple straight line to a complex squiggle—or you can join the ends to form a closed Bézier path.

## To create a Bézier curve:

1. In the Title Designer toolbox, select the Pen tool ⟨pen icon⟩ (**Figure 12.66**).

2. *Do one of the following:*
   - ▲ To create an anchor point, click in the drawing area (**Figure 12.67**).
   - ▲ To create a smooth point, drag the cursor around in the drawing area (**Figure 12.68**). If you want, drag a control handle to adjust the curve before continuing.

*continues on next page*

**3.** To create a corner point, select the Convert Point tool and drag a control handle (**Figure 12.69**).

Afterward, you must reselect the Pen tool and click the corner point. Otherwise, the next point you create will begin a new path.

**4.** Repeat steps 2 and 3 to create straight and curved segments between points (**Figure 12.70**).

**5.** *Do one of the following:*

▲ To close the path, position the Pen tool over the first control point so a circle icon appears 🖋₀ and then click (**Figure 12.71**).

▲ To leave the path open, choose the Selection tool.

## ✔ Tips

■ Don't let all the options confuse you; creating simple shapes with the Pen tool is easy. To create a line with the Pen tool, just click where you want one end of the line and then click to set the other end. To create a polygon, keep clicking to create more anchor points and then click the first point to close the shape.

■ Because the Pen tool can do everything the Line tool can and more, the Line tool isn't covered here. Besides, a line appears as an open Bézier object in the Graphic Type drop-down menu.

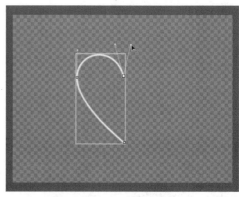

**Figure 12.69** Select the Convert Point tool and drag a smooth point's control handle independently.

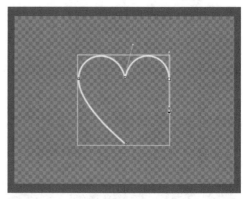

**Figure 12.70** Continue to create control points to build the path.

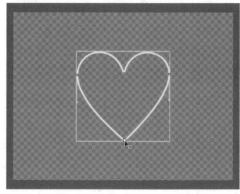

**Figure 12.71** To close the path, position the Pen tool over the first control point (a circle icon appears) and then click.

**Figure 12.72** To reshape a Bézier object, select it. Then position the Pen tool over the object.

**Figure 12.73** To move a control point, drag with the Pen tool.

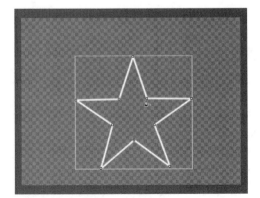

**Figure 12.74** Position the Remove Point tool over a control point...

# Reshaping a Bézier Curve

You can change the shape of a Bézier path at any time by moving, adding, or deleting its control points or direction handles.

### To move a control point:

1. Select a Bézier object.

2. Select the Pen tool 🖊 and position it over the object.

   The object's control points appear (**Figure 12.72**).

3. Drag a control point (**Figure 12.73**).

### To remove a control point:

1. Select a Bézier object.

2. Select the Remove Point tool 🖊.

3. Click a control point (**Figure 12.74**).

   The point is removed, and the path adjusts (**Figure 12.75**).

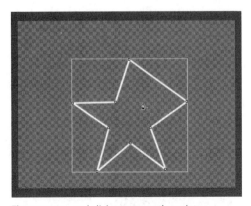

**Figure 12.75** ...and click to remove the point.

## To add a control point:

1. Select a Bézier object.

2. Select the Add Point tool ⬥₊.

3. *Do one of the following:*

   ▲ To add a point without changing the path, click the path (**Figure 12.76**).

   ▲ To add a point and change the path, drag the path (**Figure 12.77**).

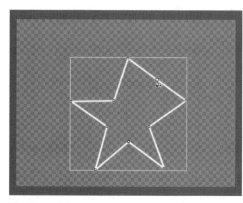

**Figure 12.76** To create a new control point, click a line segment with the Add Point tool...

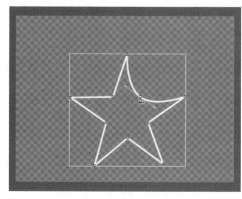

**Figure 12.77** ...or click and drag to move the new control point.

---

## Pen Pointers

If your goal is to create smooth and shapely Bézier curves, here are a few tips.

The most pleasing curves use direction handles that are about one-third the size of the curve (**Figure 12.78**).

As a rule, any line segment should use two direction lines or none at all. When only a single direction line influences a curve, one end of the curve flattens out, which looks awkward.

Use a minimal number of control points to achieve the curve you want. The curve will be smoother and easier to control.

Creating a smooth point always extends two equal and opposite direction lines. However, drag in the direction of the curve to follow.

¹⁄₃ line segments
Line segment

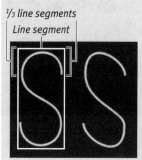

**Figure 12.78** The S shape on the left uses direction handles that follow the *rule of thirds*; the S on the right does not.

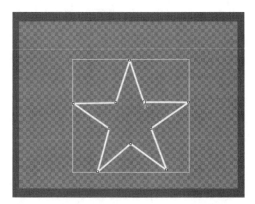

**Figure 12.79** Click a smooth point or corner point to convert it to an anchor point.

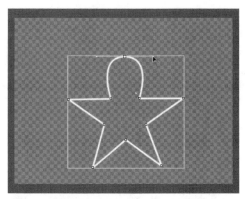

**Figure 12.80** Drag an anchor point or corner point to convert it into a smooth point.

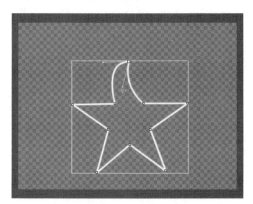

**Figure 12.81** Drag the control handle of a smooth point to convert it to a corner point.

## To convert a control point:

1. Select a Bézier object.

2. Select the Convert Point tool ⊾.

3. *Do one of the following:*

   ▲ Click a smooth point or corner point to convert it to an anchor point (**Figure 12.79**).

   ▲ Drag an anchor point or corner point to convert it to a smooth point (**Figure 12.80**).

   ▲ Drag the control handle of a smooth point to convert it to a corner point (**Figure 12.81**).

RESHAPING A BÉZIER CURVE

# Specifying Line and Path Properties

In addition to adjusting the angle and curves of line segments, you can control the appearance of the corners and ends. The *cap type* determines how the ends of a path look. You can choose butt, square, or round caps (**Figure 12.82**). The type of join determines whether a corner is mitered, rounded, or beveled (**Figure 12.83**). Framed Bézier shapes and lines have both join and cap options; filled Bézier shapes have only join options.

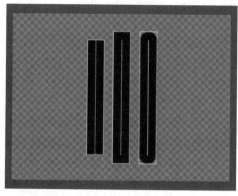

**Figure 12.82** These three thick lines have exactly the same length but use different caps: butt, square, and round (left to right).

**Figure 12.83** These Bézier shapes are exact copies, but they use different joins: rounded, mitered, and beveled. The lower star's miter limit is set to make the joins pointed rather than beveled.

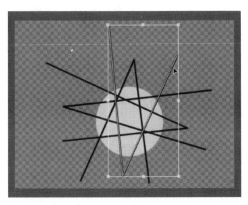

**Figure 12.84** Select a Bézier shape, including lines.

## To specify the attributes of open Bézier objects or lines:

1. Select an open Bézier object or line (**Figure 12.84**).

2. In the Object Style area, adjust the Line Width value (**Figure 12.85**).

3. For Cap Type, choose an option from the drop-down menu (**Figure 12.86**).

4. For Join Type, choose an option from the drop-down menu (**Figure 12.87**).

5. If you selected Miter as the join type, adjust the Miter Limit value.

   This value specifies when the miter switches to a bevel, expressed as a multiple of the line's stroke weight. Therefore, a miter limit of 1 results in a bevel. At the default value of 4, the miter switches to a bevel when the length of the point reaches 4 times the stroke weight.

   The object uses the properties you specified.

**Figure 12.85** Adjust the Line Width value.

**Figure 12.86** Choose an option from the Cap Type drop-down menu.

**Figure 12.87** Choose an option from the Join Type drop-down menu.

SPECIFYING LINE AND PATH PROPERTIES

# Converting Shapes to Filled Bézier Shapes

When you create a closed Bézier shape, it is framed by default—that is, empty in the middle. However, you can convert it to a filled Bézier shape by using a simple menu command.

### To convert to a filled Bézier shape:

1. Select a Bézier object or other shape (**Figure 12.88**).

2. In the Object Style area of the Title Designer, choose Filled Bézier from the Graphic Type drop-down menu (**Figure 12.89**).

   The object fills with the current fill color. If the object was an open Bézier shape, it closes and fills (**Figure 12.90**).

### ✔ Tip

■ You can open a closed Bézier shape (and vice versa) by selecting the appropriate option from the Graphic Type drop-down menu. Closed shapes such as those created with the Rectangle tool can also be opened this way. However, you won't be able to see that the shape has been opened until you drag the appropriate control point.

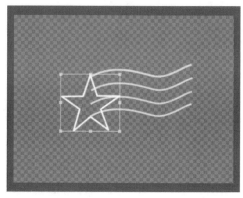

**Figure 12.88** Select a Bézier object.

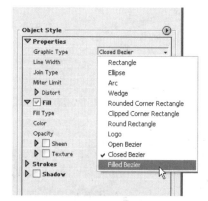

**Figure 12.89** Choose Filled Bézier from the Graphic Type drop-down menu...

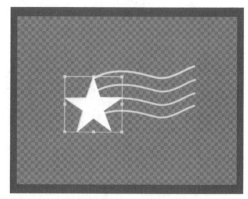

**Figure 12.90** ...to convert the object to a filled shape.

**Figure 12.91** Click the Fill option in the Object Style area. If necessary, click the triangle to expand the fill options.

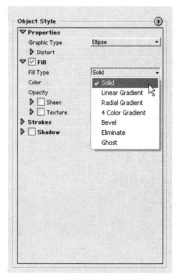

**Figure 12.92** Select a fill type from the drop-down menu.

## ✔ Tips

- A color that looks great on your computer screen may not be *NTSC safe* and may look noisy or bleed on a television. See Chapter 16, "Video and Audio Settings," for more about NTSC-safe colors.

- Naturally, choosing Eliminate as the fill type is useful only if you add a stroke to the object. See "Setting Stroke Options" later in this chapter.

# Setting Fill Options

Both text and shapes can be filled with a color. In addition to color, there are numerous other fill options.

## To set fill options:

1. Select an object in the drawing area.

2. In the Object Style area of the Title Designer, make sure Fill is selected (**Figure 12.91**).

   You may need to click the triangle next to Fill to view its properties.

3. Select an option from the Fill Type drop-down menu (**Figure 12.92**):

   **Solid:** Sets a uniform color fill.

   **Linear Gradient:** Sets a fill that gradually changes from one color to another in a linear pattern.

   **Radial Gradient:** Sets a fill that gradually changes from one color to another in a circular pattern.

   **4 Color Gradient:** Sets a gradient composed of four colors, each starting from a different corner of the object's bounding box.

   **Bevel:** Gives the object's edges a beveled appearance.

   **Eliminate:** Makes the fill transparent and unable to cast a shadow.

   **Ghost:** Makes the fill transparent yet capable of casting a shadow.

4. Set other Fill property values:

   **Color:** Use either a color swatch to select a color from a color picker or the Eyedropper tool to sample a color from the drawing area.

   **Opacity:** 100% is completely opaque, and 0% is completely transparent.

# Setting Gradient Options

As you saw in the previous section, three of the seven fill types are gradients: linear gradient, radial gradient, and four-color gradient. All the gradients change from one color to another. However, gradients can also change from one opacity level to another. For this reason, gradients use special controls to define color and transparency.

Under the Fill property heading, each color used in a gradient is represented by a *color stop*—a small box alongside a sample image of the gradient. For linear and radial gradients, the left color stop shows the starting color; the right color stop shows the ending color (**Figure 12.93**). Four-color gradients have a color box for each corner of the object (**Figure 12.94**).

**Figure 12.93** Color stops represent the starting and ending colors of a linear or radial gradient.

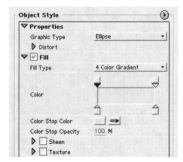

**Figure 12.94** Four-color gradients have a color stop in each corner of the gradient sample.

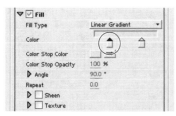

**Figure 12.95** Select a color stop by clicking the arrow above it.

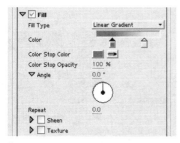

**Figure 12.96** Adjust the selected color stop by picking a color or adjusting the Color Stop Opacity value.

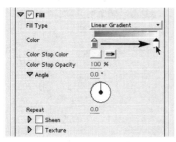

**Figure 12.97** Drag the color swatches left or right. Their relative positions affect the gradient ramp—the transition between the colors.

## To set gradient options:

1. Select an object that uses a linear, radial, or four-color gradient fill.

2. Click the arrow above the color stop you want to adjust (**Figure 12.95**).

3. To set the color stop's color, *do one of the following:*
   - ▲ Click the color swatch next to Color Stop Color to use a color picker.
   - ▲ Click the Eyedropper tool ⬌ to sample a color from the screen.

4. To set the opacity of the selected color stop, adjust the Color Stop Opacity value (**Figure 12.96**).

5. Repeat steps 2 through 4 for other color stops, as needed.

6. To adjust a linear or radial gradient's *ramp*, drag the color swatches along the gradient sample (**Figure 12.97**).

   The relative spacing of the color swatches along the gradient sample affects the transition between colors.

7. To adjust the angle of a linear gradient, adjust the Angle value.

8. To repeat a linear or radial gradient, increase the Repeat value.

## ✔ Tips

- Double-clicking a color stop also opens a color picker.

- The Render category of the Video Effects folder on the Effects palette includes an After Effects filter called Ramp. You can apply this filter to a clip to create a full-screen linear or radial gradient. The Ramp effect has Scatter and Blend with Original parameters, but no Repeat parameter.

**SETTING GRADIENT OPTIONS**

# Setting Sheen Options

Both fill and stroke options include a parameter called Sheen. Sheen makes an object seem smooth and shiny by simulating light reflecting from the object's surface.

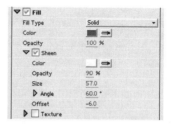

**Figure 12.98** Click the Sheen option and set its color, opacity, size, angle, and offset.

## To apply a sheen:

1. Select an object in the drawing area.

2. Apply a fill to the object, if it doesn't already have one.

   Make sure to expand the Fill property heading in the Object Style area of the Title Designer window.

3. Under the Fill property heading, click the Sheen subheading.

   A sheen appears on the object, using the default settings.

4. Click the triangle next to Sheen to reveal its properties.

5. Under Sheen, set the following options (**Figure 12.98**):

   **Color:** Sets the color of the sheen; white is the default.

   **Opacity:** Sets the opacity of the sheen.

   **Size:** Sets the width of the sheen.

   **Angle:** Sets the angle of the sheen, in degrees.

   **Offset:** Shifts the position of the sheen

   The object's sheen uses the settings you specified (**Figure 12.99**).

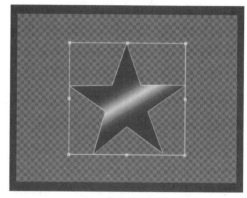

**Figure 12.99** In this example, the object's sheen implies a polished surface.

## ✔ Tip

■ The Basic 3D video effect has a parameter called *specular highlight* that also gives an object a subtle sheen.

**Figure 12.100** Select a filled object.

**Figure 12.101** Click Texture and then click the Texture swatch to open the Load Texture dialog box.

# Applying a Texture

Both the fill and stroke options include a parameter called Texture. As the name suggests, a texture gives the impression that an object has a surface composed of a given material. But you can use the Texture property to fill an object with any image.

### To apply a texture:

1. Select an object (**Figure 12.100**).

   If necessary, expand the Fill property heading in the Object Style area of the Title Designer window.

2. Click Texture.

3. Click the Texture swatch (**Figure 12.101**). A Load Texture dialog box appears.

   *continues on next page*

4. In the Load Texture dialog box, select an image to serve as the object's texture fill and then click Open (**Figure 12.102**).

   The image you chose fills the selected object (**Figure 12.103**).

5. Under the Texture property heading, set the texture's scaling, placement, tiling, and compositing options.

## ✔ Tips

■ The Texture property includes a lot of parameters, so experiment with them.

■ A texture can help you create an effect similar to the image-matte key (see Chapter 14). But unlike the image-matte key, the Texture property includes a number of settings that control the way the texture is scaled and blended with the object.

■ Premiere Pro includes several files intended to serve as textures. You'll find them in the Textures folder inside the Presets folder (which, in turn, resides in the Premiere Pro folder).

**Figure 12.102** Select the texture you want and click Open.

**Figure 12.103** The object is filled with the texture you specified.

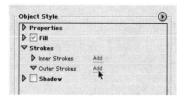

**Figure 12.104** Click the Add button next to the kind of stroke you want.

**Figure 12.105** Choose an option from the Type drop-down menu.

**Figure 12.106** Set the stroke's size, angle, and fill options.

# Setting Stroke Options

The Title Designer has full-fledged stroke options for objects, much like the ones found in dedicated graphics applications.

You can add up to 12 strokes to each object. The Title Designer lists and renders strokes in the order you create them. Each successive stroke is considered subordinate to the last stroke, in a kind of hierarchy. As a result, resizing a stroke higher in the hierarchy resizes all the strokes beneath it. At any time, you can change the hierarchy, disable strokes, or delete strokes.

## To add strokes:

1. Select one or more objects in the drawing area.

2. In the Object Style area of the Title Designer window, expand the Strokes property controls.

3. Click Add next to the type of stroke you want (**Figure 12.104**).

4. Choose an option from the Type drop-down menu (**Figure 12.105**):

    **Depth:** Creates a stroke that makes the object appear extruded and three-dimensional.

    **Edge:** Strokes the entire inner or outer edge of the object (depending on whether the stroke is an inner or outer stroke).

    **Drop Face:** Creates a stroke identical to the object, but behind the object and with its own attributes. Drop face is similar to a drop shadow, except it doesn't have a spread property.

5. Set other attributes of the stroke (**Figure 12.106**):

    **Size:** Sets the thickness of the stroke in pixels (not available for drop-face strokes).

*continues on next page*

**SETTING STROKE OPTIONS**

**Angle:** Sets the angle of the stroke in degrees (not available for edge strokes).

6. Set the fill options, including Fill Type, Color, Opacity, Sheen, and Texture.

    The stroke takes on the attributes you specified (**Figure 12.107**). For more information on using fill options, see "Setting Fill Options" earlier in this chapter.

## To change the hierarchy of strokes:

1. Select an object that contains multiple strokes (**Figure 12.108**).

2. In the Object Style area of the Title Designer window, select the stroke you want to move in the hierarchy (**Figure 12.109**).

**Figure 12.107** This example shows all three stroke types: depth (top), edge (center), and drop face (bottom).

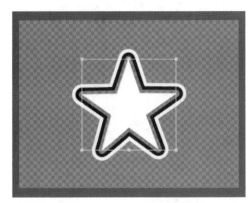

**Figure 12.108** This object has three outer strokes. The first is transparent (Eliminate fill), followed by a black stroke and then a yellow stroke.

**Figure 12.109** In the Object Style area, select the stroke you want to move in the hierarchy.

**Figure 12.110**
Choose an option from the Object Style menu. In this example, the black stroke is being promoted.

3. Choose an option from the Object Style menu (**Figure 12.110**):

**Move Stroke Up:** Moves the stroke higher in the hierarchy.

**Move Stroke Down:** Moves the stroke lower in the hierarchy.

The stroke is shifted in the hierarchy according to your choice (**Figure 12.111**).

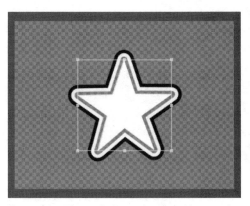

**Figure 12.111** The stroke is reordered. In this example, the black stroke becomes the outermost stroke.

## To delete a stroke:

1. Select an object that contains a stroke.

2. In the Object Style area of the Title Designer window, select the name of the stroke you want to delete.

3. From the Object Style menu, choose Delete Stroke (**Figure 12.112**).

## ✔ Tips

■ You can't specify a join type for strokes (as you can with Bézier objects, which themselves can be stroked). However, you may notice that the outer edges of outer strokes have curved obtuse angles and sharp acute angles. The inner edges of inner strokes have sharp obtuse angles, and acute angles have what might be called a *faceted* corner. So if you don't like the way strokes handle joins, use Bézier objects instead (**Figure 12.113**).

■ Experiment with strokes to create an object that looks like several concentric shapes with transparent gaps in between.

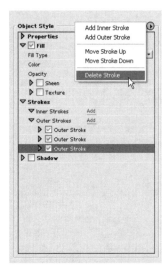

**Figure 12.112** You can also choose to delete the stroke.

**Figure 12.113** The first object uses an inner stroke, the second uses an outer stroke, and the third is actually two shapes: a Bézier object with miter joins and a filled Bézier object behind it.

SETTING STROKE OPTIONS

**Figure 12.114** Select an object to which you want to add a shadow.

**Figure 12.115** Click the Shadow option and choose the properties you want.

**Figure 12.116** This shadow's property settings are Opacity = 60%, Angle = 45 degrees, Distance = 10, Size = 0, Spread = 10.

# Adding Drop Shadows

A drop shadow can set an object apart from the background or impart a sense of depth. You can apply a drop shadow to any object.

## To apply a shadow:

1. Select an object to which you want to add a shadow (**Figure 12.114**).

2. In the Object Style area of the Title Designer window, click Shadow.

3. Set the shadow's properties (**Figure 12.115**):

   **Color:** Use a color swatch to open a color picker or the Eyedropper tool to sample a color from the drawing area.

   **Opacity:** 100% is completely opaque, and 0% is completely transparent.

   **Angle:** The direction, in degrees, from the object in which the shadow falls.

   **Distance:** The distance, in pixels, that the shadow falls from the object.

   **Size:** The shadow's size; 0 creates a shadow of the same size as the object that casts it.

   **Spread:** Blurs the shadow; 0 creates a sharp-edged shadow.

   The shadow uses the settings you specified (**Figure 12.116**).

## ✔ Tips

- You can see a shadow through a semi-transparent object (as long as the fill type isn't set to Eliminate). If a stroke or fill seems darker than it should be, the drop shadow may be showing through.

- Typically, a convincing drop shadow is anywhere from 50 to 75 percent opaque.

- A fill or stroke set to Ghost is transparent, but it can still cast a shadow.

# Inserting Logos

Titles often feature a company or brand logo. With the Title Designer, you can place a logo directly in the drawing area along with the other objects you create. This makes incorporating the logo into the design is simple.

### To insert a logo:

1. Make sure no objects are selected and then choose Title > Logo > Insert Logo (**Figure 12.117**).

   The Load Logo dialog box appears. By default, it opens the Logos folder, which is located in Premiere's Presets folder.

2. In the Load Logo dialog box, locate the logo you want to use and click Open (**Figure 12.118**).

   The logo appears in the drawing area at full size (**Figure 12.119**).

3. If necessary, adjust the logo's properties, such as position, opacity, and scale.

**Figure 12.117** Make sure that no objects are selected and choose Title > Logo > Insert Logo.

**Figure 12.118** In the Load Logo dialog box, locate the logo you want to use and click Open.

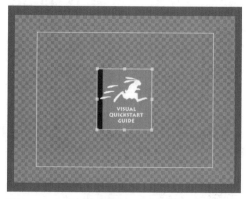

**Figure 12.119** The logo appears in the drawing area at the size it was originally created.

**Figure 12.120** Select a text box and choose Title > Logo > Insert Logo into Text.

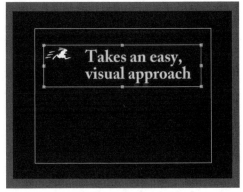

**Figure 12.121** Here, a slightly different version of the logo is inserted as a character in a text box. (Note that Show Video is selected, so the black video in the timeline serves as the background.)

## To insert a logo in a text box:

1. Select a text box and position the insertion point where you want the logo.

2. Choose Title > Logo > Insert Logo into Text (**Figure 12.120**).

3. A Load Logo dialog box appears. By default, it opens the Logos folder.

4. In the Load Logo dialog box, locate the logo you want to use and click Open.

   The logo appears at the insertion point. The logo is scaled to fit into the line of text. Changing the font size also scales the inserted logo (**Figure 12.121**).

## ✔ Tips

■ Adjusting the Slant property of text containing a logo distorts the logo, as well—probably with undesirable results. If you need to slant text, insert a logo as a separate object.

■ The graphic you insert doesn't have to be a logo per se. The Insert Logo into Text command can be a great way to create a special character that you can't get with a font.

# Transforming Objects

An object's Transform properties include its position, scale, rotation, and opacity. With the exception of opacity, you can control these properties by dragging the object in the drawing area. However, you can also adjust them in the Transform area of the Title Designer window. Even if you do transform an object by dragging, look in the Transform area to view the exact values.

You can also access Transform properties from the Title menu, but there's no need to cover that procedure here. However, the next sections will describe how to use menu commands to automatically position, arrange, and distribute objects.

### To transform an object from the Transform area:

1. Select an object in the drawing area.

2. In the Transform area of the Title Designer window, adjust any of the following values (**Figure 12.122**):

   **Opacity:** Sets the overall opacity; this setting works in combination with the object's other opacity settings.

   **X Position:** Sets the horizontal position, measured from the object's upper-left corner.

   **Y Position:** Sets the vertical position, measured from the object's upper-left corner.

   **Width:** Sets the horizontal aspect.

   **Height:** Sets the vertical aspect.

   **Rotation:** Sets the object's angle, measured from its vertical edge.

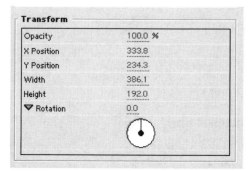

**Figure 12.122** The Transform area of the Title Designer window allows you to view and adjust a selected object's Transform properties.

## ✔ Tips

- Fill, stroke, and shadow properties each have their own opacity controls. Use these to set opacity levels relative to one another. The Opacity control in the Transform area adjusts the selected object's *overall* opacity. It controls the opacity of the entire object, but it doesn't override the relative opacity levels you set for its fill, strokes, and shadow.

- The Transform area's Opacity control doesn't affect the opacity of Texture fills. To adjust the opacity of textures, use the controls under the Texture property.

**Figure 12.123** Select the Rotation tool.

**Figure 12.124** Drag an object with the Rotation tool to adjust its angle. Here, multiple objects are selected and rotated as a group.

## To rotate an object using the rotation tool:

1. Select an object in the drawing area.

2. In the Title Designer toolbox, select the Rotation tool ○ (**Figure 12.123**).

3. Drag the selected item to rotate it freely. The object rotates around the center of the bounding box (**Figure 12.124**).

## ✔ Tip

■ Transformations—such as scaling and rotation—are calculated from the center of an object's bounding box. There's no way to change the center point (called an *anchor point* in other programs) in the Title Designer.

# Positioning Objects Automatically

You can move selected objects by dragging them with the mouse, pressing the arrow keys, or entering coordinates in the Transform area of the Title Designer window. But menu commands can quickly center objects or align objects with the bottom edge of the title-safe zone.

### To position objects using menu commands:

1. Select one or more objects in the drawing area.

2. Choose Title > Position and then choose an option from the submenu (**Figure 12.125**).

   The selected objects are positioned according to your choice (**Figure 12.126**).

### ✔ Tips

- The position commands place the bounding box, not the object within the box. If a text object doesn't look centered even after you've used the Horizontal Center command, make sure you've centered the text within the box using the Type Alignment command.

- You can copy a selected object by Alt-dragging it. A double arrow icon ↖ (like the one you'd see in Adobe Illustrator) appears when you use this keyboard shortcut.

**Figure 12.125** Choose Title > Position and then choose an option from the submenu.

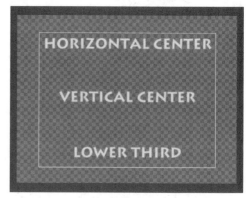

**Figure 12.126** These three text objects illustrate the Position command options. All of them are centered horizontally.

POSITIONING OBJECTS AUTOMATICALLY

**Figure 12.127** Select the object you want to move in the stacking order.

**Figure 12.128** Choose Title > Arrange and select the appropriate option...

# Arranging Objects

In addition to controlling the position of objects, you can control the way they're layered. Initially, the most recently created object appears in front of the others, but you can change the stacking order at any time.

### To change the stacking order:

1. Select an object in the drawing area (**Figure 12.127**).

2. Choose Title > Arrange and select one of the following options (**Figure 12.128**):

   **Bring to Front:** Makes the selected object first in the stack.

   **Bring Forward:** Moves the selected object one step up in the stack.

   **Send to Back:** Makes the selected object last in the stack.

   **Send Backward:** Moves the selected object back one step in the stack.

   The object's placement in the stacking order changes according to your selection (**Figure 12.129**).

**Figure 12.129** ...to change the object's relative position in the stacking order. Here, Send to Back makes the rectangle last in the stacking order, so it appears behind the text.

# Aligning Objects

Other menu commands allow you to align multiple objects with one another.

## To align objects:

1. Select two or more objects in the drawing area (**Figure 12.130**).

2. *Do one of the following:*

   ▲ Choose Title > Align Objects, and select one of the alignment options from the submenu (**Figure 12.131**).

   ▲ In the tools area of the Title Designer, select the button that corresponds to the alignment you want (**Figure 12.132**).

   The objects are aligned according to your choice (**Figure 12.133**).

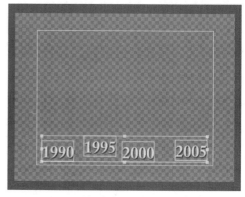

**Figure 12.130** Select two or more objects in the drawing area.

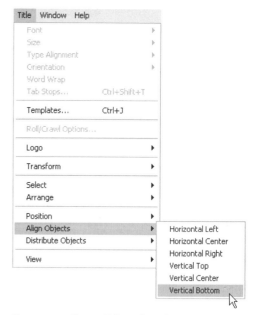

**Figure 12.131** Choose Title > Align Objects and select an option from the submenu.

**Figure 12.133** The objects are aligned according to your choice. Here, the bottom edges of several dates are aligned using Vertical Bottom.

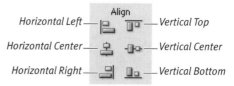

**Figure 12.132** Each Alignment option has a tool in the toolbox.

Figure 12.134 Choose Title > Distribute Objects and select an option from the submenu.

# Distributing Objects

Other menu items allow you to evenly distribute multiple objects, saving you meticulous placement or—*gulp!*—even math.

## To distribute objects:

1. Select multiple objects in the drawing area.

2. *Do one of the following:*

   ▲ Choose Title > Distribute Objects and select an option from the submenu (**Figure 12.134**).

   ▲ In the tools area of the Title Designer, select the button that corresponds to the distribution option you want (**Figure 12.135**).

   The objects are spaced according to your selection (**Figure 12.136**).

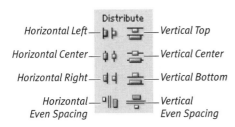

Figure 12.135 Each Distribution option has a tool in the toolbox.

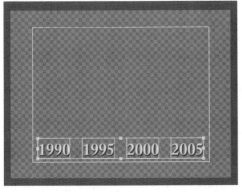

Figure 12.136 The objects are spaced according to your selection. Here, the dates from Figure 12.132 are evenly spaced horizontally.

# WORKING WITH EFFECTS

Although it's possible that the clips in your sequence require no alteration, chances are you need to modify them in some way, using effects. In Premiere Pro, the rubric effects encompasses any means by which you adjust a clip's audio or video characteristics, or properties.

Effects are categorized by function: motion, opacity, volume, and filters. By changing a clip's spatial properties, for example, you can resize the clip for use as a picture-in-picture effect or simulate a camera move over a large image. Altering a clip's opacity lets you superimpose one clip over another. You can also apply any combination of audio and video filters. Apply an EQ filter to enhance a voice-over or use reverb to imply certain acoustics. Similarly, video filters can alter an image in countless ways, from subtle color correction, to fantastic distortions, to an image composited with a background. Befitting moving media, nearly all effect settings can change over time, using a technique called keyframing. This allows you to animate motion, fade a clip's opacity or volume, or vary the character or intensity of any video or audio filter. You can even specify whether the change is constant, accelerates, or decelerates. For example, you can simulate the way the camera starts to move slowly, comes up to full speed, and then slows to a stop.

Premiere Pro 1.5 introduces the use of Bézier curves to draw motion paths, GPU accelerated effects, effects sharing with Adobe After Effects 6.5 (if installed), and the ability to save your favorite effects with all of their modifications as a *preset* for reuse in other projects.

Despite their diversity, you apply, adjust, and animate effects using only a few methods. This chapter reflects Premiere Pro's unified approach. First you'll learn to distinguish effects not only by function, but by methodology. Then you'll learn methods to view and adjust effect properties. You'll find that by first focusing on techniques common to *all* effects, you'll be prepared to tackle *any* effect.

# Comparing Effect Types

Although we describe effects by what they do, it's just as useful to classify them by how they're applied. In Premiere Pro, effects fall into two major categories: fixed effects and standard effects.

## Fixed/inherent effects

Motion effects, opacity, and volume are called *fixed effects*. This isn't meant to imply that you can't adjust or animate the settings over time; you can. *Fixed* refers to the fact that these effects let you control attributes that are inherent to the clip: its position on the screen, its level of opacity, and its volume. Better terms might be *inherent effects* or *intrinsic effects*. The upshot is that you don't have to actively apply these effects to a clip; they're always listed in the Effect Controls window (which you'll learn more about soon) (**Figure 13.1**).

Beginning with Premiere Pro 1.5 the fixed effects Motion and Opacity have been optimized for the Intel Pentium 4 and the AMD Opteron processors. The fixed effects are now two to three times faster when a clip is rendered or when it is previewed in the program view of the Monitor window.

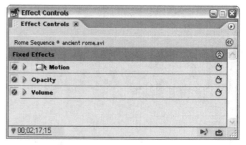

**Figure 13.1** Motion, opacity, and volume are inherent to clips and are always listed in the Effect Controls window.

## Obsolete Effects

The following effects (originally from Adobe Photoshop) are now obsolete: Cystalize, Pinch, Pointilize, Shear, Tiles, Wind, and Zig Zag. Even though you can no longer apply these effects in new Premiere Pro 1.5 projects, if you used them in projects from the previous version of Premiere Pro, they will be recognized properly if you import the project into Premiere Pro 1.5.

Figure 13.2 You add standard effects by dragging them from the Effect Controls window to a clip in the Timeline window.

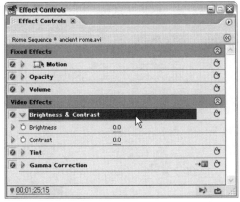

Figure 13.3 Once standard effects are applied, they appear in the Effect Controls window in the order they were added.

# Standard effects/filters

Effects you actively apply to clips are known as *standard effects*. You apply a standard effect by dragging it from the Effects palette to a clip in the timeline (**Figure 13.2**). Once the effect has been applied, you can view and adjust its parameters using the same methods you use for fixed effects (**Figure 13.3**).

Standard effects are also called *filters*, after the filters you place in front of a camera lens to filter light or distort an image. Of course, digital filters can modify both images and sound in countless ways. You can make subtle adjustments—such as color correction or audio equalization—or create more dramatic distortions and stylizations. Note that standard effects include *keying effects*, which are used to composite layers of images. On the other hand, standard effects are listed separately from transitions (which operate differently and are explained in Chapter 9, "Adding Transitions").

Standard effects are stored in Premiere Pro's Plug-Ins folder. You can add compatible filters created by other software developers to expand your collection.

If you have Adobe After Effects 6.5 installed on your PC, when Premiere Pro 1.5 launches, it will find and load 41 compatible filters from the After Effects directory.

# Setting and Animating Effect Properties

A *property* refers to any effect parameter to which you can assign a value. For example, you can specify a clip's Opacity property value from 0 percent (completely transparent) to 100 percent (completely opaque), or you can determine the intensity of the Gaussian Blur filter by adjusting its blur value. You can set any property to a single *global* value for the duration of the clip. You can also animate a property, varying its values over time.

To produce animation, you change a clip's properties over time—for example, you create motion by changing a clip's position over time. In Premiere Pro (as in other programs), you use keyframes to define and control these changes.

A *keyframe* defines a property's value at a specific point in time. When you create at least two keyframes with different values, Premiere Pro *interpolates* the value for each frame in between. In other words, Premiere Pro calculates how to progress smoothly from one keyframe value to another—or, in terms of motion, how to get from Point A to Point B (**Figure 13.4**).

As you adjust any effect, you can view it right away in the program view of the Monitor window. But as you learned in Chapter 10, "Previewing a Sequence," whether you can play it at the project's full frame rate depends on both the complexity of the effect and your system's resources.

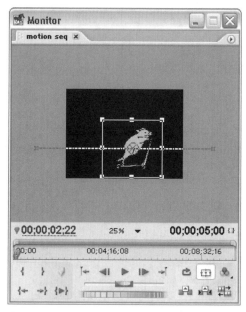

**Figure 13.4** You can vary any property's value over time using keyframes. In this example, Premiere Pro calculates the position of a clip between two keyframes to create movement.

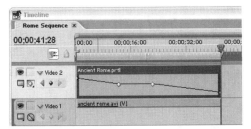

**Figure 13.5** You can view any effect's property values as a graph in an expanded track of the timeline.

## Keyframes

*Keyframe* is a term borrowed from traditional animation. In a traditional animation studio, a senior animator might draw only the keyframes—what the character looks like at key moments in the animation. The junior animators then drew the in-betweens (a process sometimes called *tweening*). The same principle applies to animating effects in Premiere Pro: If you supply the keyframes for a property, the program calculates the values in between. And you can keyframe any property, not just movement.

In Premiere Pro, you're always the senior animator, so you should supply only the keyframes—just enough to define the animation. Premiere Pro does the tedious tweening. Setting too many keyframes defeats the purpose of this division of labor. (Hence, it's even useful to thin out, or *optimize*, the keyframes created by the audio mixing process, as you learned in Chapter 11, "Mixing Audio.")

# Viewing Effect Property Values

You can view and adjust an effect's property values in several ways in an expanded track of the Timeline window, in the Effect Controls window, or (in the case of motion effect properties) in the program view of the Monitor window.

## Timeline window

In the Timeline window, expanding a track reveals additional clip data not visible when the track is collapsed. (In Chapter 7, "Editing in the Timeline," you learned how expanding a track allows you to view thumbnails and audio waveforms.) In an expanded track, you can view effect property values as a graph in which the selected property value appears as a thin black line (**Figure 13.5**). Diamond-shaped icons on the graph represent values you specify, or keyframes. Dragging a keyframe horizontally changes its position in time, whereas dragging it vertically changes the property's value at that time. The line connecting keyframes represents interpolated values. A set of buttons called the *keyframe navigator* helps you add, subtract, and cue to keyframes.

In the property graph—particularly when it represents opacity or volume—keyframes are also known as *handles*. The graph itself is often referred to as a *rubberband* view, and the keyframing process is called *rubberbanding*.

### ✔ Tip

■ In versions of Premiere and Premiere Pro prior to Premiere Pro 1.5, the rubberbands were located at the very top for 100% and at the very bottom for 0%. In Premiere Pro 1.5, the rubberbands are slightly below the top and bottom to give you a better target for dragging or adding new keyframes.

## Effect Controls window

You can also view and control effect property values in a window optimized for the task: the Effect Controls window (**Figure 13.6**). The Effect Controls window lists all the effects contained in a selected clip. You can expand each effect heading to reveal controls for each property value. To vary values over time, you can reveal a *timeline view*. The timeline view corresponds to the sequence's timeline and includes familiar controls, such as a CTI and viewing area bar.

In contrast to the Timeline window, the Effect Controls window's timeline view shows the selected clip in isolation. Under the clip, keyframes for each property appear in vertically stacked rows, or *property tracks*. As in an expanded track of the Timeline window, the Effect Controls window has a keyframe navigator for adding, deleting, and cueing to keyframes. But instead of a property graph, the Effect Controls window shows property values numerically. You can drag keyframes horizontally in time, but you change their value using numerical controls.

## Spatial controls in the program view

Because they are spatial in nature, Premiere Pro lets you view and control motion effect properties—position, rotation, scale, and anchor point—by dragging in the program view, a method Adobe likes to call *direct manipulation* (**Figure 13.7**). In the program view, animated motion appears as keyframe icons connected by a *motion path*. Direct manipulation controls complement the Effect Controls window's controls. You use the former to control the spatial properties at a keyframe; you use the latter to control the timing. Certain filters also offer direct manipulation controls, including crop, corner pin, lightning, mirror, ramp, and transform.

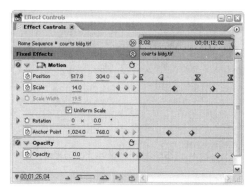

**Figure 13.6** You can view multiple effect property values at once in the Effect Controls window.

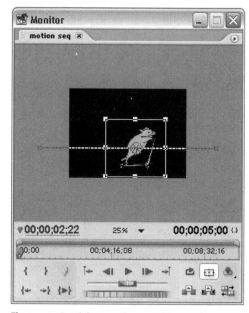

**Figure 13.7** Spatial properties—position, scale, rotation, and anchor point—can also be viewed and controlled in the program view of the Monitor window.

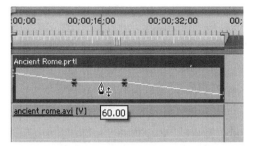

**Figure 13.8** Keyframing in the timeline—sometimes called *rubberbanding*—is best suited for controlling clip volume and opacity (shown here).

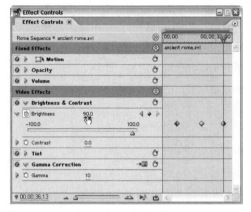

**Figure 13.9** Motion and standard effects are more easily controlled in the Effect Controls window.

## ✔ Tip

- The recommendations made in this section are reinforced by Premiere Pro's interface. In the timeline, the display of keyframes for opacity and volume can be accessed through a menu separate from other properties.

# Choosing a Keyframing Method

Although you can switch among keyframing methods freely, you'll find that each is better suited for certain tasks.

## Opacity and volume in the property graph

Rubberbanding in the timeline is ideal for making adjustments to opacity and volume values—not only because this approach is time-tested and familiar to many users, but because these values are easy to understand in graph form (**Figure 13.8**). When the graph goes up, the opacity or volume value increases; when the graph goes down, the value decreases. Properties like rotation, for instance, don't translate well to a vertical graph (and others don't translate at all). Moreover, adjusting opacity and volume requires only a single property graph, whereas motion effects and many filters include several parameters you need to adjust.

## Standard effects and motion in the Effect Controls window

For all other effects, focus on the Effect Controls window. It lets you adjust both the value and timing of several properties at once with numerical precision (**Figure 13.9**). By comparison, the graphical clarity of a single property graph provides little benefit.

For motion effects, use the Effect Controls window to activate the direct manipulation tools in the program view, and to control the timing of keyframes for the various spatial properties: position, rotation, scale, and anchor point.

# Viewing Property Values in the Timeline Window

In an expanded track of the Timeline window, you can view a value graph of any effect property. However, each clip can show only one property graph at a time. Audio tracks can show property values either for individual clips or for the entire track. The same audio track property values can be adjusted using the audio mixer, covered in Chapter 11.

### To view property values for video clips in the timeline:

1. Click the triangle next to a track's name to expand the track.

   The track expands, revealing additional track controls.

2. Click the expanded track's Show Keyframes button and choose an option:

   **Show Keyframes:** Displays keyframes for any video effect property (**Figure 13.10**).

   **Show Opacity Handles:** Display keyframes for each clip's inherent Opacity property (not an opacity property included in a standard effect, such as the transform filter).

   The Show Keyframe button's icon reflects your choice. If you choose Show Keyframes, each clip in the track includes a drop-down menu of its fixed and standard effect properties.

3. If you chose Show Keyframes in step 2, choose the effect property you want to view from the clip's effect drop-down menu (**Figure 13.11**).

   You may have to use submenus to find the property you want. The selected property's value graph appears in the expanded area of the clip. The range of values represented by the vertical position of the graph depends on the particular parameter.

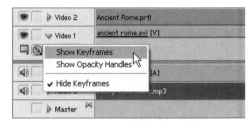

**Figure 13.10** Click the Show Keyframes button and choose an option from the menu that appears.

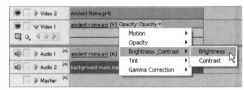

**Figure 13.11** When Show Keyframes is selected, choose the property you want to view from the clip's drop-down menu.

**VIEWING PROPERTY VALUES**

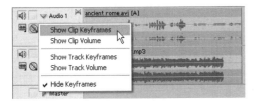

**Figure 13.12** Click the audio track's Show Keyframes button and choose an option from the menu that appears.

**Figure 13.13** When Show Clip Keyframes is selected, choose the property you want to view from the audio clip's drop-down menu.

## To view property values for audio clips in the timeline:

1. Click the triangle next to a track's name to expand the track.

   The track expands, revealing additional track controls.

2. Click the expanded track's Show Keyframes button and choose an option:

   **Show Clip Keyframes:** Displays a value graph for any audio clip's effect property (**Figure 13.12**).

   **Show Clip Volume:** Displays a value graph for each clip's inherent Volume property (not a volume property included in a standard effect, such as the volume filter).

   The Show Keyframe button's icon reflects your choice. If you choose Show Clip Keyframes, each clip in the track includes a drop-down menu of its fixed and standard effect properties.

3. If you chose Show Clip Keyframes in step 2, choose the effect property you want to view from the clip's effect drop-down menu (**Figure 13.13**).

   You may have to use submenus to find the property you want. The selected property's value graph appears in the expanded area of the clip. The range of values represented by the vertical position of the graph depends on the particular parameter.

### ✔ Tip

■ An audio track's Show Keyframes button also includes options for viewing a value graph for Track Keyframes and Track Volume. These graphs correspond to changes you make using the audio mixer, covered in Chapter 11.

# Changing Property Values in the Timeline

In the Timeline window, you can add, delete, move, and change the value of keyframes using the Pen tool. You can also add, delete, and cue the CTI to keyframes using a set of buttons in the track header area, called the *keyframe navigator*.

## To add keyframes with the pen:

1. In the Timeline window, expand the track that contains the clips with effect properties you want to adjust and view the appropriate property graph.

   For detailed instructions, see "Viewing Property Values in the Timeline Window" earlier in this chapter.

2. In the Tools window, select the Pen tool ⟨♦⟩ (**Figure 13.14**).

   Position the pen on the property graph (the thin black line) where you want to add a keyframe and Ctrl-click the line.

   Pressing Ctrl makes the pen appear with a plus sign ♦₊ (**Figure 13.15**); Ctrl-clicking adds a keyframe at that point (**Figure 13.16**).

**Figure 13.14** Select the Pen tool.

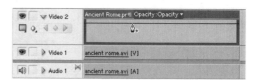

**Figure 13.15** Ctrl-clicking the graph with the Pen tool...

**Figure 13.16** ...adds a keyframe.

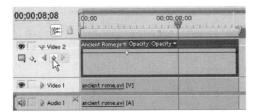

**Figure 13.17** You can also add a keyframe by setting the CTI...

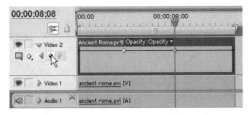

**Figure 13.18** ...and clicking the diamond icon in the keyframe navigator.

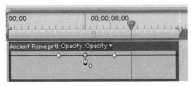

**Figure 13.19** To select a keyframe, click with the Pen tool; Shift-click to add to or subtract from the selection.

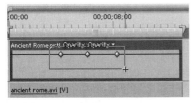

**Figure 13.20** You can also drag a marquee to select several consecutive keyframes.

## To add keyframes with the timeline's keyframe navigator:

1. In the Timeline window, expand the track that contains the clips with effect properties you want to adjust and view the appropriate property graph.

   For detailed instructions, see "Viewing Property Values in the Timeline Window" earlier in this chapter.

2. Position the CTI at the point where you want to add a keyframe to the visible property graph.

3. In the track's keyframe navigator (under the track's name), click the Add/Remove Keyframe button (the diamond-shaped icon between the Previous and Next Keyframe arrows) (**Figure 13.17**).

   A keyframe appears on the property graph at the CTI (**Figure 13.18**).

## To select keyframes:

1. Make sure the Pen tool is selected.

2. In a property graph of a clip in the timeline, *do one of the following:*

   ▲ To select a keyframe, click it with the Pen tool (**Figure 13.19**).

   ▲ To add keyframes to and subtract them from your selection, Shift-click them with the pen tool.

   ▲ To select one or more keyframes, drag a marquee around them (**Figure 13.20**).

   Selected keyframes appear yellow; unselected keyframes appear gray.

## To move keyframes in time:

1. Select one or more keyframes.

2. Drag any of the selected keyframes left or right (**Figure 13.21**).

3. To constrain the mouse to horizontal movement only, press Shift after you begin dragging horizontally.

   Shift-dragging constrains the movement, so you can't drag the keyframes vertically and thereby change their values. As you drag, a tool tip shows the sequence time of the keyframe you grabbed before you started dragging.

## To change keyframe values with the pen:

1. With the Pen tool, select one or more keyframes.

2. Drag any of the selected keyframes up or down (**Figure 13.22**).

3. To constrain the mouse to vertical movement only, press Shift after you begin dragging vertically.

   Shift-dragging constrains the movement, so you can't drag the keyframes horizontally and thereby change their position in time. As you drag, a tool tip shows the property's value at the keyframe you grabbed before you started dragging. Interpolated values (the slope of the graph) change accordingly.

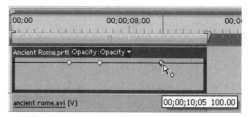

**Figure 13.21** Drag selected keyframes right or left to move them in time.

**Figure 13.22** Drag selected keyframes up to increase their value or down to decrease their value.

CHANGING PROPERTY VALUES IN THE TIMELINE

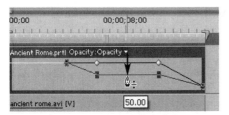

**Figure 13.23** With the Pen tool, drag the line between keyframes to shift both keyframe values by the same amount.

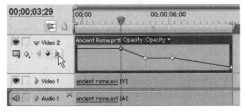

**Figure 13.24** In the track's keyframe navigator, clicking the left arrow or the right arrow (shown here)...

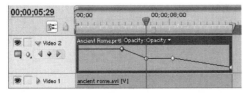

**Figure 13.25** ...cues the sequence's CTI to the previous or next keyframe, respectively.

## To change two keyframes simultaneously:

1. Position the Pen tool on the line between two keyframes in the property graph.

   The Pen tool appears with a vertical adjustment icon ⚷.

2. Drag up or down (**Figure 13.23**).

   Keyframe icons on either side of the Pen tool move up or down by the same amount. The slope of the property graph's line (interpolated values) adjusts accordingly.

## To cue the CTI to keyframes:

- In the track's keyframe navigator, *do one of the following:*

   ▲ To cue the CTI to the previous keyframe, click the Left Arrow button ◀.

   ▲ To cue the CTI to the next keyframe, click the Right Arrow button ▶ (**Figure 13.24**).

   The sequence's CTI moves to the keyframe you specify (**Figure 13.25**). The sequence's CTI moves in any window that shows the sequence, including the Timeline window and program view.

## To remove keyframes in the timeline:

1. In a track's keyframe navigator, click the Left or Right Arrow button to cue the CTI to the keyframe you want to remove (**Figure 13.26**).

   You can use any playback control to cue the CTI, but the keyframe navigator offers the easiest method.

2. Click the keyframe navigator's Add/Remove Keyframe button (the diamond between the left and right arrows).

   The keyframe at the CTI is removed from the property graph. Interpolated values (the line between keyframes) adjust accordingly (**Figure 13.27**).

## ✔ Tips

- In the property graph, the thin black line connecting keyframes represents interpolated property values. By default, values are interpolated using a linear scale. You can change the interpolation method. However, the line's slope doesn't reflect acceleration or deceleration caused by different interpolation methods. See "Specifying a Temporal Interpolation Method" later in this chapter.

- To temporarily disable an effect, you must use the Effect Controls window (as explained later in the chapter).

**Figure 13.26** Cue the CTI to the keyframe you want to remove.

**Figure 13.27** Clicking the keyframe navigator's diamond icon removes the keyframe at the CTI.

# Animating Opacity and Volume

As explained in "Choosing a Keyframing Method" earlier in this chapter, keyframing in the timeline, or rubberbanding, is ideally suited to controlling opacity and volume. In fact, in the Show Keyframes button's drop-down menu, opacity and volume are listed separately from other property keyframes. Even though the previous sections covered rubberbanding techniques, it's worthwhile to review the process in terms of opacity and volume.

But remember: to create simple video dissolves and audio fades, use a video or audio transition instead of keyframes (see Chapter 9).

## ✔ Tip

- You can also apply opacity changes using the Transform filter and volume changes using a Volume filter. Because Premiere Pro renders filters after fixed effects, using the filter version may allow you to achieve a result you couldn't get otherwise.

# Rubberbanding opacity

You can keyframe the opacity of clips in video track 2 and higher to blend them with clips in lower tracks. Lowering the opacity of clips in track 1 blends the image with black. If you want to make only parts of the clip transparent, apply a keying effect (explained in Chapter 14, "Effects in Action"). Of course, you can combine keying with fading—for example, when you want to make a superimposed title semitransparent.

## To rubberband opacity:

1. Arrange clips in the timeline so that the clip you want to superimpose is in a higher video track than the clip (or clips) that serve as the underlying image.

2. Expand the track that contains the clip you want to adjust (**Figure 13.28**).

3. Click the track's Show Keyframes button and choose Show Opacity Handles (**Figure 13.29**).

   An Opacity property graph appears for the clips in the track. The height of the property graph corresponds to clip opacity levels, so that near the top of the clip is 100 percent opaque, and near the bottom of the clip is 0 percent opaque (completely transparent).

4. Using keyframing techniques described in the previous sections, adjust the clip's opacity over time (**Figure 13.30**).

   Opacity levels affect the entire clip's overall opacity. To make certain parts of an image transparent, use a keying filter (described in Chapter 14).

**Figure 13.28** Arrange a clip you want to superimpose in a higher layer and expand its track.

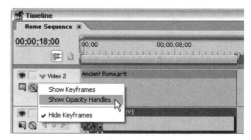

**Figure 13.29** Click the track's Show Keyframes button and choose Show Opacity Handles from the menu that appears.

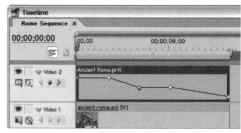

**Figure 13.30** Use the track's keyframe navigator and the Pen tool to add keyframes and adjust them in the opacity graph. In this example, the opacity starts at 100 percent, drops to 50 percent, holds at 50 percent, and then ends at 0 percent.

**Figure 13.31** Expand the track that contains audio clips you want to adjust.

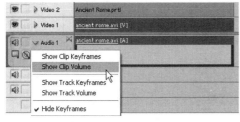

**Figure 13.32** Click the track's Show Keyframes button and choose Show Clip Volume from the menu that appears.

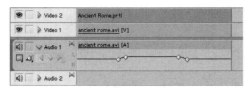

**Figure 13.33** Using the keyframe navigator and Pen tool, add keyframes and adjust them in the clip's Volume property graph. In this example, the volume starts at the normal level, or changes by 0 dB. Then the volume is boosted by +3 dB and brought back to its normal level.

# Rubberbanding volume

When you're keyframing audio, remember that you can adjust levels for individual clips or for the entire track of clips. But in general, you should use the rubberbanding method to adjust individual clips and the audio mixer to mix the tracks. Make only the adjustments you need to prepare the clips for track mixing, and be sure to avoid making redundant or conflicting adjustments.

## To rubberband clip volume:

1. To monitor the audio level output, choose Window > Audio Mixer. In the Audio Mixer window's menu, choose Master Meters only.

   A VU meter shows the output levels.

2. Expand the track containing the audio clip you want to adjust (**Figure 13.31**).

3. Click the track's Show Keyframes button and choose Show Clip Volume (**Figure 13.32**).

   A Volume property graph appears for the clips in the track (not for the track as a whole). The height of the yellow property graph corresponds to clip volume levels, so that levels are adjusted 0 dB when the graph is in the center of the clip, +6 dB near the top of the clip, and –6 dB near the bottom.

4. Using keyframing techniques described in the previous sections, adjust the clip's volume over time (**Figure 13.33**).

ANIMATING OPACITY AND VOLUME

# Adding Standard Effects

The procedure for adding a standard effect (or filter) to a clip is nearly self-explanatory: you simply drag a filter from the Effects palette directly to a compatible clip in the timeline. Clips with effects applied appear with a thin blue line under the clip's name.

On the Effects palette, video and audio are contained in separate folders and are further organized into categorized subfolders. Audio filters are sorted by channel type and must match the channel type of the clip to which they're added—after all, you can't filter a channel that isn't there (**Figure 13.34**). (You already learned how to organize and find items on the Effects palette in Chapter 9, so that information won't be repeated here.)

Nearly all filters have one or more properties that you can adjust either by using a value graph in the timeline window or by using the Effect Controls window. But as explained in "Choosing a Keyframing Method" earlier in this chapter, using the Effect Controls window is the most appropriate method for most filters. Some filters also include a settings dialog box that opens automatically when you apply the filter. You can also reopen the dialog box from the Effect Controls window.

This task summarizes the basic process of adding an effect to a clip. You'll discover that each effect has a unique set of parameters, or *properties,* that you can customize. In the following sections, you'll first learn how to apply an effect and specify *global* property values—a single set of property values for the duration of the clip. Then you'll learn how to animate any effect—fixed or standard—using the Effect Controls window.

**Figure 13.34** On the Effects palette, video filters are sorted by function, and audio filters are organized by channel type.

**Figure 13.35** Drag a filter from the Effects palette to the appropriate clip in the Timeline window.

**Figure 13.36** If a settings dialog box opens automatically, specify values for the effect's properties and click OK.

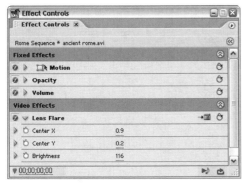

**Figure 13.37** You can select the clip in the timeline to view its properties in the Effect Controls window.

## To add an effect to a clip:

1. On the Effects palette, *do one of the following:*

   ▲ Select a video effect.

   ▲ Select an audio effect that matches the audio clip's channel type (mono, stereo, or 5.1).

   For more about organizing and locating effects, see Chapter 9.

2. Drag the effect to the appropriate clip in the Timeline window (**Figure 13.35**).

   The effect is applied to the clip and is listed on the Effect Controls palette when the clip is selected. Clips with effects applied appear with a thin blue line under the clip's name.

3. To adjust the effect's settings, *do one of the following* (depending on the particular effect):

   ▲ If a settings dialog box appears automatically, specify values for the effect's parameters and click OK (**Figure 13.36**).

   ▲ Select the clip in the timeline and adjust its effect properties in the Effect Controls window (**Figure 13.37**).

4. To vary effect properties over time, specify keyframes as explained in the task "To set keyframes in the Effect Controls window" later in this chapter.

## ✔ Tip

■ You can add audio effects to entire tracks of clips using the audio mixer. See Chapter 11 for details.

ADDING STANDARD EFFECTS

# Viewing Effect Properties in the Effect Controls Window

The Effect Controls window lists all the effects for a selected clip and provides controls for adjusting each property's value (**Figure 13.38**). Fixed video and audio effects are listed separately; standard effects are listed in the order they're applied (see the previous section, "Adding Standard Effects"). To see and adjust the timing of keyframes, use the Effect Controls window's timeline view.

You can control each effect property using familiar numerical controls that you set by dragging or by selecting and entering a value. Most property value controls can also be expanded to reveal a slider control, knob, or color picker. You'll also notice that the main panel of the Effect Controls window includes playback and zoom controls, its timeline view includes a CTI and viewing area bar, and you can toggle the time count to audio samples. By now, all these controls should be familiar to you, and they won't be reviewed here.

### To open the Effect Controls window:

◆ Choose Window > Effect Controls (**Figure 13.39**).

The Effect Controls window appears (**Figure 13.40**). You can view the effect controls in their own window or as a tab in the source view of the Monitor window.

Selected    Timeline    Property
clip        view        tracks

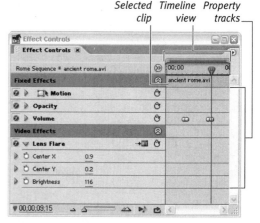

**Figure 13.38** The Effect Controls window lists all the effects for the selected clip and provides controls for adjusting their values over time.

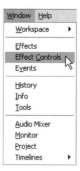

**Figure 13.39** Choose Window > Effect Controls.

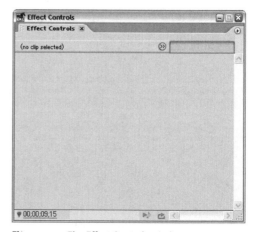

**Figure 13.40** The Effect Controls window appears.

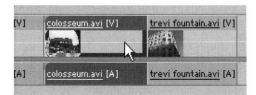

**Figure 13.41** In the Timeline window, select the clip that contains the effect properties you want to adjust.

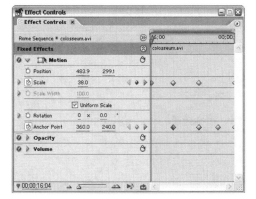

**Figure 13.42** The selected clip's effects appear in the Effect Controls window.

## To view effect properties in the Effect Controls window:

1. Make sure the Effect Controls window is open.

2. In the Timeline window, select the clip that contains the effect properties you want to adjust (**Figure 13.41**).

   The selected clip's effects appear in the Effect Controls window (**Figure 13.42**).

## To show and hide effect categories:

◆ In the Effect Controls window, click the double-chevron icon for the effect category you want to show or hide.

   Effect category headings are set against a dark gray background. When the chevrons point down ⊗, the effects under the heading are hidden from view (**Figure 13.43**); when the chevrons point up ⊗ the effects in that category are visible (**Figure 13.44**).

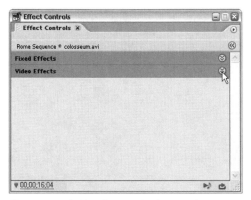

**Figure 13.43** Clicking the Double-Chevrons button toggles it between pointing down to hide effects...

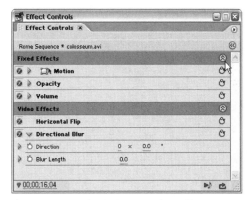

**Figure 13.44** ...and pointing up to show effects.

427

## To show and hide the Effect Controls window's timeline area:

◆ In the Effect Controls window, click the double-chevron icon in the upper-right corner of the effects list area.

When the chevrons point to the left ⊛, the timeline area is hidden (**Figure 13.45**); when the chevrons point to the right ⊛, the timeline area is visible (**Figure 13.46**).

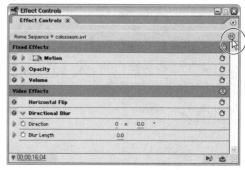

**Figure 13.45** Clicking this Double-Chevrons button toggles between hiding the timeline view...

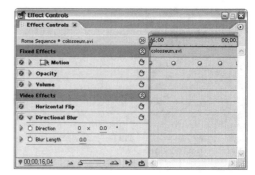

**Figure 13.46** ...and showing the timeline view.

**Figure 13.47**
Clicking an
effect's effects
icon...

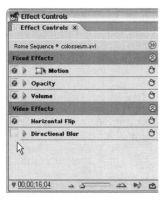

**Figure 13.48**
...makes the icon
disappear and
disables the
effect. Click again
to make the icon
reappear and
enable the effect.

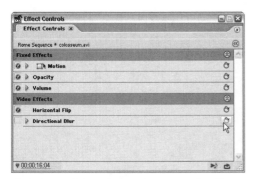

**Figure 13.49** Clicking the reset icon resets the effect
property values to their default settings.

# Disabling and Resetting Effects

Whereas you can view effect values in either
the Timeline window or the Effect Controls
window, you can disable effects or reset their
values to the default settings only in the
Effect Controls window. Disabling an effect
doesn't delete your settings; it merely turns
off the effect until you toggle it back on.
Resetting an effect, on the other hand,
removes your adjustments, replacing them
with the default property values.

## To disable or enable an effect:

◆ In the Effect Controls window, click the
effects icon 🕖 next to the effect you
want to disable (**Figure 13.47**).

The icon disappears, and the effect is disabled (**Figure 13.48**). Clicking the empty
box makes the icon reappear and enables
the effect.

## To reset any effect to its default settings:

◆ In the Effect Controls window, click the
reset icon 🕖 for the effect you want to
reset to its default property values
(**Figure 13.49**).

## To use a standard effect's custom settings:

◆ In the Effect Controls window, click a standard effect's Setup button (**Figure 13.50**).

Depending on the effect, a settings dialog box may open, or (in the case of effects like the Image Matte filter) a dialog box for choosing a file to serve as an effect source may appear (**Figure 13.51**).

## ✔ Tip

■ If you selected the option Scale Clips to Project Dimensions When Adding to a Sequence on the General panel of the Project settings, Premiere Pro may have scaled some of your clips automatically. Resetting their motion effect properties will return them to their native proportions, not their automatically scaled proportions.

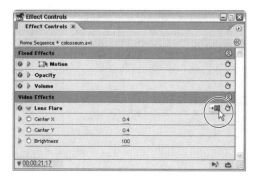

**Figure 13.50** Click an effect's Setup button...

**Figure 13.51** ...to access custom options for that effect. In this example, the Setup button reopens the Lens Flare Settings dialog box.

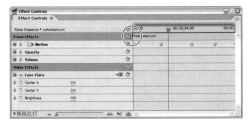

**Figure 13.52** Position the mouse between the Effect Controls window's main panel and its timeline view so that the width adjustment icon appears...

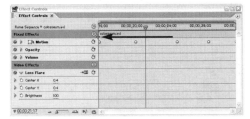

**Figure 13.53** ...and drag to adjust the relative widths of the two areas.

# Customizing the Effect Controls Window

Although you can view the Effect Controls window as a tab in the source view of the Monitor window, you may prefer to open it separately. This allows you to make the effect controls wider without adding unnecessary space to the program view. You can allocate that extra space even more efficiently by adjusting the border between the effect list area and the timeline view.

You can also customize the range of the Effect Controls window's time ruler. Selecting Pin to Clip makes the maximum visible area of the ruler correspond to the selected clip. This might make it easier for you to focus on the selected clip and prevent you from setting keyframes beyond the limits of the clip's duration. If you prefer, you can deselect the Pin to Clip option, so that the time ruler corresponds to the duration of the sequence. This allows you to see the selected clip in a wider context or set keyframes beyond the clip's duration.

## To change the relative size of the timeline area:

1. With the Effect Controls window's timeline area visible, position the mouse pointer between the area listing effects and the timeline view area.

   The mouse pointer becomes a width adjustment icon ⊞ (**Figure 13.52**).

2. Drag left or right to change the relative width of the effects list area and the timeline area (**Figure 13.53**).

## To set the zoom range of the Effect Controls window's time ruler:

◆ In the Effect Controls window's menu, *do one of the following:*

▲ Select Pin to Clip to make the maximum visible area of the time ruler correspond to the duration of the selected clip (**Figures 13.54** and **13.55**).

▲ Deselect Pin to Clip to make the maximum visible area of the time ruler correspond to the duration of the sequence (**Figure 13.56**).

## ✔ Tip

■ The Window menu includes a workspace optimized for effects editing. But as usual, you'll probably want to use it as a starting point for your own custom workspace.

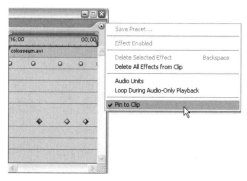

**Figure 13.54** In the Effect Controls window's menu, choose Pin to Clip.

**Figure 13.55** When Pin to Clip is selected, the maximum visible area of the time ruler corresponds to the selected clip.

**Figure 13.56** When Pin to Clip is deselected, the maximum visible area of the time ruler corresponds to the sequence's duration.

**Figure 13.57** The Mirror filter followed by the Replicate filter results in this image.

**Figure 13.58** Reversing the order of the filters in Figure 13.57 results in this image.

# Using Multiple Effects

You can add any number of effects to a clip. You can layer different effects onto a single clip or apply the same effect more than once, specifying different settings each time.

Because each filter adds to the effect of the preceding one, the order of the filters determines the cumulative effect. Changing the order of filters can change the final appearance of the clip (**Figures 13.57** and **13.58**).

## Rendering Order

When Premiere Pro renders frames for playback or export, it calculates each clip's attributes in a particular sequence, referred to as the *rendering order*.

Having interpreted your source footage according to your specifications and conformed the video frame rate and audio sample rate to match your project, Premiere Pro processes each frame. Rendering proceeds from lower-numbered tracks to higher-numbered tracks, and from nested sequences up through the hierarchy of sequences. Filters are applied in the order in which they're added—or in terms of how they're listed in the Effect Controls window, from the top to the bottom. Then fixed effects are applied: motion effects followed by opacity.

## To set the order of standard effects:

◆ In the Effect Controls palette, drag an effect up or down to change its position in the list (**Figure 13.59**).

The effect name appears in the new position (**Figure 13.60**). You can't drag a standard effect (filter) above the fixed effects (motion and opacity for video, or volume for audio effects).

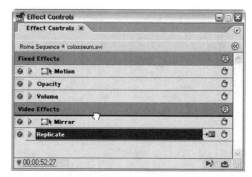

**Figure 13.59** In the Effect Controls window, drag a filter's name up or down to change the filter's position in the list.

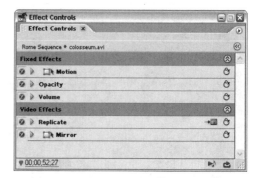

**Figure 13.60** The filter appears in the new position, and the filters are rendered accordingly.

## Subverting the Render Order

At times, the rendering order prevents you from achieving the result you want. For example, you might want to use the Replicate filter to create numerous copies of a rotating image. However, the rendering order dictates that the Replicate filter is applied before rotation. This causes the image to be replicated before it's rotated, making it appear as though all the images are rotated as a group—*not* the effect you desire. To solve the problem, you need to defy the rendering order so that the effect is applied after rotation.

Although you can't alter the rendering order, you can subvert it by using standard effects that emulate fixed effects. One such effect is the Transform filter. Its properties match those of fixed effects: anchor point, position, scale, rotation, and opacity. It also includes skew and shutter angle. By applying the Transform filter after the Replicate filter, you can adjust the properties in the order you want.

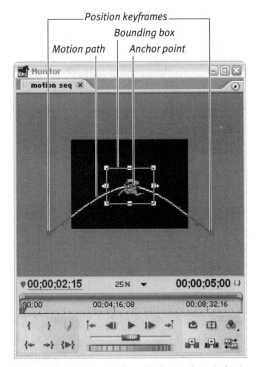

*Position keyframes*

*Bounding box*

*Motion path*      *Anchor point*

**Figure 13.61** Selecting the frame in the Monitor window's program view makes the direct manipulation controls appear.

# Viewing Motion Effects

Motion effects include the inherent spatial properties of a video clip: position, scale, rotation, and anchor point. You can adjust these properties as you would any other property, using controls in the Effect Controls window.

But because these properties are spatial in nature, it's more convenient to change them by dragging the clip in the program view, using what are called *direct manipulation controls* (**Figure 13.61**). When these controls are enabled, the selected clip appears with a bounding box and control handles. A circle with an X indicates the clip's anchor point. Dragging the clip changes its position, whereas dragging the control handles can alter the clip's scale or rotation. When you animate the clip's position, the keyframed positions appear as small x icons in the program view. The clip's route (its interpolated position values) is represented by a dotted line, or *motion path,* connecting the x icons. The spacing of the motion path's dots indicates speed: closely spaced dots correspond to slower movement, and widely spaced dots correspond to faster movement. You can change a clip's position at a keyframe by dragging the keyframe's X icon in the program view.

Whereas you can control position, scale, and rotation using direct manipulation controls, you must set the clip's anchor point using controls in the Effect Controls window. You must also use the Effect Controls window (or, if you prefer, the property graph) to adjust the timing of keyframes.

## ✔ Tip

■ Certain filters also offer direct manipulation controls. You can identify them by the direct manipulation icon 🖳 next to the effect's name in the Effect Controls window. Select the effect's name to activate the controls.

## To view spatial controls in the program view:

1. Select a clip in the timeline so that its effects appear in the Effect Controls window.

2. Cue the sequence time to anywhere within the selected clip's duration, so that it appears in the Monitor window's program view.

3. In the Effect Controls window, select the Motion category (**Figure 13.62**).

   In the program view, the selected clip appears with a bounding box and handles, and its anchor point is represented by a circle with an X. When the clip's position is animated, keyframes and a motion path also become visible (**Figure 13.63**).

## ✔ Tip

■ All effects with direct manipulation capability are activated by selecting the effect's name in the Effect Controls window and then directly manipulating the frame in the Monitor window's program view. Because it's the most commonly used effect, the Motion control's direct manipulation can also be activated by simply clicking directly on the frame in the Monitor window's program view.

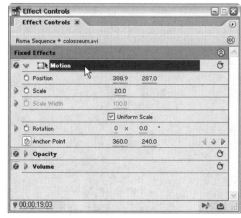

**Figure 13.62** In the Effect Controls window, select the Motion category.

**Figure 13.63** In the program view, the selected clip's spatial controls become visible.

# Setting Spatial Properties in the Program View

Once you enable the selected clip's direct manipulation controls, you can adjust its position, scale, and rotation in the program view.

Be aware that Premiere Pro calculates the position, scale, and rotation of a clip by its anchor point. In other words, the anchor point defines the position of a layer, the point around which a layer is scaled, and the pivot point of the layer's rotation. By default, a layer's anchor point is positioned in the center of the layer. In the program view, a clip's anchor point is represented by a circle with an X.

## ✔ Tip

■ Adjusting and keyframing effects in Premiere Pro works much the same as in the program's sibling, After Effects. However, there are differences, including variations in terminology. In After Effects, spatial properties (position, scale, rotation, and anchor point) are referred to as *transform* properties. And in After Effects, transform properties also include opacity. However, both programs include a Transform filter, which emulates these properties.

## Setting the position

Setting a layer's position places its anchor point anywhere inside or outside the viewable area of the program view (which corresponds to the screen). The exact position of a layer is expressed in *x, y* coordinates, where the upper-left corner of the program view is 0, 0. When the clip image doesn't fill the screen, the empty areas of the screen reveal either clips in lower tracks or (when there is no video in lower tracks) black video.

### To position a clip in the program view:

◆ In the program view, drag the clip to the position you want (**Figure 13.64**).

The Position property values in the Effect Controls window change accordingly. If the property's stopwatch icon is selected, then changing the position creates a keyframe at the current time.

### ✔ Tips

■ When you change the anchor point, it may appear as if you've also changed the clip's position. Actually, the layer's Position property remains the same; you simply changed the spot in the clip's image that determines its position on the screen.

■ The way Premiere Pro handles large images, in combination with the motion properties, make the Image Pan filter found in older versions of Premiere obsolete.

## Setting the scale

By default, a layer is set to 100 percent of its original size, or scale. You scale a layer around its anchor point. In other words, the anchor point serves as the mathematical center of a change in size. When you scale a layer by dragging, you'll notice that the handles of the layer seem to stretch from the anchor point.

Remember that bitmapped images look blocky and pixelated when they're scaled much beyond 100 percent.

### To scale a clip in the program view:

1. In the Effect Controls window, deselect Uniform Scale under the Scale property (**Figure 13.65**).

If you select Uniform Scale, dragging any handle maintains the clip's proportions, or aspect ratio.

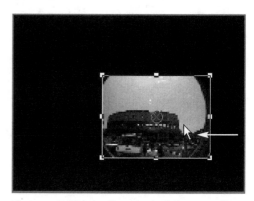

**Figure 13.64** With the direct manipulation controls active, you can drag the selected clip in the program view to change its position.

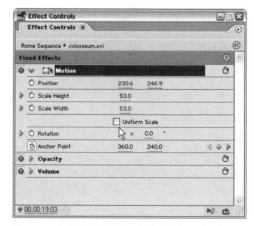

**Figure 13.65** In the Effect Controls window, deselect Uniform Scale to scale the clip's vertical and horizontal aspects separately.

Setting Spatial Properties

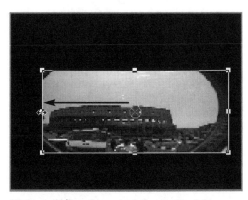

Figure 13.66 Drag the center-left or center-right handle to scale horizontally.

Figure 13.67 Drag the center-top or center-bottom handle to scale vertically.

Figure 13.68 Drag a corner handle to scale both aspects, or Shift-drag a corner handle to maintain the clip's aspect ratio as you scale.

2. In the program view, *do one of the following:*

▲ To scale the clip's horizontal aspect, drag the center-left or center-right handle (**Figure 13.66**).

▲ To scale the clip's vertical aspect, drag the center-top or center-bottom handle (**Figure 13.67**).

▲ To scale the clip horizontally and vertically, drag a corner handle (**Figure 13.68**).

▲ To scale the layer while maintaining its proportions, press Shift as you drag a corner handle (or click Uniform Scale in the Effect Controls window).

SETTING SPATIAL PROPERTIES

# Setting the rotation

When you rotate a clip, it pivots around the clip's anchor point. Therefore, make sure the anchor point is where you want it before you adjust rotation.

### To rotate a clip in the program view:

1. Position the mouse pointer near, but not on, a corner handle, so that the mouse becomes the rotation icon ↰.

2. With the rotate icon visible, drag to rotate the clip (**Figure 13.69**).

### ✔ Tips

- You can't flip a clip's image by changing its horizontal or vertical scale. However, you can achieve this effect with the Horizontal Flip or Vertical Flip filter. You can animate a flipping movement with the Transform filter or the Basic 3D filter.

- You can't use the Shift key to constrain rotational movement to 45-degree angles. To rotate the clip to exact angles, use the Rotation property controls in the Effect Controls window.

- Unlike After Effects, Premiere Pro includes no option to orient a clip tangential to its motion path automatically. You'll have to do it manually by setting rotation keyframes.

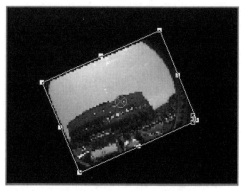

**Figure 13.69** Position the mouse just off the clip's corner handle, so that the rotation icon appears, and then drag to rotate.

## Rotational Values

Rotation is expressed as an absolute, not relative, value. You might even think of it as a rotational position. A clip's default rotation is 0 degrees; setting its rotation to 0 degrees always restores it to its original upright angle. This is true when you keyframe rotational values as well. For example, if you want to rotate a layer 180 degrees clockwise (upside down) and back again, the rotation values at each keyframe would be 0, 180, and 0. Mistakenly setting values of 0, 180, and –180 would cause the layer to turn clockwise 180 degrees and then turn counterclockwise—past its original position—until it's upside down again.

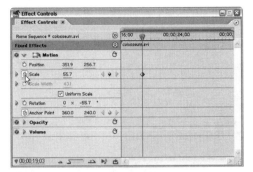

**Figure 13.70** Set the CTI to the frame where you want to specify a property value and then click the stopwatch icon to set the first keyframe at the CTI and initiate the keyframing process.

# Basic Keyframing in the Effect Controls Window

Essentially, keyframing is nothing more than repeating a two-step process: setting the current frame and setting the property value for that frame. The specific steps are outlined in this section.

If you're new to animating with keyframes, you might want to start with a simple effect property that yields results that are easy to see. For starters, try the Scale property (under the Motion category) or add a standard effect such as Fast Blur.

In later sections, you'll learn to gain greater control over your animations by manipulating the interpolation method used between keyframes.

## To set keyframes in the Effect Controls window:

1. In the Timeline window, select the clip that contains effect properties you want to adjust.

   The selected clip's effect properties appear in the Effect Controls window.

2. In the Effect Controls window, make sure the timeline view is visible.

3. Set the sequence CTI to the frame where you want to specify a keyframed property value.

4. Click the stopwatch icon ⏱ next to the layer property you want to keyframe, to activate the icon and the keyframing process (**Figure 13.70**).

*continues on next page*

The property's stopwatch icon appears selected ⏱. To the right of the property name, a keyframe navigator appears; a selected diamond indicates that the CTI is cued to a keyframe. In the property's track in the timeline view, a keyframe icon appears at the CTI.

5. Set the value for the keyframe (**Figure 13.71**).

6. Set the CTI to another frame.

7. *Do one of the following:*

   ▲ To create a keyframe with a new value, change the property's value (**Figure 13.72**).

   In the property's track of the timeline view, a new keyframe appears, and the diamond at the center of the keyframe navigator is highlighted.

   ▲ To create a keyframe without changing the property's value at that frame, click the center diamond of the keyframe navigator (**Figure 13.73**).

   If the new keyframe becomes the last keyframe for the property, it has the same value as the previous keyframe. Otherwise, the new keyframe's value is based on the previously interpolated value for that frame.

8. To create additional keyframes, repeat steps 6 and 7.

   To modify the keyframe values or to change the keyframes' position in time, use the methods explained in the following sections.

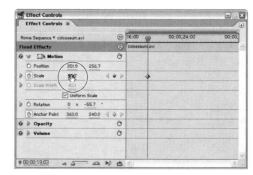

**Figure 13.71** Use the property value controls to set the keyframe's value.

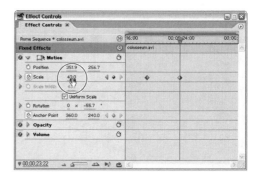

**Figure 13.72** Set the CTI to a new frame and change the property's value to set a keyframe with a new value...

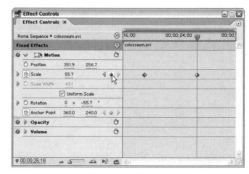

**Figure 13.73** ...or click the keyframe navigator's diamond icon to set a keyframe using the value already calculated for that frame.

**Figure 13.74** Use the playback controls or render a preview file to see the effect in motion.

9. To see the effect property values vary over time in the program view, use the playback controls in the Effect Controls window or any of the sequence playback controls you've learned about so far. You may need to render a preview file to see the effect play back at the project's full frame rate (see Chapter 10) (**Figure 13.74**).

### ✔ Tips

- Although it's possible to set a keyframe beyond the duration of the clip, doing so is usually unnecessary and will prevent you from seeing the keyframe in the timeline view of the Effects Control window when Pin to Clip is selected.

- Beginning with Premiere Pro 1.5, you can set keyframes at the edge of the transition even with Pin to Clip selected in the Effect Controls window. Pin to Clip still limits the scrolling range to just the selected clip, but it now includes the transition area.

- There's more than one way to make a property pause, or hold, at a certain value. You can create two consecutive keyframes that use the same value, or you can apply a hold interpolation method to a keyframe (explained later in this chapter). And naturally, a value is also maintained after the last keyframe.

- Property values before the first keyframe use the first keyframe's values; values after the last keyframe use the last keyframe's values. Therefore, setting the first keyframe after the beginning of the clip delays the animation, and setting the last keyframe before the end of the clip makes the value hold until the clip's Out point.

**KEYFRAMING IN THE EFFECT CONTROLS WINDOW**

## Keyframes with Interpolated Property Values

When you select the diamond in the keyframe navigator, the keyframe you create uses *interpolated* property values: values determined by calculating the progression between the keyframed values that come immediately before and after it. The mathematical term *interpolation* is the equivalent of the animation term *tweening*. For more about interpolation see "Understanding Interpolation" later in this chapter.

You usually create keyframes with interpolated values to modify an animation or, when no animation exists yet, to repeat a value. For example, adding a keyframe with interpolated values between two position keyframes lets you modify the existing motion path. When there's no difference between keyframed values, a new interpolated keyframe uses the same value. Likewise, when you make the last keyframe an interpolated keyframe, it uses the same value as the previous one.

By comparison, all keyframes you add to a value graph in the Timeline window initially use interpolated values. After all, you can add a keyframe only to the line of the value graph, which represents interpolated values.

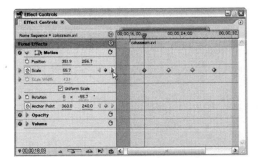

**Figure 13.75** Use the keyframe navigator's Left and Right Arrow buttons to cue the CTI. In this example, clicking the right button...

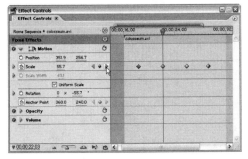

**Figure 13.76** ...cues the CTI to the next keyframe.

# Using Keyframes in the Effect Controls Window

As in the value graph, you can change the timing of keyframes by dragging them in the Effect Controls window's timeline view. However, to change the property value at a keyframe, you must cue the sequence CTI to the keyframe and then change the value using controls in the left side of the window. In the case of the position, you can also drag the keyframe's x icon in the motion path of the program view. In addition, you can copy and paste keyframes within a property, or from a property in one clip to the same property in another clip.

## To cue the CTI to keyframes:

1. Make sure that the property with the keyframes you want to see is visible in the Effect Controls window.

2. In the keyframe navigator for the property, *do one of the following:*

   ▲ To cue the current time to the previous keyframe, click the left arrow.

   ▲ To cue the current time to the next keyframe, click the right arrow (**Figure 13.75**).

   The sequence's CTI moves to the keyframe you specify (**Figure 13.76**). If no keyframe exists beyond the current keyframe, the appropriate arrow appears dimmed.

## To change a property's value at a keyframe:

1. Cue the sequence CTI to the keyframe whose value you want to adjust.

2. Adjust the property's value by using controls at the left side of the Effect Controls window or, in the case of motion properties, by dragging in the program view (**Figure 13.77**).

   Remember that changing a property value when the current time isn't cued to a keyframe creates a new keyframe at that point.

## To select keyframes:

◆ *Do one of the following:*

   ▲ To select a keyframe, click it in the timeline view (**Figure 13.78**).

   ▲ To add or subtract from your selection, Shift-click a keyframe.

   ▲ To select all the keyframes for a property, click the name of the property (**Figure 13.79**).

   Selected keyframes appear blue.

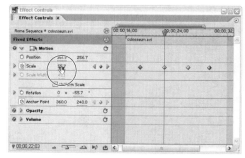

**Figure 13.77** To change the property value at a keyframe, make sure the CTI is cued to the keyframe and then change the property's value. If the CTI isn't cued to a keyframe, changing the value creates a new keyframe at that point.

**Figure 13.78** In the Effect Controls window's timeline view, click a keyframe to select it, or Shift-click to add or subtract from the selection.

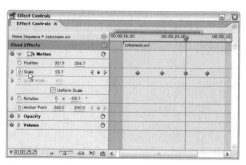

**Figure 13.79** Click the property's name to select all of its keyframes.

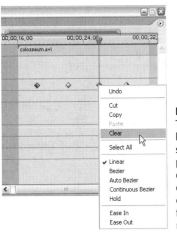

**Figure 13.80**
To delete a keyframe, select it and press Delete, or context-click it and choose Clear from the menu.

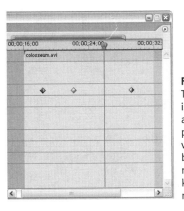

**Figure 13.81**
The keyframe is removed, and the property's values between the remaining keyframes are recalculated.

## To delete keyframes:

◆ In the Effect Controls window's timeline view, *do one of the following:*

  ▲ Select one or more keyframes and press Delete.

  ▲ Context-click a keyframe and choose Clear from the menu (**Figure 13.80**).

The keyframes are removed, and the property's interpolated values are recalculated accordingly (**Figure 13.81**).

## To delete all keyframes for a property:

◆ Deactivate the stopwatch icon for the property (**Figure 13.82**) and confirm your choice when prompted.

All keyframes disappear (**Figure 13.83**). You can't restore the keyframes by reactivating the stopwatch (doing this only starts a new keyframe process).

KEYFRAMES IN THE EFFECT CONTROLS WINDOW

**Figure 13.82** Click the stopwatch to deactivate it...

**Figure 13.83** ...and remove all the keyframes.

## To move keyframes in time:

1. Select one or more keyframes (as explained earlier in this chapter).

2. Drag the selected keyframes left or right, to a new position in time (**Figure 13.84**).

## To copy and paste keyframed values:

1. Select one or more keyframes (as explained earlier in this chapter) (**Figure 13.85**).

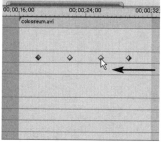

**Figure 13.84** Drag keyframes right or left to change their positions in time.

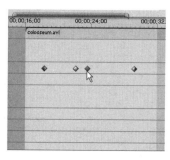

**Figure 13.85** Select one or more keyframes.

## Keyframe Icons

A property's keyframes appear in its corresponding row, or *property track*, in the timeline view. When the property heading is expanded, its keyframes appear as large icons (**Figure 13.86**). When the property heading is collapsed, the keyframes of the properties in that category appear as smaller circles and can't be modified (**Figure 13.87**).

The full-size keyframe icons vary according to the interpolation method used by the keyframe (see "Specifying a Temporal Interpolation Method" later in this chapter). Regardless of method, shading indicates that the property value either before or after the keyframe hasn't been interpolated.

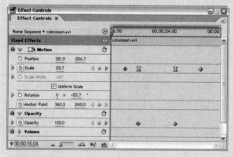

**Figure 13.86** When the property heading is expanded, its keyframe icons appear full-sized and reflect interpolation methods.

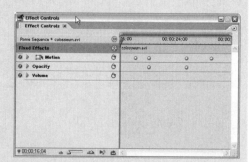

**Figure 13.87** When the property heading is collapsed, the keyframes of the properties in that category appear as smaller circles and can't be modified.

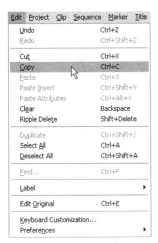

Figure 13.88
Choose Edit > Copy.

**Figure 13.89** Set the CTI to the frame at which you want the pasted keyframes to start...

**Figure 13.90**
...and choose Edit > Paste or press Ctrl+V.

**2.** Choose Edit > Copy or press Ctrl+C (**Figure 13.88**).

**3.** Set the CTI to the time at which you want the pasted keyframes to begin (**Figure 13.89**).

**4.** Choose Edit > Paste or press Ctrl-V (**Figure 13.90**).

The keyframes are pasted into the property, starting at the CTI (**Figure 13.91**).

## ✔ Tips

■ You can select multiple keyframes by dragging a marquee around them, just as you can with keyframes in the Timeline window.

■ You can paste keyframes from a property in one clip to the same property in another clip. To do this, select the new clip and set the CTI before you use the Paste command.

**Figure 13.91** The keyframes are pasted into the property, starting at the CTI.

# Understanding Interpolation

The beauty of keyframes is that they save you work. If you set the keyframes, Premiere Pro calculates the values for the frames in between, a process known as *interpolation*. Controlling the interpolation between keyframes allows you to set fewer keyframes than you could otherwise—without sacrificing precise control over your animation.

Beginning with Premiere Pro 1.5, you can use Bézier curves (the same kind of curves you used to create shapes and path text in the Title Designer) to control both *spatial* and *temporal* interpolation.

Spatial interpolation refers to the way that Premiere Pro calculates changes in position—in other words, how a layer or its anchor point moves through the visible area of the screen. Does it proceed directly from one keyframe to the next, or does it take a curved route (**Figure 13.92** and **Figure 13.93**)?

By default, Premiere Pro calculates the values between spatial keyframes—its motion path—using a curved progression, called an *auto* Bézier curve. In spatial terms, this means that there is a smooth rate of change through the keyframe. In other words, there aren't any sharp changes in direction.

Temporal interpolation refers to any property value's rate of change between keyframes. Does the value change at a constant rate from one keyframe to the next, or does it accelerate or decelerate (**Figure 13.94** and **Figure 13.95**)?

By default, Premiere Pro calculates the values between temporal keyframes using a linear progression, or *linear interpolation* method. In temporal terms, this means that property values change at a constant rate, or speed.

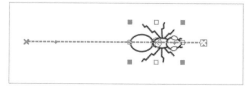

**Figure 13.92** Does it take the straight route...

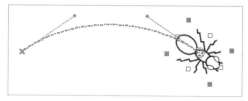

**Figure 13.93** ...or the curved path?

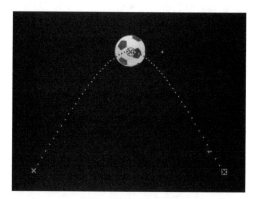

**Figure 13.94** Does the value change at a constant rate...

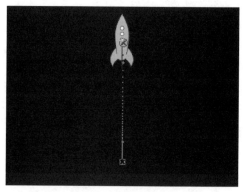

**Figure 13.95** ...or does it decelerate or accelerate (shown here).

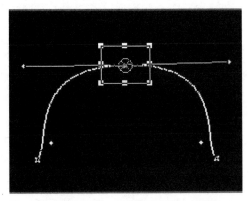

**Figure 13.96** A Bézier curve with handles showing.

Though their default settings differ, Premiere Pro calculates both spatial and temporal interpolation using a similar set of methods, or interpolation types. Controlling the interpolation between keyframes allows you to set fewer keyframes than you could otherwise—without sacrificing precise control over your animation.

## Viewing and adjusting spatial interpolation

As already discussed, spatial interpolation is represented in the program view as a motion path, a dotted line connecting keyframes. Using the Pen tool, you can change the path from a straight line—linear interpolation—to a curve, known as a *Bézier curve* (**Figure 13.96**). You'll find that editing motion paths works in much the same way as drawing shapes with the Pen tool in the Title Designer (see Chapter 12, "Creating Titles"), or as in a path-based drawing program, such as Illustrator. Although a motion path provides a rough indication of speed, it doesn't provide you with accurate control over the speed or the temporal interpolation.

# Viewing and adjusting temporal interpolation

You can also control the way that property values are interpolated *temporally*. In other words, the rate at which a value changes from one keyframe to another can remain constant, or it can accelerate or decelerate. You can even specify no interpolation, so that a keyframe value holds until the next keyframe value is reached. Simple commands convert keyframes from using one temporal interpolation type to another.

You can also adjust temporal interpolation manually by manipulating Bézier curves similar to the ones you use to adjust spatial interpolation. Because they control temporal interpolation, these Bézier curves appear in the property's value graph in the expanded track of the timeline. Adjusting the curve at each keyframe in the timeline eases in or eases out values at a custom rate (**Figure 13.97**).

Temporal interpolation is difficult to understand visually. The lines connecting keyframes in the expanded track of the Timeline window are like mathematical graphs. A straight line represents a constant speed, while a curved line shows acceleration or deceleration. But as in a motion path, a sharp corner in the graph represents an abrupt change in the rate of change, and a smooth curve indicates a gradual change.

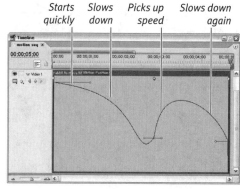

**Figure 13.97** The object this curve controls starts quickly, slowing down smoothly until it puts on a burst of speed and then slows down again.

## Temporal Interpolation in Action

It's important to understand that the temporal interpolation method doesn't affect the time between keyframes, just the value's rate of change between keyframes. For example, suppose that you composite two clips and animate their position so that they both move the same horizontal distance in one second. They both start animating at the same time, but one is set to Linear interpolation and the other to gradually accelerate (by specifying Ease Out for its first keyframe's interpolation; see the next section for more about Ease Out). When you play the clips, the first clip moves instantly and steadily toward its second keyframe position, whereas the second clip gets up to speed more slowly. Although the second clip falls behind at first, it gradually catches up, and both clips reach their destination simultaneously (**Figure 13.98**).

**Figure 13.98** Both rabbits run the same distance in the same amount of time. However, the top rabbit moves at a steady pace (Linear interpolation), whereas the bottom rabbit accelerates as it nears the final position.

# Interpolation Types

You can apply the following interpolation methods to calculate both spatial and temporal interpolation. But for the sake of clarity, the following figures illustrate them spatially. (Later, you'll learn about methods unique to temporal interpolation: Hold interpolation and the Ease In and Ease Out options.)

**Linear:** Linear interpolation dictates a constant rate of change from one keyframe to the next. Spatially, Linear interpolation defines a straight path from one keyframe to the next (**Figure 13.99**); temporally, Linear interpolation results in a constant speed between keyframes.

**Auto Bézier:** Auto Bézier interpolation automatically reduces the rate of change equally on both sides of a keyframe. Spatially, a keyframe set to Auto Bézier is comparable to a smooth point, with two equal direction lines extending from it. It results in a smooth, symmetrical curve in a motion path (**Figure 13.100**). Temporally, Auto Bézier interpolation reduces the rate of change equally before and after a keyframe, creating a gradual deceleration that eases into and out of the keyframe.

Adjusting an Auto Bézier keyframe's direction handles manually make it a Continuous Bézier keyframe.

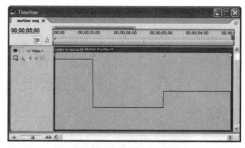

**Figure 13.99** Linear interpolation defines a straight path from one keyframe to the next.

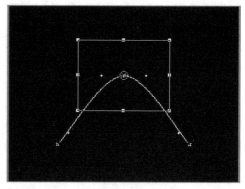

**Figure 13.100** Auto Bézier curve.

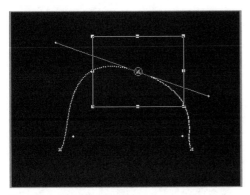

**Figure 13.101** Continuous Bézier curve.

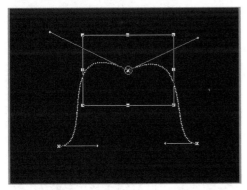

**Figure 13.102** Bézier curve.

**Continuous Bézier:** Like Auto Bézier, Continuous Bézier interpolation reduces the rate of change on both sides of a keyframe. However, Continuous Bézier interpolation is set manually, so it does not affect the incoming and outgoing rates of change equally. In the motion path, Continuous Bézier interpolation results in a smooth and continuous, but asymmetrical, curve (**Figure 13.101**). Temporally, Continuous Bézier interpolation manually and unequally reduces the rate of change before and after a keyframe.

Ctrl-clicking a Continuous Bézier keyframe's handles make it a Bézier keyframe.

**Bézier:** As with Continuous Bézier, you set Bézier interpolation manually. Bézier interpolation can either decrease or increase the rate of change on either or both sides of a keyframe. Spatially, Bézier keyframes are comparable to a corner point in a mask path. As in a corner point, the direction lines extending from the keyframe are unequal and discontinuous. In a motion path, Bézier interpolation creates a discontinuous curve, or cusp, at the keyframe (**Figure 13.102**). Temporally, Bézier interpolation can reduce or increase the rate of change before and after a keyframe.

# Specifying a Spatial Interpolation Method

Adjusting a motion path is just like editing a Bézier shape in the Title Designer—except that the curve doesn't define the shape of an object, but the path of a clip.

### To modify a motion path using Bézier curves:

1. Select one or more keyframes in the Effect Controls window (as explained earlier in this chapter) (**Figure 13.103**).

2. Context-click a selected keyframe.

3. Choose Spatial Interpolation and select an option (**Figure 13.104**):
   - ▲ Linear
   - ▲ Bézier
   - ▲ Auto Bézier
   - ▲ Continuous Bézier

4. Drag the Bézier directional handles in the Monitor window's program view (**Figure 13.105**).

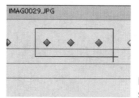

**Figure 13.103** Marquee-selected keyframes.

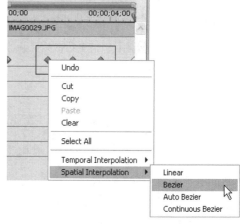

**Figure 13.104** Choose Spatial Interpolation and select one of the four options.

**Figure 13.105** Drag the Bézier directional handles in the program view.

# Specifying a Temporal Interpolation Method

As you have learned, temporal interpolation affects not the change between positions, but the rate of change between any keyframed value, and you adjust it not by altering the motion path in the program view, but by altering the value graph in the timeline. Otherwise, you can apply the same Linear or Bézier methods. (See "Interpolation Methods" earlier in this chapter.)

You can also specify an interpolation method unique to temporal interpolation: hold interpolation. In addition, you can quickly ease the incoming or outgoing interpolation of a keyframe using the Ease In and Ease Out options. These options let you achieve these common effects without having to adjust the interpolation manually. (After Effects users will compare these to After Effects' keyframe assistants.)

**Ease In:** The property value's rate of change accelerates from, or eases out of, the previous keyframe and then decelerates into, or eases into, the selected keyframe (**Figure 13.106**). Contrast this to the Auto or Continuous Bézier option, which affects both the incoming and outgoing interpolation.

**Ease Out:** The property value's rate of change accelerates from, or eases out of, the selected keyframe and then decelerates into, or eases into, the following keyframe (**Figure 13.107**). Contrast this to the Auto or Continuous Bézier option, which affects both the incoming and outgoing interpolation.

**Hold:** Although you can observe its effects both spatially and temporally, hold interpolation is a strictly temporal type of interpolation, halting changes in a property's value at the keyframe. The value remains fixed until the current frame of the composition reaches the next keyframe, where the property is set to a new value instantly (**Figure 13.108**). For example, specifying hold keyframes for a layer's Position property can cause it to disappear suddenly and then reappear in different places. When hold interpolation is applied to position keyframes, no motion path connects the keyframes displayed in the program view.

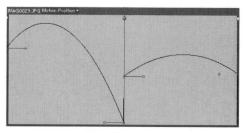

**Figure 13.106** The center keyframe set for Ease In...

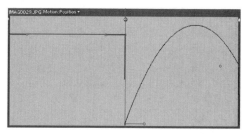

**Figure 13.107** ...Ease Out...

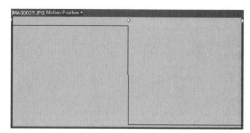

**Figure 13.108** ...and Hold.

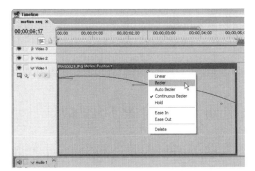

**Figure 13.109** Context-click and select a Bézier option.

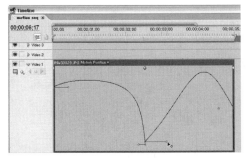

**Figure 13.110** The longer handle affects the curve farther along the path than the shorter handle.

## To set a keyframe's interpolation method in the timeline:

1. View a clip's keyframed properties in an expanded track of the Timeline window.

   By default, interpolated temporal values are calculated using a linear scale.

2. Context-click the keyframe you want to adjust and choose an option from the menu (**Figure 13.109**):
   - ▲ Linear
   - ▲ Bézier
   - ▲ Auto Bézier
   - ▲ Continuous Bézier
   - ▲ Hold
   - ▲ Ease In
   - ▲ Ease Out
   - ▲ Delete

## To adjust the temporal interpolation manually:

- ◆ In the expanded track of the Timeline window, with the property's keyframes visible (see "To view property values for video clips in the timeline" earlier in this chapter), manipulate any property's keyframe handles *by doing any of the following*:
  - ▲ Drag the handle up or down to adjust the slope of the curve.
  - ▲ Drag the handle left or right to adjust the range of the curve's influence.

  The longer the handle, the farther from the keyframe the curve is affected (**Figure 13.110**).

# EFFECTS IN ACTION

In the previous chapter, you learned how Premiere Pro's unified approach to effects lets you add and adjust a wide range of effects using a relatively small number of techniques. But although there's some truth to the saying "if you know one, you know them all," when it comes to effects, it's worthwhile to discuss some effects in a little more detail.

This chapter covers the standard video effects, or filters. Obviously, the scope of this book doesn't allow for a complete and detailed explanation of every effect—much less the infinite iterations and combinations. Nor would it be useful to attempt such a discussion. Instead, most sections briefly describe each filter category and list the filters they contain. Along the way, you'll pick up plenty of helpful tips. Special attention is devoted to the Levels filter and the Color Corrector filter. They're distinguished both by their usefulness and by their specialized controls, and therefore merit a more thorough treatment.

This chapter begins with the effect presets provided with Premiere Pro 1.5. Then it continues with a thorough discussion of a category of effects of particular interest to many users: keying. From there, the list is alphabetical, from Adjust Filters to Video Filters.

# Working with Effect Presets

In Chapter 13, "Working with Effects," you learned how to drag an effect to a clip in the timeline and modify its parameters in the Effect Control window.

It can take a lot of time and effort to get the effect you want. Luckily, beginning with Premiere Pro 1.5, you can save any combination of effects and their settings as a *preset*.

Adobe has supplied a number of presets to get you started. Many of the most common tasks, such as creating a beveled border for a picture-in-picture effect and using different effects to transition into and out of a clip, are already available in the new presets bins. You can use an existing preset, as well as modify, save, and import a preset. And because presets are saved as small files on your hard disk, it's easy to share presets with other editors. When you change the parameters of an effect in the Effect Controls window, you have the option of saving the effect as a preset in the Effect Controls window's pull-down menu. Premiere Pro stores the new preset in the root preset directory, but as you will learn later in this section, you can create custom preset bins and drag the new presets into the new bins.

### To create and save an effect preset:

1. In the Timeline window, select the clip that uses the effect that you want to save as a preset (**Figure 14.1**).

2. In the Effect Controls window, select the effect that you want to save (**Figure 14.2**).

**Figure 14.1** Select the clip that uses the effect you want to save as a preset.

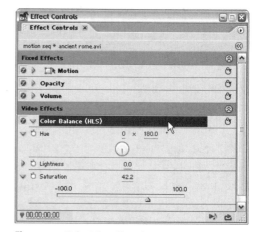

**Figure 14.2** Select the effect that you want to save.

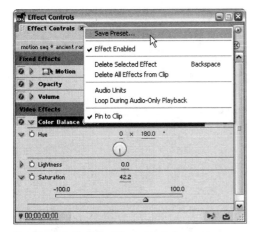

**Figure 14.3** In the Effect Controls window menu, choose Save Preset.

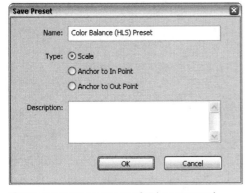

**Figure 14.4** Enter a new name for the preset and select a keyframe option.

3. In the Effect Controls window menu, choose Save Preset (**Figure 14.3**).

The Save Preset dialog box appears (**Figure 14.4**).

4. Enter a name for the preset.

Premiere Pro provides a name based on the effect that was modified. Keep the default name or enter a name that will help you remember what the preset does.

5. Determine the way the effect preset's keyframes will be applied to other clips by selecting one of the following:

▲ **Scale:** The keyframes scale proportionally to the duration of the clips.

▲ **Anchor to In Point:** The first keyframe's distance from the In point of the target clip will be the same as it was from the In point of the source clip. All other keyframes follow without scaling for the duration of the target clip.

▲ **Anchor to Out Point:** The last keyframe's distance from the Out point of the target clip will be the same as it was from the Out point of the source clip. All other keyframes precede the last keyframe without scaling for the duration of the target clip.

6. If you want, type a description of the preset in the Description field.

A description can be helpful in identifying the origin or purpose of the preset at a later time.

7. Click OK.

## To apply an effect preset:

1. On the Effects palette, expand the Presets bin (**Figure 14.5**).

2. Select a preset and drag it to a clip on the timeline (**Figure 14.6**).

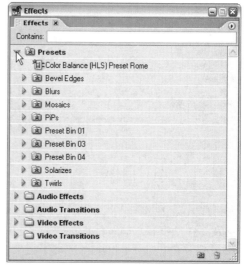

**Figure 14.5** Expand the Presets bin to expose the presets.

**Figure 14.6** Drag the preset to a clip on the timeline.

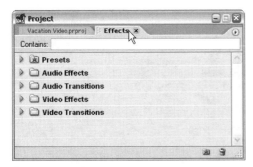

**Figure 14.7** Display the Effects palette.

**Figure 14.8** Choose New Presets Bin from the menu.

**Figure 14.9** Enter a name for the new presets bin.

## To create and rename a preset bin:

1. Click the Effects tab to display the Effects palette (**Figure 14.7**),

2. Choose New Presets Bin from the Effects palette menu (**Figure 14.8**).

   Premiere Pro names the new bin Preset Bin followed by a number.

3. Click the name of the new preset bin on the Effects palette; then click again (do not double-click) and enter a new name (**Figure 14.9**).

## To move effect presets into custom preset bins:

1. Make sure the presets you want to move and the destination bin are both visible on the Effects palette.

2. Select one or more presets (**Figure 14.10**).

3. Drag the selected items to the destination bin (**Figure 14.11**).

   The items are moved into the destination bin (**Figure 14.12**).

## ✔ Tip

■ When saving all of the effects that you spend a lot of time perfecting. get into the habit of giving them names that will make sense long into the future. If you use a modified effect in one project, chances are good that you will want to use it the same way again.

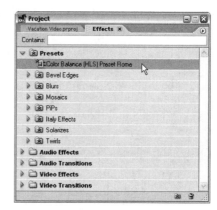

**Figure 14.10** Select one or more presets.

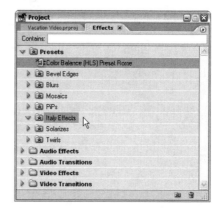

**Figure 14.11** Drag the selected items to the destination bin.

**Figure 14.12** The items are moved into the destination bin.

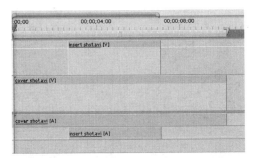

**Figure 14.13** Placing a clip in a higher track (and retaining its full opacity)...

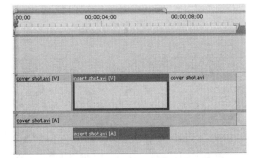

**Figure 14.14** ...has the same result as an overlay edit.

**Figure 14.15** Most often, you use the higher tracks to blend and key clips. Here, a title is keyed over video.

# Superimposing Images

One of the major techniques covered in this chapter is the use of keying filters to superimpose images. But before you learn how to use keying filters, take a moment to review how opacity works in general, and in Premiere Pro in particular.

## About track hierarchy

Video tracks 2 and higher are also referred to as *superimpose tracks*. If video clips are playing simultaneously in different tracks (and the monitor buttons are active), only the clip in the highest track is visible in the program view of the Monitor window, provided that you don't alter the clips' opacity levels. In other words, the superimpose tracks in Premiere Pro work much like layers in Adobe Photoshop (or Illustrator or After Effects).

It's possible to take advantage of track hierarchy for basic editing purposes. By placing a clip in a higher track, you can achieve an effect that looks like an overlay edit in the program view without recording over a clip in the timeline (**Figures 14.13** and **14.14**).

But in general, you use superimpose tracks as their name suggests: to superimpose the clips they contain. By layering clips in superimpose tracks, you can blend and composite images (**Figure 14.15**).

## About fading and keying

Previous chapters already introduced you to the two principal methods for superimposing clips: fading and keying.

*Fading* blends an entire clip with the clips in lower tracks. In Chapter 13, you learned that you can control a clip's overall opacity levels in much the same way that you fade audio levels. Although fading can look similar to a cross-dissolve transition, fading is generally used to blend clips for more sustained periods, not just to transition between them. And unlike with a cross-dissolve (which occurs between two adjacent clips), you can fade multiple layers of clips together (**Figure 14.16**).

In contrast to fading, *keying* makes only certain parts of a clip transparent. You encountered one form of keying in Chapter 12, "Creating Titles," where you learned that empty areas in a title become transparent automatically (**Figure 14.17**). Similarly, any areas of the screen left empty when you move a clip using a motion effect also become transparent automatically (as you discovered in Chapter 13). This behavior makes creating a picture-in-picture or split-screen effect easy (**Figure 14.18**).

**Figure 14.16** Fading blends an entire clip with the underlying image. Here, opacity has been faded to superimpose one clip over another.

**Figure 14.17** Keying makes certain parts of a clip transparent. Here, filters have been applied to the document and then the document paper has been keyed out.

**Figure 14.18** Areas of the screen left empty as a result of a motion effect are also keyed out automatically, as in this picture-in-picture effect.

*Gaspar "Tony" Bolante*

**Figure 14.19** In addition to automatically keying out an alpha channel generated by Premiere Pro, you can key out parts of an image based on other factors. Here, areas are keyed out based on a matte in the shape of a cameo.

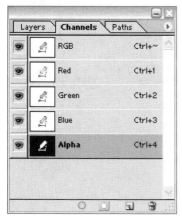

**Figure 14.20** You may be familiar with channels from Photoshop, which shows you the R, G, B, and alpha channels on the Channels palette.

As you'll see in this chapter, you can also *key out,* or remove, parts of an image based on other factors, such as a clip's brightness or color. A keying effect can also utilize a clip's preexisting alpha channel or one you define using another image (**Figure 14.19**).

Naturally, you can combine the effects of fading and keying, such as when you fade up a title over a video.

## About the alpha channel

Regardless of the method you use to change a clip's opacity, what you're really modifying is its *alpha channel.*

In 8-bit RGB color images, each channel— red, green, and blue—uses 8 bits (for a total of 24 bits), yielding millions of colors. A 32-bit file contains a fourth 8-bit channel, known as an *alpha channel* (**Figure 14.20**). Whereas the RGB channels define the amount of visible color for each pixel in the image, the alpha channel defines each pixel's level of opacity. Even when a footage file doesn't contain an alpha channel, as is often the case with video, Premiere Pro processes it as a 32-bit file.

**SUPERIMPOSING IMAGES**

**469**

The alpha channel is usually depicted as a grayscale matte in which the range from white to black corresponds to the range from opaque to transparent. You can see a clip's alpha channel as a grayscale by setting the source or program view's display mode to Alpha (see "Choosing a Display Mode" in Chapter 5) (**Figure 14.21**).

You already know several ways to modify a clip's alpha channel. Fading adjusts a clip's alpha channel's values for all of its pixels—or, in terms of the matte, changes their grayscale values anywhere from white to black. In the case of titles and motion effects, Premiere Pro automatically generates an alpha channel for empty areas and keys them out. The following sections cover numerous other keying methods.

**Figure 14.21** In Premiere Pro, you can set the source or program view's display mode to show the alpha channel as a grayscale matte.

## Keying

*Keying* makes only certain parts of a clip transparent. The terms *key* and *keying* refer to their physical counterpart, the *keyhole*. Essentially, keying cuts a keyhole in an image, making that part of the image transparent. The hole is then filled with another image—in this case, clips in lower tracks of the timeline. You can *key out*, or remove, parts of an image based on brightness or color. You can also base a key on a clip's alpha channel or even on a separate image.

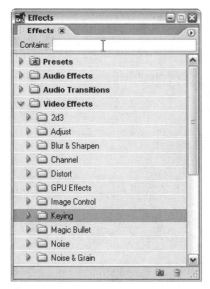

**Figure 14.22** Keying effects are listed in a folder alongside folders for other video effect categories.

# Using Keying Filters

In addition to using a clip's opacity property to make the entire image transparent, you can restrict transparency to particular areas—a technique called *keying*. Keying effects are listed among the other standard effects, and you adjust them using the methods you learned in Chapter 13 (**Figure 14.22**). But because keying effects (or simply *keys*) constitute such a useful class of techniques, they merit special attention.

Although Premiere Pro provides many keying filters, all fall into four basic categories. You can *key out*, or make parts of an image transparent, based on the clip's existing alpha channel, luminance, or chrominance, or on a separate image that defines the alpha channel's matte. You can also make these keying filters more effective by employing a *garbage matte*—a filter that crops out extraneous edges of an image.

This chapter assumes that you know how to apply a filter from the Effects palette and how to use the Effect Controls window to adjust and animate effect properties. (To review those techniques, refer to Chapter 13.) The following sections cover the key types by category, explaining the most commonly used keying filters in detail and summarizing the others.

## ✔ Tip

- Strictly speaking, a few of the keying filters may be more accurately described as *blending modes*, like the ones found in Photoshop and After Effects. Whereas keys adjust transparency, blending modes (also called *layer modes*) blend images by comparing the corresponding pixels of two images and applying a formula to get a new result. For the sake of simplicity, however, this book draws a distinction only between adjusting a clip's opacity property and applying keying filters and does not refer to these keying filters in terms of blending modes.

# Using Alpha-Based Keys

Technically, a clip's opacity is always defined by its alpha channel. The term *alpha-based keys* refers to keying methods that use either the alpha channel included in a clip or one generated by Premiere Pro.

Some footage items already contain an alpha channel. For example, you might create an image in Photoshop and define its alpha channel using that program's suite of tools. Or Premiere Pro can generate an alpha channel for a clip, for empty areas of a title or areas of the screen left uncovered by clips that have been moved with motion effects. By now, you know that adding a clip to a superimpose track automatically keys out areas based on the clip's alpha channel.

Premiere Pro applies an alpha key automatically because that's usually what you want to happen. However, sometimes you want to override the setting and ignore the alpha channel. Other times, opaque and transparent areas need to be reversed. You can also use the alpha channel as a grayscale matte. Doing so can be helpful when you want to evaluate and correct the effectiveness of a key; or you can use the matte as the source of a track matte key (see "Using Matte-Based Keys" later in this chapter). Finally, you can use a filter to adjust the clip's opacity level without using its fixed (or inherent) opacity property. This allows you to work around Premiere Pro's rendering order (see "Subverting the Render Order" in Chapter 13).

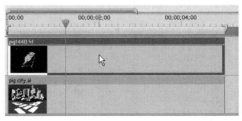

**Figure 14.23** Select the clip that contains the Alpha Adjust filter and set the CTI to a representative frame.

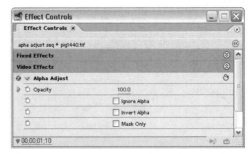

**Figure 14.24** In the Effect Controls window, specify the options you want.

**Figure 14.25** Opacity adjusts the clip's overall opacity (after the alpha key is applied). Here, the pig image is set to 75% opaque.

**Figure 14.26** Ignore Alpha prevents Premiere Pro from keying out the alpha channel.

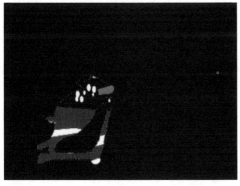

**Figure 14.27** Invert Alpha reverses the opaque and transparent areas of the clip.

**Figure 14.28** Mask Only replaces opaque areas with white.

## To use the Alpha Adjust filter:

1. In the Effects palette, drag the Alpha Adjust filter and *do one of the following*:

   ▲ Drop the effect on a clip in a superimpose track of the timeline.

   ▲ Drop the effect on to the Effect Controls window while the appropriate clip is selected.

   Make sure that the clip is selected so the effect appears in the Effect Controls window, and that the CTI is on a frame that will help you evaluate your adjustments (**Figure 14.23**).

2. In the Effect Controls window, adjust any of the filter's properties (**Figure 14.24**):

   **Opacity:** Adjusts the overall opacity levels of the clip (**Figure 14.25**).

   **Ignore Alpha:** Prevents Premiere Pro from using the alpha channel included in the clip. However, this option doesn't prevent you from fading a clip or applying other keying filters (**Figure 14.26**).

   **Invert Alpha:** Reverses the opaque and transparent areas of the clip (**Figure 14.27**).

   **Mask Only:** Ignores the RGB information included in the clip and instead shows the clip's opacity as white areas (**Figure 14.28**).

## ✔ Tip

■ Scaling or repositioning a clip using the motion effects may produce unwanted results. Inverting a resized clip's alpha channel, for example, can reveal the clip's edges. To solve problems caused by motion effects, resize the clip in a separate sequence and then use a nested version. Or resize the clip using the Transform filter.

**USING ALPHA-BASED KEYS**

# Using Luminance-Based Keys

Luminance-based keys use luminance (brightness) levels to define transparent areas. You can choose to key out either the brightest or the darkest pixels contained in the image. Luminance-based key types include Luminance, Multiply, and Screen.

The Luminance key isn't the only key type that uses luminance to define transparency, but it's probably the most commonly used (both in Premiere Pro and in traditional editing suites). You may hear luminance keys generically referred to as *luma keys*.

## To adjust the Luminance key:

◆ In the Effect Controls window, adjust the Luminance filter's property settings until the image in the program view looks the way you want (**Figure 14.29**):

**Threshold:** Sets the range of darker pixels that become transparent.

**Cutoff:** Sets the transparency of the areas defined by the Threshold value.

Areas of the clip are keyed out based on luminance levels (**Figures 14.30** and **14.31**). When the relative positions of the threshold and cutoff are reversed, the key is reversed, and lighter areas become transparent (**Figure 14.32**).

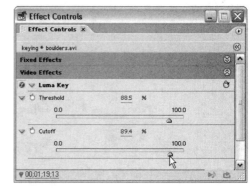

**Figure 14.29** Adjust the Luma key's Threshold and Cutoff values.

**Figure 14.30** In this example, the Luma key is applied to the rocks image; the sand dunes on the right serve as the background.

**Figure 14.31** Here, brighter areas of the clip are keyed out, revealing the underlying image.

**Figure 14.32** Reversing the relative positions of the Cutoff and Threshold values inverts the key.

**Figure 14.33** Multiply makes the clip more transparent where the bright areas of the clip and the underlying image correspond. Here, the dunes show through more where the bright areas of both images correspond.

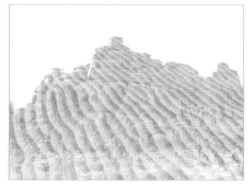

**Figure 14.34** Screen makes the clip more transparent where the dark areas of the clip and the underlying image correspond.

### ✔ Tip

- To better judge the transparency settings, use a bright color (such as a bright yellow or green) as a temporary background for the keyed clip. You can do this by temporarily placing a color matte (see Chapter 2, "Starting a Project") in the track below the clip you're keying. Then the color will show through when you preview in the program view. When you've finished, remove the color matte from the timeline (or disable it).

## Using Multiply and Screen keys

The Multiply and Screen options blend a clip with a clip in a lower track based on luminance values taken from both clips. Multiply averages the product of the pixel values of the clip and the underlying image. The resulting image is darker than both and never brighter than the original. Multiply preserves the black areas of the clip, while allowing the underlying image to show through the brighter areas (**Figure 14.33**).

Screen uses inverse luminance values in its calculations. Therefore, the resulting image is brighter than either original image and never darker than the clip to which it's applied. Screen preserves white areas of the clip and allows the underlying image to show through darker areas (**Figure 14.34**).

The best way to understand these keys is to compare them.

USING LUMINANCE-BASED KEYS

## To adjust Multiply or Screen filters:

◆ In the Effect Controls window, adjust the Multiply or Screen filter's property values (**Figure 14.35**):

**Opacity:** Sets the overall opacity, regardless of luminance values.

**Cutoff:** Sets the amount of blending, based on luminance values.

## ✔ Tip

■ Multiply and Screen keys aren't just for blending two different clips—they can also combine two copies of the same clip. For example, you can use a Screen key to quickly brighten underexposed areas of a clip.

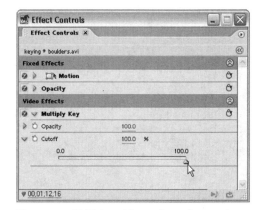

**Figure 14.35** Multiply and Screen keys allow you to adjust Opacity and Cutoff values.

**Figure 14.36** Chrominance-based keys are typically used to composite bluescreen or greenscreen footage.

# Using Chrominance-Based Keys

Chrominance-based keys use *chrominance* (color) to define the transparent areas of a clip. Chrominance-based keys are commonly used to composite moving subjects that were shot against a colored background, usually a blue or green backdrop called a *bluescreen* or *greenscreen,* respectively. Provided that the subject doesn't contain the key color, a chrominance-based key can remove the background while leaving the subject opaque.

Blue and green are standard key colors because they're relatively absent from human skin tones. Without the key color to differentiate the background from the subject, it would be difficult, if not impossible, to perfectly separate a moving subject from the background (**Figure 14.36**).

Chrominance-based key types include Chroma, Blue Screen, Green Screen, RGB Difference, and Non-Red. The following sections explain in detail how to apply the Chroma key and summarize the other color-based keys.

## To use the Chroma key:

1. In the Effect Controls dialog box, choose a key color by doing *one of the following:*

   ▲ To choose a color from the color picker, click the color swatch. In the color picker that appears, select a color and click OK to set the key color and return to the Transparency Settings dialog box.

   ▲ To select a color from the image in the program view, click and hold down the mouse on the Eyedropper tool, position the eyedropper on the color you want to use, and then release the mouse (**Figures 14.37** and **14.38**).

2. To modify the key, adjust the filter's property values (**Figure 14.39**):

   **Similarity:** Increases or decreases the range of colors similar to the key color that are keyed out.

   **Blend:** Blends the clip with the underlying clip.

   **Threshold:** Controls the amount of shadow that you keep in the range of key colors.

   **Cutoff:** Darkens or lightens shadows. Don't drag the cutoff beyond the threshold, or you'll invert the gray and transparent pixels.

   **Smoothing:** Anti-aliases (smoothes) the edges of the opaque areas. You can choose Low, Medium, or High.

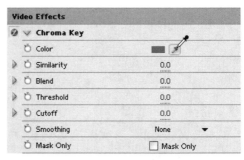

**Figure 14.37** To select the key color, click and hold down the mouse on the Eyedropper tool...

**Figure 14.38** ...and then release the mouse when the eyedropper is over the color you want to sample.

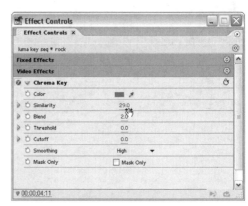

**Figure 14.39** You can adjust the Chroma key using a number of parameters.

**USING CHROMINANCE-BASED KEYS**

**Figure 14.40** The color is keyed out, revealing the underlying background image. In this example, a clear blue sky is replaced with a more dramatic one.

**3.** To see the opaque areas as white, click Mask Only.

You can use this option to see the effectiveness of the key more easily; deselect it when you're satisfied with the results. When you've finished making adjustments, the key color is transparent and reveals the underlying image (**Figure 14.40**).

## ✔ Tips

- If you want to take another color sample, you can temporarily disable the Chroma Key effect and still sample a color from the unmodified clip.

- In some areas of Premiere Pro—including the controls for selecting a key color—the color picker works a little differently than in other programs. Rather than selecting the eyedropper and then selecting a color, you must keep the mouse button down after you select the eyedropper and then release it only after you position the eyedropper over the color you want to use.

- Before you begin adjusting a Chroma key, crop out extraneous portions of the image using a garbage matte, as explained in "Using Garbage Mattes" later in this chapter. This way, you don't waste effort adjusting for parts of the background that can be eliminated at the outset.

- If your shot uses a good blue or green background, you might get better results with the Blue Screen or Green Screen key than with the Chroma key (see "Other chrominance-based keys" on the next page).

- Temporarily switch on the Mask Only option to better evaluate the effectiveness of your keying adjustments. White areas represent opaque parts of the clip, whereas black areas will be transparent. Check for unwanted holes or gray areas in the matte.

**USING CHROMINANCE-BASED KEYS**

## Other chrominance-based keys

The following list summarizes the other chrominance-based keys:

**RGB Difference key:** Works like a simpler version of the Chroma key. It provides only the Similarity and Smoothing properties. You can also use the Drop Shadow option, which adds a 50 percent gray, 50 percent opaque shadow, offset four pixels to the right and four pixels down.

**Blue Screen and Green Screen keys:** Optimized for use with true chroma blue and true chroma green, respectively. However, these keys don't provide as many controls as the Chroma key.

**Non-Red key:** Makes blue and green areas (non-red) transparent. This key type also provides a Blend property.

### Keys to the Kingdom

The results you get from chroma keying depend a great deal on the quality of your footage. Here are a few things to consider if you plan to do bluescreen work:

◆ Shoot using the best format possible. For video, choose a format with the least compression and the greatest color depth.

◆ Use a high-quality bluescreen. A good bluescreen should be painted with paint specially formulated for bluescreen work. If possible, use a shadow-free cyclorama, a background constructed from hard materials with rounded corners, to prevent shadows.

◆ Use good lighting techniques on the set. Preferably, work with someone experienced in lighting an evenly lit, shadow-free bluescreen. Use lighting to help separate the subject from the background and reduce *spill* (blue light reflected on the subject).

◆ Use a high-quality capture device. If possible, transfer the footage uncompressed, using a high-quality transfer method, such as SDI.

◆ Doing good bluescreen compositing is harder than it sounds. You may need to use software dedicated to the job, such as plug-ins like Ultimatte's Primatte keyer or the Keylight plug-in found in After Effects' Professional.

**Figure 14.41** This matte's edges perfectly match the statue in the beauty.

**Figure 14.42** This matte is designed to retain some of the beauty's background color along with the text.

# Using Matte-Based Keys

Matte-based keys use an external image to define transparent areas of a clip. A typical matte is a high-contrast grayscale image (sometimes called a *high-con*). You might think of it as an external stand-in for a clip's alpha channel.

As in an alpha channel's grayscale, brightness in the matte corresponds to opacity in the foreground clip, so that white areas specify opacity, and black areas define transparency. The matte itself never appears in the final output; it only defines the opaque and transparent areas of the foreground clip, sometimes called the *beauty*. Sometimes the matte perfectly matches the shape of the beauty; other times, the matte cuts a shape out of the beauty (**Figures 14.41**, **14.42**, and **14.43**). However, the image size of the matte should match the sequence's image size. Otherwise, the matte's relative size may not be what you expect, and the edges of the matte may be apparent.

**Figure 14.43** This matte is intended as a stencil.

**481**

Matte-based key types include Image Matte and Track Matte. The Difference Matte key also falls into this category, although it creates its own matte by comparing two clips.

## Using the Image Matte key

The Image Matte key can use any grayscale still image as the matte. Alternatively, you can use a still image that contains an alpha channel, effectively borrowing its alpha channel to define opacity in another clip. You choose the image matte from the Effect Controls window; the matte doesn't have to be used in the timeline or even imported into the project. However, once you specify a file as a matte, the project will refer to the file just as it does other clips.

You can't specify a title you created in Premiere Pro as an image matte. However, a title can serve as a matte if you use the Track Matte key (see "Using the Track Matte key" later in this chapter).

### To adjust the Image Matte key:

1. In the Effect Controls window, click the Image Matte key's Setup button →▦ (**Figure 14.44**).

   The Select a Matte Image dialog box appears.

2. In the Select a Matte Image dialog box, locate the still image you want to use as the matte and click Open (**Figure 14.45**).

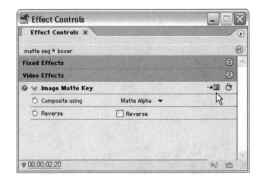

**Figure 14.44** In the Effect Controls window, click the Image Matte key's Setup button.

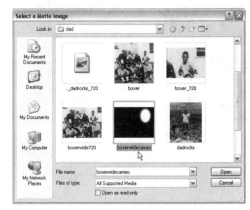

**Figure 14.45** In the Select a Matte Image dialog box, locate the still image you want to use as the matte and click Open.

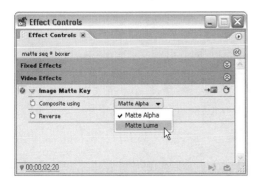

**Figure 14.46** In the Composite Using drop-down menu, select the appropriate option.

**Figure 14.47** Here, a soft-edged cameo makes the boxer opaque. Areas outside the matte become transparent, revealing a duplicate of the clip that has been filtered to appear darker and blurred.

**Figure 14.48** Selecting Reverse exchanges the opaque and transparent areas.

3. In the Effect Controls window, choose an option from the Composite Using drop-down menu (**Figure 14.46**):

   **Matte Alpha:** Uses the matte image file's alpha channel to define opacity.

   **Matte Luma:** Uses the matte image file's luminance values to define opacity.

   The specified value of the matte (alpha or luma) corresponds to opacity in the clip to which you applied the Image Matte filter (**Figure 14.47**).

4. To invert the opaque and transparent areas, select Reverse (**Figure 14.48**).

## ✔ Tip

■ Resizing a clip using motion effects also affects its matte. To avoid this, use nesting to work around the rendering order, or resize using the Transform filter.

# Using the Track Matte key

The Track Matte key uses a moving matte, often called a *traveling matte*. As with the Image Matte key, the matte can be a high-contrast, grayscale video clip or an image that you animate with motion settings, a filter, or a title roll. Or you can use a clip's alpha channel as the matte. But unlike a still-image matte that you specify with the Image Matte key, the clip that serves as the traveling matte must be arranged in the sequence with the foreground and background clips. This allows you to control the relative timing of all the elements.

To prevent the matte image from appearing in the program view, you must turn off the output of the track that contains the matte. For this reason, you can't place the matte in a track that contains clips that should appear in the final output. In fact, when you're creating effects like a track matte, consider arranging the elements in a separate sequence and then using the sequence as a clip in the main sequence. (To review nesting sequences, see Chapter 6, "Creating a Sequence.")

## To use the Track Matte key:

1. In the Timeline window, arrange the clips so that each is in a different track. The following is a typical configuration:

   ▲ Position the background clip in the lowest track among the three clips.

   ▲ Position the foreground clip in the track above the background clip.

   ▲ Position the moving matte in the track above the foreground clip.

   Because you can specify both the track that contains the matte and whether the key is reversed, each clip can occupy any track. However, be aware that you must turn off the output of the track that contains the matte clip.

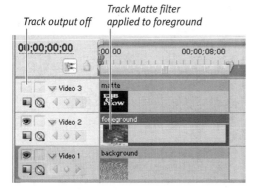

*Track output off*  *Track Matte filter applied to foreground*

**Figure 14.49** Layer the clips in separate tracks. Turn off the output of the track that contains the matte and apply the Track Matte filter to the clip that will serve as the foreground.

**Figure 14.50** Specify the track that contains the matte clip from the Matte drop-down menu.

**Figure 14.51** In the Composite Using drop-down menu, specify whether the matte's alpha channel or luminance values will define transparency.

**2.** Turn off the output of the track that contains the matte clip.

Clicking the track's Monitor button, or eye icon 👁, makes the icon disappear and excludes the contents of the track from output.

**3.** Apply the Track Matte filter to the foreground clip (**Figure 14.49**).

**4.** In the Effect Controls window, select the track that contains the matte clip from the Track Matte key's Matte drop-down menu (**Figure 14.50**).

**5.** In the Effect Controls window, choose an option in the Composite Using drop-down menu (**Figure 14.51**):

**Matte Alpha:** Uses the matte image clip's alpha channel to define opacity.

**Matte Luma:** Uses the matte image clip's luminance values to define opacity.

*continues on next page*

**USING MATTE-BASED KEYS**

The specified value of the matte (alpha or luma) corresponds to opacity in the clip to which you applied the Track Matte filter (**Figure 14.52**).

6. To invert the opaque and transparent areas, select Reverse (**Figure 14.53**).

   The matte image defines the opaque and transparent areas of the foreground clip. As the matte image moves, the foreground clip's opaque and transparent areas change accordingly.

### ✔ Tips

- If you see the matte in the output, you probably forgot to turn off the output (eye icon) for the track that contains the matte clip.

- Sometimes you can generate a useful matte by applying one or more effects to a clip. For example, you can remove color from a clip using the Black and White filter, control the range and contrast of the matte using the Levels filter, and add motion by animating the clip's motion properties.

## About the Difference Matte key

The Difference Matte key creates the transparent areas of a clip by comparing the clip with another still image and keying out the areas where the two clips match. The Difference Matte key is designed to remove a static background from behind a moving subject. By using a frame of a static background as the matte, you can key out the existing background and replace it with another. This key works only if the subject keeps moving and the camera remains static, however. This key type also provides a drop-shadow option.

**Figure 14.52** The matte defines the opaque and transparent parts of the clip that contain the Track Matte filter.

**Figure 14.53** Selecting Reverse exchanges the opaque and transparent areas.

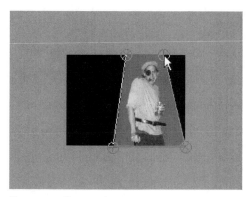

**Figure 14.54** Use a garbage matte to crop out extraneous areas of an image before you apply another key.

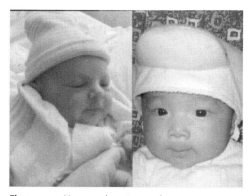

**Figure 14.55** You can also use a garbage matte to create a split-screen effect.

# Using Garbage Mattes

Garbage mattes earned their name because they're generally used to throw out extraneous areas of the frame.

You can use a garbage matte in conjunction with other keys to eliminate unnecessary elements. For example, use a garbage matte to crop out the extraneous areas of the frame before you apply a Chroma key. This way, you won't waste time adjusting the key for parts of the image you can exclude right away (**Figure 14.54**). You can also use a garbage matte to create a simple split-screen effect (**Figure 14.55**).

Beginning with Premiere Pro 1.5, the Effects palette contains 4-point, 8-point, and 16-point garbage mattes.

## To adjust the Garbage Matte filter:

1. In the Effect Controls window, select one of the Garbage Matte filters by clicking its name (**Figure 14.56**).

   A direct manipulation icon 🔲 indicates that selecting the effect activates controls in the program view. In the program view, handles appear at each corner of the selected clip.

   *continues on next page*

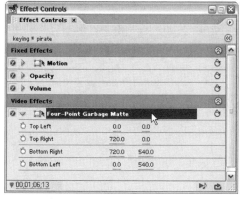

**Figure 14.56** In the Effect Controls window, select one of the garbage mattes.

**USING GARBAGE MATTES**

**487**

**2.** Drag the handles of the image to key out unwanted areas of the clip (**Figure 14.57**).

**3.** If necessary, apply other key types and adjust the clip's opacity levels.

### ✔ Tip

- You can use the new 8- and 16-point garbage mattes to create and animate sophisticated shapes, thereby eliminating some of the need for track matte animation (**Figure 14.58**).

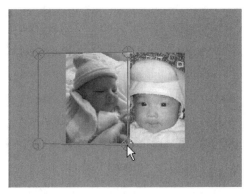

**Figure 14.57** In the program view, drag one of the garbage matte's four handles to crop out unwanted areas.

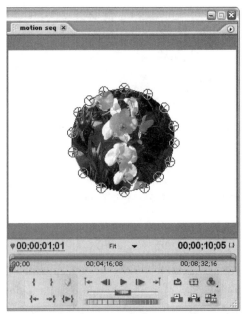

**Figure 14.58** Sixteen-point garbage mattes can be formed into many useful shapes.

# Using Adjust Filters

You may already be familiar with the Adjust category of filters from working with Adobe Photoshop or similar image-editing software. One critical difference between these programs and Premiere Pro is that Premiere Pro's Adjust filters are nondestructive. As you learned at the beginning of the book, nothing you do in Premiere Pro alters source files.

Adjust filters include the following:

◆ Auto Color

◆ Auto Contrast

◆ Auto Levels

◆ Brightness and Contrast

◆ Channel Mixer

◆ Color Balance

◆ Convolution Kernel

◆ Extract

◆ Levels

◆ Posterize

◆ ProcAmp

◆ Shadow/Highlight

## ✔ Tips

■ Adobe added the Auto Color, Auto Contrast, Auto Levels, and Shadow/ Highlight filters in Premiere Pro 1.5. These new filters are also available in After Effects 6.5 so you will not lose any effect settings if you open your Premiere Pro 1.5 project in After Effects 6.5.

■ There are usually a number of ways to adjust and correct an image. In general, filters with fewer parameters (such as Brightness and Contrast) are easiest to use but offer cruder control, whereas more complex filters (such as the Color Corrector) provide more precise control but require more knowledge to use. Naturally, learning about each filter's advantages enables you to choose the right tool for the job.

■ Editors more familiar with video gear than with Photoshop filters may find ProcAmp an attractive alternative to one of the Color Balance filters. If you're not one of these folks, ProcAmp is short for "processing amplifier," a set of controls found on decks and other video equipment used to adjust video signal levels.

## Using the Levels filter

Whether you're working in Photoshop or Premiere Pro, you'll find the Levels filter to be one of the most useful filters at your disposal. For clips that require more manual control than the Auto Levels filter provides, it's invaluable for adjusting the value range of an image.

Although it provides less control than a Curves-type filter (available in the Color Corrector filter), it's vastly superior to the crude Brightness and Contrast filter and should enable you to solve most value range problems. You may find that the Levels histogram (explained next) is as valuable as the waveform monitor and vectorscope options. Plus, you can apply what you know about the Levels filter to other programs, such as Photoshop and After Effects.

## Reading the Levels histogram

Clicking the Levels filter's Setup button in the Effect Controls window reveals a separate set of controls, including a map, or graph, of all the pixels in the image, called a *histogram*. The histogram often resembles a silhouette of distant hills, but it's actually a graph in which the darkest pixels appear on the left and the brightest appear on the right. The "mountains" represent the number of pixels at a given brightness level (**Figure 14.59**).

A high peak in the histogram indicates that a relatively large number of pixels share a brightness value. If your histogram's mountain range spans the entire horizontal scale, then your image contains a wide range of brightness values, from dark to light. A narrower range indicates that the image lacks a full range of values, which may make it a good candidate for level adjustments.

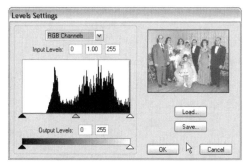

**Figure 14.59** A histogram measures all of an image's pixels and arranges them from darkest to lightest.

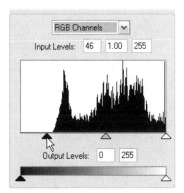

**Figure 14.60** Drag the input black triangle to the right to map more pixels to the output black value (set to 0).

# Redistributing values

The histogram represents the image, or input levels. Below the histogram, a bar with a gradient from black to white represents the output levels. The final levels of the image will depend on how you redistribute, or map, the input levels to the output levels.

Three triangles specify how the input levels are mapped. The left triangle controls input black, the right triangle controls input white, and the center triangle represents gamma. The output levels are controlled by the lower-left triangle (output black) and the lower-right triangle (output white).

As you move the input black triangle to the right, more pixels are mapped to the output black value. As you move the input white triangle to the left, more pixels are mapped to the output white value. The midtones, as indicated by the gamma triangle, move in relation to the other controls. To adjust midtones manually, drag the gamma triangle.

By default, the output black value is 0, or completely black; the output white value is 255, or completely white. Moving these controls changes the minimum and maximum brightness levels.

You can see and adjust the numeric values for all the histogram controls in the Effect Controls window.

## To increase contrast using the Levels filter:

1. Adjust the black levels by *doing one of the following:*
   - ▲ In the histogram, drag the input black triangle to the right (**Figure 14.60**).
   - ▲ In the Effect Controls window, change the input black value.

*continues on next page*

The range of input values, including the gamma point, is redistributed to the output range. In particular, all values below the input black value are mapped to the output black value.

2. Adjust the white levels by *doing one of the following:*

   ▲ In the histogram, drag the input white triangle to the left (**Figure 14.61**).

   ▲ In the Effect Controls window, change the input white value.

   The range of input values, including the gamma point, is redistributed to the output range. In particular, all values above the input white value are mapped to the output white value.

3. To adjust the midtones manually, drag the gamma triangle (**Figure 14.62**).

   Dragging left maps more pixels toward the input white value, brightening the midtones; dragging right darkens the midtones.

4. Evaluate the results subjectively by examining the output in the program view or television monitor (**Figures 14.63** and **14.64**); or make objective judgments by using the waveform monitor (see Chapter 5, "Viewing Clips in the Monitor Window").

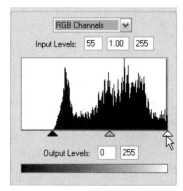

**Figure 14.61** Drag the input white triangle to the left to map more pixels to the output white value (set to 255).

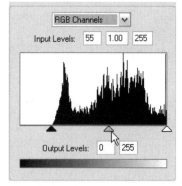

**Figure 14.62** To adjust the midtones manually, drag the gamma slider (the center triangle).

**Figure 14.63** Compare the contrast of the original image...

**Figure 14.64** ...to the image you get with the new Levels settings.

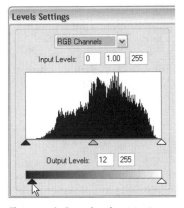

**Figure 14.65** Dragging the output black triangle to the right raises the black point.

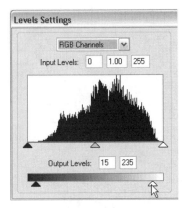

**Figure 14.66** Dragging the output white triangle to the left lowers the white point.

## To decrease the luminance range using the Levels filter:

1. To adjust the output black level, *do one of the following:*

   ▲ In the histogram, drag the output black triangle to the right (**Figure 14.65**).

   ▲ In the Effect Controls window, increase the output black value.

2. To adjust the output white level, *do one of the following:*

   ▲ In the histogram, drag the output white triangle to the left (**Figure 14.66**).

   ▲ In the Effect Controls window, reduce the output white value.

## ✔ Tip

■ You can toggle the Levels filter between enabled and disabled to compare the image before and after your adjustment. (See Chapter 13 for more about disabling effects.)

**USING ADJUST FILTERS**

## Blur and Sharpen filters

Even if you don't have any experience with image-editing software, it should be obvious that Blur filters cause an image to appear softer and out of focus, whereas Sharpen filters make an image appear crisper, with more defined edges.

Blur and Sharpen filters include the following:

◆ Antialias

◆ Camera Blur

◆ Channel Blur

◆ Compound Blur

◆ Directional Blur

◆ Fast Blur

◆ Gaussian Blur

◆ Gaussian Sharpen

◆ Ghosting

◆ Radial Blur

◆ Sharpen

◆ Sharpen Edges

◆ Unsharp Mask

### ✔ Tip

■ Compared to the resolution of printed images, video resolutions are low. To make matters worse, compression schemes add edge blockiness and other visual artifacts—features that sharpening can bring out, doing more harm than good. Thus, the message is clear: when you use a Sharpen filter, do so with care.

## Channel filters

Channel filters manipulate the individual channels of an image (R, G, B, and alpha) or their resulting color values (hue, saturation, and luminance).

Channel effects include the following:

◆ Blend

◆ Invert

### ✔ Tips

■ The Channel Blur filter is grouped with the Blur and Sharpen filters, not the Channel filters.

■ As with many of the filter categories, if you have After Effects 6.5 installed on your system, additional filters will appear on the list. The Channel category includes seven additional filters from After Effects 6.5.

■ You can use the Blend filter to achieve an effect similar to a Cross Dissolve transition but with a slightly different look. You can also use the Blend filter to simulate several blending modes: color only, tint only, darken only, and lighten only. With the exception of the Multiply and Screen keys, blending modes are unavailable in Premiere Pro.

## Distort filters

Filters in the Distort category are designed to shift pixels to deform images. But as usual, don't let the category's name limit the way you use these filters; often, a distortion may appear quite natural. For the most part, these filters are relatively straightforward and won't be discussed in detail here. Premiere Pro's effects gallery illustrates these effects nicely. Better yet, try them for yourself.

Note that the Transform effect resides in this folder—not the Transform folder. As you may recall from Chapter 13, the Transform filter allows you to apply fixed effects (position, rotation, and so on) to a clip at the effect stage of rendering. See "Subverting the Render Order" in Chapter 13 for details.

Distort effects include the following:

◆ Bend

◆ Corner Pin

◆ Lens Distortion

◆ Mirror

◆ Pinch

◆ Polar Coordinates

◆ Ripple

◆ Shear

◆ Spherize

◆ Transform

◆ Twirl

◆ Wave

◆ Zig Zag

### ✔ Tip

■ Unlike After Effects, Premiere Pro doesn't include a switch for motion blur, which blurs a moving layer (the equivalent of a clip in After Effects), simulating the effects of a camera's shutter. However, the Transform filter does have a Shutter Angle property. Animate a clip using the Transform filter; then deselect Use Composition's Shutter Angle and specify a shutter angle manually. Increasing the shutter angle increases the amount of blur. The effect can be subtle, but it still adds a touch of realism to the movement.

## Image control filters

Image control filters change the color values in a clip's image. Most of them will be familiar to you from other programs, and their controls are fairly straightforward.

Don't let this fact cause you to overlook two powerful filters innocuously tucked away here: Color Corrector and Color Match. Regrettably, the scope of this book permits only a concise review of the Color Corrector filter, but it should get you started.

Image control filters include the following:

◆ Black and White

◆ Color Balance (HLS)

◆ Color Balance (RGB)

◆ Color Corrector

◆ Color Match

◆ Color Offset

◆ Color Pass

◆ Color Replace

◆ Gamma Correction

◆ Tint

**USING ADJUST FILTERS**

# Using the Color Corrector Filter

Color-correcting a clip can involve several steps.

First, calibrate your monitor. If you're going to use the program view or the video output to a television to make subjective judgments about your color corrections, ensure that the monitor is properly calibrated so that it faithfully reproduces color and brightness.

Next, set up your video measurement tools. Customize the Premiere Pro interface for color correction by viewing the sequence both as a composite signal and through a measurement tool. You can do this by opening a reference monitor and setting it to display one of the waveform monitor and vectorscope options, whichever is most appropriate for the task at hand. See Chapter 5 for more about the waveform monitor, vectorscope, and reference monitor.

Here is an overview of the tools at your disposal:

**Black/White Balance:** These controls allow you to specify the image's black point and white point, and thereby its tonal range. You can also specify the gray point, which defines the image's midtones. In this sense, the Black/White Balance controls can achieve results similar to those from the Levels filter (see "Using the Levels Filter" earlier in this chapter).

The White Point option is analogous to the white balance on a video camcorder. Just as your camera's white balance specifies the light temperature that should be recorded as white, the white point defines which pixels should be output as white. Therefore, setting the white point is also the first step in correcting an image with an improper white balance. For example, if your camera's white balance was set for indoor (tungsten) light, sunlight gives the image a blue cast, so that white objects appear blue. Resetting the Color Corrector's white point tells Premiere Pro how to restore the whites.

**Tonal Range Definition:** This set of controls can help you select the black point and white point by identifying the darkest and lightest areas in the image. Selecting Preview makes the image appear grayscale with a limited tonal range; adjusting the Shadow and Highlight values helps bring out the image's tonal extremes. (Photoshop users might compare these controls to those in the Threshold dialog box.)

**Color and Brightness controls:** Four sets of controls—HSL Offset, HSL, RGB, and Curves—provide various methods for adjusting color and brightness. The toolset you use depends largely on your preferred color model as well as the color-correction problem at hand.

**HSL Offset:** These graphical controls are presented in the form of four color wheels: one for the master levels and one each for the shadows, midtones, and highlights of the image. Each wheel depicts hue and saturation on a circular chart. Drag the dot at the center of each wheel to make adjustments: the angle of the dot on the wheel determines hue, and the distance from the center of the wheel corresponds to saturation (**Figure 14.67**).

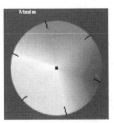

**Figure 14.67** HSL Offset controls include a color wheel for the clip's master levels and each color component. Changing the control's angle shifts hue, and adjusting its distance from the center of the wheel affects saturation.

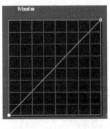

**Figure 14.68** A Curves control graphs input levels along the horizontal axis and output levels along the vertical axis.

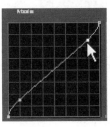

**Figure 14.69** Click the graph to add control points, and drag to alter the curve. Here, an s-curve brings up shadows and eases the highlights.

**HSL:** These numerical controls manage the image in terms of hue, saturation, and lightness (or brightness). A drop-down menu lets you specify the tonal range affected by your adjustments: master levels, highlights, midtones, and shadows. The names of some controls are more commonly used with video than with computers: for all intents and purposes, Gain controls white levels, and Pedestal controls black levels.

**RGB:** These numerical controls manage the image in terms of its red, green, and blue components. A drop-down menu lets you specify the tonal range affected by your adjustments: master levels, highlights, midtones, and shadows. The names of some controls are more commonly used with video than with computers: for all intents and purposes, Gain controls white levels, and Pedestal controls black levels.

**Curves:** There are four Curves controls (similar to those found in Photoshop and other image-editing programs): one for the master levels and one each for the red, green, and blue color components of the image. Each Curves control graphs the image's input levels along the horizontal axis and its output levels along the vertical axis. Initially, the line of the curves graph shows a slope of 1, or a 45-degree angle, indicating no adjustment (**Figure 14.68**). Clicking the line adds control points you can use to change the curve of the line, and thereby the way the input levels are output. A Curves control works much like a Levels control, but instead of controlling three parameters (white, black, and midtones), you specify points along the graph (**Figure 14.69**).

**Video Limiter:** This set of options reins in video levels to comply with the limitations of the video standard you're using. It's similar to applying a Broadcast Colors filter.

## To set up for color correction:

1. Choose Window > Workspace > Color Correction (**Figure 14.70**).

   The arrangement of windows is optimized for color correction. As usual, feel free to modify the windows to suit your preferences or system setup. You'll frequently need to use the program monitor, a reference monitor, the Effects palette, and the Effect Controls window (**Figure 14.71**).

2. In the reference monitor, click the Gang button 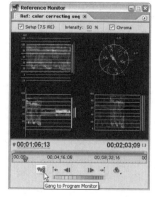 to select it (**Figure 14.72**).

   Now the reference monitor always shows the same frame as the program view, and vice versa.

3. In the Effect Controls window, select Split Screen Preview to display the selected clip's unprocessed image on the left and the color-corrected version on the right (**Figure 14.73**).

   Make sure you deselect this option when you don't need it, particularly after you're finished making adjustments to the Color Corrector filter.

**Figure 14.70** Choose Window > Workspace > Color Correction.

**Figure 14.71** For color correction, you'll need to see the program monitor and reference monitor. You'll also need the Effects palette and the Effect Controls window on hand.

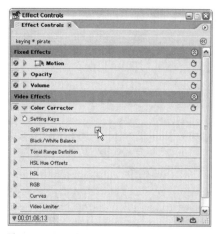

**Figure 14.73** In the Color Corrector's controls in the Effect Controls window, select Split Screen Preview to compare the unprocessed and corrected image in the program view.

**Figure 14.72** In the reference monitor, select the Gang button.

**Figure 14.74** Set the program view to show the composite image.

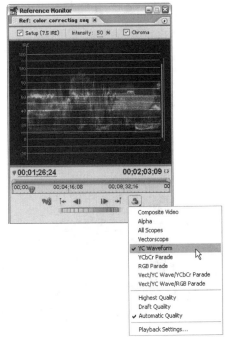

**Figure 14.75** Set the reference monitor to the appropriate measurement tool. When you're adjusting brightness, an iteration of the waveform monitor is most useful.

## To set the initial tonal range:

1. Set the program view to show the composite image (**Figure 14.74**), and set the reference monitor to Waveform to measure and evaluate master luminance levels; set it to RGB Parade or YCbCr Parade to view levels for separate components of the video signal (**Figure 14.75**).

   However, feel free to switch to another viewing mode, as appropriate. See Chapter 5 for details.

*continues on next page*

**2.** In the Effect Controls window, expand the Tonal Range Definition category and then select Preview (**Figure 14.76**).

The image becomes grayscale with a limited tonal range (**Figure 14.77**).

**3.** Adjust the Shadows and Highlights values to reveal the tonal extremes of the image.

Adjusting the Shadows value so that the image shows the least amount of black identifies the darkest areas (**Figure 14.78**); adjusting the Highlights value so that the image shows the least amount of white identifies the brightest areas (**Figure 14.79**).

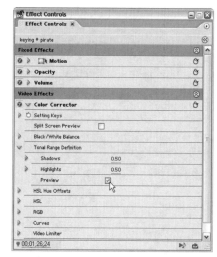

**Figure 14.76** In the Tonal Range Definition category, select Preview...

**Figure 14.77** ...to temporarily display the image as grayscale and expose its tonal extremes.

**Figure 14.79** Here, the Highlights value is set to show the minimal amount of white, thereby identifying the brightest areas.

**Figure 14.78** Here, the Shadows value is set to show the minimal amount of black, thereby identifying the darkest areas.

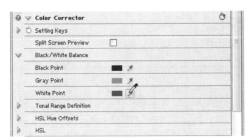

**Figure 14.80** For the black point and white point, click and drag the Eyedropper tool...

**Figure 14.81** ...and sample the appropriate point in the image. Here, the White Point eyedropper samples the bright spot identified in Figure 14.79.

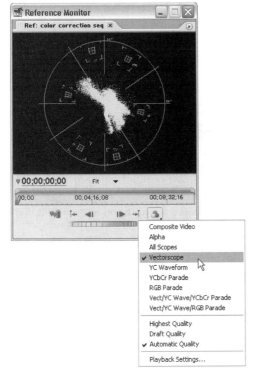

**Figure 14.82** Set the reference monitor to the appropriate measurement tool. When you're adjusting color, the vectorscope is usually most useful.

**4.** Once you've noted the darkest and brightest areas, deselect Preview.

The image appears normally.

**5.** In the Effect Controls window, expand the Color Corrector's Black/White Balance category and use the Eyedropper tool to specify the following levels (**Figure 14.80**):

**Black Point:** Samples the darkest point in the video image.

**White Point:** Samples the whitest point in the video image (**Figure 14.81**).

Generally, sampling the gray point is less critical, and you may be able to leave it at its default setting. You can also specify the colors using a color picker, but using the eyedropper is a better approach.

## To adjust color and brightness:

**1.** Set the reference monitor to Vectorscope to measure and evaluate the video's chrominance components: hue and saturation (**Figure 14.82**).

However, feel free to switch to another viewing mode, as appropriate.

**2.** In the Effect Controls window, expand the set of controls best suited to your preferences and the task at hand:

▲ HSL Offset

▲ HSL

▲ RGB

▲ Curves

Generally speaking, you should make adjustments in a systematic fashion, and you should avoid making conflicting or redundant modifications.

*continues on next page*

**Using the Color Corrector Filter**

3. For HSL and RGB controls, begin by specifying a tonal range and then make adjustments for each range (**Figure 14.83**).

   In most cases, you can proceed down the list of properties; adjust a property only if you need to.

4. For the HSL Offset controls or Curves controls, it's generally best to make adjustments to individual components first and then to the master levels, if necessary (**Figures 14.84** and **14.85**).

   For more about these toolsets, see the description at the beginning of this section.

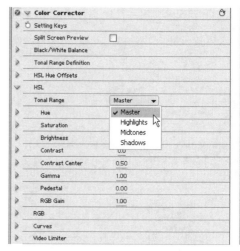

**Figure 14.83** Before you make adjustments using the HSL or RGB controls, be sure you specify the tonal range you want to affect.

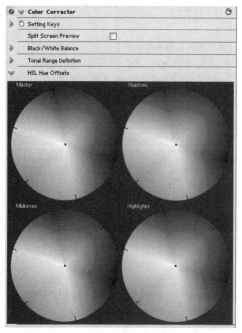

**Figure 14.84** If you opt to use the HSL Offset controls, concentrate on individual channels first and then adjust the master levels (the first color wheel).

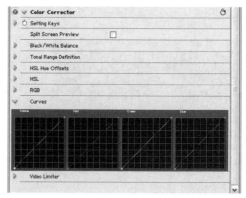

**Figure 14.85** If you opt to use the Curves controls, try to adjust color components first and then the master controls (the first curves graph).

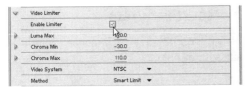

**Figure 14.86** Expand the Video Limiter category and click Enable Limiter to have Premiere Pro restrain video levels automatically.

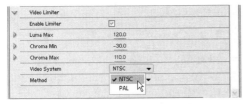

**Figure 14.87** In the Video System drop-down menu, choose the video standard you're using.

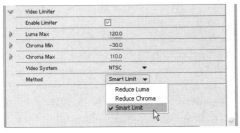

**Figure 14.88** In the Method drop-down menu, specify how you want Premiere Pro to make the levels comply to the limits of the video standard you specified.

## To limit output levels:

1. In the Effect Controls window, expand the Video Limiter category and click Enable Limiter (**Figure 14.86**).

   This option automatically restrains the image's luminance and chrominance levels according to the process you specify in the Method drop-down menu (see step 3). In most cases, you can select this option instead of entering values manually for Luma Max, Chroma Max, and Chroma Min.

2. Choose the appropriate option in the Video System drop-down menu (**Figure 14.87**):

   **NTSC:** The video standard in North America and Japan

   **PAL:** The video standard in most of Europe

3. If you selected Enable Limiter in step 1, choose an option in the Method drop-down menu (**Figure 14.88**):

   **Reduce Luma:** Corrects unsafe levels by reducing luminance.

   **Reduce Chroma:** Corrects unsafe levels by reducing saturation.

   **Smart Limit:** Allows Premiere Pro to calculate how to prevent unsafe video levels.

## ✔ Tips

- When you've finished color correcting, be sure you deselect Split Screen Preview. Otherwise, the split screen of the unadjusted and adjusted images will appear in the program view and in the exported video.

- You can save and load Color Corrector settings by expanding the Setting Keys category at the top of the effect's properties list and selecting the appropriate option.

USING THE COLOR CORRECTOR FILTER

# Other Filters

The remaining filters (presented in alphabetical order) include these categories: Noise, Perspective, Pixelate, Render, Stylize, Time, Transform, and Video.

## Noise filters

Usually, noise filters are used to add static or grain to an image. Oddly enough, the Noise filter is listed in the Stylize category. The one effect listed in the Noise category, Median, reduces detail in an image, averaging the value of adjacent pixels according to a radius you specify. It's listed here (as it is in Photoshop) because it can be used to reduce noise.

The Noise filter category includes one effect:

◆ Median

### ✔ Tip

■ Boosting saturation (or any intense image processing) can also bring out unsightly color artifacts, so image editors employ a combination of techniques to increase the color content without ruining detail. The process is too lengthy to describe here fully, but it involves two layers: an unprocessed clip and a clip with increased saturation (with Color Balance, for example) and the Median filter. Combine the clips using the color blending mode. This uses the enhanced color of one clip while retaining the detail of the other. Here's the trick: Premiere Pro doesn't support blending modes per se, but its Blend filter includes a Color Only mode. Use the filter's Blend with Original value to tweak the mix.

## Perspective filters

Perspective filters imply dimensionality in clips (or elements within a clip).

The Perspective category includes:

◆ Basic 3D

◆ Bevel Alpha

◆ Bevel Edges

◆ Drop Shadow

### ✔ Tip

■ Although the Perspective filters give the impression of three dimensions, they aren't true 3D effects (which are processed according to a 3D spatial model). For example, using Basic 3D to rotate a clip implies perspective, but the clip remains a flat plane that can't be extruded to gain thickness. Similarly, the Drop Shadow filter's parameters are convincing to an extent, but they can't cast a realistic shadow on anything but a background plane parallel to the screen. You'll have to turn to third-party software plug-ins or dedicated 3D programs to create true 3D elements.

## Pixelate filters

Videographers and editors often seek to conceal or diminish the blocky, pixilated nature of the video image. Pixelate filters, on the other hand, emphasize pixels and reduce detail in order to create a stylized effect.

The Pixelate filters include:

◆ Crystallize

◆ Facet

◆ Pointillize

## Render filters

Unlike filters that modify existing pixels, effects in this category generate their own elements.

Render filters include:

◆ Lens Flare

◆ Lightning

◆ Ramp

## Stylize filters

The Stylize category encompasses a range of filters used to make images abstract or to impart a distinctive visual character.

Stylize filters include:

◆ Alpha Glow

◆ Color Emboss

◆ Emboss

◆ Find Edges

◆ Mosaic

◆ Noise

◆ Replicate

◆ Solarize

◆ Strobe Light

◆ Texturize

◆ Tiles

◆ Wind

### ✔ Tip

■ As you discovered in Chapter 12, the Title Designer includes many options for stylizing text and objects—but adding a Photoshop-style outer glow isn't one of them. However, you can apply the Alpha Glow filter to any clip with an alpha channel to impart a glowing edge.

## Time filters

The Time category contains two effects that manipulate the playback timing of a clip's frames.

Time effects include the following:

◆ Echo

◆ Posterize Time

### ✔ Tips

■ The Echo filter isn't an audio effect, but it's the video equivalent. Instead of repeating audio, it retains video frames, causing moving objects in a clip—or a moving clip itself—to leave a trail of images.

■ The name Posterize Time may not evoke what the filter really does, which is to reduce a clip's frame rate, making motion look choppier (as in an old movie or time-lapse footage). You may know the effect as *strobe*, as it's sometimes called on camcorders and other video equipment with built-in effects. Premiere Pro's Strobe Light effect leaves the clip's frame rate intact but fills the screen with light at the frequency you specify (it's in the Stylize folder).

## Transform filters

The inherent properties of a clip—such as its opacity and spatial properties—are often referred to as *transform properties*. In the case of Premiere Pro filters, however, *transform* is used more loosely and includes filters such as Camera View, which simulates the viewfinder data in a camcorder; and Vertical Hold, which resembles a badly adjusted television set.

But if you're looking for the Transform filter, you'll find it in the Distort folder.

Transform filters include:

◆ Camera View

◆ Clip

◆ Crop

◆ Edge Feather

◆ Horizontal Flip

◆ Horizontal Hold

◆ Roll

◆ Vertical Flip

◆ Vertical Hold

### ✔ Tip

■ It's sometimes possible to use the Horizontal Flip filter to change an actor's eye line—that is, to change a person's gaze from screen right to screen left, or vice versa. Doing so can help restore a sense of continuity when, during shooting, you allowed the camera's position to jump the line established by the relative position between the characters and camera during the scene. However, flipping the image works only if elements in the shot won't give you away (as will be the case, for instance, if the logo on the character's baseball cap suddenly appears backward).

## Video filters

Filters in the Video category are designed to handle issues involving video output.

Video filters include:

◆ Broadcast Colors

◆ Field Interpolate

### ✔ Tip

■ Broadcast Colors works much like the Color Corrector filter's Video Limiter (see "Using the Color Corrector Filter" earlier in this chapter). Use Broadcast Colors when you want to ensure that luminance and saturation levels comply with video standards but you don't need all the bells and whistles of the Color Corrector. By nesting your final sequence, you can easily apply the Broadcast Colors filter to the entire sequence with a single drag and drop of the mouse.

OTHER FILTERS

# 15

# CREATING OUTPUT

At the beginning of the editing process, you asked yourself, "What is my final output goal?" Now it's time to deliver.

If your computer has an IEEE 1394 connection or analog video capture card, you can output the program directly from the timeline to a video camera or videotape recorder. Alternatively, you may want to create a stand-alone movie file to present over the Web or burn to a CD-ROM or DVD.

An exported movie may also serve as source material for a PowerPoint presentation, After Effects composition, or even another Premiere Pro project. If you're using Premiere Pro as an offline editing tool, you can export an Advanced Authoring Format (AAF) file or edit-decision list (EDL) to transfer your work to another system.

The number of export options can be daunting, and the minutiae of issues such as compression and video standards can be difficult to grasp—and boring. Luckily, recent developments have made exporting relatively simple. Exporting a DV project uses built-in settings and, in many cases, built-in hardware. To export other formats, the Adobe Media Encoder provides simple presets for MPEG1, MPEG2 (used for DVDs), QuickTime, RealMedia, and Windows Media. And, using the Export to DVD option, you can even export a sequence directly to a connected DVD burner. What's more, Premiere Pro 1.5 introduces pre-encoding and post-encoding tasks. These enable you to pre-treat clips and sequences, performing important processing tasks before encoding. Afterward, Premiere Pro can generate a log file or even upload the encoded clip using FTP.

# Choosing Export Options and Settings

You can export footage from a sequence or from an individual clip. When you export from a sequence, you can export the entire sequence or just the area below the work area bar. Similarly, you can export an entire clip or just the area between its In and Out points. Because the two procedures are essentially the same, the following sections focus on exporting a sequence.

Whatever export option you choose, the video is first processed according to the project settings. From there, the exported clip or sequence is processed according to settings you specify for the particular option. Exporting to tape is the most straightforward; the project settings were already tailored to your output goal. When you export directly to a DVD, your choices are limited by the narrow confines of the DVD specifications and simplified by a handful of helpful presets. When you export a movie file, on the other hand, your choices become more numerous, reflecting the variety of available formats. The number of options is even more expansive when you export with the Adobe Media Encoder. The Adobe Media Encoder can output a number of formats, each with its own set of extensive and complex settings.

Rather than cover export options in the order they appear on the Export submenu, this chapter covers them from the simplest (and most commonly used) to the more complex.

# Considering Output Goals

Your output goal helps determine the settings you choose. Although you've thought about it from the beginning of your project (right?), the considerations are worth reviewing.

## Videotape

Exporting to tape can be straightforward: your capture, project, and export settings all match. Video formats demand a lot from your system, however. For DV, your system must meet minimum requirements—but exceeding the minimum is recommended. For an analog-to-digital capture card, you need to familiarize yourself with the requirements of your hardware. If you're preparing your videotape for television broadcast, be sure to check with the presenter or a post-production facility to learn the requirements.

## CD-ROM

When you optimize a movie to play from a CD-ROM, your primary goal is compatibility. You also should answer the following questions:

◆ Does the movie need to be cross-platform compatible?

◆ What movie-player software will be used?

◆ What is the slowest possible CD drive that will be playing the movie?

◆ Will the movie be copied from CD to play back from a hard drive? If so, what is the slowest hard drive that will be playing back the movie?

◆ What image quality do you require?

◆ What is the total running time of the movie and will you be able to reduce the file size to fit onto a typical CD-ROM?

## DVD

Whereas a CD-ROM can contain various formats, DVDs require some implementation of MPEG2. However, MPEG2 itself contains numerous variables, many of which require advanced technical knowledge to adjust intelligently. Luckily, Premiere Pro's Export to DVD and Adobe Media Encoder each include a number of presets to help simplify the process.

The Export to DVD option outputs a sequence directly to a connected DVD burner, much as you'd export it to tape. The Adobe Media Encoder, on the other hand, can produce a DVD-compliant MPEG2 file for use with a DVD authoring program, such as the Adobe Encore DVD.

However, DVD producers face hurdles beyond exporting a DVD-compatible file. Despite the standards, it can be difficult to make a DVD that works on a wide range of players. Features like interactivity, custom menus, surround sound, and alternate audio tracks pose other challenges. A personal DVD isn't difficult to produce with Premiere Pro, an authoring program, and a DVD burner. But a complex, mass-produced DVD requires special equipment and expertise. As always, do your homework before launching a large-scale DVD project.

# Web

When you optimize movies for Web delivery, file size (and its conjoined twin, data rate) is the primary concern. To stream a movie, you need to limit the movie's data rate to the slowest anticipated connection speed. Even for fast Internet connections, that's a big limitation. You'll have to decide whether the loss in quality is worth the immediate play-back capability.

The limitations are more forgiving for movies that can be downloaded. In this case, file size influences how long the viewer will have to wait before watching your movie. Although a *progressive download* format begins playing before the movie is fully downloaded to the viewer's hard drive, file size remains an impediment—especially if the movie is more than, say, one minute in duration.

# Other programs

If you're exporting footage from Premiere Pro to use in another program, the factors you should consider depend on the format and the program. Nevertheless, you should bear in mind several common issues.

Make sure you know the file formats and compression types the program accepts. If you want to retain transparency, choose a codec that supports an alpha channel (such as Uncompressed in Windows Media, or None or Animation when exporting QuickTime). When you're exporting still frames acquired on video, be aware that video resolution translates into a mere 72 dpi, which is appropriate only for relatively small, low-quality printouts. You should also know how to deal with other aspects of translating video to other formats: color, interlacing, and image and pixel aspect ratios (see Chapter 16, "Video and Audio Settings").

# Exporting File Types

Premiere Pro exports various file formats for video, audio, or image sequences. The formats you can open and play, however, depend on your system. You can also add formats through plug-in software extensions.

## ✔ Tip

- Formats such as Windows Media and QuickTime are known as media *architectures*, which include a growing number of individual compression schemes, or *codecs*. Cinepak, for example, is a codec supported by both QuickTime and Windows Media. For more information about compression and codecs, see Chapter 16.

### Formats for Export

Video/audio formats:

- Animated GIF
- Microsoft AVI
- Microsoft DV
- MPEG1
- MPEG2
- RealMedia
- QuickTime
- Windows Media

Audio-only formats:

- QuickTime
- Microsoft AVI
- Microsoft DV AVI
- Windows Waveform

Still-image formats:

- Filmstrip
- Targa
- TIFF
- Windows Bitmap

Still-image sequence formats:

- GIF sequence
- Targa sequence
- TIFF sequence
- Windows Bitmap sequence

# Exporting to Tape

Using the Export to Tape command, you can output video to a connected camera or deck through your IEEE 1394 or other capture device. You can export any clip you open in the source view or, more likely, the selected sequence in the program view and Timeline window. Using IEEE 1394 or add-on device control, Premiere Pro can activate your deck automatically (see "Using Device Control" in Chapter 3). You can even choose where on the tape to start recording, if you can provide a timecode number at the start time. Typically, you use a *black and coded* tape—a tape with a black video signal and timecode. (For more about timecode, see "Understanding Capture Options" in Chapter 3 or "Timecode" in Chapter 16.)

The following task uses a DV camera as the recording device. Options may vary according to your hardware.

## To export to tape:

1. *Do one of the following:*
   - ▲ To export a sequence, select the sequence's tab in the Timeline window or program view of the Monitor window.
   - ▲ To export a clip, open a clip in the source view.

2. Choose File > Export > Export to Tape (**Figure 15.1**).

   The Export to Tape dialog box appears (**Figure 15.2**).

3. To have Premiere Pro automatically trigger recording using device control, select Activate Recording Device and then specify the options you want (**Figure 15.3**):

   **Assemble at Timecode:** The timecode number on the tape where you want recording to start. For you to use Assemble at Timecode, the tape must already have a timecode signal. Therefore, you can't use a blank tape.

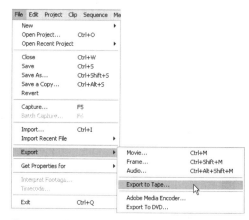

**Figure 15.1** Choose File > Export > Export to Tape.

**Figure 15.2** The Export to Tape dialog box appears.

**Figure 15.3** Select Activate Recording Device to have Premiere Pro trigger recording automatically; then specify related options.

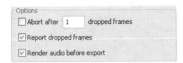

**Figure 15.4** In the Options area, specify how Premiere Pro deals with dropped frames during export and whether you want the program to render audio before exporting to tape.

| Export Status | |
|---|---|
| Dropped frames: | 0 |
| Status: | Recording... |
| Start Timecode: | 00;00;00 |
| End Timecode: | 20;12;00 |
| Current Timecode: | 00;04;15 |

**Figure 15.5** Click Record to start the export to tape and monitor the export progress in the Export Status area.

## ✔ Tips

- Your options may vary according to the device-control plug-in you're using.

- You don't need to adjust the Delay Movie Start by *x* Quarter Frames setting with most device controllers and decks. If you do need to adjust these settings, follow the recommendations that came with your device and device-control plug-in. Otherwise, you may need to experiment to find the optimal settings.

- Even though you can leave the export process unattended, it's wise to keep an eye on it. This way, you can spot problems as they occur and export again if necessary. In addition to problems with the export, you may notice problems in the sequence itself. For example, you may have inadvertently left a clip or track disabled, excluding it from the exported video. (Yes, it can happen to you.) In any case, always double-check the tape after export, especially if you're going to hand it off to a client or duplication facility.

**Delay Movie Start by *x* Quarter Frames:** The number of quarter frames by which to delay playback after you click the OK button. Some recording devices require time between receiving the record command and the video playback from the computer.

**Preroll *x* Frames:** The number of frames the camera or deck will rewind before the start time (the timecode you specified for the Assemble at Timecode setting, or the tape's current position), to ensure that the tape is up to speed when recording begins.

4. In the Options area of the Export to Tape dialog box, specify the options you want (**Figure 15.4**):

   **Abort after *x* Dropped Frames:** Allows you to set the minimum number of frames that must fail to record before Premiere Pro halts recording. For most users, even one dropped frame is unacceptable.

   **Report Dropped Frames:** Generates a report if frames are dropped during export.

   **Render Audio before Export:** Renders audio prior to exporting the clip or sequence. This can ease the on-the-fly processing demands on Premiere Pro and help prevent dropped frames; however, you must wait for audio to render before export begins.

5. Click Record.

   If you're controlling the recording device manually, make sure you trigger record mode. If you clicked Activate Recording Device, Premiere Pro triggers the recording device automatically. You can monitor the progress of the export in the Export Status area of the Export to Tape dialog box (**Figure 15.5**).

**EXPORTING TO TAPE**

# Exporting Directly to DVD

If your system is equipped with a DVD burner, you can export your sequence to DVD much as you'd export to tape. Even though you're required to process your sequence to meet the requirements of the DVD format, ready-made presets make the process relatively simple. The task in this section explains how to export to DVD using one of the built-in presets. For more guidance on selecting a preset, see the sidebar "Selecting a DVD Preset."

Note that Export to DVD is designed to produce a no-frills DVD. Although you can make chapter points at sequence markers, there are no options for other advanced DVD features, such as menus, alternate audio tracks, and the like. To create a full-featured DVD, export the sequence as a DVD-compliant file using Adobe Media Encoder (discussed later in this chapter) and then import the file into a DVD authoring program, such as Adobe Encore DVD.

### To export to DVD:

1. Select the sequence you want to export by clicking its tab in the program view or the Timeline window.

2. Choose File > Export > Export to DVD (**Figure 15.6**).

   The Export to DVD dialog box appears. Settings categories are listed on the left, and the selected category's parameters appear on the right (**Figure 15.7**).

3. In the Export to DVD dialog box, select General and specify the settings you want:

   **Disc Name:** To enter a name for the disc, choose Custom and enter a name in the dialog box (**Figure 15.8**).

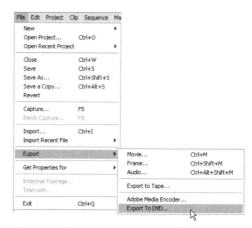

**Figure 15.6** Choose File > Export > Export to DVD.

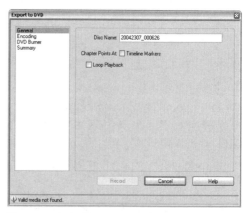

**Figure 15.7** In the Export to DVD dialog box, settings categories are listed on the left, and the selected category's settings appear on the right.

**Figure 15.8** In the General panel, choose Custom from the Disc Name drop-down menu to enter a name for the disc.

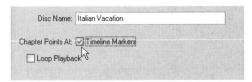

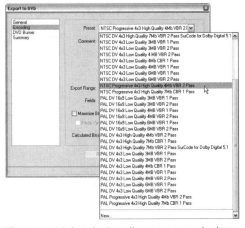

**Figure 15.9** In the General panel, specify whether to include chapter points at markers and whether you want to loop playback.

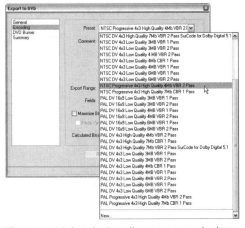

**Figure 15.10** Select the Encoding category and select an appropriate preset.

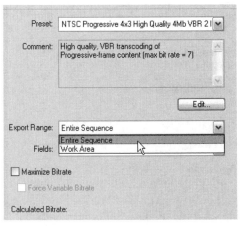

**Figure 15.11** Choose the range of the sequence you want to export from the Export Range drop-down menu.

**Chapter Points at Timeline Markers:** Select this option to translate sequence markers into chapter points (which DVD players can use to cue the video program) (**Figure 15.9**).

**Loop Playback:** Select this option to make the sequence repeat automatically when you play the DVD.

4. Select Encoding and specify the options you want:

**Preset:** Select an appropriate preset from the drop-down menu (**Figure 15.10**).

**Export Range:** Specify whether to export the entire selected sequence or just the area under the work area bar (**Figure 15.11**).

*continues on next page*

**EXPORTING DIRECTLY TO DVD**

**Fields:** Specify the dominant field, or None if you're exporting a progressive scan format (**Figure 15.12**).

**Maximize Bitrate:** Select this option to encode the specified range of the sequence at the highest bit rate that will still allow the encoded file to fit on the DVD. This setting overrides the bit rate specified by the selected preset.

**Force Variable Bitrate:** Select this option to force Premiere Pro to vary the bit rate according to the characteristics of each frame's image content. This option is available only when Maximize Bitrate is selected (**Figure 15.13**).

The dialog box displays the Calculated Bitrate value, an estimate of the resulting file's maximum bit rate.

5. Select DVD Burner and specify the options you want:

   **DVD Burner:** Select the DVD recording device you want to use from the drop-down menu (**Figure 15.14**).

   **Rescan:** Click Rescan to have Premiere Pro scan your system's DVD recorders for media.

   **Number of Copies:** Specify the number of DVDs you want to record during this export session. Premiere Pro will prompt you to insert a new, blank DVD when necessary.

   **Record Options:** Select Record to begin burning immediately after you click the Record button. Select Test Only to check the DVD media for errors without recording. Select Test and Record to burn the DVD after a successful test is performed.

6. Select Summary to review your settings.

7. When you're satisfied with your choices, make sure a blank DVD is inserted in your burner and click Record.

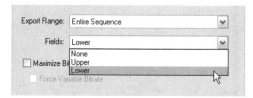

**Figure 15.12** Choose the appropriate field dominance in the Fields drop-down menu.

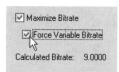

**Figure 15.13** Specify whether you want Premiere Pro to calculate a maximum bit rate or apply variable bit rate compression.

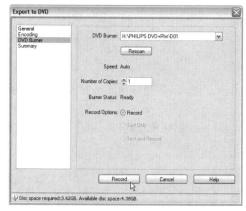

**Figure 15.14** In the DVD Burner panel, select your recording device from the DVD Burner drop-down menu. Then specify the number of copies you want and select a recording option.

## ✔ Tip

■ You can edit a preset setting by clicking the Edit button in the Encoding panel of the Export to DVD dialog box. Doing so opens the Transcode Settings dialog box, the same dialog box you use to specify settings when exporting with the Adobe Media Encoder (covered later in this chapter).

**EXPORTING DIRECTLY TO DVD**

## Selecting a DVD Preset

Without presets, exporting to DVD would force you to slog through numerous and often cryptic settings. However, don't be embarrassed if you find even a handful of presets too numerous, or you can't quite decipher their descriptive names. You probably recognize the distinction between video standards: NTSC (National Television Standards Committee) and PAL (Phase Alternation Line). However, other terms may not be so familiar. A quick rundown of the terms should help you choose the best preset for you:

**4Mb and 7Mb:** Represents the target bit rate in Mbps (megabits per second). A lower bit rate yields a smaller file (enabling you to store more on the DVD) at the expense of quality; a higher bit rate yields higher quality but a larger file (limiting the amount of content you can store).

**CBR:** (Constant bit rate.) Maintains a specified bit rate for every frame. This is a relatively inefficient but fast encoding method.

**VBR:** (Variable bit rate.) Varies the bit rate according to the content of each frame. This is a relatively efficient scheme, but one that requires more processing time.

**1 Pass:** Encodes the video in a single pass. This option is faster than two-pass encoding, but it's also a cruder compression method.

**2 Pass:** First analyzes the video's image content and then encodes the video, tailoring the compression according to the result of the analysis. Two passes yield higher quality video but take much longer than single-pass encoding.

**SurCode for Dolby Digital 5.1:** A format for encoding multichannel audio for DVD. Other preset options use either MainConcept MPEG Audio or PCM (pulse-code modulation) audio. Because PCM audio is a lossless format with a 48 kHz sample rate, it yields large files compared to the MainConcept MPEG Audio format.

**EXPORTING DIRECTLY TO DVD**

# Exporting a Movie File

You can create a single, independent file from all or part of the sequence in the timeline. You can also create a movie from a clip. This technique is useful if you want to make a movie from only one portion of a clip or create a version that uses a different format or compression type.

Just as you specify capture and project settings, you must specify the characteristics of the exported movie, such as frame size, frame rate, compression, and audio quality. The settings you choose are determined not only by your output goal but also by the capabilities of your playback device.

This chapter concentrates on the settings that are unique to output. For more in-depth explanations about compression and other technical considerations, see Chapter 16.

### To export a video file:

1. *Do one of the following:*
   ▲ To export the program from the timeline, select the sequence's tab in the Timeline window or the program view of the Monitor window.
   ▲ To export a clip, open a video clip in the source view.

2. To define the footage you want to export, *do one of the following:*
   ▲ In the sequence, set the work area bar over the range in the timeline that you want to export.
   ▲ In a clip, set the In and Out points to define the frames that you want to export.

3. Choose File > Export > Movie (**Figure 15.15**).

   The Export Movie dialog box appears. The bottom of the dialog box summarizes the current export settings.

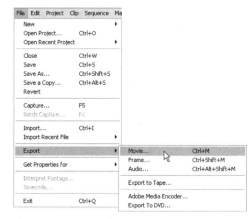

**Figure 15.15** Choose File > Export > Movie.

**Figure 15.16** In the Export Movie dialog box, click the Settings button.

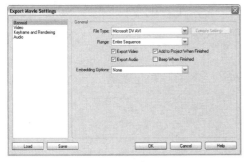

**Figure 15.17** The Export Movie Settings dialog box appears.

**Figure 15.18** Clicking a category on the left allows you to view and adjust the settings on the right.

**Figure 15.19** Specify a name and destination for the movie file and click Save.

**4.** To change the current export settings, click the Settings button (**Figure 15.16**).

The General panel of the Export Movie Settings dialog box appears (**Figure 15.17**).

**5.** To change the current export settings, specify settings in the other panels of the Export Movie Settings dialog box by selecting a category on the left side of the dialog box (**Figure 15.18**):

**General:** Specifies the movie's file type, the range of the timeline to export, which tracks to include, and whether to embed the project link.

**Video:** Specifies settings that control aspects of the video image, such as frame size and frame rate.

**Keyframe and Rendering:** Specifies keyframe options (which control how a codec uses frame differencing) and rendering options (which control which elements are included in the export, as well as video field dominance).

**Audio:** Specifies settings that control aspects of the audio, such as sample rate and bit depth.

**6.** Click OK to exit the Export Movie Settings dialog box.

You return to the Export Movie dialog box.

**7.** Specify a name and destination for your file, and click Save (**Figure 15.19**).

A progress bar appears, indicating the processing time required to make the movie.

EXPORTING A MOVIE FILE

# Specifying the General Export Settings

In the General panel of the Export Movie Settings dialog box, you can specify the range of the timeline that you want to export, which tracks to include, and whether to open the movie when it's finished. In addition, you can have Premiere Pro beep when the movie's done.

You can also embed a *project link*. Choosing this option links the movie with the project from which it was exported. When you use the movie in After Effects or Premiere Pro, you can use the Edit Original command to open the project that originated the movie to make any needed changes. All the project references must be available on the hard drive, of course, and you'll have to re-render any changes. Nevertheless, this feature does improve workflow when changes must be made.

## To specify general export settings:

1. In the Export Movie dialog box, click the Settings button to change the current settings (**Figure 15.20**).
   The General panel of the Export Movie Settings dialog box opens (**Figure 15.21**).

2. To specify a video file format, such as Microsoft DV AVI or QuickTime, choose an option from the File Type drop-down menu (**Figure 15.22**).
   The available options depend on your platform as well as on the plug-ins installed on your system.

3. Specify how much of the program you want to export by choosing one of the following options from the Range drop-down menu (**Figure 15.23**):
   **Entire Sequence:** Exports the entire program from the timeline.
   **Work Area Bar:** Exports only the part of the program below the work area bar.

**Figure 15.20** Click the Settings button to change the current settings.

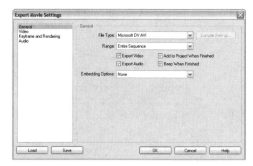

**Figure 15.21** The General panel of the Export Movie Settings dialog box opens.

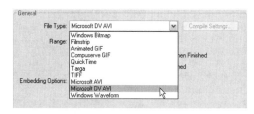

**Figure 15.22** In the File Type drop-down menu, choose a video file format.

**Figure 15.23** In the Range drop-down menu, choose whether you want to export the entire sequence or just the area under the work area bar.

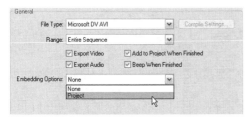

**Figure 15.24** In the Embedding Options drop-down menu, specify whether you want the exported movie to include a link to the project that created it.

4. Specify the tracks you want to export by selecting one or both of the following options:

   **Export Video:** Includes video tracks in the exported file.

   **Export Audio:** Includes audio tracks in the exported file.

   Leave an option unselected to exclude the video or audio from the exported file.

5. Set the following options:

   **Add to Project When Finished:** Imports the rendered movie into the current project automatically.

   **Beep When Finished:** Alerts you when the rendering process is complete by making your computer beep.

   If you don't want to use these options, leave them unselected.

6. Make a selection from the Embedding Options drop-down menu (**Figure 15.24**):

   **None:** Doesn't link the movie to the project from which it was exported.

   **Project:** Embeds a link in the movie to the project from which it was exported.

   When you play a linked movie in After Effects or Premiere Pro, you can choose the Edit Original command to open the original project.

7. Do one of the following:

   ▲ To close the Export Movie Settings dialog box and return to the Export Movie dialog box, click OK.

   ▲ To specify settings in another category, select a category on the left side of the Export Movie Settings dialog box.

## ✔ Tip

■ Beginning with Premiere Pro 1.5, Project link embedding is turned on by default. You can turn it off; however, an embedded link makes using the Edit Original command possible.

# Keyframe and Rendering Settings and Audio Settings

In addition to the General settings covered in the previous section, the Export Movie Settings dialog box also includes panels for Video, Keyframe and Rendering, and Audio settings. Because the options included in these settings categories arise in several areas of Premiere Pro (and digital video in general), a more detailed explanation is reserved for Chapter 16. Nevertheless, an abbreviated explanation now will help complete an overview of the process for exporting movie files.

Video settings include options that determine the characteristics of the exported video, such as the compressor (or codec), color bit depth, frame size, and so on (**Figure 15.25**). Certain codecs also allow you to control the data rate manually or set the compression's quality setting.

Keyframe and rendering options allow you to control two special aspects of the video (**Figure 15.26**). Rendering options control how video fields are processed. The keyframe options refer to compression keyframes—the frames of video a codec uses to track changes in the image. Some output options allow you to specify the frequency and placement of the keyframes and thereby influence compression quality.

Audio settings define the characteristics of the exported audio, such as the audio codec, bit depth, and sample rate (**Figure 15.27**). As you'd expect, audio settings help determine the quality of the exported audio and, hence, the file's overall data rate. As with other settings, you must understand and specify audio settings at several points in the postproduction process. Again, Chapter 16 covers each audio setting in more detail.

**Figure 15.25** Video settings determine the basic characteristics of the exported video.

**Figure 15.26** Keyframe and rendering options let you control compression keyframes and field processing.

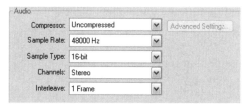

**Figure 15.27** Audio settings define the characteristics of the exported audio.

**KEYFRAME, RENDERING, AUDIO SETTINGS**

**Figure 15.28** In the Export Movie dialog box, click the Settings button.

**Figure 15.29** In the General panel of the Export Movie Settings dialog box, choose a format that supports still-image sequences.

**Figure 15.30** Choose how much of the sequence you want to export from the Range drop-down menu.

# Exporting Still-Image Sequences

You can export a program or clip as a sequence of still images. Premiere Pro numbers the frames automatically. Many animation and 3D programs can import video images only as a numbered sequence of still-image files.

## To export a still-image sequence:

1. In the Export Movie dialog box, click the Settings button (**Figure 15.28**).

   The General panel of the Export Movie Settings dialog box opens.

2. From the File Type drop-down menu, choose a still-image sequence format (**Figure 15.29**).

   CompuServe GIF, TIFF, Targa, and Windows Bitmap formats support sequences.

3. Using the Range drop-down menu, specify how much of the program you want to export (**Figure 15.30**):

   **Entire Sequence:** Exports the entire selected sequence.

   **Work Area Bar:** Exports only the part of the sequence below the work area bar.

4. Set the following options:

   **Open When Finished:** Opens the rendered movie automatically upon completion.

   **Beep When Finished:** Alerts you when the rendering process is complete by making your computer beep.

   If you don't want to use these options, leave them unselected.

*continues on next page*

**5.** If you're exporting a CompuServe GIF sequence (also called a GIF sequence), you click the Compile Settings button in the Export Movie Settings dialog box to access additional options (see "Specifying GIF Options" later in this chapter).

**6.** On the left side of the dialog box, click Video and specify the options you want, such as color depth, frame size, and frame rate.

If you're unfamiliar with these settings, consult Chapter 16.

**7.** On the left side of the dialog box, click Keyframe and Rendering to access these options.

**8.** In the Keyframe and Rendering panel of the Export Movie Settings dialog box, specify the following options:

**Fields:** Choose how to export video fields from the drop-down menu. For most DV projects, choose Lower Field First.

**Deinterlace Video Footage:** Select this option to remove interlacing from each frame before exporting. This option reduces resolution but may be desirable to remove field artifacts.

For more about video fields, interlacing, and field artifacts, see Chapter 16.

**9.** In the Export Movie Settings dialog box, click OK.

The Export Movie Settings dialog box closes, and you return to the Export Movie dialog box.

**10.** Specify a destination and file name and click Save (**Figure 15.31**).

A Rendering dialog box appears. Premiere Pro exports the range of frames as a sequence of still image files in the format you specified.

**Figure 15.31** Specify a destination and file name and click Save.

EXPORTING STILL-IMAGE SEQUENCES

Figure 15.32 Cue the clip or sequence's CTI to the frame you want to export.

# Exporting Single Still Images

You can export the current frame of video from the sequence or source clip as a single still-image file.

## To export a single frame:

1. *Do one of the following:*

   ▲ To export a frame from the sequence, cue the sequence's CTI to the frame you want to export.

   ▲ To export a frame from a clip, open a clip in the source view and cue the source view's CTI to the frame you want to export (**Figure 15.32**).

2. Choose File > Export > Frame (**Figure 15.33**).

   The Export Frame dialog box appears.

   *continues on next page*

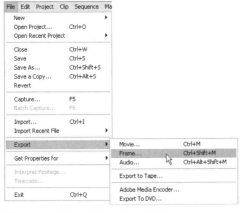

Figure 15.33 Choose File > Export > Frame.

**3.** Click Settings (**Figure 15.34**).

The General panel of the Export Frame Settings dialog box appears.

**4.** From the File Type drop-down menu, choose a still-image format (**Figure 15.35**).

**5.** *Do one of the following:*

▲ To open the exported still image automatically, click Open When Finished.

▲ To specify options for CompuServe GIF images, click Compile Settings.

**6.** To specify Video options, select Video on the left side of the Export Frame Settings dialog box.

Usually, you don't need to change these settings. However, if you want to retain alpha channel information in the still image, choose Millions+ of Colors from the Color Depth drop-down menu (**Figure 15.36**).

**7.** To deinterlace the exported frame, select Keyframe and Rendering from the left side of the Export Frame Settings dialog box and then select Deinterlace Video Footage (**Figure 15.37**).

This option removes one field from an interlaced image, which can remove the combing effect sometimes apparent in still frames taken from video that contains objects in motion. For more about interlacing, see Chapter 16.

**8.** Click OK.

The Export Frame Settings dialog box closes, and you return to the Export Frame dialog box.

**Figure 15.34** Click the Settings button.

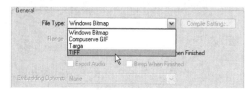

**Figure 15.35** Choose a still-image format from the File Type drop-down menu.

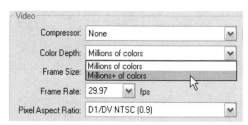

**Figure 15.36** If you want to retain alpha channel information, choose Millions+ of Colors from the Color Depth drop-down menu.

**Figure 15.37** To deinterlace the exported frame, select Keyframe and Rendering from the left side of the Export Frame Settings dialog box and then select Deinterlace Video Footage.

**Exporting Single Still Images**

**Figure 15.38** Specify a name and destination for the still image and click Save.

9. Specify a name and destination for the still image and click Save (**Figure 15.38**).

The frame you specified is exported as a still-frame file in the format and location you set.

## ✔ Tips

■ If you plan to print the still image, you should know that standard-resolution video always translates to 72 dpi, regardless of the camera's tape format. This is fine for small, low-resolution printouts. But if you want to create a press kit or other printed materials, be sure to take production stills with a film camera or a high-quality digital still camera.

■ If you plan to use the image in a still-image editing program (such as Photoshop), export the highest image quality possible. Don't resize the image or even deinterlace it. Photoshop's tool set is superior for any image editing you want to do.

■ Most stills taken from DV or other video capture cards must be deinterlaced and resized to compensate for differences in pixel aspect ratios. See Chapter 16 to learn more.

■ You can also export all or part of a clip or program as a *filmstrip* file. Appropriately enough, a filmstrip file in Photoshop looks like a filmstrip: a single still image that contains the frames of video arranged in a long column. You manipulate the frames of video using Photoshop's tools, using a technique similar to *rotoscoping* in traditional film.

**EXPORTING SINGLE STILL IMAGES**

# Specifying GIF Options

You can export animated GIFs and CompuServe GIFs from Premiere Pro as you would any other image format, except that additional options are available. You can select Animated GIF when exporting a movie file; you can select CompuServe GIF when exporting a single still image or still-image sequence.

### To specify settings for GIFs:

1. *Do one of the following:*
   - In the General panel of the Export Movie Settings dialog box, choose Animated GIF or CompuServe GIF in the File Type drop-down menu (**Figure 15.39**).
   - In the General panel of the Export Frame Settings dialog box, choose CompuServe GIF from the File Type drop-down menu.

   The Compile Settings button becomes available for use.

2. Click Compile Settings (**Figure 15.40**). The Advanced GIF Options dialog box appears (**Figure 15.41**).

**Figure 15.39** In the Export Frame Settings or Export Movie Settings (shown here) dialog box, choose Animated GIF or CompuServe GIF in the File Type drop-down menu.

**Figure 15.40** Click the Compile Settings button.

**Figure 15.41** The Advanced GIF Options dialog box appears.

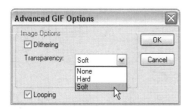

**Figure 15.42** Choose an option from the Transparency drop-down menu. To make an animated GIF play continuously, select Looping.

3. To simulate colors that aren't available on the Web-safe color palette by *dithering* (or mixing) pixels of available colors, select the Dithering check box.

   Although dithered colors look grainy, they can expand the limited color palette and improve color gradients. When Dithering is unselected, unavailable colors are replaced with the next-closest color.

4. From the Transparency drop-down menu, choose one of the following options (**Figure 15.42**):

   **None:** Exports the animated GIF or GIF sequence as opaque.

   **Hard:** Makes one color in the image transparent.

   **Soft:** Makes one color in the image transparent with soft edges.

   Click Color to open the color picker and choose the color that becomes transparent.

5. To make an animated GIF play continuously, select the Looping check box.

   Leave this option unselected to make the animated GIF play once and then stop.

# Exporting Audio-Only Files

The process for exporting audio is similar to that for exporting a movie with video and audio, except that you're limited to audio-only file formats.

## To export a video file:

1. *Do one of the following:*
   ▲ To export audio from the timeline, select the sequence's tab in the Timeline window or the program view of the Monitor window.
   ▲ To export a clip's audio, open a clip in the source view.

2. To define the footage you want to export, *do one of the following:*
   ▲ In the sequence, set the work area bar over the range in the timeline that you want to export.
   ▲ In a clip, set the In and Out points to define the frames that you want to export.

3. Choose File > Export > Audio (**Figure 15.43**).
   The Export Audio dialog box appears. The current export settings are summarized at the bottom of the dialog box.

4. To change the current export settings, click the Settings button (**Figure 15.44**).
   The General panel of the Export Audio Settings dialog box appears.

5. To change the current export settings, specify settings in the other panels of the Export Audio Settings dialog box by choosing a category from the left side of the dialog box:
   **General:** Specifies the audio file's file type, the range of the timeline to export, and whether to embed a project link (**Figure 15.45**).

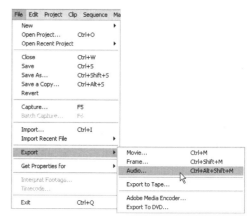

**Figure 15.43** Choose File > Export > Audio.

**Figure 15.44** To change the current export settings, click the Settings button.

**Figure 15.45** Specify the General settings.

EXPORTING AUDIO-ONLY FILES

**Figure 15.46** Specify the Audio settings.

**Figure 15.47** Specify a name and location for your file and click Save.

**Audio:** Specifies settings that control aspects of the audio, such as sample rate and bit depth (**Figure 15.46**)

See Chapter 16 for more about audio settings.

6. Click OK to exit the Export Audio Settings dialog box.

   You return to the Export Audio dialog box.

7. Specify a name and destination for your file and click Save (**Figure 15.47**).

   A progress bar appears, indicating the processing time required to make the movie.

# Using the Adobe Media Encoder

As you may suspect from its expansive title, the Adobe Media Encoder encompasses a wide range of export options, including MPEG1, MPEG2, QuickTime, RealMedia, and Windows Media. Using the Adobe Media Encoder interface, you can apply and adjust each option using similar procedures, which are covered in this section. Regrettably, the scope of this book doesn't permit a detailed discussion of each format's many settings. Fortunately, the provided presets should spare you from having to delve too deeply in most cases.

For general technical information regarding common settings, consult Chapter 16. You'll also find that the Premiere Pro Online Help system includes some of the technical details omitted from the printed user guide. But for more in-depth information, you may have to turn to documentation made available by the format's developer: Real Networks (in the case of RealMedia), Microsoft (for Windows Media), Apple (for QuickTime), or MainConcept (for MPEG). If you're still hungry for the nitty-gritty compression tools and techniques, consider consulting a book or Web site dedicated to the format or codec you're interested in using.

Premiere Pro 1.5 added pre- and post-encoding tasks that allow you to apply certain filters to the project before the encoding process—Crop, Scale, Video Noise Reduction, and Deinterlace—as well as post-encoding actions—FTP and Log File Details.

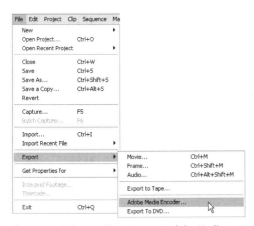

Figure 15.48 Choose File > Export > Adobe Media Encoder.

Figure 15.49 The Transcode Settings dialog box appears.

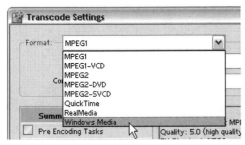

Figure 15.50 In the Transcode Settings dialog box, choose an option from the Format drop-down menu.

## To export using Adobe Media Encoder presets:

1. *Do one of the following:*
   - ▲ To export the program from the timeline, select the sequence's tab in the Timeline window or the program view of the Monitor window.
   - ▲ To export a clip, open a video clip in the source view.

2. To define the footage you want to export, *do one of the following:*
   - ▲ In a sequence, set the work area bar over the range in the timeline that you want to export.
   - ▲ In a clip, set the In and Out points to define the frames that you want to export.

3. Choose File > Export > Adobe Media Encoder (**Figure 15.48**).

   A Transcode Settings dialog box appears (**Figure 15.49**).

4. In the Transcode Settings dialog box, choose an option from the Format drop-down menu (**Figure 15.50**).

   See the sidebar "Adobe Media Encoder Formats" later in this chapter.

*continues on next page*

**5.** In the Preset drop-down menu, choose
the preset that matches your export goal
(**Figure 15.51**).

You can also modify, save, import, and
delete presets (explained later in this
chapter).

**6.** To view the settings, select a category
from the left column of the Transcode
Settings dialog box (**Figure 15.52**).

The categories that are available depend
on the format you specified in step 4.

**7.** If you chose RealMedia or Windows
Media as the format in step 4, specify
options for Metadata and Audiences, if
necessary.

Consult the Adobe Premiere Online Help
system for additional guidance on these
options, or consult resources available
from Real Networks and Microsoft.

**8.** When you're satisfied with your selections,
click OK.

A Save File dialog box appears.

**9.** In the Save File dialog box, specify an
option in the Export Range drop-down
menu (**Figure 15.53**):

▲ If exporting from the timeline, select
either Entire Sequence or Work Area.

▲ If exporting from the source view of
the Monitor window, select either
Entire Clip or In to Out.

**Figure 15.51** In the Preset drop-down menu, choose
the preset that matches your export goal.

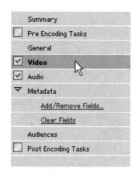

**Figure 15.52** Select a
category from the left
column of the Transcode
Settings dialog box to
view its settings.

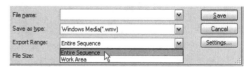

**Figure 15.53** Specify an option in the Export Range
drop-down menu.

**Figure 15.54** When you click Save, a Rendering dialog box appears, indicating the time required to render the file.

**10.** Specify a file name and destination for the exported file and click Save.

A Rendering dialog box appears, indicating the time required to render the file (**Figure 15.54**).

## ✔ Tips

■ Beginning with Premiere Pro 1.5, you can set the frame size for any MPEG-2 transcoded video and set the pixel aspect ratio for Windows Media file export.

■ The MPEG2-DVD presets have Quality set to 5. This is unnecessary for most video and causes extremely long encoding times. Unless your project has lots of extreme motion, set Quality to 3. If you see artifacts created from excessive movement, increase the Quality setting.

---

## Adobe Media Encoder Formats

**MPEG1:** A set of compression standards (developed by the Moving Picture Experts Group) designed to yield results comparable to VHS tape quality at relatively low data rates. This format is typically used for Web download, CD-ROM, or VCD.

**MPEG1-VCD:** Preset MPEG1 settings that conform to VCD (also called video CD) specifications. The VCD format supports lower quality than DVD but can be played using a standard CD-ROM player and appropriate software.

**MPEG2:** Another set of standards developed by the Moving Picture Experts Group, intended to produce high-quality, full-screen interlaced video.

**MPEG2-DVD:** Preset MPEG2 settings that conform to DVD (also called digital versatile disk) specifications.

**MEPG2-SVCD:** Preset MPEG2 settings that conform to SVCD (also called Super Video CD) specifications. SVCD supports higher-quality video and more advanced features than the VCD format.

**QuickTime:** Apple computer's multimedia architecture, which includes a wide variety of codecs designed for various applications.

**RealMedia:** Real Network's standard for low-data-rate applications, particularly downloading and streaming audio and video over the Web.

**Windows Media:** Microsoft's standard for low-data rate applications, particularly downloading streaming audio and video over the Web.

# Specifying Pre- and Post-Encoding Tasks

With the Adobe Media Encoder, you can pre-treat the video, making adjustments to a clip or sequence before you encode it. Certain processing tasks should occur before encoding to produce the best final result. For example, deinterlacing video before encoding it into a noninterlaced format removes potential field artifacts before they can be encoded—and exacerbated in the process.

After the encoder is finished, you can have Premiere Pro create a log file, or even transfer the encoded file to a server using FTP (File Transfer Protocol).

## To specify pre-encoding tasks:

1. In the Transcode Settings dialog box, select Pre Encoding Tasks (**Figure 15.55**).

2. On the right side of the dialog box, select a filter from the drop-down menu (**Figure 15.56**).

   **Deinterlace:** Removes a specified field from each interlaced video frame. Deinterlacing before encoding takes place yields better image quality you would achieve otherwise. Specify Upper, Lower, or No Fields (Progressive).

   **Video Noise Reduction:** Applies a noise reduction filter to the footage, which can improve the apparent image quality when the video is encoded to certain codecs (such as Cinepak). Higher values reduce the grain but also reduce the image sharpness.

   **Scale:** Specifies the amount (in pixels) to increase or reduce the size of the image.

   **Crop:** Specifies the amount (in pixels) to crop each side of the image.

**Figure 15.55** Check the box next to Pre Encoding Tasks.

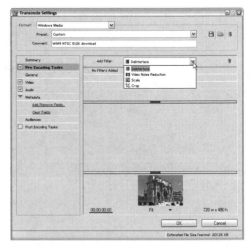

**Figure 15.56** Select a filter from the Add Filter drop-down menu.

**Figure 15.57** Filters can be added in any combination.

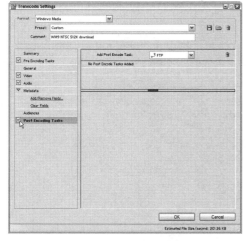

**Figure 15.58** Check the box next to Post Encoding Tasks.

Filters may selected in any order or combination (**Figure 15.57**).

3. To adjust the filters you specified in step 2, do one of the following:

▲ To deactivate or activate a filter, click the eye icon 👁.

▲ To remove a filter from the list, click the Remove button 🗑.

▲ To change the order of the filters, drag a filter's name higher or lower on the list.

## To specify post-encoding tasks:

1. In the Transcode Settings dialog box, select Post Encoding Tasks (**Figure 15.58**).

2. On the right side of the dialog box, select an item from the Add Post Encode Task pull-down menu (**Figure 15.59**).

**Log File Details:** Creates a text file listing information about your export. The file is saved to the same directory as your exported file.

**FTP:** Uses FTP to upload the exported file to a server.

3. To remove a post-render action from the list, click the Remove button 🗑.

**Figure 15.59** Select an item from the Add Post Encode Task drop-down menu.

# Modifying, Saving, and Deleting Presets

This section explains how to change, save, import, and delete presets.

**Figure 15.60** In the Transcode Settings dialog box, specify the format and preset you want to view or modify.

### To view and modify Adobe Media Encoder presets:

1. In the Transcode Settings dialog box, specify the format and preset you want to view or modify (**Figure 15.60**).

   Initially, the Summary category is selected on the left side of the dialog box, and a summary of the selected preset's settings is visible on the right.

2. On the left side of the dialog box, select the setting category you want to view:

   **Video:** Available for all formats.

   **Audio:** Available for all formats.

   **Multiplexer:** Available for MPEG1 and MPEG2 formats.

   **Metadata:** Available for RealMedia and Windows Media formats.

   **Audiences:** Available for RealMedia and Windows Media formats.

3. In the right panel, modify parameters for the selected settings category (**Figure 15.61**).

   The name in the Preset field near the top of the dialog box changes to Custom.

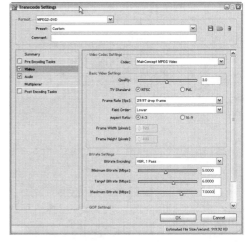

**Figure 15.61** Select a category on the left to view and adjust its settings on the right.

**Figure 15.62** Click the Save Preset button.

**Figure 15.63** In the Choose Name dialog box, specify a name for your preset and click OK.

**Figure 15.64** In the Transcode Settings dialog box, select a format and then choose the preset you want to delete.

**Figure 15.65** Click the Delete button.

**Figure 15.66** In the Delete Preset dialog box, click OK to confirm your choice.

## To save custom settings as a preset:

1. In the Transcode Settings dialog box, modify the settings according to your output goals.

   See the previous task, "To view and modify Adobe Media Encoder presets," for an overview of the process.

2. Click the Save Preset button (**Figure 15.62**). The Choose Name dialog box appears.

3. In the Choose Name dialog box, specify a name for your preset and click OK (**Figure 15.63**).

   Your preset appears in the Preset drop-down menu for the specified format.

## To delete custom presets:

1. In the Transcode Settings dialog box, select a format and then choose the preset you want to delete (**Figure 15.64**).

2. Click the Delete button (**Figure 15.65**). A Delete Preset dialog box warns you that the selected preset will be deleted and that the action cannot be undone.

3. In the Delete Preset dialog box, click OK to confirm your choice (**Figure 15.66**). The preset no longer appears in the Preset menu for the selected format.

MODIFYING, SAVING, AND DELETING PRESETS

# Exporting an AAF File

AAF (Advanced Authoring Format) is a widely accepted file exchange format used to transfer both data (video and audio files) and metadata (such as edit-decision list information, including the use of dissolves and wipes). AAF helps you retain as much of your project as possible when transferring it from one system to another. However, be aware that the AAF features and data supported by one program may not always be supported by another program. If you plan to export your project using AAF, you should research (and, ideally, test) the process to maximize the data you can transfer and to prepare to re-create the data you can't transfer.

### To export an AAF file:

1. Select the Project window.

2. Choose Project > Export Project as AAF (**Figure 15.67**).

   If the Project hasn't been saved in its current state, a dialog box prompts you to save and continue or to discontinue the export. The AAF – Save Converted Project As dialog box appears.

3. Specify the name and location of the exported AAF file and click Save (**Figure 15.68**).

   Premiere Pro creates an AAF version of your project in the location you specified.

**Figure 15.67** Choose Project > Export Project as AAF.

**Figure 15.68** Specify a name and location for the exported AAF file and click Save.

**Figure 15.69** Choose Project > Export Project as EDL.

**Figure 15.70** Specify a name and location for the exported EDL file and click Save.

# Exporting an Edit Decision List (EDL)

As you learned in the introduction to this chapter, the primary goal of offline editing is to generate an edit-decision list, or EDL. An *EDL* describes your edited program as a list of editing events. Exporting an EDL enables you to transfer your offline editing decisions to an online editing controller. Beginning with Premiere Pro 1.5, you can export an edit-decision list using the CMX3600 format. This format is the most widely accepted and most robust of the EDL formats.

You can find out more about specific EDL options (such as B-rolls and wipe codes) in the *Adobe Premiere Pro User Guide* or by consulting an online editor (the person, not the machine). Always keep in close contact with your online editing facility to ensure that you are prepared for online editing.

## To export an EDL:

1. Select the Project window.

2. Choose Project > Export Project as EDL (**Figure 15.69**).

   If the project hasn't been saved in its current state, a dialog box prompts you to save and continue or to discontinue the export. The EDL – Save Converted Project As dialog box appears.

3. Specify the name and location of the exported EDL file and click Save (**Figure 15.70**).

   Premiere Pro creates an EDL version of your project in the location you specified.

# VIDEO AND AUDIO SETTINGS

## 16

At every major step in the editing process—capture, edit, and export—you encounter settings that control the basic attributes of the video and audio. The settings you choose for one step of the process may not be the best choices for another.

To make intelligent choices, you should have a basic understanding of topics such as frame rates, frame sizes, compression, and audio quality. You should familiarize yourself not only with how these settings relate to video displayed on computers, but also with how they relate to video displayed on televisions.

This chapter will guide you in choosing settings in Premiere Pro, and it will also help you understand some of the fundamental principles of all digital video. Of course, it can offer only brief explanations of the matters directly applicable to Premiere Pro.

VIDEO AND AUDIO SETTINGS

# Choosing Settings

Perhaps the greatest advantage of using a
DV-based editing system is that it simplifies
your choice of settings. The DV format is so
consistent that systems like Premiere Pro
can include presets, sparing you the hassle
of choosing video and audio settings manually. Ignorance is indeed bliss.

If you're using a hardware capture card, your
choices are simpler, not because they're universal, but because they're specific. The settings supported by your card are the most
obvious choices for capture, playback, and
export—especially if your goal is to produce
a videotape of your final program. The documentation included with your capture card
is your best guide.

If you're editing on a different system than
you used for capture, however, you need to
understand a broader range of options. Files
that rely on a hardware card won't play back
on systems that don't have the same hardware. In fact, the files won't even open on
other systems unless they have a software
version of the capture card's compression
scheme, or *codec* (see "Codecs" later in
this chapter).

Similarly, if you want to export a final movie
to play back on other devices—such as on
another hard disk, on a CD-ROM or DVD, or
over the Web—you need to know which settings are most appropriate for each use. This
knowledge is helpful even if you plan to rely on
the presets available for many output options.

**Figure 16.1** The Custom Settings tab of the New Project dialog box includes a drop-down menu for selecting a timebase. If the editing mode is DV Playback (shown here), the list includes only 23.976 (for Panasonic 24P and 24PA footage), 25.00 frames/second (for PAL), and 29.97 frames/second (for NTSC).

# Timebase

The *timebase* of a project determines how Premiere Pro calculates time divisions, expressed in frames per second (fps) (**Figure 16.1**). Strictly speaking, you shouldn't confuse the timebase with the *frame rate*, which usually refers to the number of unique frames contained in a clip. In other words, a clip's frame rate may be conformed to the project's timebase (see the next section, "Frame Rate").

Standard video in North America and Japan complies with the NTSC standard, which uses a 29.97-fps timebase. Video in most of Europe complies with the PAL standard, which uses a 25-fps timebase. Beginning with Premiere Pro 1.5, you have the choice of using Panasonic's proprietary 24P and 24P Advanced (24PA) interlacing schemes with a 23.976-fps timebase. Choose the appropriate setting for your project.

Once you set a project's timebase, you can't change it. All sequences in the project must use the project's timebase. You can import a project into another project that uses a different timebase; however, doing so will affect Premiere Pro's time calculations, causing existing edit marks and markers to shift and changing the durations of clips. If you must convert a project in this way, double-check your edits for any misalignments.

# Frame Rate

*Frame rate* refers to both the number of frames per second contained in a source clip and the number of frames per second displayed by the program or exported movie. The frame rate of source video is determined when it's recorded or rendered. When you capture DV footage, the footage's frame rate matches the project's timebase. Other media you import, however, may use a different frame rate. You can always select a footage item in the Project window to view its frame rate and other characteristics in the preview area at the top of the window (**Figure 16.2**).

Regardless of a source clip's frame rate, the project settings determine the frame rate at which the clip is displayed in the program view and timeline. A 15-fps source, however, doesn't play back more smoothly when set to play back at 30 fps; each frame of the source is simply displayed twice. Conversely, a 30-fps source in a program set for 15 fps displays only every other frame in the program view and in the timeline. The same concept applies to speed changes you apply to a clip. Choosing a different frame rate doesn't affect the speed of the clip—only how smoothly or choppily it plays back.

If you choose to preview or export a movie at a lower frame rate, choose an even division of the full frame rate. Because NTSC video is approximately 30 fps, choose 15 fps or 10 fps when you want to export at a lower frame rate.

**Figure 16.2** Whereas the frame rate of captured footage matches the project's timebase, the frame rate of other imported footage may differ. A clip's frame rate is revealed in the preview area of the Project window, and you can decide how Premiere Pro interprets frame rates in the Interpret Footage dialog box (shown here).

# Timecode

*Timecode* is a method of counting video frames developed by the Society of Motion Picture and Television Engineers (SMPTE; often pronounced "simp-tee"). SMPTE timecode is counted in hours, minutes, seconds, and frames. It counts 30 frames per second, from 0 up to 23:59:59:29, or just under one day. Therefore, there's a timecode hour 0 but no timecode hour 24.

The advantage of timecode is that it provides an *absolute address* for each frame of video—that is, each frame has a unique and unchanging number. The number acts as an address or identity; just as a street address helps you find a specific place, timecode helps you find a specific frame.

Timecode makes offline/online editing possible. By keeping track of timecode numbers (and the reel, or tape, the source is on), you can easily re-create an offline edit.

Without timecode, frames can be counted sequentially, but they can't be identified specifically. Without timecode, you have no way to refer to a frame of video accurately—and consequently, you have no way to create an edit-decision list (EDL) or recapture a particular clip (see Chapter 3, "Capturing and Importing Footage").

A great deal of consumer video equipment doesn't read or record timecode. Even if you're using a timecode display in your project, timecode isn't necessarily present in the source clip or the source tape.

DV cameras, however, do record timecode (typically drop-frame timecode; see the following section). Computer programs like Premiere Pro can read the timecode without using additional equipment.

## ✔ Tips

■ Most consumer-level cameras start at timecode 00;00;00;00. In many cases, removing the battery, ejecting the tape, or turning off the camera for more than a few minutes resets the timecode, so that the next shot restarts at 00;00;00;00. Check the documentation included with your camera to see how it handles timecode.

■ Cameras geared toward professionals let you set the starting timecode for each tape. One advantage of this feature is that you can use the hour field to number tapes, so that the first tape's timecode starts at hour one, or 01;00;00;00; the second tape starts at 02;00;00;00; and so on. Camera tapes are usually under an hour, but if you use longer tapes, you should start each tape on an odd-numbered hour to avoid confusion. And remember: timecode counts hours 0 through 23.

# Drop-Frame and Non–Drop-Frame Timecode

Although the timebase of NTSC video is a constant 29.97 fps, SMPTE timecode counts it in two different ways—drop frame and non-drop frame:

**Non–drop-frame timecode:** Even though the true timebase of NTSC video is 29.97 fps, non–drop-frame (NDF) timecode counts 30 fps. Over time, however, the discrepancy results in a small but significant difference between the duration indicated by the time-code and the actual elapsed time (**Figure 16.3**). Nevertheless, NDF timecode is easy to understand and often is used for source tapes. Video equipment displays NDF time-code with colons between the numbers.

**Drop-frame timecode:** To compensate for the discrepancy caused by the 30-fps count-ing scheme, SMPTE developed drop-frame (DF) timecode. Drop-frame timecode also counts 30 fps, but it skips two frame num-bers (not actual video frames) at the end of every minute, except every tenth minute (**Figure 16.4**). In this way, it periodically corrects the discrepancy, preventing the timecode from drifting too far from actual elapsed time. DF timecode displays dura-tions that very closely match actual time. Premiere Pro and other video equipment display drop-frame timecode with semi-colons between numbers.

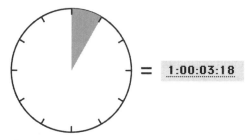

**Figure 16.3** Every hour of real-time, non–drop-frame timecode counts an extra 3 seconds and 16 frames.

**0:00:59:29**

**0:01:00:02**

**Figure 16.4** Drop-frame timecode skips two frame numbers at the end of every minute, except every tenth minute.

**Figure 16.5** You can set the display format when you start the project, on the Custom Settings tab of the New Project dialog box.

# Video Display Format

In the project settings, you can specify how you want Premiere Pro to display time in the Display Format drop-down menu. However, your choices may be limited by the editing mode you selected for the project; a DV project lets you choose only between drop-frame and non–drop-frame timecode displays (**Figure 16.5**). Choose the time display that's best suited for your project:

**24 fps Timecode:** Counts for standard film frame rates.

**25 fps Timecode:** Counts for PAL and SECAM (common standards in most countries outside North America).

**29.97 fps Drop-Frame Timecode:** Counts for NTSC video (the standard in North America, Japan, and other countries) in drop-frame format. It's displayed with semicolons between numbers.

**29.97 fps Non Drop-Frame Timecode:** Counts for NTSC video (the standard in North America, Japan, and other countries) in non–drop-frame format. It's displayed with colons between numbers.

**Frames:** Counts video frames sequentially without translating them into seconds, minutes, and hours.

# Audio Display Format

The Custom Settings tab of the New Project dialog box also lets you specify the display format used for audio (**Figure 16.6**). The display format you choose determines how audio is counted when you switch a window to display audio units:

**Audio Samples:** Counts audio samples based on the sample rate settings you specified when you started the project.

**Milliseconds:** Counts audio in milliseconds, or thousandths of a second.

The time display formats are counting systems and don't affect the timebase or frame rate, so you can change these formats whenever you wish.

## ✔ Tip

- Most consumer DV cameras record drop-frame timecode.

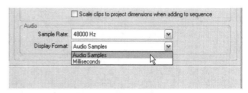

**Figure 16.6** When you start a project, you can specify the display format for audio on the Custom Settings tab of the New Project dialog box.

**Figure 16.7** Interlaced displays present a single field that includes every other line of the image...

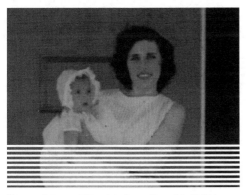

**Figure 16.8** ...and then interlaces the other field to create a full frame.

# Interlaced and Progressive Scan Video

One important difference between television and computer monitors lies in the way that they display frames of video. Television monitors display interlaced video, whereas computer monitors use a progressive scan.

In a *progressive scan,* the horizontal lines of each frame are displayed from the top of the screen to the bottom in a single pass.

*Interlaced* video divides each frame into two fields. Each field includes every other horizontal line (scan line) in the frame. A television displays one field first, drawing alternating scan lines from the top of the image to the bottom (**Figure 16.7**). Returning to the top, it then displays the alternate field, filling in the gaps to complete the frame (**Figure 16.8**). In NTSC video, each frame displays approximately 1/30 of a second; each field displays every 1/60 of a second.

The field that contains the topmost scan line is called *field 1,* the *odd field,* or the *upper field.* The other field is known as *field 2,* the *even field,* or the *lower field.* Your video equipment and the settings you choose determine which field is the *dominant* field—the field that's displayed first.

DV footage is usually lower-field dominant, which should be reflected in the Custom Settings panel of the New Project dialog box when you start a project (**Figure 16.9**). Other dialog boxes in Premiere Pro, such as the Export Movie Settings dialog box, also refer to field order (**Figure 16.10**).

As you'd expect, most video cameras record interlaced images. Capture cards designed to work with NTSC video also digitize and export interlaced video fields. Similarly, some software programs (many animation programs, for example) support *field rendering*—the ability to export noninterlaced source material as interlaced video.

On the other hand, some video cameras also offer progressive-scan video. Filmmakers have already begun using high-definition, 24-fps, progressive-scan (24P) video cameras to shoot commercial feature films. Recently, standard-definition 24P cameras have been introduced for the consumer market.

More recent home video equipment, such as higher-end DVD players and televisions, also supports progressive-scan video. You'll find a progressive scan option in Premiere Pro's Transcode Settings dialog box (when exporting video using the Export to DVD or Adobe Media Encoder) (**Figure 16.11**).

### ✔ Tips

■ Before you embrace progressive-scan video, make sure you understand its practical implications. Some cameras can capture 30 fps in progressive mode; others can record only 15 fps. Progressive-scan video is best for projects destined only for presentation on computer screens; if there's a chance that you'll want to present the project on a television, it's best to stick with interlaced video.

**Figure 16.9** When you start a project, you specify the dominant field in the Fields drop-down menu of the New Project dialog box.

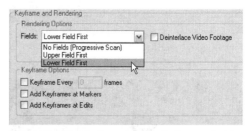

**Figure 16.10** The Keyframe and Rendering panel of the Export Movie Settings dialog box also includes a Fields drop-down menu.

**Figure 16.11** Some export formats let you export a file that uses progressive scan by specifying that option in the Transcode Settings dialog box.

■ Because its frame rate is similar to that of film, the PAL video standard shot in progressive-scan mode might make the transition to film better than interlaced video. Even so, research the pros and cons of this technique before you invest your time and money.

# Interlacing Problems

In video, problems arising from the nature of interlaced and noninterlaced images are some of the most pervasive and least understood.

Because video cameras capture each field of a frame at a different moment in time, moving objects may be in one position in one field and in a different position in the next field. You don't notice the difference as the video is playing, but it becomes apparent when you view a single interlaced frame. When a moving object is viewed as a still frame, interlacing creates *combing*, or *field artifacts*. Interlacing can also become apparent when you make a clip play in slow motion.

Just as an interlaced video image can look bad as a still, a still frame that looks fine in Photoshop can look bad on television. Certain graphic elements that look good on a progressive-scan monitor don't look good on an interlaced monitor. Interlacing makes thin horizontal details (or patterns containing thin horizontals) appear to flicker or vibrate. If a line is thin enough, it disappears with every scan of its field. Be aware that these details can include certain fonts, especially those with serifs (those little tapering feet at the ends of some letter strokes).

Disagreement between the field dominance of a video playback device and that of a recording device can cause movement in the frame to stagger or stutter in the recorded image. That's because the fields were recorded in the wrong order; the field dominance was reversed inadvertently. Applying the Backward video effect also reverses field order.

Fortunately, there are solutions for all these field-related problems.

## Solving interlacing problems

When you're exporting video, you can solve most interlacing problems by choosing the appropriate field option in the Keyframe and Rendering panel of the Export Movie Settings dialog box (Figure 16.10). Select the field dominance that matches your footage or recording device; select None if your footage isn't interlaced.

If you intend to export interlaced video to a noninterlaced format or to a still frame, you should deinterlace it. *Deinterlacing* converts two fields into a single frame, either by duplicating one field or blending the two. Some codecs deinterlace the video automatically.

When you're editing, interlacing may become apparent when you create a freeze frame or slow down a clip using the Speed command or Rate Stretch tool. The Frame Hold command includes a deinterlace option. You can solve other field rendering problems using the Field Options command. Applying this command allows you to deinterlace clips that have been slowed, interlace noninterlaced footage, or reduce flicker caused by interlacing.

## To use the Field Options command:

1. In the timeline, select a clip that requires field processing.

2. Choose Clip > Video Options > Field Options (**Figure 16.12**).

   The Field Options dialog box appears (**Figure 16.13**).

3. To eliminate the stuttering effect evident in clips that use the wrong field dominance or that use the Backward video effect, select Reverse Field Dominance.

4. In the Processing Options section, choose the appropriate option:

   **None:** Doesn't execute field processing.

   **Interlace Consecutive Frames:** Interlaces frames that aren't interlaced.

   **Always Deinterlace:** Deinterlaces the clip regardless of its playback speed.

   **Flicker Removal:** Blurs the image so that thin horizontal details don't flicker due to interlacing.

5. Select Frame Blend Speed Changes to slightly combine consecutive frames to make slow motion appear smoother.

6. Click OK to close the dialog box and apply the changes.

## ✔ Tips

- Many DV cameras offer a progressive-scan feature for capturing still images. For stills, a progressive-scan feature can save you the step of deinterlacing frames of video later. This feature may not be all that it's cracked up to be, however. Often, still images captured in video cameras don't exceed the quality of the video. For high-quality stills (for printing, for example), rely on a digital still camera or a good, old-fashioned film still camera.

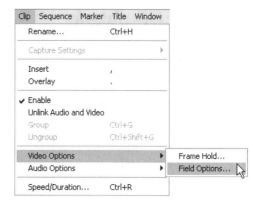

**Figure 16.12** Choose Clip > Video Options > Field Options.

**Figure 16.13** In the Field Options dialog box, specify the appropriate options and click OK to apply the changes to the clip.

- Avoid using light typefaces, thin lines, and tight patterns in images that are destined for television. If necessary, choose the Flicker Removal option in the Field Options dialog box.

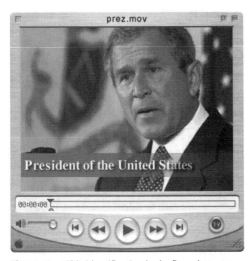

**Figure 16.14** This identification looks fine when you can see the entire image.

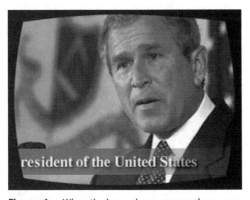

**Figure 16.15** When the image is overscanned, you may lose important elements.

# Overscan and Safe Zones

The method used to scan the image onto the screen—progressive or interlaced—is just one important difference between computer and television monitors. Whereas computer monitors display the entire video image, televisions *overscan* the video image, cropping off the outer edges of the screen. To make matters worse, the amount of overscan differs slightly from television to television (**Figures 16.14** and **16.15**).

To ensure that important elements (such as titles) remain visible when displayed on a television screen, make sure you keep these elements within television's so-called *safe zones*. You can view safe-zone guides in the source and program views of the Monitor window (see Chapter 5, "Viewing Clips in the Monitor Window") and in the Adobe Title Designer (see Chapter 12, "Creating Titles").

In video, the inner 90 percent of the complete image is considered to be *action safe*— that is, everything within that area is likely to appear on most television screens. The inner 80 percent is considered to be *title safe*. Because you can't afford to lose any of the title's content, the title-safe area includes a necessary safety margin. The safe-zone guides are for your reference only; they aren't added to the source image and don't appear in the program output.

# Safe Colors

Yet another difference between computer and video monitors lies in the way that they display colors. Video's native color model has a much narrower range, or *gamut*, than the RGB model used by computers. As a result, computer programs usually allow you to select much more saturated colors than video allows. Anything more saturated than video's *safe* colors will appear to be noisy or even bleed into areas where they doesn't belong when displayed on a video monitor.

In the color picker, a warning sign appears when you've selected a color that's not a video-safe color. Click the warning sign to shift the color to a safe color automatically when Premiere Pro renders the color (**Figure 16.16**).

You can adjust a clip's brightness and color levels for video by applying the broadcast colors effect or using the Video Limiter option in the Color Corrector filter. (See Chapter 13, "Working with Effects," to learn how to add effects to clips; see Chapter 14, "Effects in Action," for details about the Color Corrector filter.)

### ✔ Tip

■ Premiere Pro is capable of processing video using a YUV color model. See the sidebar "I Love a Parade: RGB and YCbCr" in Chapter 5.

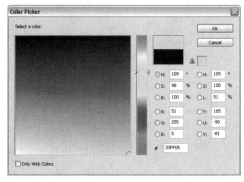

**Figure 16.16** Click the warning icon to shift the color to a video-safe color on export.

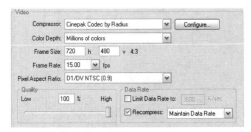

**Figure 16.17** Set the frame size in the Video panel of the New Project or Export Movie Settings (shown here) dialog box.

# Frame Size

*Frame size* refers to the number of pixels used to describe the video image. The number of pixels that equals full-screen video depends on the standard used by your capture or playback device. These are the most common frame sizes for full-screen video:

**640 × 480:** Full-screen, square-pixel standard for computers, used by some lower-end capture cards.

**720 × 486:** Nonsquare pixels used by standard-resolution professional video; also called D-1.

**720 × 480:** Nonsquare pixels used by the DV standard.

**720 × 576:** PAL video standard.

When you export frame sizes smaller than full-screen video, choose an even fraction of the full-screen pixel size (making sure to take the image aspect ratio and pixel aspect ratio into account) (**Figure 16.17**). Uneven fractions of frame sizes are more difficult for the computer to process.

## ✔ Tips

- In video, it's common to refer to frame size as *resolution*. However, the term *resolution* has a slightly different meaning for video than it does for print media. Although the number of pixels in full-screen video can differ, you can think of the display size as being fixed; it's full-screen, regardless of the size of the television screen. Therefore, it's best to think of digital video in terms of pixel dimensions, not pixels per inch.

- People who are accustomed to print media are often disappointed to learn that standard-definition video always translates to a mere 72 dpi. If you want to print large, high-quality images of your video (for a press kit or poster, for example), take production stills with a megapixel digital camera or a film camera.

# Image Aspect Ratios

*Aspect ratio* refers to the dimensions of the video frame, expressed as a ratio of the width to the height (horizontal and vertical aspects). Most video uses a 4:3 aspect ratio, but with the advent of new video standards, the 16:9 aspect ratio is becoming more common (**Figures 16.18** and **16.19**).

**Figure 16.18** Video in the 4:3 aspect ratio is still prevalent.

**Figure 16.19** Increasingly, video is shown in a 16:9 aspect ratio, which matches a common motion-picture aspect ratio. Premiere Pro supports both 4:3 and 16:9.

**Figure 16.20** When a clip and the program's aspect ratio don't match, you can scale the clip so it leaves borders...

**Figure 16.21** ...or you can scale it to crop the edges.

**Figure 16.22** Alternatively, the clip's horizontal and vertical aspects can be scaled separately, distorting the image.

Sometimes, it's necessary to resize your footage to fit in the program's image dimensions. If the source clip's aspect ratio doesn't match the program's aspect ratio, you're faced with a choice. If you scale it to fit in the confines of the program, the screen will include empty borders (**Figure 16.20**), or if you scale it to remove the borders, its edges will be cropped by the screen (**Figure 16.21**). Alternatively, you can change the source clip's aspect ratio to match the program, which results in a distorted image (**Figure 16.22**).

## ✔ Tips

- Movies shot in wide-screen formats are often *letterboxed*, or framed so that the entire width of the image fits onto a television screen. Because television's 4:3 aspect ratio isn't as wide as that of the movie, letterboxing results in a black border at the top and bottom of the screen. The Title Designer includes a preset you can superimpose over video to simulate a letterbox with a 16:9 aspect ratio.

- The 16:9 aspect ratio isn't the only aspect ratio found in film. Over the years, a number of aspect ratios have been used.

IMAGE ASPECT RATIOS

# Pixel Aspect Ratio

Different video formats can capture and display the same full-screen, 4:3 image using different pixel dimensions. Whereas certain (generally older) capture cards create a full-screen, 4:3 image using 640 × 480 pixels, DV captures the same image using 720 × 480. How is this possible? Even though their image aspect ratios are the same, their pixel aspect ratios (PARs) are different. The former uses square pixels, or a PAR of 1 (**Figure 16.23**); the latter uses nonsquare pixels, or a PAR of 0.9 (**Figure 16.24**).

Image distortion can occur when a source clip uses a pixel aspect ratio different from the one used by your display monitor. A still taken from DV footage (which uses 720 × 480 nonsquare pixels), for example, is distorted when you display it in an image-editing program that displays square pixels (**Figure 16.25**). Conversely, a still image created at 720 × 480—but using square pixels—will be distorted when it's displayed at DV resolution, which uses nonsquare pixels. Some programs, like Premiere Pro, After Effects, and Photoshop, can detect and correct for this type of distortion automatically; otherwise, you have to correct it by resizing the image. If possible, prevent the problem by using consistent image aspect and pixel aspect ratios.

## ✔ Tip

- When Premiere Pro automatically reconciles the difference between the pixel aspect ratios of the source media and the project, it does so by consulting a set of rules. You can view—and even edit— these rules by opening the text file Interpretation Rules.txt in Premiere's plug-in folder.

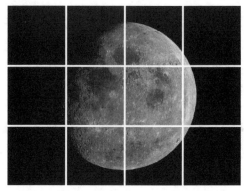

**Figure 16.23** This example illustrates how square pixels can be used to form an image with a 4:3 aspect ratio.

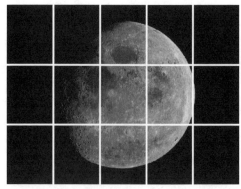

**Figure 16.24** This example illustrates how nonsquare pixels form an image with a 4:3 aspect ratio.

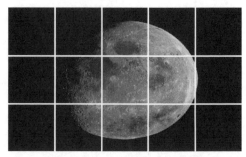

**Figure 16.25** An image created with nonsquare pixels is distorted when displayed with square pixels.

**Figure 16.26** Typically, you specify an image bit depth when you export a clip or sequence.

# Image Bit Depth

Computers store information in discrete quantities called *bits*. *Bit depth* indicates the number of bits used to describe a single pixel. A higher bit depth produces more colors in an image and, consequently, higher picture quality. The RGB color format assigns 8 bits for each color channel—red, green, and blue—for 24-bit color. A 24-bit image contains millions of colors. If an alpha channel is present, it also uses 8 bits, for a total of 32 bits—often referred to as *millions+ of colors*. Regardless of the bit depth of the source clips, Premiere Pro always uses 32 bits to process video.

Typically, you specify an image bit depth when you export a clip or sequence (**Figure 16.26**). Depending on the codec you use, you can choose any (or none) of the following bit depths:

**256 Colors (8-bit color):** Produces a grainy appearance (for people who enjoy the retro-aesthetic of a severely limited palette).

**Thousands of Colors (16-bit color):** Suitable for some multimedia.

**Millions of Colors (24-bit color):** Produces the best image quality.

**Millions+ of Colors (32-bit color):** Preserves the alpha channel.

# Compression

Simply put, *compression* is the science of storing large amounts of data in small packages. Without compression, digital video would be impractical for all but the most powerful computer systems. A single uncompressed frame of full-screen video consumes nearly 1 MB of storage. Capturing and playing back 30 uncompressed frames per second is beyond the capability of most hard disks and processors; the data rate (or flow of information) is simply too high.

Fortunately, various compression schemes have been devised to reduce the file sizes and data rates of digital video and audio. In addition, add-on capture cards and fast drives can enable your computer to process relatively high-quality, high-data-rate video files. The DV format accomplishes its compression in the camera, reducing the data rate to a level most modern computers can handle without extra hardware.

## ✔ Tips

- Technically speaking, even footage shot in the professional Betacam SP format undergoes certain types of compression when it's recorded. When it comes to editing, *uncompressed* usually means avoiding any additional compression. Uncompressed nonlinear editing systems are available but generally are used only for high-end broadcast work.

- You could fill books—others have—on the topic of compression. This chapter merely touches on the subject enough to ground your knowledge of editing with Premiere Pro.

- The term *compression* is also used in audio, to refer to the process for reducing frequency bandwidth. In the Audio Effects folder, you'll find a Multiband Compressor filter.

**Figure 16.27** Codecs for a given format are listed in the Compressor drop-down menu of the Export Movie Settings dialog box.

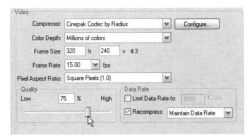

**Figure 16.28** Within each codec, use a Quality slider to control the amount of compression applied.

# Codecs

*Codec* stands for *compressor/decompressor. Compressor* refers to the method of encoding a file and is synonymous with capturing and rendering. *Decompressor* refers to the method for decoding a file and is associated with playback. *Codec* denotes a particular compression scheme—a method of compressing and decompressing a file.

In general, you have a choice of software and hardware codecs. Premiere Pro includes several software-based codecs; others are available as software plug-ins (**Figure 16.27**).

For most high-quality video capture and playback, however, you need a hardware-assisted codec. If your hardware capture card and its software are installed properly, its codec appears in the Compressor menu of the Video panel of the Settings dialog box.

When you're exporting video using a given codec, you usually can control the amount of compression applied by using a Quality slider (**Figure 16.28**). Or you can define a top limit for the data rate (see the next section, "Data Rates").

When you're exporting to videotape, choosing a codec is relatively easy. For movie output, your choice is more difficult. Fortunately, both the Export Movie Settings and Transcoder dialog boxes offer presets that can greatly simplify your choices. Presets are also available when you choose to export to DVD.

## Cards and Codecs

Some capture cards also offer a software-only version of the codec. Although the software codec usually can't enable you to play back the clip smoothly, it does allow you to open and process the file on computers that don't have the necessary hardware.

Codec technology changes rapidly. Visit the Web sites of codec developers to stay up-to-date.

# Data Rates

The file size of a clip relates directly to its *data rate*—the amount of information that the computer must process each second as it plays back the clip. Most of the video and audio settings you choose influence the data rate of clips. In addition, some video codecs allow you to define the maximum data rate for the clip's frames (**Figures 16.29** and **16.30**). You set a data rate according to the limitations of the playback device and the specifications of the codec.

**Figure 16.29** Some codecs allow you to set a maximum data rate in the Export Movie Settings dialog box.

## ✔ Tips

- Data rates are expressed in terms of data over time. But pay attention to the measurements being used. Although video data rates are most often expressed in megabytes per second (MBps), they can also be expressed in megabits per second (Mbps), kilobytes per second (KBps), kilobits per second (Kbps), or even kilobytes per frame (KB/frame). Note that MPEG2 settings typically refer to data rate as *bit rate*, in Mbps.

- The DV format has a 3.6 MBps data rate and doesn't require an exceptionally fast processor and hard disk to play back smoothly. Uncompressed (standard-resolution NTSC) video, on the other hand, has a data rate of about 900 Kb/frame (that's per frame, not per second). In addition to a hardware capture device that handles uncompressed video, you'll need a fast computer with a very fast, high-capacity hard disk.

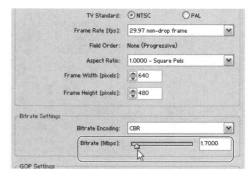

**Figure 16.30** You can limit the data rate of other codecs using similar controls in the Transcode Settings dialog box.

**Figure 16.31** In the Keyframe and Rendering panel of the Export Movie Settings dialog box, you can specify keyframing options (if the codec provides for them).

## ✔ Tips

- Other codecs include parameters similar to keyframes for controlling frame differencing. For example, MPEG codecs include controls for variables such as M Frames, N Frames, and GOPs. Consult the Adobe Premiere Pro Online Help System or other documentation dealing with MPEG compression for more information.

- You can view a data rate graph for any clip by using the Get Properties command. Choose File > Get Properties For. From the submenu, choose File to get properties for any file or choose Selection to get properties for the current selection. The graph can help you troubleshoot playback problems.

- Working with keyframes intelligently requires a strong understanding of the codec and compression, as well as a great deal of experimentation.

# Keyframes

Many codecs—especially those designed for low data rates—use keyframes to optimize compression while maintaining the highest-possible image quality. Keyframes are essential to a compression technique called *frame differencing*. (The term *keyframe* in this context has a different meaning than when it's used in reference to animation; see Chapter 13, "Working with Effects.")

In frame differencing, keyframes act as reference frames to which subsequent frames are compared. Rather than describe every frame completely, frame differencing achieves more efficient compression by describing only the changes between keyframes.

Keyframes are most effective when the image differs greatly from the preceding frame. Some codecs allow you to set the frequency of keyframes or to insert keyframes at markers and edits in the Timeline window (**Figure 16.31**). In addition, some codecs insert keyframes automatically when the image changes significantly. A greater number of keyframes tends to increase image quality as well as file size. Fewer keyframes usually results in decreased file size but lower image quality. But this isn't always the case; you should learn about the particular codec.

# Audio Sample Rate

Analog signals are described by a continuous fluctuation of voltage. The analog signal is converted to a digital signal by being measured periodically, or *sampled*. If you think of the original audio as a curve, then you can think of the digital audio as a connect-the-dots version of that curve (**Figures 16.32 and 16.33**). The more dots (samples) you have, the more accurately you can reproduce the original curve.

*Sample rate* describes the number of times audio is sampled to approximate the original analog sound. Sample rates are expressed in samples per second, or hertz (Hz); 1,000 hertz is called a kilohertz (kHz). The higher the sample rate, the larger the file.

Premiere Pro offers most standard sample rates, depending on the format you choose and on your system (**Figure 16.34**). Some of the most common sample rates are as follows:

**48,000 Hz:** Equivalent to DAT or Digital Betacam; not always supported by sound or video cards; used by some DV cameras.

**44,100 Hz:** Equivalent to CD, appropriate for music; used by some DV cameras.

**32,000 Hz:** The sample rate used by some DV cameras.

**22,050 Hz:** A good compromise between file size and quality.

**11,025 Hz:** Adequate for narration.

**8,000 Hz:** Achieves low data rates; suitable for some Web applications.

**5,000 Hz:** Achieves the lowest data rates but delivers the poorest quality; suitable for some Web applications.

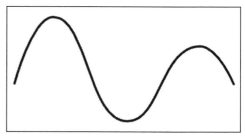

**Figure 16.32** You can think of analog audio as a continuous curve. Analog is more detailed but more difficult to copy exactly.

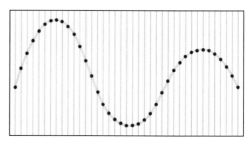

**Figure 16.33** Digital audio *samples*, or measures, the audio at discrete intervals.

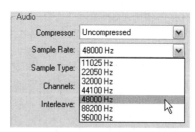

**Figure 16.34** You can find options for the audio sample rate in the Audio panel of the Export Movie Settings and Export Audio Settings dialog boxes.

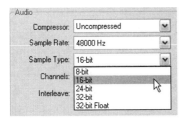

**Figure 16.35** You can specify audio bit depth in the Sample Type drop-down menu in the Audio panel of the Export Movie Settings and Export dialog boxes.

# Audio Bit Depth

*Audio bit depth* refers to the number of bits used to describe each audio sample. Bit depth affects the range of sound the audio file can reproduce, from silence to the loudest sound. This range is known as the *signal-to-noise ratio* (s/n), which can be measured in decibels (dB). Although higher bit depths may seem excessive, they're usually desirable. That's because processing audio requires the extra precision to minimize errors.

Premiere Pro and many other programs express this range as bit depth and allow you to choose the one that's most appropriate for your needs. In the Audio panel of the Export Movie Settings dialog box, bit depth is referred to as *sample type* (**Figure 16.35**). Bit depths include the following:

**8-bit:** Produces a dynamic range equivalent to 48 dB; similar to FM radio broadcasts.

**16-bit:** Produces a dynamic range equivalent to 96 dB.

**24-bit:** Produces a dynamic range equivalent to 144 dB.

**32-bit:** Achieves 24 bits of precision, which produces a dynamic range equivalent to 144 dB. The remaining 8 bits are used for overhead.

**32-bit Float:** Achieves 24 bits of precision, which produces a dynamic range equivalent to 24 bits, or 144 dB. The remaining 8 bits are used for overhead. *Float* indicates that this option uses floating-point calculations, a method that can handle extremely long numbers with great precision and, in audio applications, prevent clipping.

## ✔ Tip

- Some audio codecs reduce the sample rate and bit depth even more than the standard options do.

# Audio Channels

Multiple audio sources can be recorded and stored as a single set of data, or they can be recorded separately and stored in discrete *channels.* A monophonic (mono) audio file contains a single channel; a stereophonic audio file contains two discrete channels; 5.1 surround contains five discrete channels as well as an optional LFE (low-frequency effects) channel that contains additional low-frequency data not present in the five main channels.

As you learned in Chapter 11, "Mixing Audio," you can redistribute each audio track's channels between or among the master track's channels. Outputting the master track's channels through two or more speakers can help give the sound a sense of space, or direction.

For this reason, the main sequence's master track should contain the number of channels you want to output. You can specify a sequence's master audio track when you create it, in the New Sequence dialog box (**Figure 16.36**).

When you export audio to a file, you must specify the number of channels it will contain. Usually, the channels contained in the sequence's master track are transferred to the exported file. However, you sometimes *mix down* the channels, combining channels in the source sequence into fewer channels in the exported file. The Audio panel of the Export Movie Settings and Export Audio Settings dialog boxes contains a Channels drop-down menu (**Figure 16.37**).

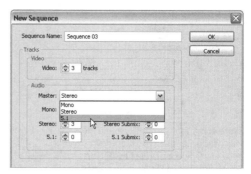

**Figure 16.36** You can specify a sequence's master audio track when you create it, in the New Sequence dialog box.

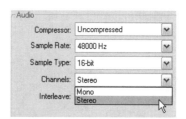

**Figure 16.37** The Audio panel of the Export Movie Settings and Export Audio Settings dialog boxes contains a Channels drop-down menu.

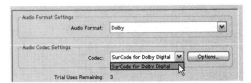

**Figure 16.38** Exporting to some formats using the Adobe Media Encoder allows you to specify Dolby audio and SurCode for Dolby Digital.

When you're exporting to MPEG1 or MPEG2 using the Adobe Media Encoder, you can specify SurCode for Dolby Digital (**Figure 16.38**). Developed by Minnetonka Audio under license from Dolby Laboratories, SurCode for Dolby Digital uses Dolby's AC-3 standard, which can encode multichannel audio into a single, low-bit-rate stream. AC-3 enables you to limit the file size of multichannel audio while retaining quality, making it ideal for use with DVDs with 5.1 surround.

### ✔ Tips

- Several audio filters manipulate audio channels. You can also use the pan controls in the timeline or in the Audio Mixer window to pan or balance audio channels. Chapter 13 discusses how to apply and adjust any filter; audio mixing is covered in Chapter 11.

- The SurCode for Dolby Digital plug-in is a trial version. You get three trial uses; to continue using it, you'll need to purchase it. To find purchasing information, click the Options button when SurCode for Dolby Digital is selected.

**AUDIO CHANNELS**

# Audio Interleave

*Audio interleave* determines how often audio information is loaded into RAM and inserted, or *interleaved*, among frames of video. Previous versions of Premiere referred to audio interleave as *audio blocks* because blocks of audio are interleaved with blocks of video.

In the Audio panel of the Export Movie Settings dialog box, you can specify the amount of audio interleave in the Interleave drop-down menu (**Figure 16.39**). A low value needs less RAM but requires the computer to process audio more often. A large value results in larger audio blocks that are processed less often but require more RAM. If the audio falters during playback, you can adjust the interleave value.

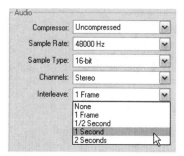

**Figure 16.39** In the Audio panel of the Export Movie Settings dialog box, you can specify the amount of audio interleave in the Interleave drop-down menu.

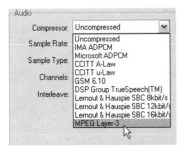

**Figure 16.40** For a given file type, you can choose an audio codec to lower file sizes and data rates. In this figure, the Compressor drop-down menu (in the Export Audio Settings' Audio panel) lists the codecs available for the Windows Waveform file type.

**Figure 16.41** A few codecs, like the QDesign 2 music codec, contain additional options for adjusting the audio compression. Click the Advanced Settings button in the Audio settings panel to access them.

# Audio Compression

If you plan to export your program to videotape, you probably don't need to compress the audio. Audio file sizes and data rates, however, often exceed the limitations of other media, such as CD-ROM or Web delivery.

Audio codecs are designed for the type of audio used in your program or clip, such as voice or music. Some codecs achieve a specific compression ratio, which is part of the codec's name (MACE 3:1, for example). Choose the codec that's best suited to your purposes (**Figure 16.40**). A few codecs offer additional options; click the Advanced Settings button in the Audio settings panel to access them. For example, the QDesign 2 music codec contains options that adjust the audio compression (**Figure 16.41**).

## ✔ Tip

- MPEG Layer-3 is the more official name for the popular MP3 format.

**AUDIO COMPRESSION**

# INDEX

/ (forward slash key), 170
3D effects, 504
4:3 aspect ratio, 21, 558
5.1 audio, 198, 312, 331–332
6.1 audio, 332
7.1 audio, 332
16:9 aspect ratio, 21, 558–559
24-bit images, 561
24P/24PA interlacing, 545
24P video, 552
32 kHz audio, 21
48 kHz audio, 21

## A

AAF (Advanced Authoring Format), 540
absolute time, 126
action-safe area, 555
actions, 12–14
adjust filters, 409, 489–495
Adobe After Effects, 226–227
Adobe Media Encoder, 532–539, 569
alert icon, 15
aliasing, 67
Align buttons, 350
Align Objects command, 404
alignment
    clips, 163
    objects, 404
    text, 366–367
    transitions, 274, 283–285
All Scopes option, 134, 136
Alpha Adjust filter, 473
alpha-based keys, 472–473
alpha channel, 106, 134, 469–470
Alpha option, 134
analog video, 36–37

anchor points, 377, 437
animated GIFs, 528–529
animation, 413, 421–423, 519
anti-aliasing, 67, 290
Application Data folder, 19
Application shortcut set, 10
Arc tool, 376
artifacts, 233, 504, 524, 553
ASIO (Audio Stream Input/Output), 310–311
aspect ratio
    image, 558–559
    pixel, 66, 105–106, 560
attributes, 356. *See also* properties
audio
    balance, 320, 330–331
    bit depth, 567
    compression, 562, 571
    countdown beeps, 76
    decibels, 315
    exporting, 530–531, 569
    gain, 315–316
    hardware options, 310–311
    In/Out points, 152
    links to, 262–263
    mixing. *See* mixing audio
    playing while scrubbing, 297
    presets, 342
    processing order, 308
    quality of, 329
    sample rates, 152, 566
    sends, 336–338
    settings, 522, 543–544, 566–571
    types of, 21, 198, 312, 331–332
    volume. *See* volume
    waveforms. *See* waveforms
audio blocks, 570
audio channels, 308, 312, 568–569

audio clips. *See also* clips
  linking, 263
  mono, 313–314
  opening, 122–123
  stereo, 313–314
  viewing property values for, 415
  volume. *See* volume
audio conform files, 113, 304
audio display format, 550
audio effects, 324, 339–343
audio files, 304, 530–531
Audio Gain command, 315–316
audio interleave, 570
audio keyframes, 344
audio mixer, 321–346. *See also* mixing audio
  automation options, 309, 333–334, 346–347
  balancing audio, 330–331
  customizing, 323–326
  described, 3, 321
  fade controls, 321, 330, 336–337
  keyframing, 309
  mixing audio, 331–332, 345–347
  monitoring tracks, 327, 345–346
  muting tracks, 327
  opening, 322
  optimizing with, 322, 344
  panning, 330
  recording with, 328–329
  routing track output, 335
  showing/hiding effects in, 325
  soloing tracks, 327
  track effects, 339–343
  VU meters, 327
  working with sends, 336–338
audio pitch, 229
Audio Playback options, 296
audio previews, 304
audio samples, 152, 191, 550, 566
Audio Stream Input/Output (ASIO), 310–311
audio tracks
  5.1, 198
  channels, 308, 312, 568–569
  effects, 339–343
  master, 21–22, 335
  monitoring, 201
  mono, 198, 312
  muting, 327
  routing output, 335
  showing/hiding, 325
  soloing, 201, 327
  specifying type, 308
  stereo, 198, 312
  submix, 312, 328, 337
  unlinking, 262
  volume, 319

audio transitions, 317–318
audio units, 152, 190–191, 236, 323
audiocassette tapes, 36
Auto-Save feature, 26–27
Automatch Time setting, 334
Automate to Sequence command, 176–178
AVID Xpress DV, 11

## B

background video, 355
backup files, 26
balance
  audio, 320, 330–331
  black/white, 496
  color, 496
Bars and Tone option, 74, 77
batch capturing, 39
batch lists, 39, 60–61
Bézier curves, 378–382, 450–456, 497
Bézier objects, 384–386
Bézier paths, 377, 381–383
bins, 96–101, 465–466
bit depth, 561, 567
bit rates, 516, 564
black and coded tape, 512
black video, 74, 77
black/white balance, 496
bluescreen, 480
blur effects, 494–495
Blur filter, 494
borders, 289–290
bounding box, 360, 376
brightness, 4, 496–497, 556
Broadcast Colors filter, 506

## C

Calculate Progress window, 112
camera/camcorder. *See* video camera/deck
Cancel button, 31
capture cards, 20, 36–37, 544, 563
Capture window, 3, 40–44, 48
capturing video, 33–61
  in background, 38
  batch capturing, 39
  capture options, 39, 42–43
  device control. *See* device control
  DV vs. digitized analog, 36–37
  optimizing system for, 38, 44
  overview, 33–35
  playback controls, 48
  setting capture location, 44
  settings, 22, 42–43

timecode option, 39
CD-ROM, outputting to, 509
Channel filters, 494
channel map transitions, 292
channels
    5.1, 312
    alpha, 106, 134, 469–470
    audio, 308, 312, 568–569
    described, 322
    LFE, 312, 331–332
    mixing down, 569
    mono, 312, 568
    output, 310
    specifying, 21–22
    stereo, 312, 568
chapter links, 210–211
Chroma key, 478–479
Chroma option, 136–137
chrominance, 140, 477–480
clapper board, 263
Clear History command, 14
clip-based editing, 308
clip instances, 120
clip markers
    adding, 154–155
    clearing, 156–157
    cuing to, 156
    numbered, 154–155, 157
    setting, 153–155
    unnumbered, 154
Clipped-Corner Rectangle tool, 376
clips
    adding by dragging, 146–147, 161–165
    adding from Project window, 164
    adding with Automate to Sequence, 176–178
    aligning, 163
    audio. See audio clips
    bins for, 96–101
    capturing. See capturing video
    contiguous, 215
    copying, 100–102, 224–227
    cuing, 126–127
    cutting, 224
    deleting, 92, 218–219
    described, 17
    dragging/dropping, 164
    duration of, 215, 229, 231
    enabling/disabling, 220
    extracting, 242
    finding, 104, 265, 271
    groups, 216–217
    importing files as, 62–63
    inserting, 239–240
    inverting, 473
    labels, 90–91

linked. See linked clips
    managing, 79–113
    match-frame, 266
    missing, 29–31
    naming/renaming, 103, 113
    navigating, 128–130
    noncontiguous, 215
    offline, 29–31, 108–109, 113
    online, 29
    organizing in bins, 96–99
    pasting, 101–102, 224–227
    playing. See playback
    positioning in program view, 438
    previewing. See previews
    properties, 107, 212
    repositioning, 473
    rotating, 440
    scaling, 430, 438–439, 473, 559
    selecting in timeline, 214–215, 217
    sequence, 120–121
    sliding, 249, 251
    slipping, 249–250
    sorting, 89, 177
    source, 118, 120–121, 153, 161, 265
    speed of, 168, 171, 228–231
    splitting, 221–223
    status of, 29
    subclips, 102
    synthetic media, 74–77
    thumbnails, 81–82
    trimming, 172, 243–245
    unused, 113
    video, 263, 414
    viewing, 119–121
    zooming in/out, 163
CMX3600 format, 541
codecs, 20, 511, 563–565, 571
color
    artifacts, 504
    balance, 496
    bleeds, 140
    borders, 289
    broadcast, 506
    chrominance, 140, 477–480
    correcting. See color correction
    dithered, 528
    gradients, 388–389
    HSL, 496–497, 502
    labels, 90–91
    NTSC-safe, 138, 140, 387
    objects, 355
    RGB, 139, 469, 480, 502
    saturation, 140, 504
    vectorscopes, 134–135, 139–140
    video-safe, 556

**INDEX**

color *(continued)*
    Web-safe, 528
    YUV, 139, 556
color bars, 77, 138–140
color correction, 496–503
Color Corrector filter, 496–503
color matte, 75
color picker, 479, 556
color stop, 388
comments, 210–211
Composite Video option, 134
compression
    audio, 562, 571
    codecs, 20, 511, 563–565, 571
    described, 562
    video, 34, 562–563
computer monitors, 551
context-clicking, 7
context menus, 7
contrast, 491–492
control points, 377, 381–383
Convert Point tool, 378, 380, 383
corner points, 378
countdown, standard, 76–77
crawling text, 373–375
Crop filter, 536
cross-dissolves, 292
cross-fades, 317–318
Crystallize effect, 408
CTI (current time indicator)
    cuing, 121, 207, 209, 419, 445
    described, 117
    snapping, 208
    splitting clips at, 223
    zooming in/out, 203
Current Style swatch, 350, 370
current time indicator. *See* CTI
curves, 378–382, 450–456, 497
Custom Settings tab, 22
custom workspaces, 5–6

## D

data rates, 34–35, 564
decibels, 315
deinterlacing, 536, 553
Delete Render Files command, 305
deleting items
    clips, 92, 218–219
    gaps, 218–219
    items in Project window, 92
    keyframes, 447
    media files, 109
    presets, 539

preview files, 305–306
ripple deletes, 218–219
strokes, 396
tracks, 198–199
device control
    cuing tape to specified timecode, 48
    described, 39
    settings, 23, 46–47
    timecode, 39
    using, 45–47
devices. *See also* video camera/deck
    audio options, 310–311
    IEEE 1394, 35
    input/output, 310
    playback via, 295–297
    viewing sequences with, 295–297
dialog, 155
Difference Matte key, 486
Dip to Black transition, 273
disks
    boot, 44
    calculating space, 112
    scratch, 44, 302–303
    space requirements, 37, 113, 304
    specifying for captures, 44
    speed of, 304
displace transitions, 292
dissolves, 273
Distort filters, 495
distortion, 495, 560
Distribute buttons, 350
Distribute Objects command, 405
distributing objects, 405
dithering, 528
Draft Quality setting, 132
drop-frame timecode, 46, 548–549
drop shadows, 397
dropped frames, 46, 548–549
DV – NTSC presets, 21
DV – PAL presets, 21
DV devices. *See* devices; video camera/deck
DV formats, 20, 37
DV Playback settings, 295–297
DV video, 36–37. *See also* video
DVCam format, 37
DVCPro format, 37
DVD
    exporting to, 509, 514–517
    presets, 517
dynamic range, 567

# E

Echo filter, 505
edges, 243
edit-decision lists (EDLs), 507, 541
editing
    clip-based, 308
    by dragging, 238–242, 254, 256
    with home keys, 175
    keyboard modifiers for, 238, 241
    in Monitor window, 146–147, 165, 168–172
    nondestructive, 17
    nonlinear systems, 293
    offline, 29
    online, 29
    split edit points, 151
    storyboard, 84, 147, 176–178
    text, 365
    in timeline, 189–233
    track-based, 308
    in Trim window, 252–257
edits
    applying trimmed edits, 257
    cuing to, 207, 209
    described, 209
    extract, 242
    four-point, 146, 166, 168, 171–172
    insert. See insert edits
    match-frame, 223
    overlay, 239–240, 246
    previewing in Trim window, 257
    rearrange, 238–239
    recycle, 238–239, 241
    ripple, 245–247, 253–254, 261, 285
    rolling, 246, 248, 254–256
    slide, 249, 251
    slip, 249–250
    split, 258–261
    three-point, 146, 166–167, 169–170
EDLs (edit-decision lists), 507, 541
Effect Controls palette, 4, 279–282
Effect Controls window
    adjusting motion effects, 413
    adjusting standard effects, 413
    changing keyframe property values, 446
    cuing CTI to keyframes, 445
    customizing, 431–432
    deleting keyframes, 447
    moving keyframes in time, 448
    opening, 426
    selecting keyframes, 446
    setting keyframes in, 441–444
    showing/hiding categories, 427
    showing/hiding timeline area, 428
    time ruler zoom range, 432

viewing properties in, 412, 426–428
effects, 407–459. See also filters
    3D, 504
    adding to clips, 424–425
    audio, 324, 339–343
    blur, 494–495
    custom settings, 430
    default settings, 429
    direct manipulation, 436
    disabling, 420, 429
    fading, 468–470
    fixed, 408
    inherent, 408
    keying, 468–471
    LFE, 312, 320
    motion. See motion effects
    multiple, 433–434
    obsolete, 408
    Opacity, 408
    order of, 433–434
    presets, 462–466
    properties, 410–420, 426–428, 443
    resetting, 429
    standard, 409, 424–425
    strobe, 505
    track, 339–343
    types of, 408–409
Effects palette, 4, 268–271
Ellipse tool, 376
Enable Record button, 328
error messages, 15
events, 15
Export to Tape command, 509, 512–513
exporting. See also output creation
    AAF files, 540
    with Adobe Media Encoder presets, 533–535
    audio, 569
    audio-only files, 530–531
    batch lists, 60–61
    to CD-ROM, 509
    to DVD, 509, 514–517
    EDLs, 541
    file types for, 511
    frames, 525–527
    movie files, 518–519
    to other programs, 510
    settings, 508, 520–522
    still images, 523–527
    video files, 518–519
    video-safe colors and, 556
    to videotape, 509, 512–513
    to Web, 510
extensions, 19, 72, 302
extract edits, 242
extract function, 166, 173, 175, 239

extract inserts, 242
extract overlays, 242
Eyedropper tool, 290, 389

**F**

Factory Defaults, 9
fade controls, 321
fades
    with audio mixer, 321, 330, 336–337
    cross-fades, 317–318
    Dip to Black, 273
    pan/fader controls, 338
    post-fader sends, 336–337
    pre-fader sends, 336–337
fading effects, 468–470
field artifacts, 233, 524, 553
Field Options command, 553–554
field rendering, 552–553
file formats. *See also specific formats*
    Adobe Media Encoder, 533–535
    DV, 20, 37
    for exporting, 511
    MPEG, 509, 535, 569
files
    audio, 304, 530–531
    audio conform, 113
    backing up, 26
    deleting, 109, 305–306
    filmstrip, 527
    GIF, 524, 528–529
    Illustrator, 67
    importing, 62–63, 67–71
    media, 109, 113, 228
    missing, 29–31
    moving, 30
    names, 30
    offline, 29–31
    Photoshop, 66, 68–71
    preview. *See* preview files
    project, 30
    properties, 107
    render, 293, 298
    source. *See* source files
fills, 386–387. *See also* gradients
filmstrip files, 527
filters, 471–506. *See also* effects; *specific filters*
    adjust, 489–495
    audio, 569
    channel, 494
    color correction, 496–503
    distort, 495
    image control, 495
    keying, 471

matte, 487–488
noise, 504, 567
perspective, 504
pixelate, 504
render, 505
standard, 307
stylize, 505
time, 505
transform, 506
video, 506
Final Cut Pro, 11
finding items
    clips, 104, 265, 271
    in Effects palette, 271
    source clips, 265
FireWire devices, 35
floating-point calculations, 567
folders
    Application Data, 19
    Auto-Save, 26–27
    My Documents, 303
    Premiere Pro Preview Files, 302–303
Font Browser, 368–369
fonts, 366–369
footage
    capturing. *See* capturing video
    interpreting, 105–106
    presets, 21
    standard, 21
    synchronizing, 263
    widescreen, 21
footage files, 113
formats. *See* file formats
forward slash key (/), 170
four-point editing, 146, 166, 168, 171–172
Frame Advance control, 124
Frame Back control, 124
frame differencing, 565
Frame Hold command, 232–233
frame rates, 34, 105, 505, 545–546
frames
    dropped, 47, 548–549
    exporting, 525–527
    freeze, 232–233
    match, 121, 266
    moving forward/backward, 124
    poster, 92, 95
    size, 557
    values, 126
freeze frames, 232–233
FTP option, 537

# G

gain, 315–316
gamut, 556
ganging, 116, 141–143, 338
gaps, 218–219
garbage keys, 487–488
Garbage Matte filter, 487–488
garbage mattes, 471, 479, 487–488
GIF files, 524, 528–529
gradient wipe transitions, 292
gradients, 388–389. *See also* fills
graphics, 398–399. *See also* images
grayscale, 134, 470
groups, 186, 216–217

# H

handles, 113, 451, 459. *See also* keyframes
head, 243
Help feature, 9
Hi8 videotape, 36
histogram, 490–493
History palette, 2, 13–14
Hold option, 458
Horizontal Type tool, 358
HSL color, 496–497, 502

# I

icon view, 81, 84–85
IEEE 1394 devices, 35
iLink devices, 35
Illustrator files, 67
image control filters, 495
image map transitions, 292
Image Matte key, 482–483
images
    aspect ratio, 558–559
    bit depth, 561
    flipping, 506
    graphics, 398–399
    letterboxed, 559
    overscanned, 555
    safe zones, 555
    still. *See* still images
    superimposing, 467–470
importing, 62–72
    batch lists, 60
    files as clips, 62–63
    Illustrator files, 67
    Photoshop files, 68–71
    projects, 64–65
    still images, 66, 72

vs. opening projects, 64
In/Out points
    adjusting, 243–245
    audio, 152
    changing in time ruler, 150
    clearing in Monitor window, 149
    duration, 148
    edges, 243
    head, 243
    marking in Monitor window, 148–149
    playing clips In to Out, 125
    poster frames and, 95
    ripple-editing, 247
    rolling edits, 248
    setting, 148–150, 152, 170
    slide edits, 249, 251
    slip edits, 249–250
    split edits, 151, 259–261
    tail, 243
    viewing in source view, 148–149
Info palette, 2
Info window, 215
informational messages, 15
insert edits
    described, 166, 178
    editing by dragging, 239–240
    keyboard modifiers, 165
    linked clips and, 170
    performing, 163–164
    vs. overlay edits, 160
insert function, 239
insert icons, 165
Institute of Radio Engineers (IRE), 135, 138
Intensity option, 136
interface, 2
interlaced video, 132, 551–554
interpolation, 444, 450–459
IRE (Institute of Radio Engineers), 135, 138

# J

J-cuts. *See* split edits
J-K-L keyboard combination, 125, 175
Japanese characters, 367
Jog Disk control, 124–125

# K

Keyboard Customization dialog box, 10
keyboard modifiers, 165, 238, 241
keyboard shortcuts
    applications, 10
    AVID Xpress DV, 11
    customizing, 10–11

keyboard shortcuts *(continued)*
  deleting, 11
  for editing, 146–147
  Final Cut Pro, 11
  J-K-L keyboard combination, 125, 175
  naming, 11
  playback controls, 125
  saving set, 11
  tools, 10
  using, 9–11
  viewing in Help, 9
  windows, 10
keyframe icons, 448
keyframe navigator, 411, 417
keyframes
  adding with keyframe navigator, 417
  adding with Pen tool, 416
  Bézier, 454–455
  changing simultaneously, 419
  changing values, 418, 446
  copying values, 448–449
  cuing CTI to, 419, 445
  deleting, 447
  described, 410–411
  interpolation, 444, 450–459
  moving in time, 418, 448
  pasting values, 448–449
  removing, 420
  selecting, 417, 446, 449
  setting in Effect Controls window, 441–444
  setting on transition edges, 443
  settings, 522, 565
  showing/hiding, 319–320, 345, 414–415
  spatial, 450
keyframing, 288, 309, 413
keying effects, 468–471
keying filters, 471
keys
  alpha-based, 472–473
  chrominance-based, 477–480
  garbage, 487–488
  luminance-based, 474–476
  matte-based, 481–486

**L**

L-cuts. *See* split edits
labels, 90–91
Latch mode, 334
latency, 310
layers
  anchor points, 437
  Photoshop files, 68–71
  position of, 437

scaling, 438–439
  sequences, 70–71
leader shots, 77
letterboxing, 559
Levels filter, 490–493
Levels histogram, 490–493
LFE (low-frequency effects), 312, 320
LFE channel, 312, 331–332
lift function, 166, 173–174, 239
lines
  attributes, 385
  direction, 377
  properties, 384–385
Link Audio and Video command, 263
link embedding, 521
linked clips
  audio/video, 161, 215, 262–263
  described, 258
  dragging, 163
  linking clips with media, 109
  linking video and audio, 263
  out-of-sync, 170, 213, 264, 266
  restoring sync, 264, 266
  split edits, 259–261
  unlinking audio and video, 262
  unlinking clips from media, 108–109
  using, 213
  working with, 258–264
links, 108–110
  to audio, 262–263
  breaking, 262
  chapter, 210
  project, 520–521
  to sequence markers, 211
  to video, 262–263
  Web, 210
list view, 81, 86–89
Load Preset, 18–19
log files, 537
logging clips for batch capture, 39
logos, inserting, 398–399
looping playback, 124
low-frequency effects. *See* LFE
luminance, 138, 493
luminance-based keys, 474–476
luminance map transitions, 292

**M**

magnification settings, 133
markers
  clip. *See* clip markers
  comments, 210–211
  described, 153

duration, 211
sequence, 153, 210–211, 515
zero, 95, 155, 232
master audio track, 21
master meters, 326
master tape, 77
master tracks, 21–22, 335
match frames, 121, 266
matte-based keys, 481–486
matte filters, 487–488
media
Adobe Media Encoder, 532–537, 569
deleting, 109
links, 108–110
synthetic, 74–77
media files, 109, 113, 228
memory, 570
MiniDV format, 36–37
mixing audio, 307–346. *See also* audio mixer
5.1 audio, 331–332
adjusting clip gain, 315–316
audio data in Timeline window, 319–320
audio hardware options, 310–311
audio processing order, 308
audio quality, 329
balancing audio, 330–331
converting mono/stereo clips, 313–314
fades/cross-fades, 317–318, 330
nesting sequences, 309
panning, 320, 330
planning for, 308–309
process for, 345–347
routing mixes, 309
routing track output, 335
submix tracks, 312
subtractive mixing, 309
track effects, 339–343
working with sends, 336–338
MJPEG format, 36
Monitor window
clearing In/Out points in, 149
described, 2
display mode, 134–138
marking In/Out points in, 148–149
modifying, 118
performing edits in, 146–147, 165, 168–172
playback controls, 124–125
using, 116–117
viewing clips in, 115–143
monitors
calibration, 496
computer, 551–552
reference, 118, 141–142
television, 131, 295, 551–552
waveform, 134–135, 138–140

mono clips, 313–314
mono mixes, 310
mono tracks, 198, 312
motion blur, 495
motion effects
adjusting in Effect Controls window, 413
problems caused by, 473
slow motion, 231
viewing, 435–436
motion paths, 435, 456
mouse pointer, 245
movies. *See also* video
exporting, 518–519
playing. *See* playback
MP3 format, 571
MPEG-2 transcoded video, 535
MPEG formats, 509, 535, 569
Multiply filter, 476
Multiply key, 475
Multitrack tool, 215
Mute button, 327
muting
audio tracks, 327
sends, 338
My Documents folder, 303

**N**

Name Key Set dialog box, 11
nested sequences, 179, 184–187, 231, 309
New item button, 351
New Project command, 18–19
New Project dialog box, 18–19, 22–23
New Style command, 372
NLEs (nonlinear editing systems), 293
noise filters, 504
noise reduction, 536
nondestructive editing, 17
nonlinear editing systems (NLEs), 293
NTSC format, 46, 136, 138, 545, 548
NTSC presets, 21
NTSC-safe color, 138, 140, 387

**O**

objects
aligning, 404
arranging, 403
Bézier, 384–386
color, 355
distributing, 405
positioning, 402
properties, 356
rotating, 401

objects *(continued)*
  stacking order, 403
  text, 357–359
  transforming, 400–401
Off mode, 333
offline clips, 29–31, 108–109, 113
offline editing, 29
offline files, 29–31
online clips, 29
online editing, 29
online help, 9
opacity, 400, 413, 421–422, 472
Opacity effect, 408
opacity handles, 414
Open Project dialog box, 27
Open Recent Project command, 28
Opteron processors, 408
optimization
  audio keyframes, 344
  computer system, 38, 44
  video capture, 38, 44
  workspace, 322
Out points. *See* In/Out points
output creation, 507–538. *See also* exporting
  Adobe Media Encoder, 532–537
  export options/settings, 508, 520–522
  exporting AAF files, 540
  exporting audio-only files, 530–531
  exporting movie files, 518–519
  exporting still images, 523–527
  exporting to DVD, 509, 514–517
  exporting to other programs, 510
  exporting to videotape, 509, 512–513
  goals of, 509–510
  optimizing for CD-ROM, 509
  for Web delivery, 510
overcranking, 231
overlay edits
  described, 166, 178
  editing by dragging, 239–240
  keyboard modifiers, 165
  performing, 162, 164
  vs. insert edits, 160
Overlay function, 239
overlay icons, 165
overscanned images, 555

## P

PAL format, 46, 545, 552
PAL presets, 21
palettes
  Effect Controls, 4, 279–282
  Effects, 4, 268–271

History, 13–14
Info, 2
viewing as tabs, 8
panning, 320, 330, 338
path text, 363–364
paths
  Bézier, 377, 381–383
  motion, 435
  properties, 384–385
  text, 363–364
pedestal, 136
Pen tools, 379–382, 416, 418
perspective filters, 504
Photoshop files, 66, 68–71, 73
Pinch effect, 408
pixelate filters, 504
pixels
  aspect ratio, 66, 105–106, 560
  bi-linear, 132
  frame size and, 557
  nonsquare, 557, 560
  square, 557, 560
Play button, 329
Play In to Out control, 124–125
Play/Stop control, 124
playback
  in Capture window, 48
  frame movement controls, 124
  jog disk control, 125
  keyboard shortcuts, 125
  looping, 124
  in Monitor window, 124–125
  movie clips, 94–95
  pausing, 125
  playing audio while scrubbing, 297
  playing clips In to Out, 125
  in Project window, 94–95
  quality of, 294–295
  Real-Time Playback options, 296
  reversing, 125, 228–229
  sequences in timeline, 207
  shuttle control, 125
  speed of, 125, 228–231
  starting/stopping, 124–125
  via DV devices, 295–296
playing work area after rendering, 301
Pointilize effect, 408
points
  anchor, 377, 437
  center, 288
  control, 377, 381–383
  corner, 378
  In/Out. *See* In/Out points
  smooth, 377
  split edit, 151

post-fader sends, 336–337
poster frames, 92, 95
pre-fader sends, 336–337
Preferences file, 19
Premiere Pro
    basics, 1–15
    factory defaults, 9
    Help feature, 9
    keyboard shortcuts. *See* keyboard shortcuts
    launching, 19
    quitting, 28
    undo feature, 12
Premiere Pro Preview Files folder, 302–303
Preroll Time feature, 47
preset bins, 465–466
presets
    Adobe Media Encoder, 532–535, 538–539
    audio effects, 342
    built-in, 21
    deleting, 539
    described, 23
    DVD, 517
    effects, 462–466
    footage, 21
    modifying, 538
    naming, 23
    NTSC, 21
    PAL, 21
    projects, 21
    saving, 23, 539
    selecting, 18
    viewing, 538
    workspaces, 5
preview files. *See also* render files
    deleting, 305–306
    described, 298
    including, 113
    managing, 302–306
    modifying, 305–306
    moving, 305
    naming, 302, 306
    obsolete, 305–306
    scratch disks for, 302–303
    storing, 302–304
previews
    audio, 304
    clips, 93–95
    edits, 257
    in Project window, 93–95
    sequences, 293–303
    video, 303
program view
    described, 2, 116
    dragging clips to, 164

image quality of, 294
positioning clips in, 438
rotating clips in, 440
scaling clips/layers in, 438–439
setting spatial properties in, 412, 437–440
using, 116
viewing spatial controls, 436
progressive-scan video, 551–553
Project command, 18
project files, 30
project links, 520–521
Project Manager, 111–113, 306
Project window, 80–113
    adding clips from, 164
    adding Effects Controls palette to, 280
    bins, 96–99
    closing, 19
    deleting items from, 92
    described, 2
    duplicating/copying items in, 100–102
    finding clips, 104
    interpreting footage, 105–106
    labels, 90–91
    preview area, 93–95
    renaming clips, 103
    selecting items in, 92
    unlinking/relinking media, 108–110
    viewing clip properties, 107
    views, 81–89
    working with, 80
projects
    auto-saved, 26–27
    backing up, 26
    closing, 28
    collecting, 111–113
    creating trimmed project, 112
    custom settings, 23
    described, 17, 29
    ending, 19
    importing. *See* importing
    location of, 19
    naming, 19, 24
    opening, 27–28, 30–31
    presets, 21
    recent, 28
    reverting to last saved version, 25
    saving, 19, 24–26
    settings, 20, 22–23
    size of, 17
    starting, 18–19
    trimming. *See* trimming
    versions, 26

properties
    clips, 107, 212
    deleting keyframes for, 447
    effects, 410–420, 426–428, 443
    files, 107
    lines, 384–385
    objects, 356
    paths, 384–385
    spatial, 412, 437–440
    text, 366–367
    titles, 356, 366–367
property graph, 413, 420
.prproj extension, 19
.PRV extension, 302

**Q**

QDesign 2 music codec, 571
Quality settings, 132, 294–295, 535
QuickTime format, 511, 535

**R**

RAM, 570
Rate Stretch tool, 230
Razor tool, 221–223
Read mode, 333
real-time editing, 293
Real-Time Playback options, 296
real-time rendering, 293–294
RealMedia format, 534–535
rearrange edits, 238–239
Rearrange function, 239
Record button, 321, 329
recording with audio mixer, 328–329
Rectangle tool, 376, 386
recycle edits, 238–239, 241
Redo command, 12
reference monitor, 118, 141–142
relative time, 126–127
render files, 293, 298. *See also* preview files
render filters, 505
rendering
    field, 552–553
    order of, 433–434
    playing work area after, 301
    real-time, 293–294
    settings, 22, 522
    work area, 298–301
Rendering window, 300–301
resolution, 132, 447, 494, 527, 560
Reveal in Project command, 265
Revert command, 14, 25
RGB color, 139, 469, 480, 502

RGB Parade option, 135, 139
ripple deletes, 218–219
ripple edits, 245–247, 253–254, 261, 285
rolling edits, 246, 248, 254–256, 285
rolling text, 373–375
rotation, 401, 440
rotational values, 440
Rounded-Corner Rectangle tool, 376
rubberbanding, 411, 413, 421–423

**S**

safe zones, 131, 354, 555
sample rates, 152, 566–567
saturation, 140, 504
Save a Copy command, 24
Save As command, 24
Save command, 24
Save Photoshop File As dialog box, 73
Save Preset command, 23
Save Project Settings dialog box, 23
Save Workspace command, 5–6
Save Workspace dialog box, 6
saving
    automatically, 26
    custom workspaces, 5–6
    keyboard shortcuts, 11
    presets, 23, 539
    projects, 19, 24–26
Scale filter, 536
Scale option, 463
scaling, 430, 438–439, 473, 559
scene detect feature, 48–49
scratch disks, 44, 302–303
Screen filter, 476
Screen key, 475
scrollbars, 133
scrubbable hot text, 126–127
scrubbing, 127, 297
segments, 377
Selection tool, 365
sends, 336–338
sequence clips, 120–121, 265–266
sequence creation, 145–187
    clip markers. *See* clip markers
    duplicating sequences, 182–183
    editing in Monitor window, 165, 168–172
    extracts, 173, 175
    lifts, 173–174
    methods for, 146–147
    multiple sequences, 180–183
    nesting sequences, 184–187
    with New Sequence command, 180–183
    overlay vs. insert edits, 160

setting In/Out points, 148–150, 152
specifying source/target tracks, 158–159
split edit points, 151
storyboard editing, 147, 176–178
sequence CTI. *See* CTI
sequence markers, 153, 210–211, 515
Sequence Zero Point option, 190
sequences
    creating. *See* sequence creation
    duplicating, 182–183
    layered, 70–71
    multiple, 179–183
    navigating, 128–130
    nested, 179, 184–187, 231, 309
    previewing, 293–303
    refining, 235–266
    source view, 184–187
    starting time, 190
    still-image, 72, 523–524
    switching, 181
    viewing in Timeline window, 181, 204–206
    viewing via DV devices, 295–297
Set Unnumbered Marker button, 210–211
settings
    audio, 522, 543–544, 566–571
    choosing, 544
    DV Playback, 295–297
    for exporting, 520–522
    general, 22
    GIFs, 528–529
    keyframe, 522, 565
    magnification, 133
    project, 20
    rendering, 22, 522
    timebase, 545
    timecode, 547–549
    transitions, 286–291
    video, 543–565
    video capture, 22, 42–43
Setup option, 136
shadows, 397, 500
shapes, 376, 386
Sharpen filter, 494
Shear effect, 408
sheen option, 390
shortcuts. *See* keyboard shortcuts
Show/Hide Keyframes button, 319–320, 345,
    414–415
Shuttle control, 124–125
signal-to-noise ratio, 567
Skip buttons, 31
slash key (/), 170
slate, 77, 263
slip edits, 249–250
smooth points, 377

SMPTE timecode, 547
snap line, 236
snapping feature
    aligning clips, 163
    edit points, 208
    Timeline window CTI, 208
    trimming and, 245
    turning on/off, 237
    using, 236–237
    work area bar, 299
Solo button, 327
sound. *See* audio
source clips, 118, 120–121, 153, 161, 265
source files, 17, 29–31, 92
source menu, 119–121
source tracks, 158–159
source view
    adding Effect Controls palette to, 280
    described, 2, 116
    dragging clips to, 164
    ganging with program view, 143
    Monitor window, 116–123
    nested sequences, 184–187
    opening sequences in, 184
    viewing In/Out points in, 148–149
spatial controls, 436
spatial keyframes, 450
spatial properties, 412, 437–440
split edits, 151, 258–261
splitting clips, 221–223
stereo clips, 313–314
stereo master track, 21
stereo mixes, 310
stereo tracks, 198, 312
still-image sequences, 66, 72, 523–524
still images
    capturing with DV camera, 554
    duration, 66
    exporting, 523–527
    importing, 66, 72
storyboard editing, 84, 147, 176–178
straight cuts, 259
strobe effects, 505
strokes, 393–396
styles, text, 370–372
stylize filters, 505
subclips, 102
submix tracks, 312, 328, 335
submixes, 335, 337
subtractive mixing, 309
subwoofer output, 332
superimposing images, 467–470
SurCode for Dolby Digital plug-in, 569
Sync to Timeline button, 355
synchronization, 213, 263–264, 266, 355

# T

Tab Stops button, 361
tabbed windows, 8
tabs, 8, 361–362
tail, 243
tape
    audiocassette, 36
    cuing, 48
    master, 77
    video. *See* videotape
target tracks, 158–159, 199
television monitors, 131, 295, 551–552
templates, title, 353
text
    alignment, 366–367
    crawling, 373–375
    creating, 358–359
    editing, 365
    fonts, 366–369
    horizontal, 359, 363, 373
    hot, 126–127
    Japanese, 367
    path, 363–364
    properties, 366–367
    rolling, 373–375
    scrubbable, 126–127
    selecting, 365
    styles, 370–372
    tabs, 361–362
    titles. *See* titles
    vertical, 358–359, 363
    word wrap, 360
text boxes, 359, 399
text objects, 357–359
texture, 391–392
three-point editing, 146, 166–167, 169–170
thumbnail viewer, 164
thumbnails
    clips, 81–82
    tracks, 192–193
    transitions, 282
Tiles effect, 408
time
    absolute, 126–127
    filters for, 505
    relative, 126–127
    scrubbing, 127
    setting, 130
time ruler
    audio units, 152, 191
    changing In/Out points in, 150
    customizing, 190–191
    display of, 128–130
    Monitor window, 128–130

setting current time, 130
    zoom controls, 206, 432
timebase settings, 545
timecode
    camera control, 39
    cuing tape to, 48
    described, 547
    device control, 39
    displays, 549
    drop-frame, 46, 548–549
    non-drop-frame, 46, 548–549
    settings, 547–549
    SMPTE, 547
timecode offset, 212
Timecode Offset feature, 47
timeline
    changing size of, 431
    deleting clips from, 216–217
    dragging clips to, 164
    editing in, 189–233
    navigating, 203–206
    removing keyframes in, 420
    selecting clips in, 214–215, 217
    trimming clips in, 243–245
    viewing sequences in, 205
    zoom controls in, 203–206
timeline view, 280–281
Timeline window
    changing property values in, 416–420
    described, 2
    monitoring tracks, 201
    showing track panning values, 320
    viewing audio data in, 319–320
    viewing clip properties, 212
    viewing property values in, 411, 414–415
Title Designer, 3, 349–405
Title menu, 350
title-safe area, 131, 354, 555
titles, 349–405
    background video, 355
    crawling text, 373–375
    creating, 351–352
    fonts, 368–369
    properties, 356, 366–367
    rolling text, 373–375
    saving, 352
    shape objects, 376
    styles, 370–372
    tabs, 361–362
    templates for, 353
    text objects, 357–359
    video safe zones, 131, 354, 555
    word wrap, 360
tool tips, 9, 212
tools. *See also specific tools*

keyboard shortcuts, 10
    Pen, 379–382, 416, 418
Tools shortcut set, 10
Tools window, 2
Touch mode, 334
track-based editing, 308
track effects, 339–343
Track Lock button, 202
Track Matte key, 484–485
Track Output button, 201
track panning values, 320
Track tool, 215
tracks
    adding, 197–198
    audio. *See* audio tracks
    deleting, 198–199
    empty, 199
    expanding/collapsing, 192
    hierarchy, 467
    locking/unlocking, 202, 215
    master, 21–22, 335
    monitoring, 201
    naming/renaming, 49–50, 197, 200
    number of, 197
    removing material from, 175
    resizing, 195–196
    source, 158–159
    submix, 335
    superimpose, 467
    target, 158–159, 199
    video, 262
    viewing, 192–194
transform filters, 506
Transform properties, 400
transforming objects, 400–401
transitions, 267–292
    adjusting, 279, 281, 283–285
    alignment, 274, 283–285
    applying, 267, 277–278
    audio, 317–318
    borders, 289–290
    center point, 288
    channel map, 292
    custom settings, 286–291
    default, 178, 276, 278
    described, 267
    Dip to Black, 273
    direction, 178, 286
    displace, 292
    duration, 274–275, 283–285
    Effect Controls palette, 279–282
    Effects palette, 268–271
    gradient wipe, 292
    image map, 292
    keyframing, 288

luminance map, 292
    names, 278
    overview, 272–273
    replacing, 278
    reversing, 288
    selecting, 267
    setting keyframes on edge of, 443
    smoothing edges, 290
    special, 292
    start/end of, 287
    thumbnails, 282
    trimming, 285
    viewing, 281
transparency, 134, 475, 510, 529
Trim window, 252–257
    applying edits in, 257
    described, 3
    preparing to edit in, 252–253
    previewing edits in, 257
    ripple edits, 253–254
    rolling edits, 254–256
    split edits, 260–261
    views, 252
trimming
    clips in Monitor window, 172
    clips in timeline, 243–245
    described, 111, 235, 243
    methods for, 243
    with Project Manager, 111–113
    snapping and, 245
    in timeline, 243–245
    transition clips, 285
type tool, 357–358

## U

Undo command, 12, 170
User interface Brightness slider, 4

## V

vectorscopes, 134–137, 139–140
video. *See also* movies
    24P, 552
    analog, 36–37
    background, 355
    black, 74, 77
    capturing. *See* capturing video
    compression, 34, 562–563
    display mode, 134–138
    DV, 36–37
    interlaced, 132, 551–554
    links to, 262–263
    magnification settings, 133

INDEX

video *(continued)*
MPEG-2 transcoded, 535
overscanned, 555
post-encoding tasks, 537
pre-encoding tasks, 536–537
previews, 303
progressive-scan, 551–553
quality of, 132, 294–295
safe zones, 132, 354, 555
settings, 543–565
video camera/deck. *See also* device control;
    devices
audio options, 310–311
FireWire, 34–35
local controls, 49
playback via, 295–297
specifying for device control, 45–47
standby mode, 48
timecode and, 39, 547
viewing sequences with, 295–297
video capture cards, 20, 36–37, 544, 563
video clips, 263, 414. *See also* clips
video display format, 549
video filters, 506
video footage. *See* footage
Video Limiter options, 497
Video Noise Reduction filter, 536
video tracks, 262
videotape
codecs, 563
cuing to specified timecode, 48
exporting to, 509, 512–513
Hi8, 36
naming, 49–50
outputting to, 509
VHS, 36
Virtual Studio Technology (VST), 339
voiceovers, 155
volume
adjusting in property graph, 413
adjusting with Clip Gain command, 315–316
animating, 413, 421, 423
audio tracks, 319
rubberbanding, 413, 421, 423
sends, 338
showing in Timeline window, 320
VU meters, 327
VST (Virtual Studio Technology), 339
VU meters, 327

**W**

warning messages, 15
waveform monitor, 134–135, 138–140
waveforms, 134–138
described, 122–123, 192
display options, 136–137
intensity, 137
showing/hiding, 123, 194, 319
Web links, 210–211
Web output, 510
Web-safe colors, 528
Wedge tool, 376
Widescreen options, 21
Wind effect, 408
windows. *See also specific windows*
keyboard shortcuts, 10
secondary, 3–4
stacking order, 6
tabbed, 8
Windows Media format, 511, 534–535
Windows shortcut set, 10
word wrap, 360
work area, 298–301
work area bar, 298–299
workspace, arranging, 5–6
Write mode, 334

**Y**

YC Waveform option, 135, 137
YCbCR Parade option, 135, 139
YUV color, 139, 556

**Z**

zero marker, 95, 155, 232
Zig Zag effect, 408
zoom controls
time ruler, 432
timeline, 203–206
Zoom Out button, 205
zoom slider, 204–205
Zoom tool, 203–206
zooming in/out, 163